The Theory of Dynamic Efficiency

This book gathers a collection of English-language essays by Jesús Huerta de Soto over the past ten years, examining the dynamic processes of social cooperation which characterize the market, with particular emphasis on the role of both entrepreneurship and institutions. The author's multidisciplinary approach to the subject is in keeping with a trend in economic thought established by the Austrian School of economics; a discourse that had witnessed a significant revival over the last thirty years.

Areas covered in this book include an introduction to the theory of dynamic efficiency as an alternative to the standard Paretian criteria, a detailed explanation of the differences between the Austrian and the neo-classical (including the Chicago School) approach to economics, a generalized definition of socialism that allows the joint application of the analysis of interventionism, a dynamic Austrian approach to the analysis of free market environmentalism, nationalism, the crisis and reform of social security and the theory of banking and economic cycles and an evaluation of the role of Spanish scholastics of the sixteenth century as forerunners of the Austrian School.

This book will be of great interest to those engaged with the study of Austrian economics, economic methodology, the theory of banking and economic cycles, and the history of economic thought.

Jesús Huerta de Soto is Professor of Political Economy at King Juan Carlos University in Madrid.

Routledge Foundations of the Market Economy
Edited by Mario J. Rizzo, New York University and Lawrence H. White, University of Missouri at St Louis

A central theme in this series is the importance of understanding and assessing the market economy from a perspective broader than the static economics of perfect competition and Pareto optimality. Such a perspective sees markets as causal processes generated by the preferences, expectations and beliefs of Economic agents. The creative acts of entrepreneurship that uncover new information about preferences, prices and technology are central to these processes with respect to their ability to promote the discovery and use of knowledge in society.

The market economy consists of a set of institutions that facilitate voluntary cooperation and exchange among individuals. These institutions include the legal and ethical framework as well as more narrowly 'economic' patterns of social interaction. Thus the law, legal institutions and cultural and ethical norms, as well as ordinary business practices and monetary phenomena, fall within the analytical domain of the economist.

Previous books in this series include:

1. The Meaning of Market Process
Essays in the development of modern Austrian economics
Israel M. Kirzner

2. Prices and Knowledge
A market-process perspective
Esteban F. Thomsen

3. Keynes' General Theory of Interest
A reconsideration
Fiona C. Maclachlan

4. Laissez-faire Banking
Kevin Dowd

5. Expectations and the Meaning of Institutions
Essays in economics by Ludwig Lachmann
Edited by Don Lavoie

6. Perfect Competition and the Transformation of Economics
Frank M. Machovec

7. Entrepreneurship and the Market Process
An enquiry into the growth of knowledge
David Harper

8. Economics of Time and Ignorance
Gerald O'Driscoll and
Mario J. Rizzo

9. Dynamics of the Mixed Economy
Toward a theory of interventionism
Sanford Ikeda

10. Neoclassical Microeconomic Theory
The founding of Austrian vision
A. M. Endres

11. The Cultural Foundations of Economic Development
Urban female entrepreneurship in Ghana
Emily Chamlee-Wright

12. Risk and Business Cycles
New and old Austrian perspectives
Tyler Cowen

13. Capital in Disequilibrium
The role of capital in a changing world
Peter Lewin

14. The Driving Force of the Market
Essays in Austrian economics
Israel Kirzner

15. An Entrepreneurial Theory of the Firm
Frédéric Sautet

16. Time and Money
The macroeconomics of capital structure
Roger Garrison

17. Microfoundations and Macroeconomics
An Austrian perspective
Steven Horwitz

18. Money and The Market
Essays on free banking
Kevin Dowd

19. Calculation and Coordination
Essays on socialism and transitional political economy
Peter Boettke

20. Keynes & Hayek
The money economy
G. R. Steele

21. The Constitution of Markets
Essays in political economy
Viktor J. Vanberg

22. Foundations of Entrepreneurship and Economic Development
David A. Harper

23. Markets, Information and Communication
Austrian perspectives on the Internet economy
Edited by Jack Birner and Pierre Garrouste

24. The Constitution of Liberty in the Open Economy
Lüder Gerken

25. Liberalism Against Liberalism
Javier Aranzadi

26. Money and Markets
Essays in honor of Leland B. Yeager
Edited by Roger Koppl

27. Entrepreneurship and Economic Progress
Randall G. Holcombe

28. The Theory of Dynamic Efficiency
Jesús Huerta de Soto

The Theory of Dynamic Efficiency

Jesús Huerta de Soto

Routledge
Taylor & Francis Group

LONDON AND NEW YORK

First published 2009
First revised edition published 2010
by Routledge
2 Park Square, Milton Park, Abingdon, Oxon OX14 4RN

Simultaneously published in the USA and Canada
by Routledge
270 Madison Avenue, New York, NY 10016

Routledge is an imprint of the Taylor & Francis Group, an informa business

© 2009 Jesús Huerta de Soto

Typeset in Times New Roman by
Taylor & Francis Books
Printed and bound in Great Britain by
CPI Antony Rowe Ltd, Chippenham, Wiltshire

All rights reserved. No part of this book may be reprinted or reproduced or utilized in any form or by any electronic, mechanical, or other means, now known or hereafter invented, including photocopying and recording, or in any information storage or retrieval system, without permission in writing from the publishers.

British Library Cataloguing in Publication Data
A catalogue record for this book is available from the British Library

Library of Congress Cataloging in Publication Data
Huerta de Soto, Jesús.
The theory of dynamic efficiency / Jesús Huerta de Soto.
p. cm. – (Routledge foundations of the market economy ; 28)
Includes bibliographical references and index.
1. Statics and dynamics (Social sciences) 2. Entrepreneurship. 3. Austrian school of economics. I. Title.
   HB145.H865 2008
   330.15'7–dc22
                    2007035206

ISBN 978-0-415-42769-2 (hbk)
ISBN 978-0-203-93060-1 (ebk)

Contents

List of tables	ix
Preface	x
Acknowledgements	xii

1 The theory of dynamic efficiency — 1
2 The ongoing *Methodenstreit* of the Austrian School — 31
3 Conjectural history and beyond — 61
4 Entrepreneurship and the economic analysis of socialism — 63
5 The crisis of socialism — 84
6 Entrepreneurship and the theory of free market environmentalism — 94
7 A theory of liberal nationalism — 100
8 A libertarian theory of free immigration — 112
9 The crisis and reform of social security — 120
10 A critical analysis of central banks and fractional-reserve free banking from the Austrian School perspective — 139
11 A critical note on fractional-reserve free banking — 148
12 The ethics of capitalism — 169
13 A Hayekian strategy to implement free market reforms — 182
14 The future of liberalism: the deconstruction of the state through direct democracy — 200

15 Juan de Mariana and the Spanish scholastics	204
16 New light on the prehistory of the theory of banking and the School of Salamanca	211
17 Ludwig von Mises' *Human Action* as a textbook of economics	229
18 In memoriam of Murray N. Rothbard	255
19 Hayek's best test of a good economist	258
20 The Ricardo effect	261
Appendix: Interview: Spanish roots of the Austrian School	263
Notes	276
Index	352

List of tables

2.1	Essential differences between the Austrian and Neoclassical Schools	32
2.2	Two different ways of conceiving macroeconomics	49
9.1	Stages in the Reform of Social security	131
9.2	Relative position of different countries	131
11.1	Essential differences between two radically different contracts	164

Preface

This book is a collection of my English-language work over the past ten years (1994–2004). Many of these articles have appeared in specialized journals, and the main purpose of this volume is to present them together in an organized manner to provide scholars and researchers with a convenient reference and to facilitate comparative analysis. Not surprisingly, the different chapters included here are all related in one way or another to the line of research I embarked on twenty-five years ago, a course of study founded on the examination of the dynamic processes of social cooperation which characterize the market, with particular emphasis on both the role entrepreneurship plays in these processes and the different institutions which make life in society possible. This patently multidisciplinary approach corresponds with the trend in economic thought established by the Austrian School of economics. In recent years, this trend has been gaining great prestige worldwide and has enjoyed a resurgence in Spain that I have had the honour to promote.

The book is divided into four distinct parts. The first comprises three chapters devoted to the study of the theoretical basis for the dynamic conception of the market. In this first part, special attention is given to the analysis of the theory of dynamic efficiency, the essential differences between neoclassical and Austrian economics, and the three-level approach (theoretical, historical and ethical) to the study of social phenomena.

The second part of the book consists of nine chapters which focus on the economic analysis of various topics from an Austrian perspective: the crisis and reform of social security, free market environmentalism, socialism, nationalism and immigration. Also included are two chapters on banking and economic cycles, issues I have found particularly absorbing in recent years. Finally, the focus shifts to the ethical aspects of capitalism, the proper role of the libertarian economist in the political milieu and the future of democracy.

The third part of the book is devoted to a series of economic history papers in which I set out to research the origins of the Austrian School in the work of the sixteenth century Spanish scholastics. The section also contains an assessment of Ludwig von Mises' economic treatise, *Human Action*, an evaluation which marks the fiftieth anniversary of its initial publication.

The volume concludes with an Appendix consisting of an interview I gave for the *Austrian Economics Newsletter*. In it, readers may detect nuances in thought which nevertheless derive naturally from the rest of the work featured here, and they may also reflect on the application of the ideas presented in this book to the most pressing economic and political problems which beset our society.

Acknowledgements

I should like to thank the *Quarterly Journal of Austrian Economics*, the *Review of Austrian Economics* and the *Journal des économistes et des études humaines* for their permission to reprint here the pieces which first appeared in their publications.

Lastly, I wish to acknowledge the enthusiasm which my students, disciples and university colleagues, at both the bachelor's degree and doctorate levels, have shown in the study and discussion of my different research projects at the School of Law and Social Sciences of Madrid's King Juan Carlos University. I should like specifically to mention Luis Reig Albiol, Ingolf Krumm, Gabriel Calzada, Juan Ignacio del Castillo, Jesús Gómez, Francisco Capella, Óscar Vara Crespo, Javier Aranzadi del Cerro, Ángel Rodríguez, César Martínez Meseguer, Miguel Ángel Alonso Neira, Philipp Bagus and Antonio Zanella. Without their help, this work would undoubtedly have fallen short of its current quality.

1 The theory of dynamic efficiency

Introduction

The traditional Pareto criteria of allocative efficiency, which have predominated in economics up to this point, are tainted with a definite static character and therefore are inadequate to be applied as normative guidelines to the rich dynamics of real-life social institutions.[1] Consequently, it is necessary to replace the traditional standards of efficiency with an alternative criterion, one which will fill the serious gaps in the traditional Pareto approach and be easily applicable to the realm of social institutions. We will call this alternative standard the 'criterion of dynamic efficiency'.

This paper comprises three distinct sections. In the first, we will review the process by which the concept of Pareto efficiency emerged. This standard was modelled on the principle of energy efficiency, which arose in nineteenth century physics and mechanics. The above explains why the traditional criterion of Pareto efficiency, which has become the pivot of all welfare economics and much of the economic analysis of law, is heavily restricted by comparative statics, and thus cannot be easily applied to the rich dynamics of institutions.

In the second section, we will present the alternative notion of *dynamic efficiency*, which followed naturally from the theory of market processes driven by the creative and coordinating potential of entrepreneurship. Although the standard of dynamic efficiency has not yet entered the mainstream of our discipline, various authors have contributed to the field. Leading economists such as Mises, Hayek and Schumpeter, along with other more recent theorists like Rothbard, Kirzner, North (with his concept of 'adaptive efficiency') and even Leibenstein (with his notion of 'x-efficiency'), have proposed or developed alternative criteria which have coincided to a varying extent with our idea of dynamic efficiency. In this section, we will study and compare the different contributions these authors have made in this area.

The third and final section of this article embodies what we see as one of its most significant and promising contributions: an analysis of the close relationship we believe exists between the proposed criterion of dynamic efficiency and the framework of ethical principles which prevails in every society. A major, auspicious field of research thus opening up for future economists consists of the systematic application of the standard of dynamic efficiency to each of society's institutions (legal, moral and economic) and the subsequent evaluation of each according to a standard other than the traditional Pareto criterion. Furthermore, our analysis will allow us to identify the ethical principles which make dynamic efficiency possible and, as a result, permit the progress and coordinated advancement of society and civilization. We thereby intend to establish a direct relationship between economics and ethics and in this way to foster a highly productive relationship between the two thus mutually strengthened disciplines.

The evolution of the standard of static efficiency: a critical analysis

Historical background

The term 'efficiency' derives etymologically from the Latin word *efficiens*, which in turn originates from the Latin verb *ex facio*, which means 'to obtain something from'.[2] The application to economics of this view of efficiency as the ability 'to obtain something from' predates the Roman world and can even be traced back to ancient Greece, where the term 'economics' (οικονομία) was first used to refer to the efficient management of the family home or estate. In *Economics*, 380 years before Christ, Xenophon attributes to Socrates the assertion that economics is 'a branch of knowledge' of a sort 'by which men can increase estates', that an estate is 'identical with the total of one's property' and that property is 'that which is useful for supplying a livelihood'.[3] Xenophon himself, upon presenting such a modern and subjectivist definition of economics, goes on to explain in the subsequent dialogues that there are two different ways to increase one's estate, and these are ultimately equivalent to two different aspects of efficiency.

One aspect coincides with that of 'static efficiency' and consists of the sound management of the available (or 'given') resources, to prevent them from being wasted. According to Xenophon, the primary way to achieve this efficient management is by keeping the home in good *order*,[4] as well as by carefully supervising the handling of one's goods, monitoring and caring for them as well as possible. Xenophon sums up the set of abilities necessary for an efficient management of 'given' resources with the wise answer offered to the great Barbarian king who

> had happened on a good horse, and wanted to fatten him as speedily as possible. So he asked one who was reputed clever with horses what is the quickest way of fattening a horse. 'The master's eye,' replied the man. I think we may apply the answer generally, Socrates, and say that the master's eye in the main does the good and worthy work.[5]

Nevertheless, along with this aspect of efficiency, which we have described as 'static', Xenophon introduces a complementary 'dynamic' facet, which consists of the attempt to increase one's estate through entrepreneurial action and by doing business with it. What is involved is the effort to increase one's goods by way of entrepreneurial creativity; that is, by trade and speculation, more than the effort to avoid wasting the resources already in one's power. Xenophon provides two examples of specific activities to illustrate this task based on entrepreneurial activity. One example entails the purchase of poorly tended or barren land with a view to improving it and later selling it at a much higher price.[6] Another example of dynamic efficiency, which makes it possible to increase one's estate and gather new resources, is found in the activity of those merchants who buy wheat where it is abundant, and therefore inexpensive, and transport and sell it at a much higher price in places where drought or poor crops have led to a shortage and hunger.[7]

This tradition of clearly distinguishing between two distinct facets of efficiency, the static and the dynamic, survived even until the Middle Ages. For example, Saint Bernardine of Siena felt that the income of merchants and craftsmen was justified on the basis of their *industry* and *pericula*: by the sound, diligent management of their (given) resources; that is, by assiduous behaviour typically oriented toward preventing waste (static efficiency); and by the acceptance of the risks and dangers (*pericula*) which arise from any entrepreneurial speculation (dynamic efficiency).[8]

The influence of mechanical physics

Nevertheless, despite these hopeful beginnings, with the arrival of the modern age the concept of economic efficiency gradually narrowed and diminished, until it came to denote merely the static aspect; in other words, diligent action aimed at preventing the waste of 'given' resources. The effect which the emergence and development of mechanical physics ultimately exerted on the evolution of economic thought, especially from the nineteenth century onward, had a decisive influence on this reductionist trend, which noticeably impoverished the concept of efficiency as Xenophon had formulated it, with its two distinct facets.

In fact, with the arrival of the modern age, physics replaced astronomy as 'science par excellence' and was ultimately built upon the idea of 'energy', an abstract concept all physicists discuss and debate about, even if they do not manage to completely agree on the precise essence of energy in the absence of empirical evidence of its effects in the form of force or movement.[9] Along these lines, the 'law of conservation of energy' came to play a key role in the development of physics, and we should not ignore its essentially static nature ('energy is neither created nor destroyed, only transformed'). Later the second law of thermodynamics stated that in all physical processes some energy is wasted, for instance in the form of heat which dissipates, and therefore physical systems are not reversible. Both laws were integral to the great evolution of physics throughout the nineteenth century and explain why most scientists think of physical phenomena almost exclusively in terms

4 The theory of dynamic efficiency

of 'energy'. Moreover, the main practical application of physics emerged in the development of mechanical engineering, which was built entirely on the (static) concept of energy efficiency, defined by engineers as the 'minimization of energy waste'. The steam engine, which became the classic capital good in the Industrial Revolution, provides an excellent example. The steam engine transforms heat into movement and the lifting of weights, the goal of all good mechanical engineers being maximum (static) efficiency, or maximum movement with minimum energy consumption or waste.

This reductionist idea of (static) efficiency came to dominate in colloquial language as well. Hence, the definition *Webster's Dictionary* supplies for 'efficient' rests on the notion of minimizing waste: 'Marked by ability to choose and use the most effective and *least wasteful means* of doing a task or accomplishing a purpose'.[10] In Spanish, the concept of efficiency is closely related to the capacity for achieving a specific outcome or yield. The *Diccionario de la Lengua Española* defines the term *rendimiento* ('yield') as 'the ratio between the product or result obtained and the means used'[11] (both of which are assumed to be given or known).

Perhaps at this time it is most important to highlight the negative influence which the static conception of energy efficiency has exerted on the development of economics. Hans Mayer[12] and Philip Mirowski have pointed out that neoclassical economics developed as a copy of nineteenth-century mechanical physics: using the same formal method, yet replacing the concept of energy with that of utility and applying the same principles of conservation, maximization of the result and minimization of waste.[13] The leading author most representative of this trend, and the one to best illustrate this influence of physics on economic thought, is Leon Walras. In his paper 'Economics and Mechanics', published in 1909, he claims that in his *Elements of Pure Economics* he uses mathematical formulas identical to those of mathematical physics, and he stresses the parallel between the concepts of force and *rareté* (which he regards as vectors), and between those of energy and utility (which he regards as scalar quantities).[14]

In short, the influence of mechanical physics eradicated the creative, speculative dimension which belonged to the idea of economic efficiency from its very origins, and all that remained was the reductionist, static aspect, which focuses exclusively on minimizing the waste of (known or given) economic resources. By way of example, let us recall the definition of 'efficient allocation' which *The New Palgrave Dictionary of Economics* provides and which it credits to Stanley Reiter: 'going as far as possible in the satisfaction of wants within resource and technological constraints'.[15] (Note the assumption that resources and technology are given.) It is both revealing and discouraging to find that the entry devoted to economic efficiency by what is undoubtedly the leading dictionary in our discipline includes absolutely no mention of the dynamic aspect of this concept. This omission is particularly illustrative and disheartening in light of the fact that neither resources nor technology are 'given' in real life, but can vary and actually do vary continually as a result of entrepreneurial creativity. Moreover, the true changing nature of these factors clearly indicates the existence of an entire, time-honoured dimension of efficiency (the dynamic dimension, which, as we have seen, can be traced back as far as Xenophon) that can only be forgotten at a high cost to the economic analysis of reality.

The reductionist conception of static efficiency also had a great impact on business organization from the beginning of the twentieth century, when Taylorism emerged. In fact, Frederick W. Taylor, in his famous book, *The Principles of Scientific Management* (1911), advocates the establishment in all industries of a 'productive efficiency' department to pursue the following aims: first, to supervise workers; second, to measure the time spent on a job; and, third, to avoid any kind of waste.[16] This reductionist concept of static efficiency actually turned into a sort of idol which seemed to command the sacrifice of everything, and this static-efficiency obsession (which might best be described as 'worship') spread even to the realm of political ideology.

The Fabian socialists Sydney and Beatrice Webb provide a compelling example of this phenomenon. This married couple were shocked by the 'waste' they observed in the capitalist system and founded the London School of Economics in an effort to champion the reform of the economic system. The object of such reform would be to eliminate waste and make the system 'efficient'. The Webbs later made no secret of their warm admiration for the 'efficiency' they believed they observed in Soviet Russia, to the point that Beatrice even declared, 'I fell in love with Soviet Communism.' Another noted author to be lured by the static conception of economic efficiency was John Maynard Keynes himself, who, in his introduction to the 1936 German edition of his *General Theory* expressly states that his economic-policy proposals 'are more easily adapted to the conditions of a totalitarian state'. Keynes also unreservedly praised the book *Soviet Communism*, which the Webbs had published in 1933.[17]

'Welfare economics' and the static concept of efficiency

The development described above peaked in the 1920s and 1930s, when the static concept of economic efficiency became the focal point for a whole new discipline which came to be known as 'welfare economics',[18] and which grew from a series of alternative approaches. According to the Pigouvian analysis, an economic system would reach maximum efficiency when the marginal utility of all factors is equalized, something which would require the redistribution of income until each actor derived the same marginal utility from his last monetary unit. Pigou thus upholds the tradition of strict utilitarianism initiated by Jeremy Bentham and later continued by the naive marginalists (Sax, Sidgwick, etc.). It is obvious that Pigou's approach involves interpersonal comparisons of utility and metascientific value judgements, and hence it was soon generally replaced with the alternative Paretian approach.

From a Paretian perspective, an economic system is in a *state* of efficiency if no one can be made better off without making someone else worse off. This view, although still essentially static, seemed to circumvent the need for interpersonal comparisons of utility and paved the way for those welfare economists (Lerner and others) who formulated the so-called 'first theorem of welfare economics', according to which a system of perfect competition attains allocative efficiency in the Paretian sense. The next step was to identify a number of 'market failures' which supposedly generated inefficiencies (in the static sense of the word) by distancing the economic system from the model of 'perfect competition'. (Initially monopolies and externalities were dealt with, followed by more sophisticated sources of static inefficiency, such as asymmetric information, moral hazard and incomplete markets.) At the same time, and as an alternative, the Kaldor–Hicks approach was presented, including the analytical principle of 'potential compensation': situation II is considered more efficient than situation I if those who benefit can compensate those who lose (Kaldor); or if those who are made worse off by situation II cannot prevent the change by 'bribing' those who stand to gain from it (Hicks).[19]

Theorists subsequently formulated the 'second fundamental theorem of welfare economics', which stated that Pareto efficiency is compatible with various initial resource allocations. This theorem requires the belief that criteria of efficiency and fairness can be considered in isolation and that they can be combined in different proportions. Bergson and Samuelson, on their part, introduced the 'social-welfare function', which, although it again lapses into interpersonal comparisons of utility, would enable us to eliminate the indeterminacy of the point of maximum efficiency among all which are Pareto efficient and make up the production possibility curve. However, Arrow later demonstrated the impossibility of obtaining a social-welfare function which satisfies certain reasonable conditions of consistency ('third fundamental theorem of welfare economics'). The economist Amartya K. Sen, another winner of the Nobel Prize, demonstrated along the same lines that it is impossible to conceive of a social-welfare function which meets both the criteria for Pareto optimality and the traditional standards of liberalism, basically because individual ordinal-utility rankings cannot be aggregated, and thus the social-welfare function cannot possibly fulfil all individual preferences.[20]

Criticism of welfare economics and the concept of static efficiency

For obvious reasons, we cannot elaborate on all existing criticisms against the different standards of static efficiency that have appeared in the area of welfare economics. These approaches have already been critically analysed in a wealth of literature which we are unable to reproduce here. Nevertheless, we will summarize the most common objections, mainly to contrast them with the one we consider by far the most significant, and which up to now has been almost entirely disregarded.

First, the different criteria of static efficiency established in the context of welfare economics involve the more or less covert introduction of value judgements devoid of scientific objectivity. As we have indicated above, this is clear of Pigou's approach and the social-welfare function, since, in order to have any operative content, both require interpersonal comparisons of utility, which are scientifically unacceptable according to the general consensus among economists since Lionel Robbins. Furthermore, it is not altogether clear that comparisons of utility can be made even by the same individual in relation to himself if they correspond to different points in time and to the contexts of different actions. In such a case, even when the same person is involved, he would often be attempting to compare diverse and heterogeneous dimensions which are scarcely comparable with one other. Moreover, not even the Paretian approach, despite the appearances, could be considered completely neutral with respect to interpersonal comparisons and value judgements: an envious person, for example, might actually feel worse in the event of a Paretian improvement (if someone were to gain without 'appearing' to worsen anyone else's situation, except, of course, that of the envious person).

Second, the assorted approaches of welfare economics contain a serious flaw: they imply that individual utility rankings and the different possibilities that open up for each actor are 'given', that is, known and unchanging. To put it another way, it is assumed that these rankings and possibilities always reflect 'utility functions', which are also presumed constant and known. This assumption is especially restrictive and objectionable in the case of Pigou, whose normative proposal of income redistribution not only involves interpersonal comparisons of utility, but its practical implementation would entail a radical change in the corresponding 'utility functions' and also profoundly impact the process of entrepreneurial coordination, a much more significant effect still, as we shall see.

Third, the notion of technical efficiency, borrowed from mechanical physics, continues to strongly influence static-efficiency criteria. This is so despite the many efforts of highly distinguished economists (Robbins, Lipsey, Alchian and Allen, etc.) to differentiate technical or technological efficiency from economic efficiency once and for all.[21] It has been contended that while technical or technological efficiency would consist of minimizing inputs in physical terms (such as tons of coal, barrels of oil, etc.) to produce a certain outcome, economic efficiency would consist of the same; that is, the minimization of inputs, yet in terms of cost (i.e. units of input multiplied by market price) instead of in physical terms. Nevertheless, if one assumes, as is assumed with all of the static-efficiency criteria mentioned, that technology and market prices are 'given', in other words, that they are known and constant, then plainly the modus operandi of economic efficiency (the static version) and that of technical efficiency would be identical: both would amount to maximization via a mere mathematical operation subject to known restrictions. We can conclude, then, that within the context of welfare economics, a striking similarity in form exists between the concept of technical efficiency and the static notion of economic efficiency. To put it another way: *the static conception of economics reduces the principle of economic efficiency to a simple technical issue of maximization*, which in any case could be resolved with a mere computer into which someone would enter the data always presumed known in the models of static efficiency.[22]

Nevertheless, regardless of the importance of the above critical assessments, they fall short of what we see as the *essential criticism* to be levelled against the different efficiency standards propounded within welfare economics: that these standards focus solely on one of the two aspects of economic efficiency, namely the static aspect, which entails the presumption both that resources are given and constant, and that the fundamental economic challenge is to avoid wasting them. Furthermore, *when, for example, a company, social institution or entire economic system is to be judged, such criteria completely ignore its Dynamic Efficiency, understood as its capacity to foster entrepreneurial creativity as well as coordination; in other words, the entrepreneurial capacity to seek, discover, and overcome different social maladjustments.*

In fact, we believe our most important goal should not be to move the system toward the production possibilities frontier (while deeming the corresponding curve 'given'), but rather to systematically apply the criterion of dynamic efficiency, which focuses on the capacity of the system to continually 'shift' the production possibilities curve to the right. Thus the importance of overcoming the traditional static criteria of economic efficiency with a more complete, alternative standard which takes into account the dynamic dimension of every economic system. In the next section, we will discuss our dynamic-efficiency criterion in greater detail.

The economic concept of dynamic efficiency

Dynamic efficiency and entrepreneurship

The standard of dynamic efficiency is inextricably linked with the concept of entrepreneurship, and, in fact, a full understanding of the economic notion of dynamic efficiency requires a prior, if brief, review of the principle and basic attributes of entrepreneurship, understood as the main driving force behind the creativity and coordination which spontaneously arise in the market.

The word 'entrepreneurship' derives etymologically from the Latin term *in prehendo*, which means 'to discover', 'to see', 'to realize' something. In this sense, we may define entrepreneurship as *the typically human ability to recognize opportunities for profit which appear in the environment and to act accordingly to take advantage of them*. Entrepreneurship therefore involves a special *alertness*. *Webster's New World Dictionary and Thesaurus* defines 'alert' as 'watchful; vigilant'.[23] Also fully applicable to the idea of entrepreneurship is the verb *to speculate*, which originates etymologically from Latin as well, in this case from the word *specula*, which referred to the towers from

The theory of dynamic efficiency 9

which lookouts could gaze into the distance and detect anything that approached.[24]

The most important features of the above concept of entrepreneurship with respect to the dynamic-efficiency criterion that interests us are as follows:

1. Entrepreneurship always generates new information; that is, every entrepreneurial act involves the discovery of new information which the actor did not previously possess (a profit opportunity that had gone unnoticed before). This information which entrepreneurs constantly create when they act is subjective, practical (in the sense that it is only created through entrepreneurial action in its corresponding contexts), diffuse (since some portion of it exists in the mind of every human being) and tacit (very difficult to articulate).
2. By its very nature entrepreneurship is fundamentally creative, which means that any social maladjustment is embodied in a profit opportunity which remains latent until entrepreneurs discover it. For example, if B finds resource R of little use, yet A has a strong need for it, clearly a social maladjustment exists and gives rise to an opportunity for profit: entrepreneur C must only recognize this maladjustment to buy the resource from B at a low price and sell it to A at a high one, thus obtaining a 'pure entrepreneurial profit'. In this way, when an entrepreneur perceives a profit opportunity that has not yet been heeded, in his mind he *creates* information which did not exist before and which, upon the completion of the entrepreneurial act, results in a pure entrepreneurial profit.
3. Entrepreneurship transmits information. If entrepreneur C inexpensively buys resource R from B, who has plenty and makes poor use of it, and then C sells the resource at a high price to A, who needs it urgently, C *transmits* to A and B the information that resource R is available and should be saved. He also communicates to the entire market, in consecutive waves, that someone is willing to pay a good market price for R (market prices constitute very strong signs in that they convey a large amount of information at a very low cost).
4. Entrepreneurship exerts a coordinating effect. In consequence of the entrepreneurial act we have been describing, A and B learn to govern and coordinate their behaviour in terms of the other's needs: in fact, once the social maladjustment has been discovered and eliminated, B saves resource R, which he took no advantage of before, in order to hand it over to A, who needs it urgently.
5. Entrepreneurship is competitive. The word 'competition' derives from the Latin term *cum petitio*, which denotes the concurrence of multiple requests for the same thing, which must be allotted to an owner. Entrepreneurship is competitive in the precise sense that once a certain entrepreneur has discovered or created an opportunity for profit, that same

opportunity, with its specific coordinates of time and place, cannot be created, discovered or seized by another entrepreneur. This makes the entrepreneurial process one of rivalry, one of pure competition in which entrepreneurs vie with each other to be the first to discover and take advantage of the opportunities for profit which are created in the environment. *Webster's Revised Unabridged Dictionary* provides this definition for the verb 'to compete': 'to contend emulously; to seek or strive for the same thing, position, or reward for which another is striving; to contend in rivalry, as for a prize or in business; as tradesmen compete with one another'.[25] The above notion of competition patently has nothing in common with the so-called 'model of perfect competition', in which multiple suppliers perform the same actions and sell the same good at the same price; that is, a model in which, paradoxically, no one can be viewed as competing.

6. Lastly, the entrepreneurial process never stops nor ends. Though one might think that the social process driven by entrepreneurship could reach a state of equilibrium – in other words, that it could stop or end once entrepreneurs had discovered and seized all of the profit opportunities which embody social maladjustments (and, in fact, most members of our profession regard such a 'final state of rest' as the only object of study worthy of research) – there is no question that the entrepreneurial process of coordination is unbroken and never-ending. The truth is that as the entrepreneurial act coordinates, it creates new information which in turn *modifies within the market the involved actors' general perception of ends and means. New maladjustments ensue, and entrepreneurs begin to discover and resolve them, and in doing so produce coordination in an ongoing process of creativity and ever-expanding knowledge and resources. A constantly increasing population sustains the process, which tends to be as coordinated as humanly possible in each set of historical circumstances* (coordinated social 'Big Bang').

Now that we have described the fundamental characteristics of the entrepreneurial process, we are in a position to better grasp the economic concept of dynamic efficiency as well as the positions of the assorted authors who, in the history of economic thought, have approached the topic.

The economic concept of dynamic efficiency: creativity and coordination

From a dynamic standpoint, an individual, a company, an institution or an entire economic system will be more efficient the more it fuels entrepreneurial creativity and coordination as we have explained them.

From this dynamic perspective, the truly important goal is not so much to prevent the waste of certain means considered known and 'given' (the prime objective from the viewpoint of static efficiency) as to continually discover and create new ends and means, and thus to foster coordination while accepting that in any entrepreneurial process new maladjustments will always appear and *hence a certain amount of waste is inevitable and inherent in any market economy.*

Consequently, we can affirm that the dynamic aspect of efficiency is the most important. Even though an economic system may not have achieved a point on the production possibilities frontier, all of its agents may profit if entrepreneurial creativity constantly shifts the curve outward and hence improves everyone's possibilities with a continuous, creative flow of new ends and means which, prior to their entrepreneurial discovery, had yet even to be envisioned.

It is also true, and highly significant, that the dynamic aspect of economic efficiency incorporates the static aspect: for *the same entrepreneurial force which propels dynamic efficiency through the creation and discovery of new profit opportunities is precisely the one which achieves the highest degree of static efficiency humanly possible at each moment by coordinating pre-existing maladjustments.* (Nevertheless, given the endless flow of new maladjustments, Pareto optimality can never conceivably be reached in a real market economy, as we have stated, and the possibility that existing resources may be wasted cannot be totally eliminated.)

Next we will comment on the contributions of various authors who, from one perspective or another, have approached the above concept of dynamic efficiency. It is not surprising that many of these authors have been heavily influenced by the Austrian economic tradition which, if known for anything, is known precisely for the emphasis it places on the dynamic conception of the market and on the leading role of entrepreneurship in market processes. For a more extensive treatment of these views, we refer the reader to the principal works of Mises and Hayek on the conception of the market as a dynamic process driven by entrepreneurship (Mises) and on the notion of competition as a process of discovery (Hayek).[26]

Israel M. Kirzner and the idea of dynamic efficiency

Kirzner is the great contemporary scholar who, following in the footsteps of Mises and Hayek, has developed *in extenso* the analysis of entrepreneurship. He is also one of the most remarkable theorists to study the economic concept of dynamic efficiency, which he defines as the 'ability to encourage entrepreneurial alertness to valuable knowledge the very existence of which has not previously been suspected'. Kirzner sees the entrepreneurial act as extraordinarily coordinating and views social coordination not in a static or Paretian sense, but in a dynamic sense; that is, as a 'process during which market participants become aware of mutually beneficial opportunities for trade and, in grasping these opportunities, move to correct the earlier errors'.[27]

In addition, Kirzner has been careful to point out that his dynamic-efficiency criterion, which is based on creativity and entrepreneurial coordination, is free of all value judgement and therefore totally *wertfrei*: anyone who wishes to promote coordination must encourage and foster free entrepreneurship; in contrast, anyone who prefers social maladjustments and conflicts must place all sorts of obstacles in the way of entrepreneurship.[28] Economic theory alone cannot label ends good or bad, although it undoubtedly helps people to more fully grasp the ethical choices they face and to more easily adopt a consistent moral position.

Kirzner's idea of dynamic efficiency is also unaffected by the other criticisms we have outlined against the different static-efficiency standards prevalent until now. Finally, Kirzner indicates that, from an analytical standpoint, the dynamic aspect of efficiency is a particularly useful tool for producing comparative analyses of different institutions and legislative possibilities. Indeed, the dynamic-efficiency analysis makes it possible to perform an evaluation which leads to a much clearer and in many cases much different position than the one which usually follows from a mere static-efficiency analysis.[29]

Murray N. Rothbard and the myth of static efficiency: Roy E. Cordato's attempt at summation

Rothbard has also made valuable contributions to the field of dynamic-efficiency analysis. This author has stressed that the 'static-efficiency' ideal, to which the theorists of welfare economics attach primary importance in their studies, is no more than a *myth*, since its operative management requires a given framework of ends and means which can never come to exist, much less be known, in the constantly changing social environment of the real world. Furthermore, Rothbard is perhaps the author who has most plainly revealed the connection between the dynamic conception of economic efficiency and the sphere of ethics. Considering the lack of knowledge of the ends, means and utility functions that truly exist in society, Rothbard finds it imperative to first establish an appropriate ethical framework which stimulates dynamic efficiency. This framework comprises the set of rules which govern property rights and permit voluntary trade in which the different economic agents invariably demonstrate their true preferences. Rothbard maintains that *ethical principles* alone can act as a standard of efficiency by which to make decisions.[30]

Roy E. Cordato has published an interesting book in which, from the perspective of welfare economics, he examines the main contributions of Austrian economists in general, and of Mises, Rothbard, Hayek and Kirzner in particular. Cordato arrives at the conclusion that, rather than the achievement of 'optimum' results (the objective of static efficiency), the chief goal in the market should be the predominance of a suitable institutional framework which furthers entrepreneurial discovery and coordination. Economic policy must be directed toward identifying and removing the artificial obstacles which interfere with voluntary trade and the entrepreneurial process.[31] Cordato's attempt is especially valuable in that through it he aims

Joseph Alois Schumpeter and the 'process of creative destruction'

Joseph Alois Schumpeter is perhaps one of the most widely known authors to apply a distinctive conception of the dynamic angle to the analysis of economic efficiency. Schumpeter initiated his program of research in this area as early as 1911, when he published the first German edition of *The Theory of Economic Development*.[32] In this book, Schumpeter, following a traditional Austrian line of research, writes of the entrepreneur as innovator, one who imagines and discovers new goods, combinations of goods and sources of supply, and who introduces technological innovations while constantly creating new markets and expanding the existing ones. Thirty years later, in 1942, Schumpeter continued in the same line of research in his book *Capitalism, Socialism and Democracy*, particularly in chapters 7 and 8. This last chapter is even entitled 'The Process of Creative Destruction', and in it the author describes the process of economic development which triggered the evolution of capitalism and thus gave rise to the tension inherent in the two dimensions of efficiency, the dynamic and the static. Schumpeter is very critical of the traditional static-efficiency principle employed in neoclassical economics and concludes that 'perfect competition is not only impossible but inferior and has no title to being set up as a model of ideal efficiency'.[33]

Our primary criticism of Schumpeter is that he continues to hold that the basic point of reference in economic analysis should be the equilibrium model, since he considers that the economic world would usually be in a state of routine flow if it were not for entrepreneurs. Hence, Schumpeter sees the entrepreneur as a solely distorting or unbalancing factor. In other words, he focuses on only one of the facets of the entrepreneurial process, that which he refers to with the now stock expression 'the process of creative destruction'. Schumpeter overlooks the fact that, as we have set out in the preceding sections, economic analysis should concentrate on the dynamic entrepreneurial process rather than on the model of equilibrium. For at the same time that the real market process driven by entrepreneurship possesses a capacity for 'creative destruction' (the only feature Schumpeter mentions), it also has an essentially coordinating capacity which tends to drive the social process toward a state of equilibrium, though this state never arrives because new maladjustments continually emerge as it approaches. Schumpeter regards the entrepreneurial process as a sort of explosive force which, due to entrepreneurial creativity, distorts the pre-existing order, yet he fails to realize that *the same force which provokes creative destruction tends to coordinate the system and therefore make the social 'Big Bang' as harmonious as possible in all historical circumstances.* In contrast with the outlook of

Schumpeter, who sees the entrepreneur as a wholly unbalancing factor, our dynamic approach begins with a view of entrepreneurship as both a creative and coordinating driving force which continuously urges the market and civilization forward.

Harvey Leibenstein's concept of x-efficiency

Harvey Leibenstein first introduced the concept of x-efficiency in his article 'Allocative Efficiency vs. X-Efficiency', published in 1966.[34] In this paper, Leibenstein conceives x-inefficiency as the degree of inefficiency which arises in the market because many of the contracts which govern entrepreneurial relationships are incomplete, above all because they fail to properly specify the tasks each person must complete. Leibenstein also identifies as sources of inefficiency the psychological pressure the different economic agents face and the burden of the habits, inertia and routines which confine to an indefinite state of inefficiency many tasks that could yield improved results.

We should note that Leibenstein's concept of x-efficiency is rather ambiguous, or at least was in its initial formulations. It seems as if Leibenstein had intuited an important idea (that there exists a type of inefficiency which goes unnoticed in equilibrium models), yet he is unable to articulate it with total clarity. Ten years later, in an article ironically entitled 'The Existence of X-Efficiency',[35] Stigler (1976) responded to Leibenstein that in any case, the amount of ignorance and inertia existent in the market will always be optimum, since the effort to overcome them will cease right when the marginal cost derived from them begins to exceed the expected marginal revenue. Later, Kirzner offered support to Leibenstein with the argument that there would always be at least one important source of x-inefficiency, namely the genuine entrepreneurial error which arises precisely when one fails to recognize a profit opportunity in the market. Such an opportunity then remains in a latent state for other entrepreneurs to discover and seize.[36]

To put it another way, Kirzner makes the basic point that when we admit that, by definition, x-inefficiency does not exist in a context of equilibrium and perfect information (such was Stigler's patently irrelevant argument), the only way to preserve the concept of x-efficiency in an analytical and operative sense is to equate it with the concept of dynamic efficiency presented here, an idea which Leibenstein himself seems to have ultimately accepted. Ironically, the father of x-efficiency has been obliged to admit that his originally hazy concept can only retain its (high) degree of relevance if we eliminate its vagueness and ambiguity and identify it with the concept of dynamic efficiency as defined in this paper.[37]

Douglas C. North and his concept of 'adaptive efficiency'

A Nobel Laureate in Economics, Douglas C. North has criticized the merely allocative, Paretian concept of efficiency prevalent among neoclassical economists, and he proposes the alternative idea of *adaptive efficiency*, which he defines as 'the willingness of a society to acquire knowledge and learning, to induce innovation, to undertake risks and creative activity of all sorts, as well as to resolve problems and bottlenecks of the society through time'.[38]

As is evident, North includes in this definition a number of attributes which fully agree with those we have already analysed in connection with dynamic efficiency: the acquisition of knowledge, creativity, innovation, etc. Moreover, and perhaps more characteristic of North, the author focuses particularly on the *institutional framework* of guidelines which further different societies' creativity and ability to adapt, and he speaks of Europe and the United States as historical models of flexibility and adaptive capacity.

Our chief criticism of Douglas C. North is that he neglects to expressly mention entrepreneurship as the vital force behind all market processes. That is to say, North concentrates almost solely on the ability of societies in general to *adapt* to the 'external' changes and shocks which affect them and which are supposedly always of external origin, and it is precisely this viewpoint that leads North to suggest the term '*adaptive* efficiency'. Thus North's approach is much more reactive than proactive. In fact, North does not appear to realize that the entrepreneurial drive which characterizes dynamic efficiency and its coordinating capacity is precisely that which simultaneously provokes the (endogenous rather than external) changes and shocks that trigger the problems to which different societies must adapt.

Hence, North and Schumpeter work from totally opposite perspectives. While Schumpeter focuses exclusively on the aspect of entrepreneurial creativity and its destructive power (the process of 'creative destruction'), North concentrates on the other aspect; that is, the adaptive or coordinating capacity of entrepreneurship, and *he overlooks the simultaneously creative facet it invariably possesses. In this sense, we may consider that our theory of dynamic efficiency fuelled by entrepreneurship appropriately combines the creative and coordinating dimensions which Schumpeter and North have studied separately and partially, in a reductionist manner, each excluding important elements.*

Dynamic efficiency and Ronald H. Coase's transaction costs theory

It now seems fitting to make a few remarks about the possible relationship between the concept of dynamic efficiency and Ronald H. Coase's transaction costs theory, which has gained considerable influence in many areas of economic analysis, especially in the study of law and institutions.[39]

Perhaps the essential difference between the two approaches is the one Israel Kirzner has noted. According to Kirzner, the main obstacle to dynamic efficiency is not posed by transaction costs, but by what he calls 'pure or genuine entrepreneurial error', which appears in the market in the absence of sufficient entrepreneurial alertness.[40] To put it another way, even if we could imagine a hypothetical nirvana[41] or 'ideal world with zero transaction costs', such a system would fail to achieve the ideal of dynamic efficiency if, due to pure or genuine entrepreneurial errors, multiple opportunities for profit remained undiscovered or were not created or seized. Ultimately, despite the appearances, the transaction costs approach has many of the deficiencies we covered with respect to the static dimension of efficiency. Specifically, a comparative institutional analysis based on the different transaction costs of each institution implies the assumption that these costs are given and known, and that it is even possible to redesign an institution to modify the transaction costs in any particular situation. Nonetheless, the entire structure of transaction costs that is chosen as a frame of reference in the analysis can change radically and without warning if an act of pure entrepreneurial creativity leads to the discovery of new alternatives, production possibilities and, in general, new solutions which entrepreneurs had completely overlooked up to that point.

Consequently, as we shall see in detail, the initial distribution of property rights can never be irrelevant from the perspective of dynamic efficiency, rooted as it is in creativity and entrepreneurial coordination (not even in the extreme case of a complete lack of transaction costs, as the Coase theorem erroneously implies). In fact, the distribution of property rights, within the ethical framework which makes dynamic efficiency possible and which we will analyse later, is precisely what determines, in each specific time and place, who will be motivated by the particular incentives necessary to awaken entrepreneurial activity, with its dual aspects of creativity and coordination. In other words, from the standpoint of dynamic efficiency based on entrepreneurship, Coase's theorem, regardless of how it is interpreted, is scientifically invalid, since not even in a hypothetical, institutional scenario with no transaction costs will the distribution of property rights be irrelevant when dynamic efficiency is the goal.[42]

The concept of dynamic efficiency in economics textbooks

The dynamic aspect of economic efficiency has been virtually ignored by most writers of economics textbooks. Once again, this reveals the fixation with comparative statics and equilibrium prevalent thus far among economists and exposes the resultant urgent need for a paradigm shift to bring in the dynamic analysis of markets, along with the concept of dynamic efficiency.

From a sample of twenty economics manuals chosen among the best known in English, Spanish, French, German and Italian, only four included explicit mentions of dynamic efficiency. Furthermore, most of these honourable exceptions provided only a very limited discussion of the concept and failed to consistently incorporate the discussion into an overall analysis to permit the evaluation in terms of dynamic efficiency of the different institutions and alternatives covered by each textbook. An overview of the most striking approaches to dynamic efficiency follows.[43]

Although Gwartney and Stroup's textbook *Economics: Private and Public Choice*[44] does not explicitly include the term 'dynamic efficiency', it does explain that the world is in a permanent state of change as a consequence of entrepreneurial creativity and the process of competition among entrepreneurs. According to the authors, this constant change obliges economists to reassess traditional notions of static efficiency.

Dolan and Lindsay[45] provide a much more explicit analysis of dynamic efficiency, especially with respect to the distinctions between static efficiency and dynamic efficiency, which they define as 'a measure of the rate at which the production possibility frontier shifts outward over time'. In contrast, they describe static efficiency as 'a measure of how close an economy comes to its production possibility frontier'. Moreover, Dolan and Lindsay refer to Schumpeter's pioneering contributions in the area of dynamic efficiency, and they consider innovation and technological discoveries the main forces behind it, though they do not neglect to mention the creative power of entrepreneurship, nor that the recognition of it has been a fundamental contribution of Austrian theorists. In fact, the authors of this manual go so far as to estimate the possible losses to the American economy in static efficiency from the Second World War to today, and they deem this figure equal to an average of 2.5 per cent of the US gross domestic product. In addition, the authors state their belief that these losses have been more than amply compensated for by the gains in dynamic efficiency which over the same period have resulted from the creativity and coordinating force of American entrepreneurship.

In 1998, Wolfgang Kasper and Manfred E. Streit published an important manual on the economic analysis of institutions. In this book, the authors define dynamic efficiency as 'an inherent quality to adapt, respond or develop new knowledge'.[46] As we see, in this book Kasper and Streit come very close to the theory of dynamic efficiency we have presented. Furthermore, these authors join Demsetz in criticizing the 'nirvana approach', which is typical of the neoclassical methodology and revolves around comparisons of reality with the utopia of static efficiency. Kasper and Streit conclude that many supposed 'market failures' cannot be considered as such from a dynamic standpoint, since they either foster creativity and the introduction of new technology (as would be the case of 'monopolies') or constitute the most basic characteristic of real markets (as is the case with 'asymmetric information', uninsurable moral hazard inherent in each entrepreneurial act, etc.). Therefore, according to these authors, the analyst must compare actual institutions not with ideal, unattainable models (as welfare-economics theorists have done up to now), but with alternative institutions which are feasible and promote creativity and the coordinating power of entrepreneurship. Hence, Kasper and Streit supplement Demsetz's intuitions with Hayek's theory on the emergence and creation of the knowledge which entrepreneurs continually discover in market processes.

Along the same lines, O'Driscoll and Rizzo explain in their book *The Economics of Time and Ignorance* that it is inappropriate to criticize the real market process, as neoclassical economists often do, for falling short of the production possibility curve; that is, because supposed market 'failures' prevent it from being statically efficient. According to these authors, such criticism implies that we can come to know information which emerges only from the real market process and which, if we knew it a priori, would render the process unnecessary and redundant. In other words, no one can be acquainted with the production possibility curve because it is not given, but is always being disrupted and shifted to the right by entrepreneurial creativity. To find fault with the market because it fails to reach a limit which no one has knowledge of and which varies continually not only constitutes a serious methodological error, but can also lead to the absurd justification of interventionist economic policies which ultimately hinder the real market process, when this very process is the driving force behind the perpetual quantitative and qualitative increase in the possibilities of the production frontier.[47]

Finally, we would not wish to conclude this review of the manuals that have covered, even if superficially, the notion of dynamic efficiency, without mentioning the curious case of the textbook by Wonnacott and Wonnacott, who insist on defining 'dynamic efficiency' in strictly 'static' terms; that is, as the 'optimal' rate of technological change. The reference rate used to determine whether or not an economic system is approaching the 'optimal' rate is left unspecified. These authors contend that it is the model of perfect competition which stimulates dynamic efficiency, to the extent that it obliges companies to rapidly implement new technologies. They also point out that a certain amount of debate exists over whether competition or monopoly is the system which most encourages the creation and discovery of new technologies. In any case, Wonnacott and Wonnacott's handling of dynamic efficiency is not only entirely dependent upon their static view of the economy, but also quite confusing (and disconcerting). It appears as if the authors inserted the corresponding paragraph in the textbook to cover a topic considered important, yet they neglected to support it with any dynamic analysis of the real market processes that are driven by entrepreneurship.[48]

In conclusion to this brief overview of the scientific literature most widely used in teaching, we can affirm that, despite the isolated exceptions cited above, economists are still very far from generally accepting the principle of dynamic efficiency, and from beginning to systematically implement it and consider its ramifications. When they do, and no study in applied economics excludes the aspect of dynamic efficiency, its analysis will eventually filter into the textbooks and become essential, standard material in all economics manuals, to be used by students worldwide.

The relationship between ethics and dynamic efficiency

Introduction

We mentioned in the second section that the 'second fundamental theorem of welfare economics,' developed within the static framework of neoclassical theory, depicts efficiency and ethics as two distinct dimensions which may be combined in different ways.[49] In fact, from the perspective of welfare economics, multiple Pareto optimums exist (represented by each and every point on the production possibility curve), and every one of these points could correspond to a unique ethical model of income redistribution. Thus, for example, in the Bergson–Samuelson view, a hypothetical 'social-welfare function' would potentially embody the socially acceptable model of redistribution and would lead us to the 'optimum optimorum' at the point of intersection between the social-welfare function and the production possibility curve. This type of analysis has convinced many thinkers of the theory's supposed vagueness as a tool for evaluating an economic system, since they consider such an evaluation ultimately dependent on value judgements which lie outside the scope of economic theory.

This entire mainstream paradigm is disrupted completely if we introduce the dynamic conception of economic efficiency: for, as we shall see, not all ethical systems of income redistribution are compatible with dynamic efficiency understood as entrepreneurial creativity and coordination. Thus the economics theorist encounters a fascinating field of research that centres precisely on determining which principles of social ethics or distributive justice drive and are compatible with the market processes that characterize dynamic efficiency.

Ethics as a necessary and sufficient condition for dynamic efficiency

Most of the stances on distributive justice and social ethics which up to now have predominated and have formed the 'ethical foundation' of important political and social movements (of a 'socialist' or social democratic nature) are rooted in the static conception of economic efficiency. The established paradigm of neoclassical economic theory rests on the idea that information is objective and given (either in certain or probabilistic terms), and thus that it is possible to make cost–benefit analyses based on it and, as we have indicated, that the issues of utility maximization have absolutely no connection with moral considerations, and hence the two can be combined in different proportions. Furthermore, the dominant static viewpoint led almost inexorably to the conclusion that resources are in a sense given and known, and therefore the economic problem of their distribution was deemed separate and distinct from the issue of their production. Granted, if resources are given it is vitally important to inquire into the best way to allocate among different people both the available means of production and the final result of the different production processes.

This whole approach collapses like a stack of cards in light of the new dynamic conception of market processes, which hinges on the theory of entrepreneurship and on the notion of dynamic efficiency we have been examining. From this perspective, every person possesses an innate creative capacity that enables him to perceive and discover the profit opportunities which arise in his environment, and to act accordingly to take advantage of them. Therefore, entrepreneurship consists of the typically human ability to perpetually create and discover new ends and means. From this point of view, resources are never given, but, instead, both ends and means are continually devised *ex novo* by entrepreneurs, who always wish to reach new objectives that they *discover* to be of value. At the same time, this creative power of entrepreneurship combines, as we have seen, with its capacity for coordination. Therefore, if ends, means and resources are not 'given', but are continually created from nothing as a result of the entrepreneurial action of humans, clearly the fundamental ethical question ceases to be how to fairly distribute 'what exists', and becomes how, in view of human nature, to best foster entrepreneurial coordination and creativity.

Consequently, in the field of social ethics, we arrive at the fundamental conclusion that the conception of human beings as creative, coordinating actors involves the axiomatic acceptance of the principle that *each person has the right to appropriate the results of his entrepreneurial creativity*. That is, the private appropriation of the fruits of entrepreneurial creation and discovery is a tenet of natural law, because if an actor were not able to claim what he or she creates or discovers, his or her capacity to detect profit opportunities would become blocked, and his or her incentive to act would disappear. Moreover, the above principle is universal in that it can be applied to all people at all possible times and in all conceivable places.

The precept we have just set out, which provides the ethical basis for all market economies, offers other decided, characteristic advantages. First, it possesses a strong, intuitive and universal attraction: it seems obvious that if someone creates something from nothing, he has the right to appropriate it, since in doing so he does no harm to anyone.[50] (Before he invented his creation, it did not exist, and thus its invention harms no one, and it benefits at least the creative actor, when it does not also benefit many other people.) Second, the above is a universally sound ethical principle which is closely related to the traditional precept of Roman law regarding homesteading or the original appropriation of resources that belong to no one (*occupatio rei nullius*). In addition, it offers a solution to the paradox represented by 'Locke's proviso', which places the following limit on original appropriation: a sufficient 'number' of resources must be left for other people. The principle we defend, which rests on creativity, renders 'Locke's proviso' unnecessary: no product of human creativity exists prior to its entrepreneurial discovery or creation, and therefore its appropriation cannot hurt anyone. Hence, Locke's condition makes sense only in a static environment in which it is presumed that resources already exist (and thus are 'given'), that they do not change and that they must be distributed among a predetermined number of people.

If we conceive the economy as a dynamic, entrepreneurial process, the ethical principle which must govern social interactions rests on the view that the fairest society is the one which most energetically promotes the entrepreneurial creativity of all of its members. To achieve this goal, it is imperative that a society provide each member with the a priori guarantee that he will be permitted to appropriate the results of his entrepreneurial creativity and that no one will expropriate these results, either partially or totally, much less the public authorities.

We must conclude that the aforementioned basic principle of social ethics, one which hinges on the private ownership of all that is entrepreneurially created and discovered, and thus on the voluntary exchange of all goods and services, is both the necessary and the sufficient condition for dynamic efficiency. This principle is a necessary condition, because to impede the private ownership of the fruits of each human action is to remove the most powerful incentive to create and discover profit opportunities as well as the fundamental source of creativity and coordination that propels the system's dynamic efficiency (i.e. the rightward movement of the corresponding production possibility curve). However, the ethics of private property constitute not only the necessary condition for dynamic efficiency, but also the sufficient condition. Given the vital drive which characterizes all human beings, an environment of freedom in which they are not coerced and in which their private property is respected constitutes a sufficient condition for the development of the entrepreneurial process of creativity and coordination which marks dynamic efficiency.

To hinder free human action to any degree by impairing people's right to own what they entrepreneurially create is not only dynamically inefficient, since it obstructs their creativity and coordinating capacity, but also fundamentally immoral, since such coercion prevents the actor from developing that which is by nature most essential in himself, i.e. his innate ability to create and conceive new ends and means and to act accordingly in an attempt to achieve his objectives. To the extent that state coercion impedes entrepreneurial human action, people's creative capacity will be limited, and the information or knowledge necessary to coordinate society will not emerge or be discovered. Thus socialism and the economic interventionism of the state in general are not only dynamically inefficient but also ethically reprehensible.[51]

It is precisely for the above reasons that not only is socialism an intellectual error, since it stops people from generating the information needed by the regulatory agency to coordinate society via coercive commands, but also, as we have indicated, it conflicts with human nature and is ethically unacceptable. In other words, the analysis up to this point exposes the socialist, interventionist system as immoral, because it is built upon the use of force to prevent each person from claiming the product of his own entrepreneurial creativity. Thus we see not only that socialism is theoretically impossible and dynamically *inefficient*, but that at the same time it is an essentially *immoral* social system, since it contradicts the most intimate aspect of human nature by keeping people from acting freely and appropriating the results of their own entrepreneurial creativity, and thus from realizing their potential.[52]

22 *The theory of dynamic efficiency*

Hence, according to our analysis, nothing is more (dynamically) efficient than Justice (in its proper sense). If we perceive the market as a dynamic process, then dynamic efficiency, understood as coordination and creativity, emerges from the behaviour of human beings who follow certain moral laws (regarding the respect for life, private property and the fulfilment of contracts). In this way, the exercise of human action subject to these ethical principles gives rise to a dynamically efficient social process such as we have been describing. It is now easy to see why, *from a dynamic standpoint, efficiency is not compatible with different models of equity or justice (as the second fundamental theorem of welfare economics erroneously stated), but instead arises exclusively from one (that based on the respect for private property and entrepreneurship)*. Therefore, the contradiction between efficiency and justice is false. What is just cannot be inefficient, and what is efficient cannot be unjust. A dynamic analysis reveals that justice and efficiency are but two sides of the same coin, which also *confirms the consistent, integrated order that exists in the social realm*. Consequently, our study of dynamic efficiency allows us to discover which ethical principles make this type of efficiency possible. Even more significant and ambitious, however, is that our study permits an objective and scientifically uniform handling of all social problems.[53]

Dynamic efficiency and the principles of personal morality

Up to this point, we have looked at social ethics and discussed the key principles which provide the framework that makes dynamic efficiency possible. Outside that sphere we find the most intimate principles of personal morality. The influence of such principles on dynamic efficiency has rarely been studied, and in any case they are considered part of a realm that is separate and distinct from that of social ethics. Nevertheless, we believe this separation to be completely unjustified. In fact, a number of ethical and moral principles are of great importance to the dynamic efficiency of social processes, and with respect to these standards the following paradox arises: the failure to meet them on a personal level entails a staggering cost in terms of dynamic efficiency; however, the attempt to impose them on people via the coercive force of the public authorities also generates severe inefficiency from the dynamic standpoint. Hence, certain social institutions carry major significance in transmitting and encouraging the observance of these personal moral principles which, by their very nature, cannot be imposed by force but are nevertheless of vital importance to the dynamic efficiency of society. Through religion and the family, for example, people internalize these principles and thus learn to uphold them habitually and to transmit them to the next generation.[54] The principles which relate to sexual morality, the creation and indefinite preservation of the family institution, faithfulness between spouses and the care of children, the control of atavistic urges and, specifically, the overcoming and restraint of unhealthy envy, etc. are all of crucial importance to the successful working of the social process of creativity and coordination, and to its fostering dynamic efficiency in society as well as possible.

When an individual fails to observe moral principles, this lack of compliance ultimately and invariably results in some appalling human cost which affects not only the person who triggers it but also a large group of third parties who have a direct or indirect connection with him. In fact, such behaviour can even come to block much of the dynamic efficiency of an entire social system. Much more serious is the spread of immoral behaviours through the systematic processes of moral corruption which can eventually and completely paralyse the healthy, efficient social process. Therefore, the study, from the perspective of the economic theory of dynamic efficiency, of the role of personal moral principles and the different social institutions which make possible and encourage their fulfilment and preservation in society opens up an extremely significant field of research for scholars, one we hope will exert a decisive influence in the future.

For an illustration of the possibility and value of examining personal moral principles in terms of dynamic efficiency, let us consider the behaviour spouses should, with consistent effort, aspire to and maintain, to keep their marriages going and preserve the institution of the family, for their own benefit and especially for that of their children. For example, if a family man begins to give way to a more or less frivolous desire for an attractive, young companion over all else, he could very likely end up divorcing his wife, precisely when she is getting older and the children are nearly grown. If such behaviour becomes widespread, then before women decide to marry and start a family they may very well begin to reflect on the high risk that their husbands may abandon them just as they are wrapping up a period of long years spent raising children, and precisely at a time when their age and abilities put them at a disadvantage in the labour market. As a result, not only will a larger number of marriages and families be broken up but, even more significantly, the rate at which new marriages and families are started will decline, and women will tend to prolong their single life to ensure their professional careers and independent means of support, all of which will lead to a dramatic drop in the birth rate. In the absence of migratory trends to ease the decrease in the birth rate and the consequent aging of the population, the social process of entrepreneurial creativity and coordination which fuels dynamic efficiency will suffer. Both the progress of civilization and economic and social development require a constantly expanding population capable of sustaining, among a continually increasing number of people, the steady growth in the volume of social knowledge which entrepreneurial creativity generates. Ultimately, dynamic efficiency depends on people's creativity and capacity for coordination, and, other things being equal, it will tend to increase as the number of human beings increases, which can only happen within a certain framework of moral laws to govern family relationships.

It is easy to see that in the context of family relationships the principles of personal morality take on crucial importance to dynamic efficiency. Nevertheless, it is also true and only apparently paradoxical that the state must not use coercive force to impose such principles in a manner similar to that in which it defends, for example, the legal regulations of criminal law. The latter mainly prohibit certain behaviours which involve the criminal use of violence or deception against other people; that is, physical violence or the threat of it, or the criminal achievement of some end via deceit or fraud. In contrast, the coercive imposition of personal moral principles would cripple dynamic efficiency: personal family relationships, for example, belong to the most private sphere of human life, and it is practically impossible for an outsider to obtain all of the information necessary to make well-informed judgements about them, much less to resolve conceivable problems when the involved parties lack sufficient desire or willingness to solve them. The promotion of the entire framework of personal moral principles, insofar as they can be imposed by force, to the rank of legal regulations would only give rise to a closed, inquisitorial society that would deprive the population of nearly all of the individual freedoms which comprise the foundation of entrepreneurship, the only possible inducement to dynamic efficiency in the whole social process.

The above considerations reveal the importance of alternative, non-coercive methods of social guidance which expose people to the most intimate and personal moral precepts and encourage their internalization and observance. Religious feelings and principles, which are acquired at an early age within the family, play an indispensable role in this regard (together with the social pressure exerted by other members of the family and community). Religious precepts provide direction under which to act, they help people control their most atavistic impulses and they serve as a guide in the selection of those people with whom we decide to build an intimate relationship or even a family and the rest of our lives. Other things being equal, the firmer and more enduring a person's moral principles appear, the greater the esteem that person should inspire.[55]

The evolution of ethical principles: institutions essential to dynamic efficiency

Elsewhere we have defined the concept of 'institution' as 'any generalized pattern of conduct or behavior',[56] and in this sense it is easy to deduce from the analysis thus far that the social process of creation and coordination of which dynamic efficiency consists must be guided; that is, it must be subject to ethics and law or, in other words, to a series of moral principles and legal rules.

In fact, as we have seen, the basic entrepreneurial act consists of buying at a low price and selling at a high one, and thus grasping a profit opportunity and coordinating the initially maladjusted behaviour of social agents. This act would be thwarted or would fail to take place if all participating parties did not guarantee the fulfilment of their commitments; or, for example, if some circumstance rendered the contract void, or if any of the contracting parties consented due to fraud or deception, at the time either of payment or of the delivery of the good, of the quality promised. For this reason, basic legal principles, such as the respect for life, peacefully acquired ownership, the fulfilment of contracts and, in general, compliance with the *legal regulations which have evolved through custom and which comprise civil and criminal law provides the basic institutional structure or prerequisite for dynamic efficiency*. The same can be said of the personal moral principles we discussed in the last section, of the natural right to own private property and of the implications of this right, all of which compose the foundation of basic social ethics which is entirely responsible for sustaining dynamic efficiency.

Although these principles have emerged through an evolutionary process, they form part of human nature. To put it another way, human nature manifests itself through a process of evolution, and, with the benefit of hindsight and the use of reason, man is then able to refine the principles which arise from his errors in logic and contradictions, to strengthen these principles, and through careful study to apply them to the new areas and challenges that develop in society. Therefore, any scientific analysis of the dynamic aspect of social efficiency must begin with the acknowledgement that such a study can never be conducted in an institutional vacuum; that is, that the theoretical analysis of dynamic efficiency is inseparable from the study of the institutional framework in which entrepreneurial behaviours take place. As a result, we should be particularly critical of the existing economic theory of nirvana developed by neoclassical welfare economists, the majority of whom insist on judging real market processes in a complete institutional vacuum; in other words, with a total disregard for real-life human interactions.

Hence, a vast field of research is opening up for specialists in applied economics and involves the examination and re-evaluation of each and every social institution (economic, juridical, moral, ethical and even linguistic) with a view to analysing the capacity of each to trigger dynamic efficiency and the role each plays in the encouragement of it. Elsewhere we have explained that the theorist who embarks on this task must be particularly thorough and prudent, above all because he attempts to analyse highly complex, real-life features of society which have evolved over time, are accompanied by a huge volume of experience and information, compose human nature and are not often easily understood via the conceptual tools of the analyst.[57]

In the next and last section of this chapter, we will provide some examples of practical applications to illustrate, or at least sketch, the direction in which we believe the economic analysis of social institutions may evolve in the future if the dynamic concept of economic efficiency we have presented is consistently applied.

Several practical applications

We will now touch upon several specific areas which we believe could be enriched by the systematic application of the dynamic-efficiency approach we have proposed in this chapter. As is logical, we will not attempt here to perform an analysis, much less a thorough one. Our only goal is to suggest a few provisional ideas on some lines of research which appear quite promising and remain available for the future efforts of those scholars who ultimately determine that the study of the dynamic conception of economic efficiency can be productive and compelling:

1. We must mention *taxation theory*. We have already observed the vital role that (pure) entrepreneurial profits (and losses) play in terms of guiding the creative and coordinating action of entrepreneurs. In fact, such profits are the primary sign that directs and drives the market process which leads to dynamic efficiency. The distortion of entrepreneurial profits due to fiscal causes can seriously effect the entire process of dynamic efficiency (i.e. creativity and coordination), and thus generate a high cost in the shape of a reduction in dynamic efficiency. This cost would be additional to the one theorists refer to as 'excess burden', which, from the perspective of the economic analysis of equilibrium, corresponds to the loss of static efficiency, the only loss accounted for up to now by optimal tax theory.[58] Consequently, the ideal goal would be to avoid taxing pure entrepreneurial profits, in order to foster dynamic efficiency. It is important to recognize that this economic-policy goal presents significant practical problems which stem from the fact that under nearly all true circumstances pure entrepreneurial profits are inseparable from other sources of income (labour, capital, land, etc.). Nevertheless, these difficulties should challenge those analysts and researchers who wish to promote dynamic efficiency, and encourage them to search for new tax procedures and to develop fiscal reforms that minimize the negative impact on pure entrepreneurial profits and thus on entrepreneurial creativity and coordination.[59]
2. The *theory of regulation and interventionism* (i.e. the economic analysis of institutional coercion) could also be enriched by the systematic application of the dynamic approach. The objective here would be to examine all acts of regulation and economic intervention so that, as they take the shape of restrictions on the free exercise of entrepreneurship, their possible effects can be studied in terms of dynamic inefficiency. Moreover, the diagnosis of the inefficiency problems caused by economic interventionism should make it possible to devise reforms which can be more or less gradually implemented with the purpose of removing the existing obstacles to creativity and coordination, and of thus fostering the dynamic efficiency of the system.
3. The dynamic-efficiency approach suggests a completely different angle from which to view *antitrust legislation*. From the perspective of dynamic

market processes driven by entrepreneurship, and in the absence of institutional hindrances to free human action in any entrepreneurial environment, the process of rivalry between entrepreneurs often culminates in the temporary dominance of only a few producers (or even just one) in the market at a particular time and place. Far from indicating a (supposed) 'market failure', this occurrence would constitute one of the most typical manifestations of the success of these entrepreneurs at satisfying better than anyone else the desires of consumers (i.e. at discovering and conceiving new products of increasing quality and placing them on the market at decreasing prices). Thus, restrictive legislation designed to 'defend' competition could generate high costs in terms of dynamic efficiency, to the extent that potential entrepreneurs take for granted that, should they be successful (at introducing a certain innovation, or launching a product, or capturing the market), the public authorities may requisition or even partially or totally expropriate the results of their creativity. The cases of Microsoft and others are topical and currently in everyone's mind, so it is not necessary to go into detail about them. An observation similar to the above can be made concerning many other practices, such as price agreements among suppliers, market sharing, the joint sale of goods, exclusive-distribution agreements, etc. Even though these may be seen as restrictive measures from the standpoint of static efficiency, which until now has permeated antitrust legislation, they may make all the sense in the world from the perspective of dynamic efficiency, which plays a central role in real market processes.[60]

4. The *economic theory of development* is another sphere in which the application of the theory of dynamic efficiency is of great importance. Here the primary objective of economic policy would be to consider which possible reforms could remove obstacles and boost entrepreneurship in developing countries. Let us not forget that the entrepreneur is undoubtedly the leading figure in any process of economic development. For this reason, one cannot help being surprised at the sheer volume of pages which have been written in vain on the economic theory of underdevelopment because the authors have completely overlooked the key player in economic growth processes (the entrepreneur) and have made no mention of the role entrepreneurship plays in both its creative and coordinating facets. In this sense, neoclassical academics of the theory of growth and underdevelopment are to a great extent responsible, by omission and commission, for the failure of many economic policies in developing countries to include the necessary measures to protect, foster and encourage indigenous as well as foreign entrepreneurs who decide to stake their assets upon those countries which most need investments, as their inhabitants live near subsistence level.

5. The adoption of the dynamic-efficiency view could also enrich *macroeconomics* in general and *monetary theory* in particular. We have known from the time of Carl Menger that money evolved through custom and

that its development was stimulated by the entrepreneurial ingenuity of those few who first realized that they could attain their goals more conveniently by demanding in return for their goods and services a medium of exchange easily tradable in the market. As this pattern of behaviour became generalized and habitual, money emerged as a generally accepted medium of exchange. In fact, money would be unnecessary in a hypothetical, static and perfectly efficient model of equilibrium, because such an unreal scenario would involve no future uncertainty, and thus no one would need to maintain any cash balances at all. However, real life is unpredictable, in great part precisely due to entrepreneurial creativity, which results in the constant generation of new information and in the modification of all market parameters, and thus it is essential that people maintain liquid balances to cope with an ever-changing and uncertain future. Hence, money has its origins in the uncertainty entrepreneurial creativity produces, and, at the same time, it makes it possible for humans to exercise their creative and coordinating entrepreneurship, since it permits them to face a consistently uncertain future with an open set of alternatives. From this standpoint, it is important that monetary institutions not hamper the processes of entrepreneurial coordination and thereby make the goal of dynamic efficiency difficult to reach. For example, if the creation of money in the form of credit expansion permits the initial financing of investment projects at a rate out of all proportion to that of the real increase in society's voluntary saving, then a severe inter-temporal discoordination or maladjustment will arise between the behaviour of investors and consumers. This maladjustment will first manifest itself in a speculative investment bubble financed through an over-issue of fiduciary media which will ultimately result in a disproportionate rise in the prices of capital goods. This expansionary process will sooner or later reverse in the form of an economic recession which will reveal the entrepreneurial errors committed and the need to convert and restructure the investment processes initiated in error.[61] Thus, an interesting field of research is now opening up to scholars and involves the evaluation of the current monetary and credit institutions in light of the concept of dynamic efficiency presented here. In time, these scholars will design a series of reforms which will foster entrepreneurial creativity and also further inter-temporal coordination, thus impeding the artificial maladjustments which up to now have recurrently attacked market economies since the development of the modern fractional-reserve banking system in the early nineteenth century.

6. Lastly, perhaps more than any other sphere of economics *the economic analysis of law, legal regulations and social institutions,* which up to this point has rested exclusively on the traditional postulates of the economic analysis of equilibrium, needs to be completely reworked in light of the new intuitions and contributions which only the dynamic conception of efficiency can offer. This new perspective will make it possible to evaluate

the different legal regulations and social institutions in a totally new manner, i.e. in terms of their capacity to drive entrepreneurial creativity and coordination. The dynamic approach will dramatically enrich the economic analysis of contract law, of civil liability, of patent, copyright and trademark law, of the family, etc., and in general it will exert the same effect on any other economic analysis of the laws and institutions closest to the actual social environment which is always fundamentally dynamic by its very nature.

As is logical, the above examples and illustrations do not come even close to exhausting the possible applications of the dynamic conception of economic efficiency, an approach which, as we have indicated, can and should be applied in all areas of economics, both theoretical and applied. It is our fervent hope that these illustrations act as an incentive for young scholars and researchers in our discipline, and that, as a result of their effort, they see their contributions enriched and crowned with success.

Conclusions

We have arrived at the following main conclusions in this paper:

1. Dynamic efficiency may be described as the capacity of an economic system to stimulate entrepreneurial creativity and coordination.
2. Nevertheless, the dynamic aspect of efficiency has been almost completely overlooked up to now by the majority of professional economists, who have focused almost exclusively on the merely allocative or static dimension of economic efficiency.
3. However, dynamic efficiency is the most important aspect of the economic concept of efficiency, especially in the real world, where equilibrium can never be reached and the ideal of allocative or static efficiency is by definition unattainable.
4. Many behaviours and institutions which appear to be inefficient by short-term allocative or static criteria are actually able to vigorously stimulate dynamic efficiency. This idea opens up an interesting field to scholars and researchers and challenges them to analyse the possible trade-offs between the two dimensions of efficiency and to design reform proposals which tend to promote entrepreneurial creativity and coordination.
5. Dynamic efficiency is far from compatible with different models of ethical behaviour and instead emerges from only one of them: the one that most respects private property, specifically the appropriation of the results of entrepreneurial creativity. In this way, ethics and the dynamic concept of efficiency appear as two sides of the same coin. Moreover, we have put forward the original argument that the basic principles of personal morality which have prevailed throughout the evolution of mankind also tend to foster dynamic efficiency. Hence, our dynamic view of economic

analysis permits a uniform, scientific handling of all social problems, and in this context the dimensions of efficiency and justice are not separate at all, but self-explanatory and mutually strengthening.

6. In conclusion, we believe that no economic-efficiency analysis should exclude the dynamic aspect. In other words, in all applied-economics studies, the analyst should always consider, from the perspective of dynamic efficiency, the possible effects of the practice, institution or reform proposals in question. In this way, dynamic efficiency will become a key factor to be considered in every economics study, and this change will not only open up a vast and hopefully very productive field of research to the future scholars in our discipline, but we also feel sure that it will lead to a much more fruitful and dynamically efficient development of our discipline in the service of humanity.

2 The ongoing *Methodenstreit* of the Austrian School[1]

> What distinguishes the Austrian School and will lend it immortal fame is precisely the fact that it created a theory of economic action and not of economic equilibrium or non-action.
>
> Ludwig von Mises[2]

Introduction

The fall of real socialism a few years ago and the crisis of the welfare state has meant a heavy blow for the mainly neoclassical research programme that has supported social engineering to date, at the same time as the conclusions of the Austrian theoretical analysis on the impossibility of socialism seem to be largely confirmed. In addition, 1996 was been the 125th anniversary of the Austrian School, which, as we know, came into official existence in 1871 with the publication of Carl Menger's *Grundsätze*.[3] It seems, therefore, that this is the appropriate moment to return to an analysis of the differences between the two approaches, Austrian and neoclassical, together with their comparative advantages, in the light of both the latest events and the most recent evolution of economic thought.

This article is divided into the following sections. First, the characteristics that distinguish the two approaches (Austrian and neoclassical) will be explained and discussed in detail. Second, a summarized account of the *Methodenstreit* which the Austrian School has been maintaining from 1871 to date will be presented discussing its different 'rounds' and implications. A reply to the most common criticisms made of the Austrian approach, together with an evaluation of the comparative advantages of the two points of view, will conclude the article.

The essential differences between the Austrian and Neoclassical Schools

Perhaps one of the main features which is lacking in the study programmes of the schools of economics is that, to date, they have not given a complete integrated view of the essential elements of the modern Austrian paradigm *vis-à-vis* the mainstream neoclassical approach. In Table 2.1, I have tried to

Table 2.1 Essential differences between the Austrian and Neoclassical Schools

Points of comparison	Austrian paradigm	Neoclassical paradigm
1 Concept of the economic point of view (essential principle)	Theory of human action understood as a dynamic process (*praxeology*)	Theory of *decision:* rational and based on constraint maximization
2 Methodological starting point	*Subjectivism*	Stereotype of *methodological individualism* (objectivist)
3 Protagonist of the social processes	Creative *entrepreneur*	*Homo oeconomicus*
4 Possibility that the actors err *a priori* and nature of entrepreneurial profit	Pure or sheer entrepreneurial error and *ex post* regret exist; pure entrepreneurial profits arise from alertness	There are no regrettable errors because all past decisions are explicable in terms of cost–benefit analysis; profits are considered the payment for the services of a factor of production
5 Nature of information	Knowledge and information are *subjective, disperse* and *change* constantly (entrepreneurial creativity); radical distinction between scientific knowledge (objective) and practical knowledge (subjective)	Complete, objective and *constant* information on ends and means is assumed; there is no distinction between practical (entrepreneurial) knowledge and scientific knowledge
6 Reference point	General process with a coordinating tendency; there is no distinction between micro and macro: all economic problems are studied in relation to each other	Model of *equilibrium* (general or partial).; separation between microeconomics and macroeconomics
7 Concept of 'competition'	Process of entrepreneurial rivalry	Situation or model of 'perfect competition'
8 Concept of cost	*Subjective* (depends on the alertness of the entrepreneur for the discovery of new alternative ends)	Objective and constant (it may be known by a third party and measured)
9 Formalism	*Verbal* logic (abstract and formal) which allows the integration of subjective time and human creativity	*Mathematical* formalism (symbolic language typical of the analysis of constant atemporal phenomena)
10 Relation with the empirical world	*Aprioristic-deductive* reasoning; radical separation and, at the same time, coordination between theory (science) and history (art); history cannot prove theories	*Empirical* falsation of hypotheses (at least rhetorically)

Table 2.1 continued.

Points of comparison	Austrian paradigm	Neoclassical paradigm
11 Possibilities of specific prediction	Impossible, since what will happen depends on future entrepreneurial knowledge which has not yet been created; only qualitative and theoretical 'pattern predictions' on the discoordinating consequences of interventionism may be made	Prediction is a deliberately sought objective
12 Who is responsible for the prediction	The entrepreneur	The economic analyst (social engineer)
13 Present situation of the paradigm	Notable *re-emergence* over the last thirty years (especially after the crisis of Keynesianism and the fall of real socialism)	Situation of accelerated *crisis and change*
14 Amount of 'human capital' invested	*Minoritary*, but growing.	*Majority*, although it shows signs of dispersal and division
15 Type of 'human capital' invested	Multidisciplinary theorists and philosophers; radical libertarians	Specialists in economic intervention (piecemeal social engineering); very variable degree of commitment to freedom
16 Most recent contributions	• Critical analysis of institutional coercion (socialism and interventionism) • Theory of free banking and economic cycles • Evolutionary theory of institutions (juridical, moral) • Theory of entrepreneurship • Critical analysis of 'Social Justice'	• Public Choice theory • Economic analysis of the family • Economic analysis of Law • New classical macroeconomics • Economics of 'information'
17 Relative position of different authors	Rothbard, Mises, Hayek, Kirzner	Coase Demsetz-Blaug Buchanan-Samuelson Stiglitz-Friedman-Becker

fill this gap in a way that is complete but, at the same time, clear and concise, so that it is possible to understand at a glance the different opposing points between the two approaches, which I then discuss briefly.

Theory of action (Austrians) versus theory of decision (neoclassicals)

For the Austrian theorists, economic science is conceived as a theory of action rather than a theory of decision and this is one of the features that most clearly distinguishes them from their neoclassical colleagues. In fact, the concept of human action covers the concept of individual decision and much more. In the first place, for the Austrians, the relevant concept of action includes not only the hypothetical process of decision in an environment of 'given' knowledge of the ends and means but, above all, and this is the most important point, 'the very perception of the ends–means framework within which allocation and economizing is to take place'.[4] Moreover, the most important factor for the Austrians is not that a decision is taken, but that it is taken in the form of a human action in the *process* of which (that may or may not be culminated) there is a series of interactions and processes of coordination the study of which constitutes, for the Austrians, precisely the research subject of economic science. Therefore, for the Austrians, economics, far from being a theory on choice or decision, is a theory on the processes of social interaction, which may be coordinated to a greater or lesser extent depending on the alertness shown by the different actors involved in each entrepreneurial action.[5]

Consequently, the Austrians are especially critical of the narrow conception of economics that originates from Robbins and his well-known definition of it as a science which studies the utilization of scarce resources which may be put to alternative uses in order to satisfy human needs.[6] Robbins' conception implies given knowledge on ends and means, and therefore the economic problem is reduced to a mere technical problem of allocation, maximization or optimization, subject to known constraints. In other words, the conception of economics in Robbins corresponds to the core of the neoclassical paradigm and is completely foreign to the methodology of the Austrian School as it is understood today. In fact, the Robbinsian man is an automaton or caricature of the human being, who merely reacts passively to events. As opposed to Robbins' conception, the position of Mises, Kirzner and the rest of the Austrians should be highlighted. They consider that what man really does, rather than allocating given means to given ends, is to constantly seek new ends and means, learning from the past and using his imagination to discover and create (by action) the future. Therefore, for the Austrians, economics is subsumed under or integrated into a much more general and broad science, a general theory of human *action* (not of human decision). According to Hayek, if for this general science of human action 'a name is needed, the term *praxeological* sciences, now clearly defined and extensively used by Ludwig von Mises, would appear to be most appropriate'.[7]

Subjectivism (Austrians) versus objectivism (neoclassicals)

A second aspect which is of capital importance for the Austrians is *subjectivism*.[8] For the Austrians, the subjectivist conception consists of the attempt to build economic science on the basis of the real human being of flesh and blood, considered as the creative and leading actor in all social processes. This is why, for Mises,

> economics is not about things, tangible material objects. It is about men, their meanings and actions. Goods, commodities and wealth and all other elements of conduct are not elements of nature; they are elements of human meaning and conduct. He who wants to deal with them must not look at the external world. He must search for them in the meaning of acting men.[9]

Therefore, for the Austrians, and to a great extent unlike the neoclassicals, the constraints in economics are not imposed by objective phenomena or material factors of the external world (for example the oil reserves), but by human entrepreneurial subjective knowledge (the discovery, for example, of a carburettor that doubles the efficiency of the internal combustion engine *has the same economic effect* as the duplication of all the physical oil reserves).

Entrepreneur (Austrians) versus homo oeconomicus (neoclassicals)

Entrepreneurship is the force which plays the leading role in Austrian economic theory, while, on the contrary, it is conspicuous by its absence in neoclassical economic science. In fact, entrepreneurship is a typical phenomenon of the real world, which is always in disequilibrium and cannot play any part in the models of equilibrium that absorb the attention of the neoclassical authors. Furthermore, the neoclassicals consider entrepreneurship as simply one more production factor which may be allocated in accordance with its expected costs and benefits, without realizing that, when analysing the entrepreneur in this way, they make an insoluble logical contradiction: to demand entrepreneurial resources in accordance with their expected benefits and costs implies the belief that some information is available today (the probable value of the future costs and benefits) *before it has been created* by entrepreneurship itself. In other words, the main function of the entrepreneur consists in creating and discovering new information that did not previously exist and cannot be known, meaning that it is humanly impossible to make any neoclassical prior decision on allocation on the basis of expected costs and benefits.

In addition, today there is unanimity among all Austrian economists in classifying the belief that entrepreneurial profit arises from the simple assumption of risks as a fallacy. Risk, to the contrary, merely gives rise to another cost of the production process, which has nothing to do with pure entrepreneurial profit.[10]

Entrepreneurial error (Austrian) versus ex post rationalization of all past decisions (neoclassical)

The very different role played by the concept of *error* in the Austrian and Neoclassical Schools is not usually appreciated. For the Austrians, it is possible to commit sheer entrepreneurial errors[11] whenever an opportunity for gain remains undiscovered by the entrepreneurs in the market. It is precisely the existence of this type of error that gives rise to pure entrepreneurial profit. On the contrary, for the neoclassicals, there are never pure entrepreneurial errors which may subsequently be regretted (*regrettable errors*). This is due to the fact that the neoclassicals rationalize all decisions taken in the past in terms of a supposed cost–benefit analysis made within the framework of a constrained maximization. Therefore, pure entrepreneurial profits have no reason to exist in the neoclassical world and, when they are mentioned, are considered merely as payment of the services of a production factor or as income arising from the assumption of a risk.

Subjective information (Austrians) versus objective information (neoclassicals)

Entrepreneurs are constantly generating new *information*, which is essentially subjective, practical, disperse and difficult to articulate.[12] Therefore, the subjective perception of information is an essential element in Austrian methodology that is absent in neoclassical economics, since the latter always tends to handle information objectively. In fact, most economists do not realize that, when Austrians and neoclassicals use the term *information* they are referring to radically different things. In effect, for the neoclassicals, information, like commodities, is something that is objective and is bought and sold in the market as a result of a maximizing decision. This 'information', which may be stored on different supports, is not in any way *information in the subjective sense* of the Austrians: relevant practical knowledge that is created, interpreted, known and used by the actor in the context of a specific action. This is why the Austrians criticize Stiglitz and other neoclassical theorists of information for not having been able to integrate their information theory with entrepreneurship, which is always its source protagonist, as the Austrians have done. Furthermore, for the Austrians, Stiglitz does not fully understand that *information* is always subjective and that the markets he calls 'imperfect', rather than generating 'inefficiencies' (in the neoclassical sense), give rise to the formation of potential opportunities of entrepreneurial gain, which tend to be discovered and made use of by the entrepreneurs in the coordination process that they are continually stimulating in the market.[13]

Entrepreneurial coordination (Austrian) versus general and/or partial equilibrium (neoclassical)

The models of equilibrium of the neoclassical economists usually ignore the coordinating force that entrepreneurship has for the Austrians. In fact, this force not only creates and transmits information but, more importantly, also drives the coordination between the unadjusted behaviours of agents in society. Effectively, all social discoordination materializes in an opportunity for gain which remains latent until it is discovered by the entrepreneurs. Once the entrepreneur realizes that the profit opportunity exists and acts to take advantage of it, it disappears and there is a *spontaneous process of coordination*, which explains the trend towards equilibrium that exists in any market economy. Moreover, the coordinating nature of entrepreneurship is the only factor which makes it possible for economic theory to exist as a science, understood as a theoretical *corpus* of laws of coordination which explain the social processes.[14] This approach explains why the Austrian economists are interested in studying the *dynamic* concept of competition (understood as a process of *rivalry*), while the neoclassical economists concentrate exclusively on the models of equilibrium which are typical of the comparative *statics* ('perfect' competition, monopoly, 'imperfect' or monopolistic competition).[15] For Mises, as we see in the quotation at the beginning of this article (see p. 31), there is no sense in the construction of economic science based on the model of equilibrium, in which it is assumed that all the relevant information for drawing the corresponding functions of supply and demand is considered 'given'. The basic economic problem for the Austrians is quite different: to study the dynamic process of *social coordination* in which the different individuals are continually generating new information (which is never 'given') when they seek the ends and means that they consider relevant in the context of each action in which they are involved, thus establishing, without realizing it, a spontaneous process of coordination. For the Austrians, therefore, the basic economic problem is not technical or technological, as it is usually conceived by the theorists of the neoclassical paradigm when they assume that the ends and means are 'given' and pose the economic problem as if it were a mere technical problem of maximization. In other words, for the Austrians, the basic economic problem does not consist of the maximization of a known target function subject to constraints that are also known. It is, on the contrary, strictly economic: *it emerges when there are many ends and means competing among themselves, when knowledge of them is neither given nor constant, but is dispersed over the minds of innumerable human beings who are continually creating and generating it ex novo and, therefore, all the possible alternatives which exist, all those which will be created in the future and the relative intensity with which each of them will be pursued cannot even be known.*[16]

Moreover, it is necessary to realize that even what appear to be merely maximizing or optimizing human actions always have an entrepreneurial component, since the actor involved in them must have realized previously that this course of action, which is so automatic, mechanical and reactive, is the most advisable in the specific circumstances in which s/he has found him/herself. *In other words, the neoclassical approach is merely a specific case, of relatively minor importance, which is included and subsumed under the Austrian conception, which is much more general, richer and more explicative of the real world.*

Furthermore, for the Austrians, there is no sense in separating microeconomics and macroeconomics into two watertight compartments as the neoclassical economists do. On the contrary, economic problems should be studied together on an interrelated basis, without distinguishing between their micro and macro components. The radical separation between the 'micro' and 'macro' aspects of economic science is one of the most characteristic insufficiencies of modern introductory manuals and textbooks on political economy. Instead of providing a unified treatment of economic problems, as Mises and the Austrian economists try to do, they always present economic science as divided into two different disciplines ('microeconomics' and 'macroeconomics') with no connection between them and which, therefore, can be studied separately. As Mises rightly says, this separation originates from the use of concepts which, like the *general price level*, ignore the application of the subjective and marginalist theory of value to money and continue anchored in the pre-scientific stage of economics, when it was still attempted to make analyses in terms of global classes or aggregates of goods, rather than in terms of incremental or marginal units of them. This explains the fact that, to date, a whole 'discipline' based on the study of the mechanical relationships which supposedly exist between macroeconomic aggregates has been developed, the connection of which with individual human action is difficult, if not impossible, to understand.[17]

In any case, the neoclassical economists have converted the model of equilibrium into the focal point of their research. In this model, they assume that all information is 'given' (either in certain or probabilistic terms) and that the different variables are perfectly adjusted. From the Austrian point of view, the main disadvantage of this methodology is that, as it assumes that all the variables and parameters are perfectly adjusted, it is easy to draw erroneous conclusions on the cause and effect relationships between different economic concepts and phenomena. *Thus, the equilibrium would act as a sort of veil that would prevent the theorist from discovering the true direction that exists in the cause and effect relationships of economic laws.* For the neoclassical economists, rather than laws of tendency that go in a single direction, what exists is a mutual (circular) determination between the different phenomena, the initial origin of which (human action) remains concealed or is considered of no interest.[18]

Subjective costs (Austrians) versus objective costs (neoclassicals)

Another essential element of Austrian methodology is its purely subjective conception of costs. Many authors believe that it would not be very difficult to incorporate it into the mainstream neoclassical paradigm. However, the neoclassicals only include the subjective nature of costs rhetorically and, in the final analysis, although they mention the importance of the concept of cost of opportunity, they always incorporate it into their models in an objectivized form. However, for the Austrians, cost is the subjective value that the actor places on the ends which he renounces when he decides to undertake and follow a certain course of action. In other words, there are no objective costs. Costs must, rather, be discovered through the entrepreneurial alertness of each actor. In fact, many possible alternatives may go unnoticed but, once they are discovered, they radically change *the subjective perception* of costs on the part of the entrepreneur. Objective costs which tend towards determining the value of the ends do not, therefore, exist. The real situation is the exact opposite: costs are assumed as subjective values (and, therefore, are determined) depending on the subjective value of the ends really sought (consumer goods) by the actor. Therefore, for the Austrian economists, it is the final prices of consumer goods, as the materialization of subjective valuations in the market, that determine the costs which the actor is willing to incur in order to produce them and not, as the neoclassical economists so often imply, the opposite.

Verbal formalism (Austrians) versus mathematical formalism (neoclassicals)

Another aspect of interest is the different position of the two schools regarding the utilization of mathematical formalism in economic analysis. From the origins of the Austrian School, its founder, Carl Menger, took care to point out that the advantage of verbal language is that it can express the essences (*das Wesen*) of economic phenomena, something that mathematical language cannot do. In fact, in a letter he wrote to Walras in 1884, Menger wondered: 'How can we attain to a knowledge of this essence, for example, the essence of value, the essence of land rent, the essence of entrepreneurs' profits, the division of labour, bimetalism, etc., by mathematical methods?'[19] Mathematical formalism is especially adequate for expressing the states of equilibrium that the neoclassical economists study, but it does not allow the inclusion of the subjective reality of time and, much less, the entrepreneurial creativity which are essential features of the analytical reasoning of the Austrians. Perhaps Hans Mayer summed up the insufficiencies of mathematical formalism in economics better than anyone when he said that:

> In essence there is an immanent, more or less disguised, fiction at the heart of mathematical equilibrium theories: that is, *they bind together in simultaneous equations, non-simultaneous magnitudes operative in genetic-causal sequence as if these existed together at the same time.* A state of affairs is *synchronized* in the 'static' approach, whereas in reality we are dealing with a *process*. But one simply cannot consider a *generative*

> *process* 'statically' as a *state of rest*, without eliminating precisely that which makes it what it is.[20]

This means that, for the Austrians, many of the theories and conclusions of the neoclassical analysis of consumption and production do not make sense. This is true, for example, of what is called the 'law of equality of weighted (by prices) marginal utilities', the theoretical foundations of which are very doubtful. In fact, this law assumes that the actor is capable of *simultaneously* valuing the utility of all the goods at his disposal, ignoring the fact that any action is *sequential* and creative and that goods are not valued at the same time, making their supposed marginal utility equal, but rather one after another, in the context of different stages and actions for each of which it is not only that the corresponding marginal utilities may be different, but that they are not even comparable.[21] In short, *for the Austrians, the use of mathematics in economics is defective because they synchronically bind together magnitudes which are heterogeneous from the points of view of time and entrepreneurial creativity.* For the same reason, for the Austrian economists, neither do the axiomatic criteria of rationality often used by the neoclassical economists make sense. In effect, if an actor prefers A to B and B to C, it is perfectly possible that s/he prefers C to A, which does not make him or her 'irrational' or inconsistent if s/he has simply changed his/her mind (even if this only lasts the hundredth part of a second that posing this problem lasts in his/her own reasoning).[22] For the Austrians, the neoclassical criteria of 'rationality' tend to confuse the concepts of constancy and consistency.

Relation with the empirical world: the different meaning of 'prediction'

Lastly, the different relationship with the empirical world and the differences regarding the possibilities of prediction place the paradigm of the Austrian School in radical opposition to that of the neoclassicals. Effectively, the fact that the 'observing' scientist cannot obtain the practical information which is being constantly created and discovered in a decentralized way by the 'observed' actors-entrepreneurs explains the theoretical impossibility of any type of empirical verification in economics. In fact, the Austrians consider that the same reasons that determine the theoretical impossibility of socialism explain that both empiricism and the cost–benefit analysis or utilitarianism in its strictest interpretation are not viable in our science. It is irrelevant whether it is a scientist or a governor who vainly tries to obtain the practical information that is relevant to each case in order to verify theories or endow his commands with a coordinating nature. If this were possible, it would be viable to use this information either to coordinate society through coercive commands (socialism and interventionism) or to empirically verify economic theories. However, for the same reasons, first, in view of the immense volume of information in question; second, due to the nature of the relevant information (disseminated, subjective and tacit); third, because of the dynamic nature of the entrepreneurial process (information which has not yet been generated by the entrepreneurs in their process of constant innovating creation cannot be transmitted); and, fourth, due to the effect of coercion and of scientific 'observation' itself (which distorts, corrupts, impedes or simply makes the entrepreneurial creation of information impossible), both the socialist ideal and the positivist or strictly utilitarian ideal are impossible from the point of view of Austrian economic theory.

These same arguments are also applicable in order to justify the Austrians' belief that it is theoretically impossible to make *specific predictions* (i.e. referring to determined coordinates of time and place with a quantitative empirical content) in economics. What will happen tomorrow can never be scientifically known today, as it largely depends on knowledge and information which have not yet been entrepreneurially generated and which, therefore, cannot yet be known.

In economics, therefore, only general 'trend predictions' can be made (what Hayek calls *pattern predictions*). These are of an essentially theoretical nature and relative, at most, to the forecast of the disorders and effects of social discoordination produced by institutional coercion (socialism and interventionism) on the market.

Moreover, we must remember that objective facts which may be directly observed in the external world do not exist, due to the circumstance that, according to the Austrian subjectivist conception, economic research 'facts' are simply *ideas* that others have on what they pursue and do. They may never be observed directly, but only interpreted in historical terms. In order to interpret the social situation which constitutes history, a prior theory is necessary and, moreover, a non-scientific judgement of relevance (*Verstehen* or understanding) is required. This is not objective but may vary from one historian to another, converting his or her discipline (history) into a true art.

Finally, the Austrians consider that empirical phenomena are constantly variable, so that there are no parameters or constants in social events and everything is a 'variable'. This makes the traditional objective of econometrics difficult, if not impossible, together with any of the versions of the positivist methodological programme (from the most ingenuous verificationism to the most sophisticated Popperian falsationism). As opposed to the positivist ideal of the neoclassicals, the Austrian economists aim to construct their discipline through apriorism and deduction. The question is, in brief, to prepare an entire logical-deductive arsenal[23] on the basis of self-evident knowledge (axioms such as the subjective concept of human action itself, with its essential elements) which arises by introspection in the personal experience of the scientist or is considered evident because nobody can argue the axioms without contradicting him- or herself.[24] This theoretical arsenal is, according to the Austrians, indispensable for an adequate interpretation of the apparently unrelated mass of complex historical phenomena which constitute the social world and for drawing up a history towards the past or predicting events towards the future (which is the typical mission of the entrepreneur) with a minimum degree of consistency, guarantees and chances of success. It is now possible to understand the great importance that the Austrians in general place on history as a discipline and on their attempt to differentiate it from economic theory while relating it appropriately thereto.[25]

Hayek calls the undue application of the method appropriate for natural sciences to the social science field *scientism*. Thus, in the natural world, there are constants and functional relations that allow the application of mathematical language and the performance of quantitative experiments in a laboratory. However, for the Austrians, in economics, unlike the world of physics and the natural sciences, functional relations (and, therefore, functions of supply, demand, costs or of any other type) do not exist. Let us remember that, mathematically, according to set theory, a function is merely a correspondence between the elements of two sets which are called the 'initial set' and the 'final set'. Given the innate creative capacity of the human being, who is continuously generating and discovering new information in each specific circumstance in which he acts in respect of the ends he aims to pursue and the means to attain them he considers to be within his reach, it is evident that there is none of the three elements necessary for a functional relationship to exist: (1) the elements of the initial set are not given or constant; (2) the elements which constitute the final set are not given or constant; and (3), and this is the most important point, *neither are the correspondences between the elements of the two groups given, but rather they vary continually as a result of the action and creative capacity of the human being.* Thus, in our science, according to the Austrians, the use of functions requires that a *presupposition of constancy* be introduced into the information, radically eliminating the protagonist of the whole social process: the human being endowed with an innate creative entrepreneurial capacity. The great merit of the Austrians consists in having shown that it is perfectly possible to create the whole corpus of economic theory logically,[26] without any need to use functions or to establish assumptions of constancy which are contrary to the creative nature of the human being, who is the sole true protagonist of all the social processes studied by economic science.

Even the most well-known neoclassical economists have had to recognize that there are important economic laws that cannot be empirically verified (such as the theory of evolution and natural selection).[27] The Austrians have placed special emphasis on the insufficiency of empirical studies to drive the development of economic theory. Effectively, at most, empirical studies may provide some information on certain aspects of the results of the social processes which occur in reality. They do not, however, provide information on the formal structure of said processes, the knowledge of which constitutes precisely the research subject of economic theory. In other words, statistics and empirical studies cannot provide any theoretical knowledge (the error of the historicists of the nineteenth century German School consisted precisely of this and is, to a great extent, repeated today by the Neoclassical School economists). Furthermore, as Hayek rightly said in his speech on receiving the Nobel Prize, aggregates which can be measured in statistical terms often lack theoretical sense and, *vice versa*, many concepts with great theoretical significance cannot be measured or treated empirically.[28]

In short, the main criticisms that the Austrian economists make of the neoclassicals are the following: in the first place, they concentrate exclusively on states of equilibrium through a maximizing model which assumes that the agents have full information on the target functions and their constraints; second, the often random choice of variables and parameters for both the target function and constraints tends to include the most obvious ones and forget others which, although they are of great importance, are more difficult to handle empirically (moral values, customs, etc.); third, they concentrate on models of equilibrium that they treat with the formalism of mathematics and which hide the real cause and effect relationships; fourth, they raise to the level of theoretical conclusions what are merely interpretations of the historical situation and, although they may be relevant in some cases, cannot be considered to have universal theoretical validity, as they only involve historically contingent knowledge. The above considerations do not mean that all the conclusions of the neoclassical analysis are erroneous. On the contrary, a great many of them are probably appropriate and valid. The only matter to which the Austrians wish to draw attention is that there is no guarantee of the validity of the conclusions reached by the neoclassical economists and that those which are valid may perfectly well be drawn from the dynamic analysis that the Austrians advocate. This analysis has, in addition, the advantage that it allows erroneous theories (which are also very numerous) to be isolated, as it shows up the defects and errors that are currently concealed by the empirical method based on the model of equilibrium developed by the neoclassical economists.

The rounds of the *Methodenstreit*

The Austrian School has been refining its methodological positions from its foundation in 1871 until today – in other words, over a very long time period – almost always driven by the numerous doctrinal polemics in which it has taken part. In fact, it may be considered that the *Methodenstreit*, or polemic concerning the methods, has been evolving since the very beginning of the Austrian School and has affected and continues to affect very significantly the development of economic science. We will now study the most important stages of the *Methodenstreit* of the Austrian School which have taken place to date.

First round: Carl Menger versus the German Historical School[29]

There is no doubt that the Austrian School of Economics was born in 1871 with the publication of Menger's *Principles of Economics*. The most original and important distinctive idea of Menger's contribution consisted in trying to construct economics using the human being, considered as the creative actor and protagonist in all social processes, as a starting point (*subjectivism*). The fruits of this conception were Menger's two most important ideas. In the first place, and for the first time in economic science, Menger theorized on the basis of a process of action formed by a series of *intermediate stages* ('economic goods of higher order') that the actor undertakes, carries out, and tries to culminate until the end or final consumer good is attained ('economic goods of first order'). Specifically, Menger concludes:

> when we have the complementary goods of some particular higher order at our command, we must transform them first into goods of the next lower order, and then by *stages* into goods of successively still lower orders until they have been fashioned into goods of first order, which alone can be utilized directly for the satisfaction of our needs.[30]

Menger's second essential contribution is his economic theory on the emergence of *social institutions*. Menger discovered that institutions result from a social process formed by multiple human actions and led by a series of human beings (entrepreneurs) who, in their particular historical circumstances of time and place, are able to discover before other people that they attain their ends more easily if they adopt certain guided behaviours. In this way, a decentralized trial and error process is put into action, in which the forms of behaviour that best coordinate the social disorders tend to prevail, so that, through an unconscious social process of learning and imitation, the leadership initiated by the human beings who are most creative and successful in their actions extends and is followed by the rest of the members of society. Thus, guided behaviours or *institutions* which make life in society possible emerge in the economic field (money), legal field (rules and moral behaviour) and linguistic field.[31]

The fact that the professors of the German Historical School not only did not understand his contribution but also considered it a dangerous challenge to historicism must have caused Menger great frustration. Effectively, instead of realizing that Menger's contribution was the theoretical support that the evolutionist conception of social processes needed, they considered that the abstract and theoretical nature of the analysis was incompatible with the narrow historicism they advocated. This was the beginning of the first and perhaps most famous polemic in which the Austrians have been involved, the *Methodenstreit* (polemic I), which occupied Menger's intellectual energy for several decades.[32]

One of the most important by-products of the *Methodenstreit* was Menger's incipient articulation of the methodology appropriate to economic science. This is made up of a series of theories that constitute the 'form' (in the Aristotelian sense) which expresses the essences of economic phenomena and is discovered by a process of internal reflection (*introspection*) in the course of a logical process based on deductive reasoning. History accompanies theory and is made up of the empirical facts that form 'matter' (in the Aristotelian sense). No theories may be extracted directly from history but, on the contrary, a prior theory is necessary in order to interpret it appropriately. In this way, Menger established the foundations of what was to be the traditional methodology of the Austrian School.[33]

A number of recent studies have shown how, in fact, what Menger did was to take up, through Say, a much older tradition of thought that had been cut short precisely as a consequence of the negative influence of Adam Smith and the English Classical School. I refer to the continental Catholic tradition which, on a secular basis, had constructed all the essential elements that constitute the paradigm of the present Austrian School. Thus, with regard to the spontaneous emergence of institutions, we can, as Bruno Leoni has shown, go back to the juridical tradition of the Romans,[34] the Spanish scholastics,[35] like Juan de Lugo and Juan de Salas,[36] and the French theorists: Balesbat in 1692, the Marquis D'Argenson in 1751 and above all Turgot, who, long before Adam Smith, had already articulated the disperse nature of the knowledge incorporated into social institutions understood as spontaneous orders. Thus, in 1759, Turgot concluded that

> there is no need to prove that each individual is the only competent judge of the most advantageous use of his lands and of his labour. He alone has the particular knowledge without which the most enlightened man could only argue blindly. He learns by repeated trials, by his successes, by his losses, and he acquires a feeling for it which is much more ingenious than the theoretical knowledge of the indifferent observer because it is stimulated by want.

Likewise, Turgot refers to the 'complete impossibility of directing, by invariant rules and continuous inspection a multitude of transactions which by their immensity alone could not be fully known, and which, moreover, are continually dependent on a multitude of ever changing circumstances which cannot be managed or even foreseen'.[37] The subjective theory of value is also developed by the Spanish scholastics in the sixteenth century, particularly by Diego de Covarrubias y Leyva.[38] Luis Saravia de la Calle was the first of them to expressly demonstrate that prices determine costs, not *vice versa*. The Spanish scholastics also apply this subjectivist concept to the theory of money (Azpilcueta Navarro and Luis de Molina), likewise including the concept of entrepreneur which had earlier been developed by San Bernardino of Siena and Sant' Antonino of Florence and would later become the centre of the research of Cantillon, Turgot and Say.

This whole tradition was cut short by the negative effects of the Protestant reform, which, to a certain extent, explains the regression that was implied by Adam Smith and that has recently been summarized by Leland B. Yeager in his 'Review' of Rothbard's posthumous book on the history of economic thought with the following words:

Smith dropped earlier contributions about subjective value, entrepreneurship and emphasis on real-world markets and pricing and replaced it all with a labour theory of value and a dominant focus on the unchanging long run 'natural price' equilibrium, a world where entrepreneurship was assumed out of existence. He mixed up Calvinism with economics, as in supporting usury prohibition and distinguishing between productive and unproductive occupations. He lapsed from the laissez-faire of several eighteenth century French and Italian economists, introducing many waffles and qualifications. His work was unsystematic and plagued by contradictions.[39]

Second round: Böhm-Bawerk versus John Bates Clark (and also versus Marshall and Marx)

The leading player in the second round in the Austrian School's *Methodenstreit* was Böhm-Bawerk. This second round materialized in a polemic which was, for our purposes, extremely significant (the polemic with John Bates Clark, polemic II) and the debates of lesser importance with Marshall (polemic III) and Marx (polemic IV).

John Bates Clark was radically opposed to the dynamic concept of action introduced by Menger and, above all, to the Mengerian concept of action formed by a series of successive stages. As a consequence, Clark considered that capital was a homogeneous fund that reproduced itself alone, so that production (i.e. human action) was instantaneous and did not involve time. Clark's thesis is indispensable in order to justify his conclusion that the interest rate is determined by the marginal productivity of capital. This requires not only that the latter be considered as a fund that reproduces itself alone instantaneously, but also a perfectly adjusted static environment (in equilibrium), together with the determination of the values of capital goods by their historical cost of production. Clark himself explicitly acknowledges that his thesis only makes sense in a perfectly adjusted static environment in equilibrium when he says that

> in a dynamic condition of society ... time is required before any goods are ready for consumption, and during this interval owners must wait for their expected products. After the series of goods in various stages of advancement has once been established, the normal action of capital is revealed.[40]

Böhm-Bawerk criticized Clark's thesis,[41] describing it as *mystical* and *mythological* and showing that it meant, apart from a radical attack on Menger's dynamic conception, the definitive enthronement of the static paradigm of equilibrium in the world of economics. In Böhm-Bawerk's opinion, which was subsequently confirmed by the facts, this would have very serious consequences for the future development of economics. Subsequently, the neoclassical authors, following Clark, again realized that, in order to maintain their whole theoretical edifice, it was indispensable to eliminate the dynamic concept of action constituted by a series of temporal stages introduced by Menger. This happened, for example, to the founder of the School of Chicago, Frank H. Knight, who, in the 1930s, reproduced with Hayek and Machlup the polemic that had taken place between Clark and Böhm-Bawerk at the end of the nineteenth century.[42] Clark's influence was very negative for the subsequent evolution of economic thought because he upheld a position against the American institutionalists which appeared to acknowledge that the Austrians were right in their polemic with the German Historical School. However, *in reality, his defence of the paradigm of equilibrium and frontal attack on Menger's dynamic conception of action meant that the mainstream of our science forked off in a direction which was radically opposed to the path that the Austrians had initiated.*

Apart from the polemic with Clark (which we will call polemic II to distinguish it from polemic I between Menger and the historicists), Böhm-Bawerk was involved in two other polemics, one with Marx and another with Marshall, that also reflected different aspects of the Austrian School: with Marx, due to the fact the latter did not take the subjectiveness of *time preference* into account, which eliminated the potentiality of the Marxist analysis of surplus-value or exploitation;[43] with Marshall, because he tried to rehabilitate Ricardo, at least with regard to the supply side, defending the idea that the latter was determined above all by considerations related to the *historical cost of production* and being incapable of incorporating the Austrian concept of the subjective cost of opportunity, with all its implications.[44]

Third round: Mises, Hayek and Mayer versus socialism, Keynes and the neoclassicals

The third round of the Austrians' methodological controversies commenced with the third generation of Austrian School economists led by Mises. In this phase, the most important polemic was the one initiated by Mises on the *theoretical impossibility of socialism* (polemic V). Effectively, for Mises, the theorem of the theoretical impossibility of socialism was an immediate consequence of the subjectivist and dynamic conception developed by the Austrians. In fact, if the source of all wants, valuations and knowledge is to be found in the creative entrepreneurial capacity of the human being, any system which, like socialism, is based on the use of violent coercion against free human action will prevent the creation and transmission of the information necessary to coordinate society. Moreover, Mises is perfectly aware that, if the neoclassical economists are not capable of understanding the theorem of the impossibility of socialism, this is due to the fact that they have not been capable of accepting the Austrians' subjectivist and dynamic conception. Effectively, for Mises, the illusion that a rational order of economic management is possible in a society based on public ownership of the means of production owed its origin to the value theory of the classical economists and its tenacity to the failure of many modern economists to think through consistently to its ultimate conclusions the fundamental theory of the subjectivist theory. ... In truth it was the errors of these schools that made the socialist ideas thrive.[45]

Thus, as an example, we can again mention the founder of the School of Chicago, Frank H. Knight, who even said that 'socialism is a political problem to be discussed in terms of social and political psychology, and economic theory has relatively little to say about it'.[46] And, in fact, even today, the neoclassical economists still do not understand the profound theoretical reasons for the impossibility of socialism and, at most, have tried to explain the fall of socialism *a posteriori*, either by resorting to the 'error' committed in the interpretation of the statistical data which came from the real socialist systems and was accepted by the 'profession' with insufficient critical spirit, or by the argument that the role played by 'incentives' in economic life had been assessed unsatisfactorily.[47] Fortunately, the former socialist economists have seen the facts better than their Western neoclassical colleagues and have realized that Oskar Lange and the other neoclassical socialists 'never succeeded in confronting the Austrian challenge'.[48] It is, however, hopeful to mention how, more recently, a neoclassical author of the level of Joseph E. Stiglitz has finally recognized that 'the standard neoclassical models were partly to blame for the disastrous situation in which so many Eastern European countries found themselves. A strong case could be made for the proposition that ideas about economics have led half the world's population to untold suffering'.[49]

The polemic with the macroeconomists, particularly against Keynes and the theorists of Cambridge (polemic VI), which was basically led by Hayek on the Austrian side, also arose naturally from placing the conceptions belonging to the analysis made exclusively in terms of macroeconomic aggregates in opposition to the dynamic conception of the market developed by the Austrians. Logically, we cannot deal with the specific development of this whole polemic here,[50] but Table 2.2 shows a summary of the different distinguishing aspects which exist between the Austrian School and the Neoclassical School (constituted, for our purposes, by the monetarists, the Keynesians and all their different successors) with regard to macroeconomics.[51]

These theoretical discussions, which took place in the period between the two world wars, finally convinced the Austrians that their supposed victory in the *first round of the Methodenstreit* with the German Historical School had been a pyrrhic, or even strictly nominal, victory, as occurred to the Currency School theorists with Peel's Law in 1844. So, as Kirzner has said, one of the most important by-products of the controversy on the impossibility of socialism was that it forced the Austrians to refine their methodological position even further, realize its profound implications and, above all,

Table 2.2 Two different ways of conceiving macroeconomics

Austrian School	Neoclassical School (Monetarists and Keynesians)
1 *Time* plays an essential role	1 The influence of time is ignored
2 'Capital' is considered as a *heterogeneous* set of capital goods that are constantly being used up and must be *reproduced*	2 Capital is considered as a *homogeneous* fund that reproduces itself alone
3 The productive process is *dynamic* and broken down into multiple *vertical* stages	3 There is considered to be a *horizontal* and *one-dimensional* productive structure in *equilibrium*
4 Money affects the process by modifying the structure of *relative* prices	4 Money affects the *general* price level; changes in relative prices are not considered
5 Explains macroeconomic phenomena in *microeconomic* terms (changes in relative prices)	5 The *macroeconomic aggregates* prevent the analysis of the underlying microeconomic situations
6 Has a theory on the *endogenous* causes of economic crises that explains their *recurring* nature	6 Has no endogenous theory of cycles; crises occur due to *exogenous* reasons (psychological and/or errors in monetary policy)
7 Has a developed *theory of capital*	7 Has no theory of capital
8 Saving plays a leading role and determines a *longitudinal* change in the productive structure and the type of technology that will be used	8 Saving is *not* important; capital reproduces itself *laterally* (more of the same thing) and the *production function* is fixed and is given by the state of the art
9 The demand for capital goods varies *inversely* to the demand for consumer goods (any investment requires saving and therefore a sacrifice of consumption over time)	9 The demand for capital goods varies in the *same* direction as the demand for consumer goods
10 It is assumed that production costs are *subjective* and are not given	10 Production costs are *objective*, real and are considered to be given
11 Market prices are considered to tend to determine production costs, not *vice versa*	11 It is considered that historical production costs tend to determine market prices
12 The interest rate is considered as a market price determined by subjective valuations of time preference; it is used to discount the present value of the future flow of yields towards which the market price of each capital good tends	12 The interest rate is considered to tend to be determined by the marginal productivity or efficiency of capital and is conceived as the internal return rate which makes the expected flow of yields equal to the historical production cost of capital goods (which is considered given and invariable); the rate of interest is considered to be a mainly monetary phenomenon

become fully aware of the methodological abyss that separated them from the neoclassicals.[52] Thus, little by little, the Austrian economists commenced a second version of the *Methodenstreit*, this time against the emerging neoclassical paradigm, and began a redefinition of their methodological positions, set forth basically in the works of Mises, Mayer and Hayek which came out in the 1930s, 1940s and 1950s (polemic VII). Thus, Mises specified and established the methodology opposed to the use of mathematics in economics and to positivism in the different methodological works that are summarized in the first part of his *Human Action*. Hans Mayer, in an extensive work that has still not been answered, made a devastating criticism of the functional and mathematical analysis of the neoclassical theory of prices. Mayer's article has only recently been published in English, thanks to Israel M. Kirzner, with the title 'The Cognitive Value of Functional Theories of Price: Critical and Positive Investigations Concerning the Price Problem'.[53] Finally, Hayek summarizes and articulates his methodological criticisms of both the empiricism originating from Saint Simon and the narrow utilitarianism of the neoclassical cost–benefit analysis in his book *The Counter-Revolution of Science*, published in 1952.[54] Unfortunately, the following year, Milton Friedman's work *Essays in Positive Economics*[55] was published and achieved great popularity, providing the use of positivist methodology in our science with a great impetus.

Although Hayek's abovementioned work anticipated, answered and criticized the most important points of Friedman's almost simultaneous book to a great extent, Hayek later said:

> one of the things I often have publicly said is that one of the things I most regret is not having returned to a criticism of Keynes' treatise (*The General Theory*), but it is as much true of not having criticized Milton Friedman's *Essays in Positive Economics*, which in a way is quite as dangerous a book.[56]

Fourth round: neo-Austrians versus the mainstream and methodological nihilism

The last round of the methodological discussion has been taking place over the last twenty-five years. In this round, the Austrian economists have become convinced that their position is correct, having confirmed how the neoclassical models (of general equilibrium) have been used to justify the theoretical possibility of socialism. Moreover, many positivist neoclassical theorists have believed that, in the final analysis, only empirical considerations could move the balance definitively in favour of either the capitalist economic system or the socialist one,[57] utterly disregarding all the *a priori* theoretical teachings of the Austrian School that demonstrate the impossibility of socialism and unnecessarily condemning a large part of humankind to enormous suffering for many of the decades of the last century. For the

Austrians, not only were a large number of the members of the Neoclassical School especially responsible for this suffering because they ignored the content of the Austrian analysis on the impossibility of socialism, but the positivism that continues to influence our science and which preaches that only experience, regardless of any theory, is able to demonstrate the chances of survival of any social system was also to blame.

The notable re-emergence of the Austrian School over the last twenty-five years is, therefore, explained, together with the effort made by its members to rework the most important contributions of our discipline in accordance with the subjectivist methodology and dynamic approach initiated by Menger, purifying it of the errors that the positivist paradigm of equilibrium tends to surreptitiously introduce into the *corpus* of our science. Furthermore, the extension of the refined methodological nihilism that originated since the teachings of Karl Popper has given rise to a new polemic (polemic VIII) which, this time, has taken place even within the sphere of the Austrian School itself. The triumph of methodological pluralism appeared, at the beginning, to favour the Austrians, since their method, which had been almost cast into oblivion by a large part of the scientific community, again began to be 'respected' (like any other). However, many Austrians have finally realized that the 'anything goes' in methodological terms which has come so much into fashion today radically contradicts the criteria of methodological rigour and the research agenda for the scientific truth that the Austrians have traditionally defended. This explains the recent reaction of many Austrian economists against the nihilism and methodological pluralism originating from the hermeneutical post-modernist position of authors who, like Deirdre McCloskey and Don Lavoie, believe that the scientific truth depends to a great extent on the cultural context in which the argument between its leading players takes place. Israel Kirzner[58] and Hans-Hermann Hoppe[59] have even mentioned the fact that the extension of hermeneutics in economic methodology means, in a certain way, a resurrection of the old errors of the German Historical School, as it makes the criteria for scientific truth depend on contingent external situations.

Replies to some criticisms and comments

We are now going to reply to some of the critical comments on the Austrian paradigm that are habitually made and which, for the reasons we will set forth, we believe to be unfounded. The most common criticisms against the Austrians are as follows:

> The two approaches (Austrian and neoclassical) do not exclude each other but are, rather, complementary.

This is the thesis upheld by many neoclassical authors who would like to maintain an eclectic position which does not enter into open conflict with the Austrian School. However, the Austrians consider that, in general, this thesis is merely an unfortunate consequence of the nihilism typical of methodological pluralism, according to which any method is acceptable and the only problem of economic science is to choose the most appropriate method for each specific problem. We consider that this thesis is merely an attempt to immunize the neoclassical paradigm against the powerful critical arguments launched against it by Austrian methodology. The compatibility thesis would be founded if the neoclassical method (based on equilibrium, preference constancy and the narrow concept of rationality) corresponded to the real way in which human beings act and did not tend to invalidate, to a great extent, the theoretical analysis, as the Austrians believe. This is the reason for the great importance of reworking the neoclassical theoretical conclusions using the subjectivist and dynamic methodology of the Austrians, in order to see which of the neoclassical theoretical conclusions continue to be valid and which should be abandoned due to theoretical defects. The neoclassical method is essentially erroneous from the Austrian point of view and, therefore, creates serious risks and dangers for the analyst, which tend to lead him or her further away from the truth.[60]

Finally, we should remember that, according to Hayek's theory on the hierarchy of spontaneous orders depending on their degree of complexity, a certain order may explain, include and give account of relatively simpler orders. But what cannot be conceived is that a relatively simple order can include and give account of others that are composed of a more complex system of categories.[61]

If this Hayekian insight is applied to the methodological field, it is possible to conceive that the Austrian approach, which is relatively richer and more complex and realistic, could subsume and include the neoclassical approach, which could be accepted at least in the relatively infrequent cases where human beings choose to behave in the more reactive and narrowly maximizing way considered by neoclassicals. But what cannot be conceived is that human realities, like creative entrepreneurship, which far exceed the conceptual scheme of neoclassical categories, can be incorporated into the neoclassical paradigm. The attempt to force the subjective realities of the human being that the Austrians study to fit within the neoclassical straitjacket leads inevitably to either a clumsy characterization of them or to the healthy failure of the neoclassical approach itself, overcome by the more complex, richer and more explicative conceptual scheme of the Austrian point of view.

> The Austrians should not criticize the neoclassicals for using simplified assumptions which help to understand reality.

The Austrian economists reply to this so commonly used argument by saying that it is one thing to simplify an assumption and another to make it completely unreal. What the Austrians really object to in the neoclassicals is not that their assumptions are simplified but, precisely, that they are contrary to the empirical reality of how the human being reveals himself to be and acts (dynamically and creatively). It is, therefore, the essential unreality (not the simplification) of the neoclassical assumptions which tends, from the Austrian point of view, to endanger the validity of the theoretical conclusions that the neoclassicals believe they reach in the different applied economics problems they study.

The Austrians fail when formalizing their theoretical propositions.

This is, for example, the only argument against the Austrian School that Stiglitz sets forth in his critical treatise on the models of general equilibrium.[62] We have already explained (pp. 39-40) the reasons why, from the start, the majority of Austrian economists have been very distrustful of the use of mathematical language in our science. For the Austrian economists, the use of mathematical formalism is a vice rather than a virtue, since it consists of a symbolic language that has been constructed in accordance with the demands of the worlds of natural sciences, engineering and logic, in all of which subjective time and entrepreneurial creativity are noticeably absent. It therefore tends to ignore the most essential characteristics of the human being, who is the protagonist of the social processes that economists should study. Thus, for example, Pareto himself reveals this serious disadvantage of mathematical formalism when he acknowledges that all his analysis is made without taking the real protagonist of the social process (the human being) into account and that, for the purpose of his mathematical economics analysis, 'the individual can disappear, provided he leaves us his photograph of his tastes'.[63] In the same error falls Schumpeter when he states that 'one needs only "enquire" of individuals the value functions of the consumption goods, and one thereby obtains everything else'.[64]

In any case, the mathematicians' response (if they can provide one) to the challenge of conceiving and developing a whole new 'mathematics' able to include and allow the analysis of the human being's creative capacity with all its implication, without resorting, therefore, to the assumptions of constancy that come from the world of physics and which have been the driving force behind all the mathematical languages known to date, is still pending. In our opinion, however, the ideal scientific language for including this creative capacity is precisely the language that human beings have spontaneously created in their day-to-day entrepreneurship, which materializes in the different verbal languages and forms of speech which prevail in the world today.

The Austrians carry out very little empirical work.

This is the most common criticism that the empiricists make of the Austrians. Although the Austrians place an extraordinary importance on the role of history, they recognize that their field of scientific activity-theory, which it is necessary to know before it is applied to reality or illustrated by historical facts – is very different. For the Austrians, there is, on the contrary, an excess production of empirical works and a relative lack of theoretical studies that enable us to understand and interpret what really happens. Moreover, the methodological assumptions of the Neoclassical School (equilibrium, maximization and preference constancy), although they appear to facilitate empirical studies and the 'verification' of certain theories, often conceal the correct theoretical relations and, therefore, may induce serious theoretical errors and an erroneous interpretation of what is really happening at any given moment or under any historical circumstance.

The Austrians renounce prediction in the economic field.

We have already seen that the Austrian theorists are very humble and prudent with regard to the possibilities of making scientific predictions of what will happen in the economic and social fields. They are, rather, concerned with constructing a scheme or arsenal of theoretical concepts and laws that allow reality to be interpreted and help acting human beings (entrepreneurs) to make decisions with a greater chance of success. Although the Austrians' 'predictions' are only qualitative and are made in theoretical terms, there exists the paradox that, in practice, as the assumptions of their analysis are much more realistic (dynamic and entrepreneurially creative processes) their conclusions and theories greatly increase the chances of making successful predictions in the field of human action in comparison with the possibilities of the Neoclassical School.[65]

The Austrians do not have empirical criteria to validate their theories.

According to this criticism, often made by the empiricists affected by the complex of St Thomas the Apostle that 'if I don't see it, I don't believe it', only through the empirical reality can one become certain of which theories are correct or otherwise. As we have seen, this point of view ignores the fact that, in economics, the empirical 'evidence' is never indisputable as it refers to complex historical phenomena that do not permit laboratory experiments in which the relevant phenomena are isolated and all aspects which could have an influence are left constant. In other words, economic laws are always laws *ceteris paribus* but in reality the other things never remain equal. According to the Austrians, the validation of theories is perfectly possible through the continual elimination of defects in the chain of logical-deductive reasoning of the different theories and by taking the greatest care when, at the moment of applying the theories to reality, it is necessary to evaluate whether the *assumptions* contained in the theory therein exist or not in the specific historical case analysed. Given the uniform logical structure of the human mind, this continual validation activity proposed by the Austrians is more than sufficient to reach an agreement between the different protagonists of scientific labour. Moreover, in spite of appearances, in practice, this agreement is usually more difficult to reach in relation to empirical phenomena, which, in view of their very complex nature, are always subject to the most widely differing interpretations.

The Austrians are dogmatic.

This is an accusation which, to a great extent, thanks to the notable re-emergence of the Austrian School and the fact that it is better understood by the economics profession, is fortunately being employed less often. However, in the past, many neoclassical economists fell into the easy temptation of globally discrediting the whole Austrian paradigm and describing it as 'dogmatic', without making any detailed study of its different aspects or attempting to answer the criticisms it raised.[66]

Bruce Caldwell is especially critical of this neoclassical attitude of disdaining and not even considering the positions of the Austrian methodologists, describing it, likewise, as dogmatic and anti-scientific and reaching the conclusion that it is in no way justified from a scientific point of view. In fact, and in relation to Samuelson's position, Caldwell wonders:

> What are the reasons behind this almost anti-scientific response to praxeology? There is, of course, a practical concern: the human capital of most economists would be drastically reduced (or made obsolete) were praxeology operationalized throughout the discipline. But the principal reason for rejecting Misesian methodology is not so self-serving. Simply put, the preoccupation of praxeologists with the 'ultimate foundations' of economics must seem mindless, if not perverse, to economists who dutifully learned their methodology from Friedman and who therefore are confident that assumptions do not matter and that prediction is the key. ... Regardless of its origins, such a reaction is itself dogmatic and, at its core, anti-scientific.[67]

The habitual way in which the neoclassical economists present what they consider to be the essential point of view of economics is much more arrogant and dogmatic. They base it exclusively on the principles of equilibrium, maximization and constancy of preferences. Thus, they intend to take on a monopoly of the conception of the 'economic point of view', extending the law of silence to the other alternative conceptions that, like the one represented by the Austrians, dispute the field of scientific research with them with a much richer and more realistic paradigm. We hope that, for the good of the future development of our discipline, this disguised dogmatism will gradually disappear in the future.[68]

Fortunately, some neoclassical authors have recently begun to recognize the narrowness and constraints of their traditional conception of the 'economic point of view'. Thus, Stiglitz has said that the criticism of neoclassical economics is not only that it fails to take into account the broader consequences of economic organization and the nature of society and the individual, but that it focuses too narrowly on a subset of human characteristics – *self-interest, rational behaviour*.[69]

However, this more open conception has not yet become general and therefore most of the neoclassicals are earning the well-deserved accusation of 'scientific imperialism' when they try to extend their narrow concept of rationality to spheres which, like the family, criminality and the economic analysis of law, are becoming increasingly broad. In this respect, Israel M. Kirzner has recently said that 'modern economists have seemed to permit the narrowest formulations of the rationality assumption to dictate social policy in what critics could easily perceive to be a highly dangerous fashion. It is not surprising that all this has stimulated sharply critical reaction'.[70]

Conclusion: evaluating the successes and failures of the two approaches

What we have said up to now does not mean that all, or even the majority, of the theoretical conclusions of the neoclassical economists should be rejected. Our recommendation should rather lead to a review and, if appropriate, a reworking of the neoclassical doctrines using the Austrian approach. In this way, the important valid conclusions contributed by the theorists of the Neoclassical School would be reinforced, while the errors which have remained latent and have surreptitiously been concealed from the theoretical 'spectacles' of the neoclassical researcher would come to light.

We have not yet mentioned what is a very relevant aspect, especially for all libertarian economists interested in stimulating research into the theory and practice of human liberty. The fact is that the neoclassical methodology based on a narrow concept of rationalism, the utilitarian cost–benefit analysis and the assumptions of constancy and full availability of the necessary information (in determinist or probabilistic terms), one way or another, very easily ends up justifying coercive measures of state intervention. In other words, the typical 'social engineering' approach that the neoclassicals naturally adopt leads them, almost without realizing it, to become 'analysts' who are easily prone to giving an interventionist prescription to the different specific problems they diagnose in the real world. This, which is precisely what gives the appearance of greater 'operational' success to the Neoclassical School, is also what, on many occasions, usually ends up justifying important measures of state interventionism. The problem is posed now with special virulence among our neoclassical allies of the School of Chicago, whose devotion and effort in the defence of liberty are indisputable, although their theoretical conclusions are often far from what would be considered desirable from the libertarian point of view, as they are influenced by the scientistic conception of the Neoclassical School, which they follow with what is, if possible, even greater devotion. Thus, as early as 1883, Menger, in his criticism of Adam Smith, showed how those who tried to scientifically create and improve the social institutions were headed towards interventionist conclusions.[71] And more recently, one of the distinguished members of the libertarian Mont Pelèrin Society regretted that 'it is frustrating when our Chicago allies employ their manifest talents in helping the state do more efficiently that which it either shouldn't be doing or of which it should be doing much less'.[72] The fact is that the neoclassical theorists who want to be libertarians are often victims of what we could call the 'paradox of the libertarian social engineer': effectively, they fully share the scientistic paradigm of the neoclassical social engineers and, at the same time, try to justify, with the same analytical perspective and instruments, supposedly more 'libertarian' policies, which are frequently in contradiction with the essential principles of freedom. In the long run, they end up, often without realizing it or wanting to, encouraging the institutional coercion which is typical of state intervention. This happens not only because the analytical innovations which they stimulate, in the hands of theorists who are less scrupulous or have a lower commitment to freedom, are easy to use to justify measures of intervention, but also because, as in the case mentioned by Crane, they themselves propose recipes that, although they appear to lead in the right direction, often finally reinforce the interventionist role of the State. This tension between the scientific approach of the neoclassicals and libertarianism arises time and again throughout the history of economic thought and perhaps the most illustrative example is Jeremy Bentham, who, in spite of his initial libertarian sympathies, ended up justifying important measures of interventionism.[73] In any case, it is evident that the social engineering approach which the mainstream neoclassical paradigm has been encouraging has, to a large degree, been responsible for the extension of the State in the last century. We should, therefore, consider that Hans-Hermann Hoppe is right when he says that the neoclassical-positivist methodology has often ended up by becoming 'the intellectual cover of socialism'.[74]

The fall of real socialism and the crisis of the welfare state, considered the most ambitious social engineering attempts made by the human being in the twentieth century, will have a profound impact on the future evolution of the neoclassical paradigm. It is obvious that something critical had failed in neoclassical economics when it was not able to analyse or predict such a significant historical event previously. Thus, the neoclassical Sherwin Rosen has had to acknowledge that 'the collapse of central planning in the past decade has come as a surprise to most of us'.[75] And we have already seen the critical comments on the standard neoclassical models made by Stiglitz in his *Whither Socialism?* Fortunately, it is not necessary to start methodologically from scratch: a large part of the analytical instruments necessary to reconstruct economic science along a more realistic path have already been articulated and perfected by the theorists of the Austrian School, who have prepared, explained, defended and refined them throughout the successive controversies in which we have seen they were in dispute with the theorists of the neoclassical paradigm. Some of the latter, like Mark Blaug, have shown a great deal of courage and have recently declared their abandonment of the model of general equilibrium and the static neoclassical-Walrasian paradigm, concluding: 'I have come slowly and extremely reluctantly to view that they (the Austrian School) are right and that we have all been wrong'.[76] Furthermore, the healthy influence of the present circumstances has begun to make itself felt in the mainstream paradigm in a series of research (the theory of auctions, the theory of financial markets, the economic analysis of information, the theory of industrial organization and the theory of games and strategic interactions). However, some words of warning on these more or less recent developments are necessary: to the extent that they merely introduce somewhat more realistic assumptions while maintaining the neoclassical methodology intact, it is possible that we will see the replacement of one series of methodologically defective models by others which are equally erroneous. In our opinion, only the introduction into the new fields of the dynamic approach based on the market processes, subjectivism and entrepreneurial creativity that the Austrians have developed will allow the development of economic science to be fruitfully stimulated in the new era that is commencing.

The evaluation of the comparative success of the different paradigms is usually made by the neoclassical economists in strictly empirical and quantitative terms, in line with the essence of their methodological point of view. Thus, for example, they usually consider that the *number* of scientists who follow a methodological point of view is a criterion which determines its 'success'. They also often refer to the *quantity* of specific problems that have apparently been 'solved' in operational terms by the point of view in question. However, this 'democratic' argument relative to the number of scientists who follow a certain paradigm is not very convincing. It is not only the fact that, in the history of human thought, even in the natural sciences, a majority of scientists have often been wrong, but, in the economic field, there is the additional problem that empirical evidence is never indisputable and therefore erroneous doctrines are not immediately identified and cast aside.

Moreover, when the theoretical analyses based on equilibrium receive an apparent empirical confirmation, even if their underlying economic theory is erroneous, they may be considered valid for very long periods of time. Even if the theoretical error or defect they include finally comes to light, given that they were prepared in relation to the operational solution of specific historical problems, the theoretical error committed in the analysis goes unnoticed or remains, to a great extent, concealed for the majority when the problems are no longer current.

If we add to the foregoing the fact that, to date, there has existed (and will continue to exist in the future) an ingenuous but significant demand on the part of many social agents (above all, the public authorities, social leaders and citizens in general) for specific predictions and empirical and 'operational' analysis relative to the different measures of economic and social policy which may be taken, it is obvious that this demand (like the demand for horoscopes and astrological predictions) will tend to be satisfied in the market by a supply of analysts and social engineers who give their clients what they want with an appearance of scientific respectability and legitimacy.

As Mises rightly says,

> the development of a profession of economists is an offshoot of interventionism. The professional economist is the specialist who is instrumental in deciding various measures of government interference with business. He is an expert in the field of economic legislation, which today invariably aims at hindering the operation of the market economy.[77]

If the behaviour of the members of a profession of specialists in intervention is, in the final analysis, the definitive judge who must pass judgement on a paradigm which, like the Austrian one, shows that their interventionist measures are not legitimate, it invalidates the 'democratic' argument. If, furthermore, it is recognized that, in the economics field, unlike the engineering and natural sciences fields, rather than a continual advance, there are sometimes important regressions[78] and errors which take a long time to be identified and corrected, then neither can the number of apparently successful 'operational' solutions be accepted as a definitive criterion, since what today appears 'correct' in operational terms may tomorrow be seen to be based on erroneous theoretical formulations.

As opposed to the empirical success criteria,[79] we propose an alternative *qualitative* criterion. According to our alternative criterion, a paradigm will have been more successful if it has give rise to a greater number of correct theoretical developments which are important for the evolution of humanity. In this respect, it is evident that the Austrian approach is clearly superior to the neoclassical approach. The Austrians have been capable of drawing up a theory on the impossibility of socialism which, if it had been taken into account in time, would have avoided enormous suffering for humankind. Moreover, the historical fall of real socialism has illustrated the accuracy of the Austrian analysis. Something similar occurred, as we have seen, in relation to the Great Depression of 1929 and also in many other areas in which the Austrians have developed their dynamic analysis of the discoordinating effects of state intervention. This is the case, for example, in the monetary and credit field, the field of the theory of economic cycles, the reworking of the dynamic theory of competition and monopoly, the analysis of the theory of interventionism, the search for new criteria of dynamic efficiency to replace the traditional Paretian criteria, the critical analysis of the concept of 'social justice' that has been constructed on the basis of the static neoclassical paradigm and, in short, of the better understanding of the market as a process of social interaction driven by entrepreneurship. All these are examples of significant qualitative successes of the Austrian approach that contrast with the serious insufficiencies (or failures) of the neoclassical approach, among which its confessed inability to recognize and make provision for the impossibility and harmful consequences of the socialist economic system in time should be highlighted.

What is clear is that, in order to overcome the inertia implied by the constant social demand for specific predictions, recipes for intervention and empirical studies, which are easily accepted in spite of the fact that they include significant defects from the theoretical point of view, hidden in an empirical environment in which it is very difficult to obtain indisputable proof of the conclusions presented, it will be necessary to continue to extend and deepen the subjective and dynamic approach proposed by the Austrian School in the field of our science. In this respect, we should recall the much quoted phrase of Hayek that 'it is probably not exaggeration to say that every important advance in economic theory during the last hundred years was a further step in the consistent application of subjectivism'.[80] If Hayek is right, only the consistent application of the Austrian subjectivist method can make economic science advance in the future.

The ongoing *Methodenstreit* will continue while human beings still prefer doctrines that satisfy them to those that are theoretically true and while the rationalist fatal conceit of the human being, which leads him to believe that he has, in each specific historical circumstance, information which is much greater than that he can really possess, prevails. Against these dangerous trends in human thought, which inevitably will appear time and time again, we only have the much more realistic, richer and more humanistic methodology developed by the theorists of the Austrian School, which I, here today, cordially invite the maximum number of freedom-loving scientists possible to join.

3 Conjectural history and beyond[1]

Professor Hayek states on page 20 of his work *The Fatal Conceit* that 'reluctant as we may be to accept this, no universally valid system of ethics can ever be known to us'. In this brief comment we aim to criticize this claim on the part of Professor Hayek and, in turn, to expound a theory of the compatibility of three different levels of approach to the study of this same human reality.

A first level of approach would be constituted by what Hayek, following Hume, terms 'conjectural history'.[2] Conjectural history consists in interpreting the processes of evolution and in analysing their results (customs, morals, laws and institutions). This first area of research has its origin in the tradition that begins with Montesquieu and Hume and culminates in Hayek's most significant works, and especially in *The Fatal Conceit.* This level of approach is highly multidisciplinary and must include studies from sociology, political science, anthropology, etc. In short, this approach to the study of human reality is the first to have sprung up in the history of scientific thought, and it aims to explain the evolution and emergence of 'real or positive law'. The main risk facing the researcher in this area lies in how easy it is to commit errors when it comes to interpreting the phenomena of historical evolution, especially when an erroneous theory is used, either implicitly or explicitly, in this process of interpretation.

The second level of approach to the study of human reality emerges much later in time, with the appearance of economic science towards the end of the eighteenth century and culminating in the contributions of the Austrian School of Economics, which focuses its scientific research programme on the formal study of the spontaneous and dynamic processes resulting from human interaction. This level consists, therefore, in the development of a formal theory of the social processes, or, if you prefer, in the attempt to rationalize these social processes in a detailed manner. This second field of research gives rise to praxeology (a formal theory of social processes), which has its beginnings with Menger, continues with Mises and is even developed by Hayek himself in his earlier works and more recently by the members of the Neo-Austrian School. In Montesquieu's terminology this second level of approach would aim to discover in a rational way the laws of nature in the social field. The main risk in this second level of approach (constituted by economic science) lies in what Hayek terms constructivism, as it is extremely easy for the economist to fall into the error of not restricting himself to interpreting and studying the social process logically and formally, but instead falling into the fatal conceit of believing it possible and advisable to use this knowledge to rebuild and design society *ex novo*.

Finally, the third level of approach would consist in the development of a formal theory of social ethics. This level of approach is precisely what Hayek appears to deny in the quotation included at the outset of this commentary. Yet we believe that, just as we can progress in the rationalization of the social processes (economics), it is possible to carry out a certain formal rationalization of social ethics. We would therefore be engaged in the discovery and justification of 'natural law', thereby following the tradition of Locke, which has found continuation today in such authors as Nozick and Rothbard. Naturally, as was the case with economics, the main risk in this third level of approach lies in constructivism. However, this should not lead us to give up directly attempts to rationalize a formal theory of social ethics, insofar as it lies within our scope. Thus, one has the levels of real or positive law, the law of nature and natural law, understood (respectively) by conjectural history, praxeology and the formal theory of ethics. Each level is complementary to the others; each also has its dangers (theoretical error for the first level, constructivism for the second and third). In this respect, an important practical rule may be to be on one's guard whenever the rationalist conclusions of the second and third level seem to be in open contradiction with the conclusions of the first level (conjectural history). In this case, one will have to take the utmost care not to fall into constructivism.

Hayek's work is especially praiseworthy for its contributions both in the second level (economic theory) and in the first level (the theory of evolution and the critique of constructivism). However, we feel that it could have been enriched even further if Professor Hayek had, on a supplementary basis, applied his ample wisdom to the third level (the theory of social ethics).

4 Entrepreneurship and the economic analysis of socialism[1]

In this article, I try to show the way in which the theory of entrepreneurship, as developed by Israel M. Kirzner, must be an essential element of any analysis of the impossibility of socialism. As a consequence of my analysis, I propose a new definition of socialism, based on the concept of entrepreneurship, which seems to be more general and analytically fruitful than the standard definition. In the first section, I explain my interpretation of the essence of entrepreneurship and, in the second, I introduce my new definition of socialism; thereafter I develop the analysis of its impossibility from the point of view of entrepreneurial theory. A critique of the alternative and traditional concepts of socialism is included in the final section.

The essence of entrepreneurship

In a general or broad sense, entrepreneurship coincides with *human action* itself.[2] In this respect, it can be said that any person who *acts* to modify the present and obtain his objectives in the future is practising entrepreneurship. Although, at first sight, this definition may appear to be too broad and out of line with current linguistic usage, it must be remembered that it corresponds to a concept of entrepreneurship which is being constantly worked upon and studied by economic science[3] and which, moreover, is fully in line with the original etymological meaning of the term *entrepreneur*. In fact, both the English word *enterprise* (in French *entreprise*, in Spanish *empresa*) and the French and English *entrepreneur* (in Spanish *empresario*) have their etymological origin in the Latin verb *in prehendo-endi-ensum*, which means, discover, see, perceive, realize, trap; and the Latin expression *in prehensa* clearly implies the idea of *action*, meaning take, grasp or seize. In short, the Spanish word *empresa* is synonymous with action and in France the term *entrepreneur* has been used since medieval times to refer to people entrusted with the performance of important actions, generally connected with warfare or with great projects for the construction of cathedrals. In English, *The Oxford English Dictionary* defines *enterprise* as the '*action* of taking in hand' and also as 'the bold, arduous, or momentous undertaking'.[4] And in Spanish, one of the meanings of *empresa* given in the *Dictionary* of the

Spanish Royal Academy is 'arduous and difficult *action* which is valiantly commenced'. This word was also used in medieval times to refer to the insignias of certain orders of knighthood, which indicated the pledge, under oath, to carry out a certain important *action*. In any case, the meaning of *enterprise* as action is necessarily and inexorably linked to an enterprising, go-ahead attitude, which consists of continuously seeking, discovering, creating or becoming aware of new ends and means (all of which is in line with the etymological meaning stemming from the Latin verb *in prehendo*).

Entrepreneurship and alertness

Entrepreneurship, in the strict sense of the term, consists basically of discovering and appreciating (*prehendo*) the opportunities of attaining an end or, if one prefers, of obtaining a gain or profit, which arise in one's environment, acting in consequence in order to take advantage of them. Kirzner says that the performance of entrepreneurship implies a special *alertness* (in Spanish *perspicacia*), i.e. continually being *alert*, which makes it possible for the human being to discover and become aware of what is happening around him.[5] Perhaps Kirzner uses the English term 'alertness' because the term *entrepreneurship* is of French origin and does not automatically imply in the Anglo-Saxon language the idea of *prehendo* which is present in the continental European romance languages. In any case, in Spanish the adjective *perspicaz* is most appropriate to describe entrepreneurship, as it applies, according to the *Dictionary* of the Spanish Royal Academy, 'to the very acute glance or look which is far-reaching'. Furthermore, *speculator* etymologically comes from the Latin noun *specula*, which means watchtower or high vantage point from which to discover or see in the distance. This idea fits in perfectly with the activity carried out by the entrepreneur when deciding what actions he will take and estimating the effect thereof in the future. Being alert is also acceptable as a feature of entrepreneurship as it implies the idea of attention or watchfulness.

Information, knowledge and entrepreneurship

The nature of entrepreneurship in the form in which we have been discussing it cannot be understood in depth without understanding how it modifies or produces changes in the information or knowledge which the actor possesses. First, perceiving or becoming aware of new ends and means leads to a modification of the actor's knowledge, in the sense that he creates or discovers new information. Second, this discovery modifies the whole map or context of information or knowledge which the subject possesses. We may, therefore, pose the following essential question: what are the relevant characteristics of the information or knowledge discovered by the performance of entrepreneurship? We will study in detail six basic characteristics of this type of knowledge: (1) it is subjective knowledge of a practical, non-scientific nature; (2) it is private or exclusive knowledge; (3) it is dispersed over the minds of all men; (4) most of it is tacit knowledge and, therefore, is not articulable; (5) it is knowledge which is created *ex nihilo*, from nothing, precisely by entrepreneurship; and (6) most of it is transmissible in a form which is not conscious, through very complex social processes the study of which constitutes the research subject of Economic Science.

Subjective and practical non-scientific knowledge

First, the knowledge we are analysing, the most important or relevant to the practice of human action, is, above all, *subjective* knowledge of a *practical*, non-scientific, nature. Practical knowledge is all knowledge that cannot be formally represented, but that the subject acquires or learns through practice, i.e. from human action itself carried out in its corresponding contexts. It is, as Hayek says, the knowledge relevant to all kinds of particular circumstances as regards its subjective coordinates in time and space.[6] In short, we are talking about knowledge of specific human valuations, i.e. both of the ends desired by the actor and of his knowledge about the ends which he believes other actors desire or pursue. In the same way, it is practical knowledge of the means which the actor believes to be within his reach to attain his ends and, in particular, of all the circumstances, personal or otherwise, which the actor considers may be relevant within the context of each specific action.[7]

Private and dispersed knowledge

Practical knowledge has an exclusive and dispersed nature. This means that each human actor possesses only some of what we could call 'atoms' or 'bits' of the information which is globally generated and transmitted at the social level, but which, paradoxically, only he or she possesses, i.e. which only s/he consciously knows and consciously interprets. Therefore, each person who acts and practises entrepreneurship does so in a strictly personal and unrepeatable way, as his or her starting point is an attempt to attain ends or objectives in accordance with a vision and knowledge of the world which only s/he possesses with all its richness and variety of nuances and which cannot be exactly repeated in any other human being. Therefore, the knowledge to which we refer is not something which is *given*, available to everybody by some material means of information storage (newspapers, specialized journals, books, computers, etc.). On the contrary, the relevant knowledge for human action is basically practical and strictly exclusive, which can only be 'found' spread over the mind of all and every one of the men and women who act and constitute humanity. In Figure 4.1, we will introduce some stick people, with the sole objective of helping us make the analysis contained herein more graphic.

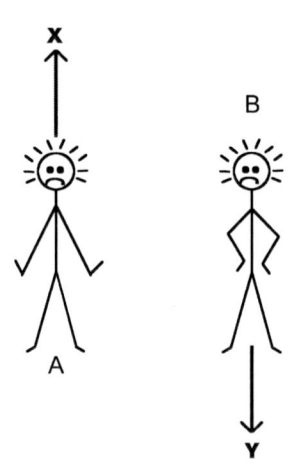

Figure 4.1

In this figure we wish to represent two real human beings of flesh and blood, whom we call A and B. Each of the people represented by A and B possesses his or her own exclusive knowledge, i.e. knowledge which the other does not have; what is more, from the point of view of an external observer, we may say that there 'exists' knowledge we, as observers, do not possess and which is dispersed between A and B, inasmuch as A has part of it and B another part. Thus, for example, let us assume that the information which A has is that she aims to attain an end X (which we represent by the arrow above her head pointing towards X) and that, with a view to attaining this end, possesses certain practical information which is relevant in the context of the action (this knowledge or practical information is represented by the 'halo' which A has around her head). B's case is similar, except that the end he pursues is very different, in this case, Y (represented by the arrow at his feet pointing towards Y); the practical information which the actor B considers relevant in the context of his action is also represented by the 'halo' around his head.

In some simple actions the actor, individually, possesses the information necessary to attain the proposed end without the need to relate to other actors at all. In these cases, whether or not the action is undertaken is the result of an *economic calculation* or estimative judgement made by the actor, weighing up and *directly* comparing the subjective value s/he places on the end s/he aims to attain with the cost or value s/he places upon what s/he renounces if s/he pursues the chosen end. However, the actions on which the actor can take this type of decisions directly are few and very simple. The majority of actions in which we are involved are much more complex, as we will now explain. Let us imagine, as represented in Figure 4.1, that A has a great desire to reach end X but, in order to do so, requires the existence of a means M which she does not have at her disposal and which she *does not know* either where or how to obtain. Simultaneously, let us suppose that B is somewhere else, that he aims to attain a very different end (end Y), to which he devotes all his efforts, and that he knows, or 'knows of' or has at his disposal a large quantity of a means M which he does not consider useful or suitable for attaining his end but which, by coincidence, is the means which A would need to enable her to reach the objective she desires (X). What is more, it must be emphasized that, as is true in most real cases, X and Y are *contradictory*, i.e. each actor pursues different ends, with a different degree of intensity and with a relative degree of knowledge regarding the ends and regarding the means within his or her realm which do not coincide with or are not adjusted to his or her needs (this explains the disconsolate expression with which we have drawn our stick people). Later on, we will see how the practice of entrepreneurship makes it possible to overcome this kind of contradictory or *uncoordinated* behaviour.

Tacit, inarticulate knowledge

Practical knowledge is mostly *tacit* and *inarticulate*. This means that the actor knows how to do or carry out certain actions (*know how*) but does not know what the elements or parts of what he is doing are, or if they are true or false (*know that*).[8] Thus, for example, when a person learns to play golf, he is not learning a set of objective, scientific rules which permit him to make the necessary movements as a result of the application of a series of formulae of mathematical physics, but the learning process rather consists of the acquisition of a series of practical habits of conduct. In the same way, we may quote, as Polanyi does, the example of the person who learns to ride a bicycle, trying to keep his balance by moving the handlebar to the side towards which he is beginning to fall, thus causing a centrifugal force which tends to keep the bicycle upright. However, practically no cyclist is aware of or knows the physical principles on which his ability is based. On the contrary, the cyclist is rather using his 'sense of balance', which, in some way, indicates to him the way in which he should behave at any given moment in order not to fall. Polanyi even states that tacit knowledge is, in fact, the dominant principle of all knowledge.[9] Even the most highly formalized and scientific knowledge is always the result of an intuition or act of creation, both of which are simply manifestations of tacit knowledge. Apart from the fact that the new formalized knowledge, which we can acquire thanks to formulae, books, graphs, maps, etc., is, above all, important because it helps to reorganize all our contexts of information from different, richer and more productive points of view, which opens up new possibilities for using creative intuition.

A type of inarticulable knowledge which plays an essential role in the development of society is that which is made up of a set of habits, traditions, institutions and legal rules which constitute law and make society possible and which humans learn to obey without being able to theorize or articulate

68 *Entrepreneurship and socialism*

in detail the precise role played by such rules and institutions in the different situations and social processes where they intervene. The same may be said of language and also, for example, of the financial and cost accounting used by the entrepreneur to guide his actions and which is simply a practical knowledge or technique which, used within a determined context of market economy, is a generalized guideline for entrepreneurs to help them attain their objectives, without their being able, in the majority of cases, to formulate a scientific theory of accounting and, even less, to explain how such a theory helps in the complicated processes of coordination which make life in society possible.[10] We can, therefore, conclude that the practice of entrepreneurship as we have defined it (the capacity to discover and appreciate opportunities for profit, undertaking a conscious line of behaviour in order to take advantage thereof) consists of a type of knowledge which is basically tacit and inarticulable.

The essentially creative nature of entrepreneurship

Entrepreneurship does not require any means for its execution. This means that entrepreneurship does not imply any cost and, therefore, is essentially creative. The creative nature of entrepreneurship is shown by the fact that it gives rise to profits which, in a certain sense, arise from nowhere and which we will call *pure entrepreneurial profits*. To obtain entrepreneurial profits it is not necessary, therefore, to have any prior means available, but merely to practise entrepreneurship well. We can illustrate this fact starting from the situation described in Figure 4.1. It is sufficient to *become aware of* the situation of *lack of adjustment or of coordination* which exists between A and B for the opportunity of pure entrepreneurial profit to arise. Thus, in Figure 4.2 it is assumed that it is a third person, in this case C, who practises

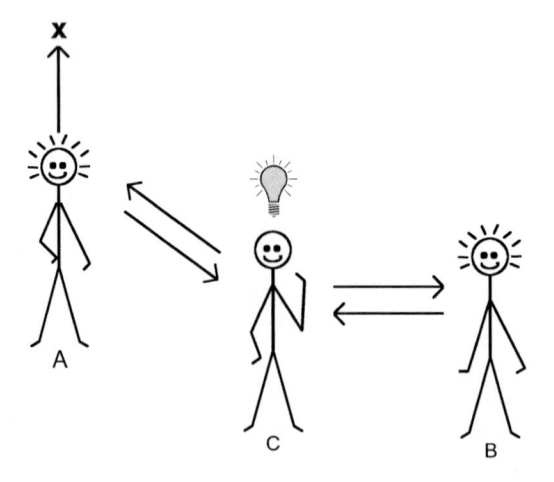

Figure 4.2

entrepreneurship on discovering the lack of adjustment or of coordination shown in Figure 4.1 (we represent the fact that C becomes aware of such opportunity by a 'bulb' which lights up). Logically, in practice, entrepreneurship could be practised by A or B or by both of them simultaneously, with the same or differing intensities, although, for our purposes, it is more illustrative to consider that it is carried out by a third person C.

In fact, it is sufficient for C to contact B and offer to buy the resource, which the latter possesses in abundance and upon which he places practically no importance, for a certain amount, let us say 3 monetary units, which B will find enormously satisfactory, as he never imagined he could obtain so much for his resource. Later, once the exchange has been made, C will be able to contact A and sell her the resource which A so intensely needs to attain the end she is pursuing, selling it to her for, let us say, 9 monetary units (if C does not have any money, he can obtain it, for example, by persuading someone to make him a temporary loan). As a consequence, therefore, of the practice of entrepreneurship by C, he has obtained, *ex nihilo*, pure entrepreneurial profit of 6 monetary units.

It is now of special interest to emphasize that, as a consequence of this act of entrepreneurship, there have been three effects of extraordinary importance. First, entrepreneurship has *created* new information which did not exist previously. Second, this information has been *transmitted* throughout the market. Third, as a consequence of the entrepreneurial act, the economic agents involved *have learnt* to act in accordance with each other. These consequences of entrepreneurship are so important that it is worth studying each of them separately in detail.

Creation of information

All entrepreneurial acts imply the creation *ex nihilo* of new information. This creation takes place in the mind of the person, in our example the person represented by stickman C, who is the first to practise entrepreneurship. Effectively, when C becomes aware that there exists a situation such as the one described, in which A and B are involved, new information, which he did not previously have, is created in his mind. But moreover, once C undertakes the action and enters into contact with A and B, new information is also created in the minds of A and B. Thus, A becomes aware of the fact that the resource which she lacked and of which she had such a need in order to attain her end is available in other parts of the market in greater abundance than she thought and that, therefore, she may undertake, now without problems, the action which she did not begin due to the lack of the resource. B, on his part, becomes aware that the resource which he possessed in such abundance and upon which he placed no value is very much wanted or desired by other people and that, therefore, he can sell it at a good price. Moreover, part of the new practical information which originated in the mind of C on practising entrepreneurship and which later arises in the minds of A and B, is included, in a very summarized form, in a series of *prices* or historical exchange *ratios* (i.e. B sold at 3 and A bought at 9).

Transmission of information

The entrepreneurial creation of information implies a simultaneous *transmission* thereof in the market. In fact, transmitting something to someone is to make that person generate or create in his own mind part of the information which we created or discovered previously. In our example, strictly speaking, not only the idea has been transmitted to B that his resource is important and should not be wasted, and to A the idea that he may go ahead with the pursuit of the end he desired but could not pursue in view of the lack of such resource, but also, through the respective prices, which are a potent transmission system, since they transmit a large amount of information at very low cost, it is communicated to the whole market or society that the resource in question should be kept and saved, as there is a demand for it and, simultaneously, that all those who do not undertake actions because they think the said resource does not exist can obtain it and go ahead with their respective plans of action. Logically, the relevant information is always subjective and only exists within the persons which are capable of interpreting or discovering it, meaning that it is always human beings who create, perceive and transmit information. The erroneous idea that information is objective originates from the fact that part of the entrepreneurial-created subjective information is set out 'objectively' in signals (prices, institutions, rules, 'firms', etc.) which may be discovered and subjectively interpreted by many people in the context of their specific actions, thus facilitating the creation of new subjective information, richer and more complex. However, in spite of appearances, the transmission of social information is basically tacit and subjective, i.e. it is not express and articulated, and takes a very summarized form (in fact, the minimum information indispensable to coordinate the social process is transmitted and subjectively captured), which, in addition, permits full advantage to be taken of the limited capacity of the human mind to constantly create, discover and create new knowledge.

Learning effect: coordination and adjustment

Finally, it is necessary to stress how agents A and B have learnt to act in accordance with each other. In other words, B, as a consequence of the entrepreneurial act originally undertaken by C, does not now squander or waste the resource he has at his disposal but, in his own interest, keeps and conserves it. A, as he has the resource at his disposal, can attain his end and undertake the action which he did not undertake previously. Both, therefore, learn to act in coordination, i.e. to modify and discipline their behaviour in accordance with the other human beings. Moreover, they learn in the best possible way: without realizing that they are learning and *motu proprio*, i.e.

voluntarily and within the context of a plan in which each of them pursues his own ends and interests. This, and nothing else, is the *nucleus* of the process, both marvellous, and simple and effective, which makes life in society possible. Finally, we observe that the practice of entrepreneurship by C makes possible not only a coordinated action between A and B which did not exist previously, but also that the latter two carry out an *economic calculation* in the context of their respective actions, with data or information which they did not have before and which permits them to attain, with a much greater chance of success, their respective ends. In short, the economic calculation by each actor is made possible thanks precisely to the information generated in the entrepreneurial process. Or, in other words, without the practice of entrepreneurship, the information necessary for each actor to calculate or estimate appropriately the value of each alternative course of action is not generated. That is, without entrepreneurship, economic calculation is not possible.[11]

The above observations constitute the social science teachings which are, at the same time, the most important and the most elementary and which allow us to conclude that entrepreneurship is, without any doubt, the social function par excellence, given that it makes life in society possible, as it adjusts and coordinates the individual behaviour of its members. Without entrepreneurship, it is impossible to conceive of the existence of any society.

The essential principle

Now the really important point from a theoretical point of view is not who, specifically, practises entrepreneurship (although, in practice, this is precisely the most important point), but that, as there are no institutional or legal restrictions on the free practice of entrepreneurship, each person may put into practice his or her entrepreneurial activities as best s/he can, creating new information and taking advantage of the practical, exclusive information which s/he has discovered in the circumstances of any given moment.

It does not correspond to the economist, but rather to the psychologist, to study in detail humankind's innate force which moves people entrepreneurially in all their fields of action. Here and now, we are only interested in stressing the essential principle that people tend to discover the information which is of interest to them and, therefore, if there is freedom with regard to the attainment of ends and interests, these will act as an incentive and will make it possible for the person practising entrepreneurship, motivated by such incentive, to continuously perceive and discover the relevant practical information for the attainment of the proposed ends. And, *vice versa*, if for any reason the field in which entrepreneurship may be practised is limited or closed in a determined area of life in society (by legal, institutional or traditional restrictions), then human beings will not even consider the possibility of attaining or reaching ends in these forbidden or limited areas, and, therefore, as the end is not possible, it will not act as an incentive and, in consequence, no practical relevant information for the attainment of such end will be perceived or discovered. What is more, not even the affected persons *will be conscious* under these circumstances of the enormous value and great number of ends which cannot be attained as a result of the situation of institutional restriction. That is, within the stick people scheme of Figures 4.1 and 4.2, we realize how, if there is freedom for human action to be carried out, the 'entrepreneurial bulb' can freely light up in any circumstance where there is lack of social adjustment or coordination, thus producing the process of creation and transmission of information which will lead to the coordination of the disorder, allowing and making possible life in society. On the other hand, if in a certain area the practice of entrepreneurship is prevented, it is never possible for the 'entrepreneurial bulb' to light up, i.e. it is not possible for the entrepreneur to discover the existing situation of discoordination, which, therefore, will be able to continue unaltered indefinitely or may even get worse.

Entrepreneurship and the concept of socialism

Our discussion of entrepreneurship in the first section was necessary because we propose a new definition of socialism which is based on the concept of entrepreneurship. In fact, we will define socialism as any *system of institutionalized aggression against the free practice of entrepreneurship*. Aggression or *coercion* must be understood to mean any physical violence or threat of physical violence which is originated towards and performed on an individual by another human being or group of human beings. As a consequence of this coercion, the individual, who would otherwise have freely carried on his or her entrepreneurship, is, in order to avoid a greater evil, forced to act differently to the way s/he would have acted under other circumstances, thus modifying his or her behaviour and adapting it to meet the ends of the person or persons who are coercing him or her.[12] We may consider aggression, thus defined, to be the anti-human action par excellence. This is so because coercion prevents a person from freely carrying on his or her entrepreneurship, i.e. from seeking the objectives s/he has set using the means which, according to his or her information and to the best of his or her knowledge, s/he believes or considers to be accessible to him or her for reaching these objectives. Aggression is, therefore, an evil because it prevents the human being from carrying on the activity which is most characteristic of him or her and which essentially and most intimately corresponds to him or her.

There are two types of aggression: systematic or institutionalized and non-systematic or non-institutionalized. The latter type of coercion, which is, in nature, dispersed, arbitrary and more unpredictable, affects the carrying on of entrepreneurship to the extent that the individual considers there to be a greater or lesser probability that, in the context of a specific action, force will be used upon him or her by a third party, who may even appropriate the results of his or her entrepreneurial creativity. Although non-systematic outbreaks of aggression are more or less serious, depending on the circumstances, institutionalized or systematic aggression is far more serious as regards coordinated human interaction. As we have seen, this type of aggression constitutes the essence of our definition of socialism.[13] In fact, institutionalized coercion is characterized by being highly predictable, repetitive, methodical and organized. The main consequence of this systematic aggression against entrepreneurship is to make largely impossible and perversely divert the carrying on of entrepreneurship in all the areas of society where said aggression is effective. In Figure 4.3, we show the typical situation resulting from the systematic practice of coercion.

In Figure 4.3 we assume that, in an organized and systematic way, the free human action of C in relation to A and B in a specific area of life in society is prevented by coercion. This is represented by the lines which separate C from A and B. As a consequence, it is not possible, as systematic coercion prevents it by the threat of serious evils, for C to discover and take advantage of the profit opportunity which he would have if he could interact freely with B and with A. It is very important to clearly understand that the aggression does not only prevent him from taking advantage of the profit opportunity, but even prevents the discovery of this opportunity. The possibility of obtaining gains or profits acts as an incentive to the discovery of these opportunities. Therefore, if a determined area of life in society is restricted by systematic coercion, the actors tend to adapt to said situation, they take it for granted and, therefore, do not even create, discover or

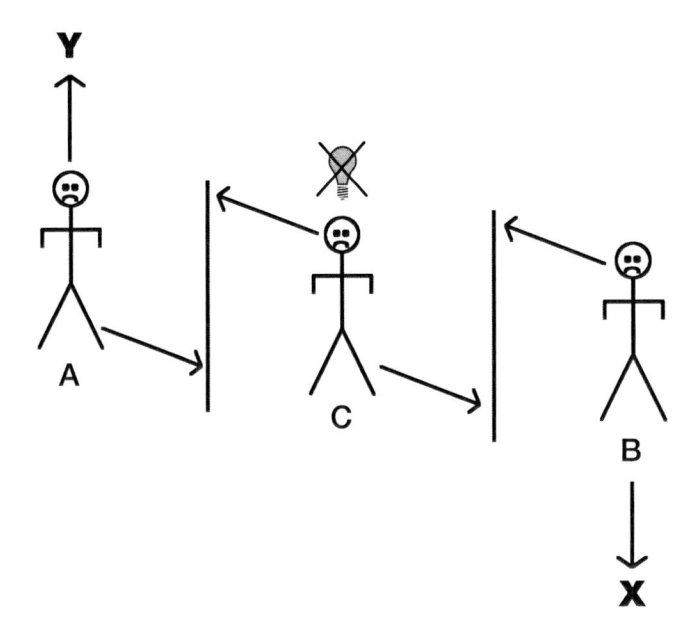

Figure 4.3

become aware of the opportunities which are latent. We represent this situation in the figure by crossing out the light bulb which, in accordance with our convention, indicates the creative act of pure entrepreneurial discovery.

If the aggression falls systematically upon one social area and, as a consequence, entrepreneurship cannot be carried out in that area, none of the other effects typical of the pure entrepreneurial act explained in the first section of the article will take place. In fact, in the first place, new information will not be created; nor will it be transmitted from actor to actor. Second, and this is a cause for even more concern, the adjustment necessary in cases of a lack of social coordination will not occur. As the discovery of opportunities for profit is not permitted, there will be no incentive for the actors to become aware of situations of lack of adjustment or coordination which arise. In short, information will not be created, it will not be transmitted from one agent to another and the different human beings will not learn to discipline their behaviour in accordance with that of their peers.

Thus, in Figure 4.3, we see how, as C cannot carry on entrepreneurship, the system is maintained continuously uncoordinated: A cannot pursue end Y due to lack of a resource which B has in abundance and does not know what to do with. He therefore squanders and misuses it, unaware that an A exists and needs it urgently. In accordance with our analysis, we can, therefore, conclude that the main effect of socialism, as we have defined it, is to prevent the action of the coordinating forces which make life in society possible. Does this mean that the proposers of socialism are advocating a chaotic or uncoordinated society? On the contrary, apart from a few exceptions, the proposers of the socialist ideal defend it because, tacitly or explicitly, they believe or suppose that the system of social coordination not only will be undisturbed by the existence of the institutionalized and systematic violence which they favour, but will be made much more effective by the fact that the systematic coercion is performed by a controlling organism which is supposed to possess knowledge (regarding both the ends and the means) and valuations which are better, both quantitatively and qualitatively, than those which the coerced actors may possess at a lower level. From this perspective, we may now complete the definition of socialism given at the beginning of this section, stating that *socialism is all systematic and institutionalized aggression which restricts the free performance of entrepreneurship in a determined social area and which is carried out by a controlling organism which is in charge of the tasks of social coordination necessary in said area.* Under the following heading we will analyse the point to which socialism, in the terms we have defined it, is or is not an intellectual error.

Socialism as an intellectual error

Life in society is possible thanks to the fact that individuals, spontaneously and without realizing it, learn to modify their behaviour, adapting it to the needs of other people. This unconscious learning process is the natural result

Entrepreneurship and socialism 75

of the practice of entrepreneurship by human beings. This means that, upon interaction with his peers, each person spontaneously initiates a process of adjustment or coordination in which new information – tacit, practical and dispersed – is continually being created, discovered and transmitted from one mind to others. The problem posed by socialism is whether it is possible, by the coercive mechanism, to verify the processes of adjustment and coordination of the conduct of different human beings, which depend upon each other and which are indispensable if life in society is to function; all the foregoing taking place within a framework of constant discovery and new creation of practical information which makes it possible for civilization to advance and develop. The ideal put forward by socialism is, therefore, highly daring and ambitious,[14] as it implies the belief that not only may the mechanism of coordination and social adjustment be made effective by the controlling organism which performs the institutionalized coercion in the social area in question but that, in addition, this adjustment may even be improved by the coercive procedure.

Figure 4.4 is a schematic representation of the concept of socialism as we have defined it. On the 'lower level' are human beings, endowed with knowledge or practical information, who, for this reason, try to interact freely among themselves, although such interaction is not possible in some areas due to institutionalized coercion. This coercion is represented by the vertical lines which separate the figures forming each group. On the 'upper level', we show the controlling organism which, as an institution, practices coercion in determined areas of life in society. The vertical arrows in opposite directions, which come from the figures on the left and right of each

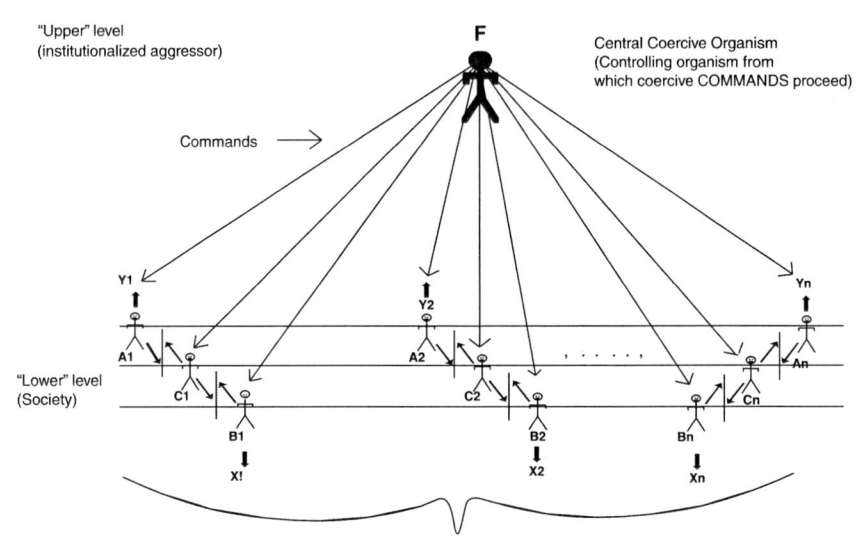

Figure 4.4

group, represent the existence of unadjusted personal plans which are typical of a situation where there is a lack of social coordination. Cases of lack of coordination cannot be discovered and eliminated by entrepreneurship because of the barriers imposed by the effect of institutionalized coercion on entrepreneurship. The arrows which go from the head of the controlling figure towards each human being on the lower level represent the coercive commands which comprise the aggression typical of socialism, aimed at compelling the citizens to act in a coordinated way and to pursue end F which is considered 'right' by the controlling organism.

The command may be defined as any specific instruction or stipulation, the contents of which are clearly defined, which, regardless of the legal form it takes, prohibits or compels determined actions to be taken under specific circumstances. The command is characterized by the fact that it does not allow the human being to freely carry on his or her entrepreneurship in the social area it refers to.

Commands are, moreover, deliberate decisions of the controlling organism practising institutionalized aggression and are aimed to force all the actors to fulfil or pursue, not their personal ends, but the ends of those who govern or control.

In view of the foregoing, socialism is an intellectual error because it is not theoretically possible that the organism in charge of practising institutionalized aggression possess sufficient information to endow its commands with contents of a coordinating nature. We will examine this simple argument in a certain amount of detail; it can be developed from two different, but complementary, points of view: first, from the overall perspective of the human beings who constitute society and who are coerced; second, from the standpoint of the coercive organization which practises aggression systematically. Below we analyse separately the problem posed by socialism from each of these viewpoints.

The impossibility of socialism from the perspective of society

The static argument

First, from the point of view of human beings who interact among themselves and constitute society (the so-called 'lower' level of Figure 4.4), it must be remembered that each of them possesses exclusive practical and dispersed information, the majority of which is tacit and, therefore, cannot be articulated. This means that it is logically impossible to conceive of its possible transmission to the controlling organism (the so-called 'upper' level in Figure 4.4). In fact, it is not only that the total volume of practical information sensed and handled by all human beings at an individual level is so enormous that its conscious acquisition by the controlling organism is inconceivable, but, above all, that this volume of information is disseminated among the minds of all men in the form of tacit information which cannot be articulated and, therefore, cannot be formally expressed or explicitly transmitted to any controlling centre.

We already saw in the second section how information relevant to life in society is created and transmitted implicitly in a disseminated way, i.e. neither consciously nor deliberately. In this way the different social agents learn to discipline their behaviour in relation to that of other people but are not aware that they are the protagonists of this learning process or that, therefore, they are adapting their behaviour to that of other human beings: they are simply conscious that they are acting, i.e. trying to obtain their personal ends using the means they believe to be within their reach. Therefore, the knowledge we are discussing is a knowledge which is only possessed by human beings acting in society which, in view of its intrinsic nature, cannot be explicitly transmitted to any central controlling organism. As this knowledge is indispensable if different individual behaviours are to be coordinated socially, thus making society possible, and cannot be transmitted to the controlling organism given the fact that it cannot be articulated, it is logically absurd to think that a socialist system can work.

The dynamic argument

Socialism is impossible not only because the information possessed by the actors is intrinsically unable to be transmitted explicitly, but because, moreover, from a dynamic point of view, human beings, on carrying out entrepreneurship, i.e. on acting, constantly create and discover new information. It would be very difficult to transmit to the controlling organism information or knowledge which has not yet been created, but which is continually arising as a result of the social process itself to the extent that the latter is not attacked.

Figure 4.5 represents the actors who are continually creating and discovering new information throughout the social process. As time, in its subjective sense, elapses, those who perform their entrepreneurship in interaction with their peers are constantly becoming aware of new profit opportunities, of which they try to take advantage. Consequently, the information possessed by each of them is constantly undergoing modification. This is represented in the figure by the different bulbs which light up as time passes. It is clear not only that it will be impossible for the controlling organism to have all the information necessary to coordinate society by commands at its disposal, given that this information is, as we have seen, dispersed, exclusive and impossible to articulate, but also that, moreover, this information will be continually modified and will arise *ex nihilo* as time passes. It is highly unlikely that it is possible to transmit to the controlling organism information which is at each moment indispensable for the coordination of society but which has not yet even been created by the entrepreneurial process itself.

Thus, for example, when it looks rainy at dawn or there is any other series of meteorological circumstances, the farmer realizes that, as a result of the

78   Entrepreneurship and socialism

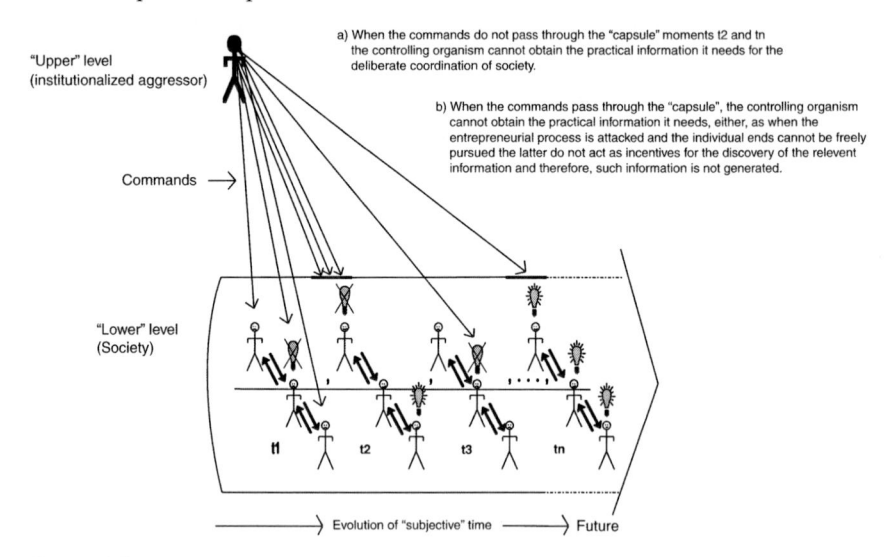

Figure 4.5

"Upper" level (institutionalized aggressor)

Commands →

a) When the commands do not pass through the "capsule" moments t2 and tn the controlling organism cannot obtain the practical information it needs for the deliberate coordination of society.

b) When the commands pass through the "capsule", the controlling organism cannot obtain the practical information it needs, either, as when the entrepreneurial process is attacked and the individual ends cannot be freely pursued the latter do not act as incentives for the discovery of the relevent information and therefore, such information is not generated.

"Lower" level (Society)

t1   t2   t3   tn

→ Evolution of "subjective" time → Future

change in the situation, s/he will have to modify his or her decision on the different tasks that should be done on the farm on that day, without being able to articulate formally the reasons why s/he is taking such a decision. It is not possible, therefore, to transfer this information, which is the result of many years of experience and work on the farm, to a hypothetical controlling organism (for example a Ministry of Agriculture in the capital) and await instructions. The same may be said of any other person who carries on his or her entrepreneurship in a determined environment, be it a decision as to whether s/he should invest or otherwise in a certain company or sector, or whether s/he should buy or sell certain stocks or shares, or contract certain persons to collaborate in his or her work, etc., etc. We may, therefore, consider that the practical information not only is, as it were, in a capsule, in the sense that it is not accessible to the controlling organism which practises institutionalized aggression, but, in addition to being in a capsule, is continually being modified and regenerated in a new form, as the future is created and made step by step by the actors.

Lastly, let us remember that, to the same extent as the socialist coercion is practised on a more continual and effective basis, the free pursuit of individual ends will be made increasingly impossible and, therefore, the latter will not act as an incentive and it will not be possible to discover or generate the practical information necessary to coordinate society through entrepreneurship. The controlling organism is, therefore, faced with a dilemma impossible to eradicate, as it has an absolute need of the information generated in the social process, which it cannot obtain under any circumstance, as if it intervenes coercively in such process it will destroy the capacity to create information and if it does not intervene it will not obtain the information either.

In short, we may conclude that, from the perspective of the social process, socialism is an intellectual error, as, for the following reasons, it is not possible to conceive that the controlling organism in charge of intervening with commands can obtain the information necessary to coordinate society: first, because of the volume (it is impossible for the intervening organism to consciously assimilate the enormous volume of practical information which is spread over the minds of human beings); second, given the fact that the necessary information is essentially impossible to transfer to the central organism (as it is tacit and impossible to articulate); third, because, in addition, it is not possible to transfer information which has not yet been discovered or created by the actors and which only arises as a result of the free process of the practice of entrepreneurship; and, fourth, because the practice of coercion prevents the entrepreneurial process from discovering and creating the information necessary to coordinate society.

The impossibility of socialism from the perspective of the controlling organism

Second, now from the perspective of what we have called the 'upper' level in the figures, i.e. from the standpoint of the person or group of persons, organized to a greater or lesser extent, who, systematically and institutionally, carry out aggression against the free practice of entrepreneurship, we should make a series of considerations which confirm, even more, if that is possible, the conclusion that socialism is simply an intellectual error.

We will begin by accepting for dialectic purposes, as did Mises,[15] that the controlling organism (regardless of whether it is a dictator or leader, an elite, a group of scientists or intellectuals, a ministerial department, a group of representatives elected democratically by 'the people' or, in short, any combination, of a greater or lesser complexity, of all or some of these elements) is endowed with the maximum technical and intellectual capacity, experience and wisdom, together with the best intentions, which is humanly conceivable (we will soon see that these hypotheses are not true in reality and the reason for this). However, what cannot be accepted is that the controlling organism is endowed with superhuman capacities or, specifically, that it has the gift of omniscience,[16] i.e. that it is capable of assimilating, knowing and interpreting simultaneously all the scattered and exclusive information which is dispersed over the minds of all the beings who act in society and which is continually being generated and created *ex novo* by these beings. The reality is that the greater part of the controlling organism, sometimes also called the planning organism or organism of central or partial intervention, does not know or only has a very vague idea as to the knowledge which is available dispersed among the minds of all the actors who may be submitted to its orders. There is, therefore, a small or non-existent possibility that the planner may come to know, or discover where to look for and find, the elements of dispersed information which are being generated in the social process and of which it has such a great need in order to control and coordinate such process.

Moreover, the controlling organism will unavoidably have to be composed of human beings, with all their virtues and defects, who, like any other actor, will have their own personal ends which will act as incentives and lead them to discover the information relevant to their personal interests. Most probably, therefore, the men who constitute the controlling organism, if they use their entrepreneurial intuition correctly from the point of view of their own ends or interests, will generate the information and experience necessary to, for example, keep themselves in power indefinitely and justify and rationalize their acts to themselves and to third parties, practise coercion in an increasingly sophisticated and effective way, present their aggression to the citizens as something inevitable and attractive, etc., etc. To the contrary of the 'well-intentioned' hypothesis set out at the beginning of the preceding paragraph, these will generally be the most common incentives and will prevail over others, particularly over interest in discovering the practical, specific and relevant information which exists at each moment dispersed over society and which is necessary to make the coordinated functioning of the latter possible through commands. This lack of motivation will determine, moreover, that the controlling organism does not even realize, i.e. become conscious, of the degree of its own ineradicable ignorance, sinking into a process which distances it more and more from the social realities which it is trying to control.

In addition, the controlling organism will become incapable of making any kind of economic calculation, inasmuch as, regardless of its ends (and we may again imagine that they are the most 'human' and 'morally elevated' ones), it cannot know whether the costs incurred in pursuing such ends have, for itself, a value even greater than the value which it attributes subjectively to the ends pursued. The cost is merely the subjective value which the actor attributes to what s/he must renounce in pursuit of a determined end. It is obvious that the controlling organism cannot obtain the knowledge or information necessary to become aware of the true cost incurred in accordance with its own scale of values, as the information necessary to estimate costs is spread over the minds of all the human beings or actors who make up the social process and who are coerced by the controlling organism (democratically elected or otherwise) in charge of systematically practising aggression against the body of society.

In this respect, if we define the concept of responsibility as the quality of the action which is executed once the actor has come to know the cost thereof and takes such cost into account by the corresponding estimated economic calculation, we may conclude that the controlling organism, regardless of its composition, system of choice and value judgements, as it is unable to see and appreciate the costs incurred, will always tend to act irresponsibly. There exists, therefore, the unresolvable paradox that the more the controlling organism tries to plan or control a determined area of life in society, the fewer possibilities it will have of reaching its objectives, as it cannot obtain the information necessary to organize society, creating, moreover, new, serious imbalances and distortions to the precise degree that its coercion is carried out more effectively and limits the entrepreneurship of human beings. We must, therefore, draw the conclusion that it is a serious error to think that the controlling organism can make economic calculations in the same way as the individual entrepreneur. On the contrary, the more developed the socialist organization, the more practical first-hand information which is indispensable for economic calculation will be lost, making economic calculation completely impossible to the precise degree to which obstacles to free human action are placed by the organism practising institutionalized coercion.

Criticism of the alternative concepts of socialism

Traditionally, socialism has been defined as the system of social organization based on state ownership of the means of production. This definition has for a long time been the most generalized definition for historical and political reasons. It was the original definition used by Mises in his critical treatise on socialism in 1922[17] and was later considered by Mises and the rest of his school as a reference point throughout the subsequent controversy as to the impossibility of socialist economic calculation.

However, since its origin, this traditional definition of socialism could be seen to be unsatisfactory. First, it was of an evidently static nature, as it depended on the existence or otherwise of a determined legal institution (property rights) in relation to a specific economic category (the means of production). Therefore, the use of this definition of socialism required a prior explanation of what was understood by property rights and the implications of such concept in the economic area. Moreover, the controversy on the impossibility of socialism showed how the different scientists involved had serious communication difficulties among themselves, precisely due to the different meaning and contents they considered implicit in their concept of property rights. Finally, the traditional definition appeared to exclude interventionism and economic control from its scope. However, notwithstanding the fact that it did not demand full state ownership of the means of production, interventionism produced effects of lack of coordination which were qualitatively very similar. For all these reasons, it seemed advisable to continue searching to find a definition of socialism which went to the very root of its essence, was as free as possible of concepts liable to ambiguous interpretation and which, as was the case with the social processes to which it would be applied, had a markedly dynamic nature.

Second, one of the most important consequences of the controversy on the impossibility of socialist economic calculation was the development and refinement by the economists of the Austrian School (Mises, Hayek and, above all, Kirzner) of a theory in which entrepreneurship appeared as the protagonizing and creative force of all social processes. The discovery that it was precisely the innate entrepreneurial capacity of humankind, visible through humans' own creative action, which made life in society possible, as it discovered social imbalances and created and transmitted the information necessary for each actor to learn to discipline their own behaviour in accordance with that of their peers, indicated definitively the path along which the preparation of a truly scientific concept of socialism should travel.

The following most important step in the process of the formation of a definition of socialism was given by Hans-Hermann Hoppe in 1989.[18] Hoppe has shown that the essential characteristic of socialism is that it is based on an aggression or institutionalized interference against property rights. His definition is more dynamic and, therefore, much more operative than the traditional definition. He does not talk about the existence or otherwise of something called property rights, but about whether institutionally, i.e. in a repetitive and organized way, coercion or physical violence is practised against property rights. Although we consider Hoppe's definition to be an important advance, it does not seem completely satisfactory as, first, it requires that what is understood by property rights be explained or defined *ab initio* and, second, it does not make any mention of the practise of entrepreneurship as the essential protagonist of all social processes.

Combining Hoppe's definition, in the sense that all socialism implies the systematic use of coercion, with the contributions in the field of the theory of entrepreneurship of Professor Kirzner, we reach the conclusion that the most appropriate definition of socialism is that which has been proposed and used in this article, according to which socialism is any organized system of institutionalized aggression against entrepreneurship and human action. This definition has, in the first place, the advantage of being easily understood by anybody, without the need for an *a priori* detailed explanation of what is understood by property rights and what their contents should be. Anybody can understand that human action may or may not be aggressive and that, when it is not so, except in the specific case of a person defending himself from arbitrary non-systematic external aggression, such action is the most intimate and typical manifestation of the human being and, therefore, is something completely legitimate which must be respected.

In other words, we consider our definition of socialism to be the most appropriate because it is established in terms of the concept of human action and, therefore, in terms of the most intimate essence of humankind. Moreover, socialism is conceived as an institutionalized aggression against the precise forces which make life in society possible and, in this respect, it is only apparently paradoxical to state that there is nothing more anti-social than the socialist system itself. Bringing this reality to light is one of the greatest virtues of the definition of socialism we propose. Without any doubt, the process of social interaction free from aggression requires compliance with a whole series of rules, guidelines or behaviour habits. All of these together constitute law in the traditional sense, i.e. the framework within which human actions may pacifically be carried out. Law, however, is not something which arises prior to the practise of human action, but a result of the evolution and customs of the social process of interaction itself. Therefore, according to our definition, socialism is not a system of institutionalized aggression against an evolutionary consequence of entrepreneurship (property rights), but a system of aggression against human action or entrepreneurship itself. Our definition of socialism allows the theory of society to relate directly to a theory on law, its origins, development and evolution. Moreover, it is perfectly compatible with our posing the questions, on a theoretical level, of what property rights arise from a non-coercive social process, what the just property rights are, and to what point socialism is ethically admissible or otherwise.

Socialism and interventionism

Another advantage of the definition of socialism we have proposed is that it includes or incorporates within its scope the social system based on interventionism. In fact, whether interventionism is considered as one of the typical features of socialism or, as is more usual, as an intermediate system between 'real socialism' and the free social process, it is evident that, as any interventionist measure consists of an institutional aggression coercively practised in a certain social area, interventionism, regardless of its degree, type or cause, is socialism from the standpoint of our definition.

The use of the terms socialism and interventionism as synonyms, far from being an unjustified broadening of the sense which they normally have, is an analytic requirement for the theory of social processes. In fact, although originally the first Austrian School theorists who dealt with interventionism considered it to be a different conceptual category from socialism,[19] as the controversy on the impossibility of socialist economic calculation advanced the borderlines between the two concepts were erased and this definition process has continued up to the present day, when it has become evident to those who cultivate the theory of entrepreneurship that there is no qualitative difference between socialism and interventionism,[20] although it may be admitted that, in colloquial usage, one term or the other is sometimes used to refer to the different degrees to which the same reality becomes manifest.

In addition, the proposed definition of socialism permits science to play the important role of revealing the attempts, very habitual nowadays in many political, social and cultural spheres, to immunize interventionism against the natural and inevitable effects of the economic, social and political decay of 'real socialism', which is, in fact, its predecessor and intellectual inspiration. Real socialism and interventionism are, at most, only two manifestations of different degrees of intensity of the same coercive and institutionalized reality and they fully share the same essential intellectual error and the same pernicious social consequences.

5 The crisis of socialism[1]

There is nothing more practical than a good theory. Therefore I intend to explain in theoretical terms what socialism is and why it is an intellectual error, a scientific impossibility. I will show why it (or at least real socialism) collapsed, and why the socialism which still exists in the form of economic intervention in Western countries is the main source of the tensions and conflicts we experience. We live in a world which is essentially socialist, despite the fall of the Berlin Wall, and we continue to suffer the effects which, according to theory, are typical of state intervention in social life.

To define 'socialism', we must first understand the concept of 'entrepreneurship'. Economic theorists conceive 'entrepreneurship' as an innate human ability. I am not referring to the typical entrepreneur who gets a business off the ground. I am referring to that innate ability all human beings have to discover, create and recognize the profit opportunities which arise in their environment, and to act accordingly to take advantage of them. In fact, etymologically speaking, the word 'entrepreneur' evokes the discoverer, someone who realizes something and grasps it. It is the light bulb which lights up.

Entrepreneurship is humankind's primary capacity. This ability to create and discover goals and means is what, by nature, most distinguishes us from the animals. In this general sense, humans are more *homo empresario* than *homo sapiens*. Who, then, is an entrepreneur? Mother Theresa of Calcutta, for instance. I am not talking merely about Henry Ford or Bill Gates, who have been most certainly great entrepreneurs in the area of business and economics. Every person with a creative, revolutionary vision is an entrepreneur. The mission of Mother Theresa was to help the most needy, and she sought the means to accomplish it creatively, by pushing and harmonizing the efforts and wishes of many different people. Hence, Mother Theresa of Calcutta was a paradigmatic example of an entrepreneur. Let us view entrepreneurship as the most intimate characteristic of our nature as human beings, a quality responsible for the emergence of society as an extremely complex network of interactions. These consist of exchange relationships between people, and we establish them because we somehow realize that they benefit us. And our entrepreneurial spirit is the driving force behind them all.

Every entrepreneurial act involves three stages. The first stage consists of the creation of information; when an entrepreneur discovers or creates a new idea, s/he generates in his or her mind information which did not exist before. Then, one way and another, this information is transmitted in successive waves, which leads to the second stage. Here I see a cheap resource which is poorly used, and there I discover an urgent need for the same resource. I buy cheap and sell dear. I transmit the information. Finally, in the third stage, economic agents who act in a discoordinated manner learn; they discover that they should save a resource because someone else needs it. Those are the three stages which complete the process: the creation of information, the transmission of information and, most importantly, the effect of coordination or adjustment. From the time we wake up in the morning until the time we go to bed at night, we discipline our behaviour in terms of the needs of others, of people we never even meet, and we do this *motu proprio*, because when we act in our own entrepreneurial self-interest, we realize that this is to our advantage. It was important to present this idea first, because now, in contrast, we will consider the nature of socialism.

Socialism must be defined as 'any system of institutional, methodical aggression against the free exercise of entrepreneurship'. It consists of a forcible imposition, via all the coercive means of the state. A socialist regime may place certain objectives in a positive light, but it will have to impose them and thus aggressively interfere with the process of social coordination which entrepreneurs spearhead. Therefore, in a socialist system, the state acts using coercion, and this is the main characteristic of socialism. It is very important to keep this in mind, because socialists invariably wish to conceal their coercive side, the essential feature of their system. Coercion consists of the use of violence to force someone to do something. There are two types of coercion: that of the criminal who robs people in the streets and that of the state, the sort of which characterizes socialism. In the case of asystematic coercion, the market has mechanisms to provide, as far as possible, a definition of property rights and a defence against crime. However, in the case of systematic, institutional coercion by a state with all the tools of power at its disposal, we have very little hope of avoiding it or defending ourselves against it. It is then that socialism reveals its true essence in all its harshness.

I am not defining socialism based on whether ownership of the means of production is public or private. That is an archaism. The essence of socialism is coercion, institutional state coercion, by which a governing body is meant to perform the tasks necessary to coordinate society. The responsibility passes from ordinary people, who are in charge of their entrepreneurship, seek ends and attempt to create the circumstances most favourable to achieving them, to a government body, which 'from above' strives forcibly to impose its particular view of the world or its particular objectives. Moreover, in this definition of socialism, the issue of whether or not the governing body has been democratically elected is irrelevant. The theorem of the impossibility of socialism remains intact and totally unchanged, regardless of whether the governing body which tries to forcibly impose the coordination of society is of democratic origin.

Now that I have defined socialism, I will explain why it is an intellectual error. Socialism is an intellectual error because the governing body in charge of exercising coercion to coordinate society cannot possibly obtain the information it needs to give its commands a coordinating effect. That is the problem of socialism, its great paradox. It requires information, knowledge, data for its desired coercive outcome – the organization of society – to be successful. But the governing body can never obtain such information. Mises and Hayek, theorists of the Austrian School of Economics, formulated four basic arguments during their twentieth century debate with the theorists of neoclassical economics, who were never capable of fathoming the problem posed by socialism. Why were they incapable of fathoming it? The answer is that they believed the economy functioned as explained in first-year economic textbooks, yet what is explained in first-year economic textbooks concerning the functioning of a market economy is radically incorrect and false. The writers of these textbooks explain the market in terms of mathematics and perfect adjustment. That is, they portray the market as a sort of computer which automatically and perfectly adjusts the desires of consumers and the action of producers in such a way that the ideal model is that of perfect competition, which is described by Walras' system of simultaneous equations.

In my first economics class as a student, the professor began with a surprising statement: 'Let us suppose that all information is given'. He then began to fill the blackboard with functions, curves and formulae. That is the supposition neoclassicals use: that all information is given and unchanging. However, that supposition is wildly unrealistic. It contradicts the most typical characteristic of the market: information is never given.

Knowledge of data emerges continually as a result of the creative activity of entrepreneurs: new ends, new means. Thus, that supposition cannot provide the basis for a valid economic theory. Neoclassical economists deemed socialism possible because they assumed that all of the data necessary to formulate the system of equations and find the solution were 'given'. They were unable to perceive the real-world events they should have researched scientifically; they could not see what was really happening.

The Austrian School alone – led by Ludwig von Mises – followed a different paradigm. Austrians never assumed information to be given; they viewed the economic process as one driven by entrepreneurs who continually change and discover new information. Only members of the Austrian School managed to realize that socialism was an intellectual error. They grounded their position on four arguments, two 'static' and two 'dynamic'.

The first argument asserts that, for reasons of volume, the governing body cannot possibly obtain the information it needs to give its commands a coordinating effect. Human beings handle an immense volume of information, and what 7 billion people have in their minds cannot possibly be managed. The neoclassicals might be able to understand this argument, but it is the weakest, the least important. After all, the computer capacity available to us nowadays permits us to process immense volumes of information.

The second argument is much more profound and convincing. The information people work with in the market is not objective; it is not like the information printed in the telephone book. Entrepreneurial information is of a radically different nature. It is subjective, not objective. It is tacit. In other words we know something, the *know how*, but we do not know in detail what it consists of, the *know that*. To put it another way, it is like information on how to ride a bicycle. A person could try to learn a bicycle by studying the formula of mathematical physics which expresses the equilibrium the cyclist maintains when he pedals. However, the knowledge necessary to ride a bicycle is not obtained in this way, but through a learning process which usually contains setbacks, but which eventually enables the rider to experience a sense of equilibrium on a bicycle and teaches him or her that s/he must lean to one side in the curves to avoid falling. In all probability, Lance Armstrong is unfamiliar with the laws which enabled him to win the Tour de France seven times, but he knows how to ride a bicycle. Tacit information cannot be expressed in a formalized, objective manner, nor can it be transferred anywhere, much less to a governing body. Only univocal information, which does not lend itself to misunderstandings, can be transmitted to a governing body, be assimilated and used by it in the coercion of society, and give coordinating quality to its commands. Nevertheless, most of the information upon which the success of our lives depends is not objective; it is not like the information printed in the telephone book, but is subjective, tacit information.

Still, these two arguments – that the information is huge in volume and also of a tacit nature – are not sufficient. Two other arguments exist, which are dynamic and much more convincing as well, and they highlight the impossibility of socialism.

Human beings are endowed with an innate creative capacity. We constantly discover 'new' things, 'new' ends, 'new' means. Information or knowledge that entrepreneurs have not yet 'created' can hardly be transmitted to a governing body. The governing body is determined to build 'social nirvana' through coercion and the Official State Gazette. However, to do so, it must know what will happen tomorrow. And what will happen tomorrow will depend on entrepreneurial information which has not yet been created today, and thus cannot be transmitted today so that our authorities can coordinate us effectively tomorrow. This is the paradox of socialism, the third argument.

However, that is not all. There is a fourth argument which is definitive. By its very nature, socialism – which, as we have stated, rests on coercion of civil society as a whole – blocks, hampers or renders impossible, precisely where it affects society and to the extent that it affects society, the entrepreneurial creation of information, which is precisely what the authorities need to issue coordinating commands.

This is the explanation of socialism's theoretical impossibility in scientific terms: the authorities cannot acquire the information they need to give their commands a coordinating quality. And this is a purely scientific and objective analysis. We should not think the problem of socialism is that 'bad people are in power'. Not even the best person in the world, with the best intentions and the greatest human knowledge, could organize a society according to the coercive socialist model; s/he would make it hell, since, *given human nature, it is impossible to achieve the socialist objective or ideal.*

All of these characteristics of socialism have consequences we can identify in our everyday lives. To begin with, socialism is attractive. In the most intimate part of our nature lies the risk of succumbing to socialism, because its ideal tempts us, because humans rebel against their own nature. To live in a world with an uncertain future disturbs us, and the possibility of controlling that future, of eradicating uncertainty, attracts us. In *The Fatal Conceit*, Hayek writes that socialism is actually the social, political and economic manifestation of humankind's original sin, pride. Humankind wants to be God, that is, omniscient. Therefore, generation after generation, we will have to persistently guard against socialism and accept that our nature is creative and entrepreneurial. Socialism is not a simple matter of acronyms or political parties in specific historical contexts. It will always seep furtively into communities, families, neighbourhoods, conservative and liberal parties ... We must resist that temptation towards statism, because it is the most original danger we face as human beings, our greatest temptation to believe we are God. The socialist considers him- or herself as overcoming this problem of radical ignorance which fundamentally discredits his (or her) social system. Hence, socialism is always a result of the sin of intellectual pride. Within every socialist there lies a pretentious person, a prideful intellectual.

Furthermore, socialism has some characteristics we could call 'peripheral': social discoordination and disorder. The pure entrepreneurial act coordinates, but socialism distorts it though coercion and causes discoordination. The entrepreneur realizes a profit opportunity. He buys cheap and sells dear. He transmits information and coordinates. Two people who initially acted against their respective interests now, without realizing it, act in a coordinated or adjusted manner. Because socialism forcibly prevents this exchange, it causes maladjustment to a greater or lesser extent. To top it all, when socialists observe the maladjustment they have caused, the discoordination, the conflict and the worsening of the problem, far from reaching the reasonable conclusions we have presented, they demand more socialism, more institutional coercion. And we enter a process in which problems, rather than being solved, worsen indefinitely and produce yet further increases in the weight of the state. The socialist ideal requires that the tentacles of the state reach every gap in society, and it triggers a process which leads to totalitarianism.

Another characteristic of socialism is its lack of rigour. Criteria are tried and changed, problems are observed to worsen, and a new political direction is taken, and thus coercion is erratic. Why? Because the effects of interventionist measures usually bear little resemblance to the effects sought. The minimum wage, for instance, is intended to raise the standard of living. Its result? More unemployment and more poverty. The worst hit? Social groups which are entering the labour market for the first time, i.e. young people, women, ethnic minorities and immigrants. Another example: a community agricultural policy is designed, and the European Union (EU) is flooded with products via subsidies or political prices. The consumer pays higher prices, and poor countries are placed at a disadvantage because international markets fill with surplus products from the EU at prices with which they cannot compete.

In addition, socialism acts as a sort of drug, like an inhibitory opium. It generates poor investments, because it distorts the signs which indicate where investments should be made if the desires of consumers are to be satisfied. Socialism exacerbates problems of scarcity and provokes the systematic irresponsibility of governments, and because it is impossible to acquire the information necessary to act responsibly, costs cannot be known. The authorities can only act wilfully and leave a record of their mere wishes in the Official State Gazette. However, as Hayek asserts, that is not 'LAW' in capital letters, but 'legislation' or rules which are usually excessive and useless, even when they are claimed to be based on objective data. Lenin held that the entire economy should be organized like the postal service, and that the most important department in a socialist system is the National Institute of Statistics. The word 'statistics' derives etymologically from 'state'. Therefore it is a term we must be cautious of if we wish to avoid socialism, a suspicious concept. Jesus was born in Bethlehem because the emperor had ordered a statistical study concerning taxes. The first duty of every great libertarian should be to request the elimination of the National Institute of Statistics. Since we cannot keep the state from doing harm, let us at least blindfold it so that the damage will occur more at random when the state errs, as invariably it will.

Socialism also plainly exerts a terrible effect on the environment. The only way to protect the environment is to define property rights clearly and to defend them effectively. No one rings someone else's doorbell and then throws garbage in his face. This only happens in 'common areas'. An old Spanish saying goes '*lo que es del común es del ningún*', or 'what belongs to everyone belongs to no one'. The tragedy of the commons – first described by Ludwig von Mises in 1940 – whether it be polluted water, disappearing schools of fish or the extinction of the rhinoceros, is always the result of a state restriction on the property rights required by a market economy. For instance, there is hunting where mountain land is privatized, but not where it is publicly owned. And elephants survive where they have been privatized. Fighting bulls still exist because bullfighting entrepreneurs look after them. The only way to preserve the environment is through a market economy, a capitalist system which implies well-defined property rights. Where these principles disappear, the environment suffers. English rivers are privatized, for example. They are clean and there is fishing in them: members of different fishing clubs, cheap, expensive and moderately priced, fish in them. But try to find fish in Spanish rivers ...

And then there is corruption. Socialism corrupts. Those who experienced the socialist economies which hid behind the Berlin Wall became aware of the huge lie that whole world represented. And let us not rest on our laurels and think that we have overcome it, that the huge lie has no power here. It is still present, though in varying degrees. Why does socialism corrupt? For several reasons. Coerced people in a socialist system quickly realize that, in order to reach their goals, it is more effective for them to devote their effort and ingenuity to influencing the authorities, rather than seeking opportunities to make a profit and to serve others. This is the origin of special interest groups, which strive to influence the decisions of the governing body. The socialist governing body attracts all sorts of perverse, corrupting influences like a magnet. It also sets in motion a struggle for power. When the socialist model predominates, the issue of who is in power, whether it is someone from 'my group' or not, is vital. A socialist society is always very politicized, unlike Switzerland, for instance, where people most likely do not know the name of their defence minister or even of the president. In fact, it does not even matter to them, because the question of who is in power is not crucial.

Human beings should dedicate most of their efforts to living successful lives, without this sort of intervention. This process of struggle for power, of interventionism, provokes a gradual change in man's habits of moral behaviour. People manifest behaviour that is increasingly amoral and less subject to principles. Our behaviour becomes more and more aggressive. The goal is to gain power so we can impose our wishes on others. This also applies mimetically to the behaviour of individuals and, consequently, we discipline our behaviour less and less and disregard the customary framework of moral laws. Morality is the automatic pilot of freedom. Thus, the above serves as another example of the corrupting influence of socialism.

Furthermore, the more prevalent socialism is, the more the underground economy or black market develops. However, as people in the countries of Eastern Europe used to say, in a socialist setting, the underground economy is not the problem but the solution. For instance, in Soviet Moscow there was no gasoline, but everyone knew that in a certain tunnel gasoline was sold on the black market. As a result, people were able to drive.

Still, obviously, socialist governments cannot simply accept all of these criticisms, so they resort to political propaganda. It is claimed that the state detects every problem in time and solves it immediately. Again and again, political propaganda is systematically disseminated in all spheres in an attempt to deflect criticism and, as a consequence, a culture of the state is created, a culture which bewilders and disorients the citizenry, who come to believe that, when faced with any problem, the state will take care of everything. And this strictly socialist way of thinking is passed down from generation to generation through the education system, which is always controlled by the state.

Propaganda leads to megalomania. Bureaucratic organizations, public officials, politicians, etc., are not subject to a profit and loss statement. For them, poor management does not mean expulsion from the market. Authorities and public officials are only accountable to a budget and a set of regulations. There is no personal malice involved. At least, not necessarily. They are like any one of us, but in the institutional environment in which they live, their actions are perverse. Their activity within the state leads them to request more public officials and a larger budget, and to assert that their work is vital. Can you think of a single public official, politician or bureaucrat who, after a profound analysis, has arrived at the conclusion that the agency for which s/he works is useless or entails costs which exceed the benefit it provides society, a single individual who has proposed that his or her government superior and minister eliminate the corresponding budget item? Not one. On the contrary, in all contexts and governments, each official invariably considers his or her own role in the state 'vital'. Socialism is megalomaniac and infects all of society with this quality. Culture, transformed into cultural policy, is one example, and it was defined by a very distinguished representative of the European Union, when speaking with a fellow party member who was head of the Ministry of Culture, as follows: 'Lots of public money, lots of parties for the young people and awards for the pals'.

In addition, socialism leads to the prostitution of the concepts of law and justice. Law, in the classical view, is simply a set of abstract, substantive rules or laws which are generally applied equally to all. Justice consists of judging whether or not individual behaviours have been in keeping with this framework of objective and abstract laws. These are blind laws. Thus, justice has traditionally been portrayed blindfolded. In Leviticus 19,15 we read: 'Do not pervert justice; do not show partiality to the poor nor favouritism to the great, but judge your neighbour fairly'. The moment we violate general legal principles, even if we do so 'for a good cause' (because we are moved by an eviction for unpaid rent, or because a minor theft in a large department store will have no significant effect on the income of the company involved), we do terrible damage to justice. Judges who act in this way, who neglect to apply the law, fall prey to the fatal error of intellectual conceit, of believing themselves gods. They replace the law with their impression of the particular circumstances of the case and they open the door to those whose goal it is for the judged to be moved, not to administer justice. Each suit becomes a lottery ticket which may be a winner if one is lucky in court, and a snowball effect is triggered and overloads judges, who issue increasingly flawed rulings and encourage the process with their arbitrariness. Legal certainty disappears and justice is corrupted.

Of course, the solution is not to provide the judicial system with more resources, but that is precisely what will be required by public officials.

Ultimately, the most perverse effect of socialist corruption is the mimetic influence it exerts on the sphere of individual moral actions. To people of good faith, socialism is very attractive: if there are problems, the state will provide the necessary resources and impose a solution. Who could oppose the achievement of such a worthwhile, praiseworthy objective? The problem is the ignorance which lies at the heart of this argument. The state cannot know what it would need to know to act in this manner; it is not God, even if some people believe it is. This belief disturbs the entrepreneurial process and aggravates problems. Instead of acting automatically and according to dogmatic principles which are subject to law, the state acts arbitrarily, and that is what most demoralizes and corrupts society. The illegal battle fought against terrorists in Spain while the Spanish Socialist Workers' Party (PSOE) was in power provides the perfect example. It was a colossal mistake. Principles are not an obstacle which prevents us from achieving desired results, but the only road which can lead us to them. As the English proverb teaches, 'honesty is the best policy', i.e. honesty is a principle which should always be followed. This is precisely where socialism fails, for in the socialist model for choosing the best combination of means and ends, the leaders play God and it is thought that the 'optimal' course of action is to violate moral principles.

Socialism is not only an intellectual error, but is also a truly antisocial force, because its most intimate characteristic consists of its coercive restriction, to a varying degree, of people's entrepreneurial freedom, in its creative and coordinating capacity. As this freedom is humanity's distinguishing attribute, socialism is an unnatural social system which conflicts with man's true nature and aspirations.

In his encyclical letter 'Centesimus Annus (IV, 42)', Pope John Paul II, when considering whether capitalism is the social system most compatible with human nature, writes:

> If by 'capitalism' is meant an economic system which recognizes the fundamental and positive role of business, the market, private property and the resulting responsibility for the means of production, as well as free human creativity in the economic sector, then the answer is certainly in the affirmative.

Nevertheless, he immediately adds 'But ... ' Why? Because Pope John Paul II spent his life warning of the effects of an unbridled 'capitalism' detached from moral, ethical and legal principles. But if we take into account that what is reprehensible is egoism, immorality, etc., true capitalism as a social system is neutral at worst. In fact, a system of voluntary exchanges promotes morality, the distinction between good and evil, as opposed to the moral corruption which *always* accompanies socialism.

Finally, whatever happened to socialism? Has it failed? Has it disappeared? Has it vanished into thin air? Yes and no. That certainly has been the fate of 'real socialism', but our societies are still deeply imbued with socialism. The differences between so-called left-wing and right-wing parties are differences of degree, although Spain did make some progress between 1996 and 2004 in the area of freedom under the leadership of the right-wing Popular Party. First came the abolition of that twentieth century form of slavery, compulsory military service. Military service became voluntary, and that is of vital importance – incidentally, may I mention that the socialists opposed this? Second, there was a timid tax cut, and then the principle of a balanced budget was adopted, and some liberalization and privatization occurred. It was not really much to get excited about, but we must remember that the vast majority of those 11 or 12 million people who voted for the Popular Party then in power were, in fact, also socialists according to the definition we have offered here. Not much else could be done.

Now the mission falls to us, the university professors, the intellectuals and the 'second-hand dealers of ideas'. We are responsible for gradually changing the spirit of the times, especially among the young, who are willing to take to the streets boldly to defend their ideals. Today socialism continues to prevail: between 40 and 50 per cent of the gross domestic product of the countries in the modern Western world is in the hands of government. Our only hope lies, as always, in the power of ideas and in the intellectual honesty of the young.

6 Entrepreneurship and the theory of free market environmentalism[1]

In Professor Jacques Garello's long and fruitful effort to stimulate studies related to liberty, the analysis of free market environmentalism and its different implications has played a relevant role. In fact, my first personal contact with Professor Garello took place as the result of a seminar on this subject which he organized in Aix-en-Provence in September 1985, to which the present author had the honour of being invited.[2] Therefore, perhaps one of the best homages which may be rendered to Professor Garello is to summarize and re-evaluate, from today's standpoint, more than ten years after that seminar, the main items and implications of the modern theory of free market environmentalism.

Introduction

Free market environmentalism[3] is a new discipline which began to emerge incipiently at the beginning of the last decade and which today, twenty years later, has reached a remarkable level of development.[4]

In the final analysis, what has been developed by the theorists of free market environmentalism is a theory of the intimate relations which exist between economics and environmentalism. These relations, moreover, are obvious, above all taking into account that the most modern definition of economic science is the theoretical study of the dynamic processes of interaction which take place between human beings,[5] while environmentalism could be defined as 'the science which studies the relations of human beings with each other and with their environment'.[6] It becomes evident, therefore, that the conception of the two disciplines is absolutely parallel, as are the subjects they study, the subject of economics being based on the analysis of the *market* understood as a decentralized spontaneous order and that of environmentalism on the study and monitoring of *ecosystems* conceived, like the market, as evolutionary decentralized processes in which the different species undergo spontaneous adaptations and modifications in accordance with a multitude of specific circumstances of time and place which nobody is capable of fully predicting or knowing.[7]

The most significant discovery of the free market environmentalism theorists is that there exist spontaneous processes, impelled by the creative force of human entrepreneurship, which assist the economic and social development of the human race so that we may efficiently and respectfully coordinate with and adjust to the rest of the species and elements of the natural environment. It has been discovered, in short, that the most important aggressions against the natural environment, the problems of pollution, the threat of the extinction of many species, the deterioration of natural resources and of the environment in general, far from being an inevitable result of economic development, the operation of the market and the spontaneous system of social organization based on free enterprise, appear when the state intervenes systematically, institutionally and coercively and, to a greater or lesser extent, impedes the spontaneous process of coordination and adjustment which arises from the market and from the free practice of entrepreneurship in all the areas in which human beings relate to each other and to other species and natural resources.

Coercion, property rights and the environment

It should be emphasized that the problems of environmental deterioration constitute, from this point of view, one of the most typical examples of the perverse effects of the systematic practice of institutional coercion or aggression against human action or entrepreneurship.[8] The non-intervened and uncoerced practice of entrepreneurship spontaneously gives rise to the emergence of a series of institutions, understood as established patterns of behaviour which emerge from the entrepreneurial process itself and, at the same time, make it possible.[9] Among these social institutions which, like ecosystems, emerge and develop in an evolutionary, decentralized and adaptive way, perhaps one of the most important, together with language and money, is that which is constituted by private law in general and, specifically, by contracts and property rights. In fact, few human actions would be carried out if the creative result thereof, instead of being appropriated by the actors themselves, were coercively expropriated by a third party (i.e. by someone whose action was not in accordance with the law) or if other persons could be attacked or harmed by such actions, as happens when the cost of opportunity incurred on acting is not duly taken into account. It is, therefore, essential, and this constitutes one of the fundamental bases of the institutional network of the free enterprise system, to establish the necessary property rights, with regard to all those items which may in some sense, under each historical circumstance, become scarce in relation to the attainment of any end. These property rights, first, allow the external costs incurred on acting to be internalized[10] and, second, guarantee to each entrepreneurial actor the attainment, within the framework of the rules established by property law, of the corresponding ends discovered, created and achieved entrepreneurially.[11]

It is easy to realize, looking at the situation of the natural environment, that it is precisely in those areas where the definition and/or defence of the corresponding property rights and, therefore, the free practice of entrepreneurship subject to the traditional principles of private law, are prevented where the tragic effects of deterioration and expoliation of the environment, so often criticized by nature lovers, occur most virulently. In fact, if we had to give a theoretical definition of *deteriorated or threatened natural environment*, we could say that it is a combination of the following two types of species or natural resources: in the first place, those resources which were extremely abundant up to now in relative terms but, due to circumstances, are now becoming scarce, to a greater or lesser extent, from the point of view of certain specific actions. They are, for example, the resources which are on the *border* between what we could call 'free goods' and the resources which are scarce in relative terms with regard to the satisfaction of human needs and which, inevitably, must be allocated in economic terms. The fact is that, inasmuch as the definition of property rights in relation to these 'border resources' is prevented, as has occurred frequently with regard to traditionally free resources which have become scarce (as happened, for example, with the prairies of the American West in the nineteenth century), there is a tragic effect of overexploitation or deterioration, which Garrett Hardin describes with the now generally accepted expression 'tragedy of the commons'.[12] The second type of resources is constituted by all those species and resources which are, in fact, already scarce, but to which the state has, for certain reasons, prevented the extension of private contractual law and property rights, and, in consequence, they are considered as 'public property' from a legal and administrative point of view.

The origin of these two types of resources, which inexorably cause the overexploitation of the natural environment, may be found either in the granting of a privilege by the state to certain private entities, enabling them to violate the property rights of others with impunity (such is the case with many industrial polluters who are protected from the consequences of their aggression in the interests of an incorrectly understood defence of industrial progress), or in the development of an erroneous doctrine of 'public goods'[13] with regard to certain scarce resources, which is used to justify the brake on their spontaneous privatization, blocking the entrepreneurial spirit necessary to use them appropriately and thus making it impossible to discover and introduce the technological innovations necessary to correctly define and defend the corresponding property rights.

Environmentalism and the impossibility of economic calculation under socialism

In this way the force of entrepreneurship is destroyed and its impetus and creative spirit are perversely diverted. Moreover, it is clear that environmental problems constitute a special case which illustrates the theory of the impossibility of socialist economic calculation to perfection, socialism being defined, as we have seen, as a coercive system which, to a greater or lesser extent, systematically impedes the free practice of entrepreneurship. In fact, the existence of areas reserved as public or communal property prevents, in the first place, the *economic calculation* necessary to assign resources with the necessary knowledge of the facts.[14] We should understand economic calculation to be any estimate of the value of different courses of action. Thus, when the free market is prevented from operating and property rights are not assigned, the information necessary to act rationally cannot be created and not even the most radical environmentalists can be sure that the specific measures they advocate do not provoke even greater environmental damage than that which they are intended to avoid. How can we, for example, be certain that the obligatory establishment of SO_2 purifiers for factories which use coal will not produce secondary and indirect effects which have a higher environmental cost? It may be the case that the cost of producing and installing the purifiers, in terms of economic and environmental resources, is much higher than that of other alternatives which could be discovered entrepreneurially if entrepreneurs were allowed to experiment in an environment of well-defined and protected property rights (for example, instead of installing purifiers, coal with a lower sulphide content could be used).

In the second place, the extension of the legal concept of public property to natural resources does not only prevent, as we have seen, rational economic calculation, but also perversely diverts the practice of entrepreneurship, as it modifies in general the incentives which stimulate entrepreneurs. It is clear that if the air is declared public property the definition of property rights over it is prevented and anyone can pollute it as much as he likes. Thus the incentive for all entrepreneurs to pollute it emerges, as those with a more environmentalist conscience who decide to install a purifier will increase their costs and will not be able to compete with others who merely dirty the air, meaning that the former will be expelled from their business. Therefore, the phenomenon of the 'tragedy of the commons', which threatens all the areas in which the practice of entrepreneurship is not allowed, where property rights are not appropriately defined or defended or where the free operation of the market is coercively intervened, is again explained to perfection. The fact is that, in the case of any area declared to be publicly owned, each actor internalizes all the profits derived from its use, without assuming or being responsible for all the costs incurred, which are not even seen or discovered and which are diluted over all the present and future potential users, meaning that there will always be an incentive to damage or overexploit. As the saying goes, 'what belongs to everybody belongs to nobody' and, effectively, for example, if the poacher does not kill the buffalo or the elephant today to remove its skin or its tusk, he knows that another poacher will very probably do so tomorrow. The inexorable result of public ownership is the disappearance of the elephant, the buffalo, the whale or the publicly owned natural resource in question.

Moreover, it is of little use to try to uphold the publicly owned or communal nature of the resource without defining private property rights over it, while establishing the conditions governing its use through state regulations.

This is due to the fact that the operation of political systems is highly inefficient, as the theoretical analysis of the School of Public Choice has rightly demonstrated in detail. Governmental decisions substitute the free network of voluntary contracts in which all the parties gain (because, if not, they would not be made) by the political struggle between interest groups, in which some gain and some lose ('zero sum games'). Public management is composed by an incomprehensible legislative network or tangle which makes the management of resources tremendously inefficient, not only because it is the result of a political consensus, but also because of its arbitrary nature and, above all, due to the position of ineradicable ignorance in which, in the final analysis, the legislator or bureaucrat is always situated with regard to individual actors. In fact, the information relative to any phenomenon of society, in particular to natural species and resources, is information which is exclusive, dispersed, subjective and difficult to articulate and which varies at each specific coordinate of time and place and can only be known, that is to say, discovered and interpreted, by each individual entrepreneur in the context of his action. Therefore, not only is it impossible to transfer such information to the controlling governmental organism, but, moreover, the coercive intervention of the administration prevents the practice of entrepreneurship, thus blocking the emergence of the information necessary to allocate and manage natural resources appropriately. How can we know, for example, what type and composition of babies' diapers are the most suitable from an environmentalist viewpoint? Given that the collection and treatment of garbage is a government responsibility financed through taxes, there is no way in which the consumers can internalize the costs of processing the different types of rubbish, meaning that diaper manufacturers do not have any incentive to consider the environmental aspects of their product. The same thing occurs in all the fields where the state intervenes, although in most cases we do not realize it.[15]

The entrepreneurial solution to environmental problems

How, then, could the environmental problems which threaten us today be solved? One of the most notable virtues of the free market environmentalist theorists is that they repeatedly insist that the only real and definitive solutions which may be provided to the environmental problems are institutional solutions. Or, in other words, that what is really important is to put the entrepreneurial processes tending to solve the problems into operation. This means that no specific technical recipes can be given, as they will have to be discovered, taking into account the specific circumstances of time and place of each environmental problem, by the force of entrepreneurship, within a context of free enterprise and the correct definition and defence of property rights.[16] The fact is that only entrepreneurial creativity will be able to find solutions to introduce the technological innovations necessary to make the definition and defence of property rights possible in areas where this has not been possible so far. Thus, for example, perhaps the mention of private roads will surprise many people, but it is a perfectly viable possibility from a technical point of view and would mean an enormous increase not only in the safety of the roads, but also in their acoustic and atmospheric cleanliness. And, in the same way, the problems posed by the different natural resources may be systematically analysed, ranging from those related to the natural parks to those posed by water, air, garbage, pollution and species threatened by extinction. The dynamic theory of market processes based on entrepreneurship may be applied to all these areas and indications given of the possible solutions which, by analogy to what has already been created entrepreneurially in other similar areas, or because they have already begun to be timidly conceived, the entrepreneurs would be able to develop and implement to solve effectively the problems which threaten us today.[17]

Therefore, the practical strategy to defend the natural environment is based, above all, on the privatization of public property and a redefinition of the role of the state, which should devote all its efforts to fomenting and favouring the definition and defence of property rights over both publicly owned scarce resources and the 'border resources' which have been free so far, but which now are beginning to become scarce.[18] Making possible the definition of property rights, establishing an effective legal system and defending appropriately the correctly defined property rights are the most important and urgent measures which the government should take if it wishes to conserve and improve the natural environment.[19] In short, the new theory of *free market environmentalism* has shown that, theoretically, public ownership of the natural environment is unjustified. The problems which may supposedly justify its existence create an extremely strong incentive for their solution through entrepreneurial creativity. In this dynamic perspective, therefore, whenever the circumstances which give rise to so-called communal property arise, the spontaneous forces which tend to eliminate them come into operation, meaning that this kind of public property as a whole also becomes empty of content.[20]

I am writing the last lines of this article in Formentor, one of the most beautiful ecosystems in Spain. Observing the reality which surrounds me, the overexploitation of the bay by the boats, forest fires which place the existence of millions of pine trees in danger, the crowded beaches and water which, although they are still clean, are increasingly threatened, I realize, when I apply the *free market environmentalism* theory, that this privileged natural environment of Mallorca can only be conserved for future generations, free from abuses and increasingly cared for and pure, if its exploitation in accordance with the typical criteria of the free market is permitted and all the natural resources involved are completely privatized, in such a way that they become property rights which are well defined and defended by the public organisms. And we are sure that all well-intentioned nature lovers who read the present article with an open mind will reach the same conclusion as I have reached in agreement with the *free market environmentalism* theorists.

7 A theory of liberal[1] nationalism[2]

Introduction

The problem of nationalism and the existence of nations leads, in general, to great unease among today's liberal thinkers. On the one hand, they acknowledge that nationalism has played a healthy leading role, creating a favourable atmosphere for the fall of the communist regimes of Eastern Europe and opposing, on many historical occasions, interventionist and centralizing statism. Moreover, important European liberal leaders have recently defended the role of the nation as an irreplaceable element of equilibrium to combat the interventionist and centralizing trends which, for example, are becoming evident in the process of European unification. Finally, it may be observed how, in many specific circumstances, nationalist decentralization brings a process of spontaneous competition into operation in order to reduce the regulatory and interventionist measures the majority of which originate from the central bodies of state power.[3]

However, on the other hand, it must be acknowledged that nationalism has had, on many occasions, important consequences which are inconsistent with the freedom of human beings. Thus, without needing to go back to the tragedy implied by the upsurge of national socialism in Germany and Italy during the first half of the last century, it is easy to recall the tragedy of the war which took place between the nations of the former Yugoslavia or, for example, the way in which the freedom of choice in education is being trampled on by the present Catalonian government.

It seems, therefore, evident, that it is necessary to develop a theory of nationalism which allows these problems to be explained and makes it possible for liberals to adopt a consistent position on the problems posed by the concept of nation, nationalism and the relationship between different nations.

Concept and characteristics of the nation

The nation may be defined as a subgroup of civil society. It is a spontaneous and living order of human interactions, which is constituted by a determined series of guided behaviours of a cultural, linguistic, historical, religious and, with much less importance, racial nature. From among all the behavioural habits which constitute the national essence, the tongue or language shared by the national group stands out and constitutes one of the most important signs of national identity.

The essence of the concept of nation which we have just described fits in perfectly with the theory on the origin, nature and development of social institutions which we owe to the Austrian School of Economics.[4] In fact, the Austrian School explains the evolutive and spontaneous emergence of the social institutions (ethical, moral, economic and linguistic) as the result of a decentralized process of human interactions, led by the people who, in each historical circumstance, enjoy the greatest entrepreneurial alertness and perspicacity when discovering the most appropriate forms of behaviour to achieve their particular objectives. These forms of behaviour, which are tested in a social process of trial and error through the social mechanisms of learning and imitation, extend throughout the social body. This means that the social institutions are in a constant process of evolution and that, in the specific case of the nation, together with all the linguistic and cultural signs which constitute it, they are constantly changing, overlapping and competing with other national orders which also continuously emerge, grow, develop and, perhaps, may stagnate or even disappear when they are absorbed by other nationalities and languages which are more advanced, rich or broad. In short, nations are simply evolutive social realities, basically united by a common language and other historical or cultural characteristics, which emerge spontaneously and through evolution and which constantly compete in a much broader (worldwide) 'market' of nations, with no possibility of knowing *a priori* what the historical destiny of each nation will be or, much less, which specific nations will prevail or subsist in the future.[5]

It is important to acknowledge the intimate relations which exist between the juridical and economic institutions and the subgroup of civil society which we have called *nation*. In fact, society is simply a very complex process of human interactions, which are basically relationships of exchanges made by human beings using a tongue or language which is often common to them and which constitutes the basic substratum of any nation. Moreover, the human interactions are carried out in accordance with standards, rules or behavioural habits which constitute not only law in the material sense, but a whole constellation of guided behaviours of a moral type, rules of education, of courtesy, of dressing habits, of beliefs, etc., which, in the final analysis, constitute and are included in the concept of nation. The social groups which adopt guided behaviours most appropriate for obtaining the objectives they pursue will prevail over the rest through a selective and spontaneous process which is in constant change and evolution. The human being lacks the necessary information to consciously design these complex social processes, as they incorporate an enormous volume of information and practical knowledge constituted by what human beings who act in society are continually learning and discovering. Therefore, the use of coercion or physical violence to impose certain guided behaviours of a national type is condemned to failure, precisely for the same reasons which make it impossible, from a theoretical viewpoint, to coordinate life in society through coercive commands. In other words, the theorem of the impossibility of socialism discovered by the theorists of the Austrian School (Mises and Hayek) is fully applicable to the objective of forcing or violently imposing a determined result of the social process in the field of nationalities.[6]

The foregoing explanation, together with the constantly dynamic nature of national reality, makes it impossible to accept the principle that a political state with specific fixed borders must correspond to each nation. In fact, if we understand the nation as a subgroup of civil society in continual evolution and experimentation, it is evident that there will always exist an important volume of human beings in the process of national experimentation, that is, influenced, to a greater or lesser degree, by different national behaviours, without it being possible to know whether, in the final analysis, they will end up being absorbed by the culture of one nation or another, or whether they will finally constitute a new one. We know that nations are constantly competing, changing, evolving and overlapping, which, from the viewpoint of the conception of nationality as a historical reality of a dynamic nature, prevents them from being tied to a determined geographical space in a rigid and paralysed way. Any attempt to violently fix such a changing social reality as a nation within pre-established borders will only generate, in the final analysis, unsolvable conflicts and wars, with a great human and social cost which will ultimately endanger the existence of the national reality itself. On the contrary, nationalities understood as subgroups of civil society may only have guarantees of survival in a competitive *international* process developed in an environment of freedom, with the essential governing principles that we analyse in the next section.

Essential principles of liberal nationalism

There are three essential principles which govern a healthy, pacific and spontaneous relationship between the different nations: the principle of self-determination, the principle of complete freedom of trade between nations, and the principle of freedom of emigration and immigration. We will analyse each of these principles in what follows.

The principle of *self-determination* means that each national group must have, at all times, the possibility of freely deciding in which political state it wishes to be included. In other words, each subgroup of civil society must be free to decide to which political group it wishes to belong. Thus, it is possible that a single nation is, in accordance with the freely expressed will of its members, dispersed over several states. This is the case, for example, with the Anglo-Saxon nation, perhaps the most advanced, lively and fruitful nation at the present time in history, which is dispersed over different political states of which the United States of America and the United Kingdom are, without doubt, the most important. The German-speaking nation may also be mentioned, with more than 100 million members distributed over three important European states: Federal Germany, Austria and part of Switzerland. It is also possible for different nations to form a single state. Thus, Switzerland includes a series of cantons which belong to three different nations, the German, the French and the Italian. Likewise, in the case of Spain, at least three national groups may be considered to exist: the Castilians, the Catalonians and the Basques.[7]

With regard to the principle of self-determination, it is, however, necessary to make two observations. In the first place, the decision as to whether or not to form part of a certain political state does not necessarily have to be an explicit decision (although neither should we discard the idea that, in certain historical circumstances, a secession may be decided by referendum, as has recently occurred in the case of the Czech and Slovak nations). On many occasions, the decision to form part of a certain state is shown through custom, that is, through the wish of a certain nation to form part of and live within a specific state which has implicitly been upheld historically by the majority of its members. The second observation is that the principle of self-determination does not refer exclusively to the possibility that, applying the majority criterion, the human beings who reside in a certain geographical environment should decide whether or not they wish to belong to a certain state in accordance with their national affiliation, but such principle must also be applied in general, at all levels and for all the subgroups of civil society, whether or not they are linked together by their nationality. This means that the existence of nations which freely decide to become dispersed over different states is perfectly compatible with the principle of self-determination and, in addition, it must also be accepted that, within one same nation and state, minority groups decide to secede, separate or join another state, depending on their particular interests. Therefore, it is necessary to avoid the situation where a certain national group, which has decided to secede from a state where it was in a minority, also use the systematic coercion which it previously suffered to subdue other minority national groups contained within it.

The second essential principle which must govern the relationship between nations is complete *freedom of trade* between them. In fact, if nations are determined to fix specific geographical frontiers which separate them, place obstacles on freedom of trade and create protectionist measures, then, inevitably, the need to organize their economy and society on the basis of the principle of self-sufficient autarky will emerge. Autarky is not viable from the economic standpoint as, today, with the high level of development of the international division of labour, no geographical area possesses all the resources necessary to maintain a modern economy, meaning that a protectionist nation will be continuously directed towards forcing the expansion of its borders in order to gain more economic, material and human resources. This means that protectionism in the national field inevitably generates the logic of conflict and war, which are justified by the aim to expand the borders and gain more markets and productive resources. Therefore, in the final analysis, national protectionism destroys and sacrifices the national realities themselves in an inevitable war of all nations against all nations. It is easy to understand that the great wars have always originated from protectionist nationalism and that, in addition, the national conflicts which we know today (Yugoslavia, the Middle East, etc.) would disappear in an environment where there existed a common market with complete freedom of trade between all the nations involved.

In relation to this principle, the following economic law must be taken into account. Other things being equal, the smaller the state to which a nation is affiliated, the more difficult it will be for it to impose the centralist protectionism which generates conflicts and the more it will be forced to accept free trade. This is so because the smaller the state in question, the more its inhabitants will feel the impossibility of acceding to foreign markets and resources if there is not a complete freedom of trade. And, to the contrary, the larger the state organization, both geographically and in human terms, the easier it will be to organize its economy from the point of view of autarky, without the citizens being able to identify everything they are losing through the absence of free trade. This important economic law is, without any doubt, a *prima facie* argument in favour of decentralization and the political organization of nations in the smallest units possible.[8]

Freedom of trade is not sufficient if there is not a complete parallel *freedom of emigration and immigration*. If freedom to emigrate and immigrate does not exist, important disparities in income may continuously exist between some social groups and others, originating from the existence of a protectionist monopoly in the labour market (constituted, precisely, by the frontiers and regulations which prevent freedom of immigration). In the final analysis, all this may give rise to important disturbances and violence between different social groups. However, the freedom of emigration and immigration must, in turn, be subject to a series of rules and principles which prevent it from being used for coercive and interventionist ends contrary to the free interaction between nations. Thus, immigration must not be subsidized by the 'welfare state'. The people who immigrate must do so at their own risk. If this is not the case, the compulsory transfers of income from certain social groups to others will attract artificial immigration like a magnet and this will not only abort the redistributive processes but will, moreover, cause important social conflicts. The great threat to the 'welfare state' constituted by immigration is perfectly understandable, as is the fact that the 'welfare state' is mainly responsible for the construction of barriers to immigration in modern times. The only solution for political cooperation between nations consists, therefore, in dismantling the 'welfare state' and establishing complete freedom of immigration.[9]

In the second place, freedom of immigration should not, under any circumstance, imply that the political vote will rapidly be granted to the immigrants, as this would lead to political exploitation by the nationalities involved in the corresponding emigration flows. Those who emigrate must be aware of what they are doing in moving to a new cultural environment, where they will presumably improve their living conditions, but this should not give them the right to use the mechanisms of political coercion (represented by the democratic vote) to intervene and modify the spontaneous processes of the national markets which they enter. Only when, after a long period of time, they are considered to have fully absorbed the cultural principles of the society which receives them, may the grant of the corresponding political right to vote be considered.[10]

In the third place, the emigrants or immigrants must be able to demonstrate that they accede to the social group which receives them in order to contribute their labour, technical or entrepreneurial capacity; in other words, that they will have independent means to live from, will not be a burden to charity and can, in general, support themselves.

Finally, in the fourth and last place, and this is the most important principle which should govern emigration, the emigrants must scrupulously respect, in general, the material law (especially the criminal law) of the social group which receives them and, in particular, the private property rights in force in their new society. In this way, the phenomena of massive occupation (such as, for example, the *favelas* in Brazil, which have always been built on land belonging to third parties) will be avoided. The most visible problems provoked by immigration usually originate from the fact that there is no clear pre-existing definition and/or defence of the property rights involved, meaning that the people who arrive inevitably cause a significant number of external costs to those who are already there, which finally leads to outbreaks of xenophobia and violence with a high social cost. These conflicts are minimized and completely avoided precisely to the extent that the process of privatization of all the resources which exist in the social body advances.

Economic and social advantages of liberal nationalism

Provided the principles which we have set out in the preceding section are fulfilled, the ideas of nation and nationality, far from being prejudicial to the process of social interaction, are highly positive from a liberal viewpoint, as they enrich, reinforce and deepen the spontaneous and pacific process of social cooperation. Thus, for example, let us consider an environment in which the three basic principles mentioned are applied, particularly the principles of freedom of trade and freedom of emigration, as is the case of the present European Economic Community (today, the European Union). It is clear that, in this environment, no state-nation alone may adopt interventionist measures or measures of institutional coercion. Thus, for example, we see how nationalism in Europe acts as a true escape valve against the socialist and interventionist forces embodied in important sectors of the

Eurocracy, such as those represented by Jacques Delors and other Eurofanatics. We must remember that, when it is attempted to establish more restrictive regulations or higher taxes in a certain state or region, investments and citizens immediately tend to flee from the area and move to other states or nations with rules which are less interventionist and more favourable. This is, for example, what happened recently with the labour and tax regulations in Dijon, France, which caused the most important companies and factories in the area to abandon it and close their facilities in order to move to other, more favourable, areas of the European Economic Community, in Scotland and other parts of the United Kingdom. The fact that such a conspicuous liberal as Margaret Thatcher, leader of the so-called Eurosceptic liberals (among whom I am included) has defended the liberal nationalism model against the centralism of Brussels in the European Community is not, therefore, a whim or contradiction, as the competition between nations in a free trade environment tends to make the most liberal measures and regulations of each of them extend and be applied to the rest, by the force of the competition between them.[11] On the other hand, the intuition of the socialists and interventionists who defend the creation of a powerful federal European state, heavily centralized in Brussels, may now be understood perfectly. In fact, no interventionist measure (in the labour, social or taxation fields) will be successful if it is not imposed simultaneously in all the states and nations belonging to the European Community. The Socialists, therefore, have no alternative but to move the centre of gravity of the political decisions away from the state-nations towards the centre of Europe, giving an increasing number of powers and prerogatives to the organizations in Brussels, to the detriment of the state-nations which comprise the Community. A curious fact is the great short-sightedness of many socialist politicians who, like Felipe González, have not yet realized that in a heavily centralized federal state the importance of their own states and nations is reduced to a minimum expression. Has anyone ever heard of the head of state of Texas? It will be equally absurd to consider the role of a head of state or king in the United Kingdom or Spain within a few decades if the centralizing forces in favour of Brussels, moved by the spirit of interventionist European socialism, finally prevail.

Another example of a free trade environment in which there are different nations competing between themselves is Spain itself. It is evident that freedom of trade and immigration exists between the different regions and nationalities of Spain. This has lead to the fact that, in many fields, the competition between different areas has provoked a certain deregulation, which has not advanced further due to the great weight that the Socialist Party, heavily interventionist and centralizing, has had in all the regions of Spain up to now. Thus, recently, the local Basque Treasury has eliminated inheritance tax, to which the rest of the citizens of Spain (except in Navarra) are subject, and has also permitted a restatement of balance sheets, in flagrant defiance of the fiscal voraciousness shown by the socialist centralism of

Madrid. Mention must also be made of the case of Navarra, which, for historical reasons, has a sole local administration and collects its own taxes and which, although up to now it has used its historical prerogatives very timidly, is, in the final analysis, the model of 'entirely decentralized administration' which should be extended to the rest of the regions and nationalities of Spain as soon as possible.

The role of the state in liberal nationalism

The model of competition between nations in an environment subject to the three principles mentioned (self-determination, freedom of trade and of immigration) should be extended both upwards and downwards on the scale of the different levels of the state organization. This is the case, *upwards*, in relation to the state-nations which constitute the European Economic Community within the model of liberal competition between them defended, as we have seen, by Margaret Thatcher. The competition between nations will ineludibly lead to the increasing liberalization, with more and more limitations and difficulties, of the regulatory socialism of Brussels. But the application of the model must also be defended *downwards*, that is, in relation to the regions and nations which constitute the different states of Europe. This would be the case, for example, with Spain and the process of the autonomous communities which, in our opinion, must end in an *entirely decentralized administration* for each of the regions and nations of Spain that so choose (with its contents in accordance with the model of the Community of Navarra, which is, without doubt, as decentralized as possible).

What would be, therefore, the role of the state in the liberal system of competing nationalities which we defend? If the state is to have any role, it must be precisely that of the juridical incarnation of the three basic principles which make voluntary and pacific cooperation between the different nations possible. Thus, in the case of Spain, the Crown and State will only find their *raison d'être* if they guarantee and assure the essential principles of liberalism, that is, of complete freedom of trade, enterprise and emigration, within single areas and between different ones. And the same may be said, within a wider scope, of the only legitimate *raison d'être* of the European Union which is fully in accordance with its original founding spirit included in the Treaty of Rome. Moreover, the principle that no state organization should have attributions and competencies which may be assumed by smaller state organizations which are lower on the political scale should be defended. This implies that, in accordance with the principle we are defending, the higher we rise on such a scale, the more the specific political contents of the state organizations should decrease, with competencies which are increasingly of a strictly jurisdictional nature (human rights court, engaged basically in the defence and guarantee of the principles of freedom of enterprise and trade). To these jurisdictional competencies, as an additional security valve, competencies regarding the establishment of the maximum limits of regulation and taxation which may be imposed by the lower political organizations should also be added. In short, the question is to prevent the decentralized regions from subduing their citizens with impunity, as has happened in Catalonia, despite the formal existence of freedom of trade and immigration between the different areas. Therefore, it is convenient that, in addition to the spontaneous processes of competition between different nations which will *normally* lead to the dismantling of interventionist measures, maximum limits of regulation and taxation which are fixed by the states and higher political organizations should exist, in such away that only downward competition is permitted with regard to taxes and regulation, and the decentralized entities cannot, under any circumstance, exceed the maximum levels of taxation and regulation established by each state.[12] Therefore, the process of legal harmonization established in the European Community, through which the interventionist measures of each country are usually imposed on the rest, must be abandoned and substituted by a process of deregulatory competition between the different nations, in which the European Economic Community only plays a jurisdictional role (protection of personal rights and vigilance of the freedom of trade and immigration) and, in any case, establishes maximums for the capacity of economic, social and fiscal intervention and regulation of each state.

Liberal nationalism versus socialist nationalism

It is easy, therefore, to understand that the origin of the present evils which are generally associated with nationalism originate in failure to apply the three basic principles of liberal nationalism which have been analysed. In other words, that nationalism ceases to be a positive force for the pacific process of social cooperation and becomes, as has happened to a greater or lesser degree with the present government of Catalonia, a seedbed of conflicts and sufferings precisely when it ceases to be liberal and becomes an interventionist or socialist nationalism. That is to say, the error is in socialism, in interventionism and the systematic use of coercion, and not in nationalism *per se*. Although it must be acknowledged that, on many occasions, the interventionists and socialists resort to and prostitute the idea of nation to nourish and justify their coercive measures. It may be fully understood that the origin of the problems and conflicts is in socialism and interventionism, and not in nationalism, by analysing any given case of national conflict. Thus, the Yugoslavian war would immediately disappear if complete freedom of immigration were established, together with a common market of goods and services in which property rights were respected. The conflict created by the government of Catalonia in the educational field originates from the fact that education is public, it is financed by taxes and the decision as to which language it will take place is political, thus systematically coercing broad sectors of the population. In an environment of freedom of education (with a school voucher or some similar system which guaranteed the citizens freedom of choice), the whole conflict created by the government of Catalonia in the language area would completely disappear.[13]

Is it possible for the national socialists to be converted to liberal nationalism?

The analysis of liberal nationalism which we have made up to now has, moreover, the virtue of providing very powerful arguments to the defenders of the nationalist ideal who have so far misinterpreted its requirements and expressed it, to a greater or lesser degree, through interventionism or socialism.

Thus, it may be argued to a nationalist who truly loves the idea of the nation that there are only two models of cooperation between the different nations: either the model based on the principle of freedom of trade, immigration and self-determination which we have already seen, or the model based on protectionism, intervention and systematic coercion. It is, moreover, easy to explain to any nationalist that the model of coercive protection and intervention against other nations is inevitably doomed to failure. The autarky to which it gives rise generates dynamics of war and destruction which, in the final analysis, enormously weaken the nation it seeks to defend. The protectionist model of relations between different nations is not, therefore, at all viable. The only viable alternative, which is generally beginning to be recognized by the nationalists themselves, is that nations must compete on an equal level based on the principles of freedom of trade and immigration.

Subsequently, assuming that freedom of trade and of immigration between nations is accepted, a further step may be taken in the theoretical argument with the nationalist, explaining that, if he chooses to be, within the scope of his own nation, an interventionist and protectionist nationalist (that is, socialist to a greater or lesser extent), his regulatory measures will be doomed to failure if he does not somehow have them applied simultaneously in all the nations with which he is competing in a broad geographical area. In other words, it is absurd to establish regulatory and interventionist measures in a sole state-nation (for example of the European Economic Community) without the same intervention being imposed, through a directive or rule from Brussels, on the rest of the state-nations and regions of the Community. Therefore, the nationalist with interventionist and socialist fancies, if s/he pursues his or her objectives of intervention with perseverance and efficiency, will ultimately only achieve the transfer of the centre of gravity of the political and economic decisions from the nation s/he claims to defend to the political centre of the state or the broadest political organization to which his or her nation belongs (Madrid or Brussels). That is, we again realize that the socialist intuition of people like Jacques Delors, Felipe González and other Eurofanatics is correct when, in the final analysis, they seek a continuous reinforcement of the powers of Brussels. But what seems paradoxical and contradictory is that many nationalist leaders have also defended, to the detriment of their own nations, the expansion of the state power centres when they have pursued interventionist-type policies.

From this perspective, it is no risk to say that a great part of the responsibility for, for example, the centralism of Madrid originates from Catalonian nationalism, which, historically, when seeking and obtaining privileges in its favour (of a protectionist nature etc.), has never doubted to come to Madrid to make 'pacts' and obtain state laws which are binding on all the Spanish regions, ultimately increasing the power of the capital to the detriment of the nation which it claims to defend.[14] Nobody is, therefore, historically more responsible for the centralism of Madrid than the short-sighted Catalonian nationalists themselves.[15] And this paradoxical historical result seems to be being repeated in relation to the wider field of the European Economic Community, to which the leaders of the different regions and nationalities ingenuously resort, thinking that it will lead to a reduction in the power of the state-nations, without realizing that the federal reinforcement of the Community leads to the expansion of a centralist power, the power of Brussels, which may finally be much worse. Thus, the ingenuous nationalists, who defend the expansion of Brussels to the detriment of the state-nations, and the ingenuous European enthusiasts (like Felipe González and others), whose socialist intuition leads them to reinforce the power of Brussels, become strange fellow travellers, without either of them realizing that this takes place both at the cost of a continuous weakening of the Spanish national idea and of its most important symbols, such as that constituted by the monarchy itself, and at the cost of a progressive weakening of the national ideal at a regional level (whose decisions are of increasingly less importance in comparison with those taken in the Community).

In this field, as in others, we see how the erroneous and ingenuous interests of nationalists and socialists converge and damage the true liberal spirit which should govern the pacific, harmonious and fruitful relations between different nations.

In any case, we must not renounce the use of rational argument with the nationalists with interventionist tendencies, as those for whom the nationalist ideal prevails over interventionist or coercive ideology may finally understand that what are most contrary to the idea of the nation which they defend are interventionist policies in all spheres (economic, cultural, linguistic, etc.), which, up to now, they have favoured.

Perhaps one of the most plausible explanations for interventionist nationalism comes from the inferiority complex and lack of self-confidence of many nations. And this is why precisely the nations in greatest regression and, therefore, most lacking in confidence are those which react most violently against their own fate. In principle, we could say that the greater the state of regression of a nation (having been absorbed by others which are richer and more dynamic), the more violent will its death rattle be (as shown by the case of the Basque nation and, to a lesser extent, by that of the interventionism of the Catalonian nation in the linguistic field). A nation which is sure of itself, which believes in its future and which does not fear competition on an equal level from other nations, will be a nation in which the spirit of liberal cooperation which we have described in this article will prevail.[16]

Conclusion: in favour of a liberal nationalism

The conclusion of the analysis of liberal nationalism which we have made in this article has allowed us to clarify to what point the policy of the Eurosceptics initiated by Margaret Thatcher in relation to the European Economic Community is consistent and correct, as opposed to the ingenuous enthusiasm of the European politicians with socialist tendencies (Felipe González, Jacques Delors, etc.). Let us defend, therefore, nations in an environment of freedom of trade, market and immigration, as this is the best life insurance against control, coercion and interventionism. Likewise, let us make the short-sighted nationalists of each state see that anything which is not the development of the national ideal in an environment of complete freedom will, ultimately, be detrimental to the idea of nation which they claim to defend. The lack of self-confidence and confidence in the value of the cultural and linguistic principles of their nationality leads them to impose by force linguistic, cultural and economic protectionism which, in the final analysis, weakens their own nation and endangers the process of liberal competition with other nations. The nation may only be developed and fortified in an environment of freedom and the sooner the nationalists become aware of these essential principles, the sooner they will abandon the tragic policies which they have adopted up to now, to the detriment of their own nations and of the other nations with which they are forced to live. Liberal nationalism is not merely the only conception of nationalism compatible with the development of the nations, but also constitutes the only principle of harmonious, pacific and fruitful cooperation between all social groups for the future.

8 A libertarian theory of free immigration[1]

The problems posed by the free emigration and immigration of human beings often lead to confusion among libertarian theorists and lovers of freedom. In the first place, libertarian doctrine traditionally declared itself, with no qualifications or reservations, in favour of the principle of complete freedom of emigration and immigration. This position is based on the recognition that the establishment of political frontiers is a flagrant act of interventionism and institutional coercion on the part of the state, tending to hinder or even prevent the free movement of human beings. Moreover, many border controls and immigration laws emerge as the result of the political action of privileged interest groups, like the trade unions, that aim to restrict the labour supply in order to raise wages artificially. To the extent that these interventionist rules on emigration or immigration hinder or prevent the voluntary agreements reached between the parties (natives and foreigners), there is no doubt that they violate the basic principles which should govern any libertarian society. Furthermore, these interventionist immigration policies particularly affect nationals of foreign countries, since the principle of free movement of people within each state has, in general, been accepted.

However, the coercive action of the state manifests itself not only in hindering the free movement of people, but, at the same time, in forcing the integration of certain groups of people against the wishes of the natives of a given state or region. This coercive action on the part of the state occurs both intranationally and internationally. Thus, within each nation, measures for the integration of certain minorities and groups are often imposed by force, such as anti-discrimination laws, affirmative action legislation, or busing laws. At the international level, many states, either legally or *de facto*, open up their frontiers to foreigners indiscriminately and allow them to use the public goods (roads, parks, beaches, government health care, educational and welfare services) as free riders. In this way, the state generates significant external costs for the natives, who are obliged to accept the forced integration of the foreigners against their wishes or under conditions that they do not desire.[2]

In light of their apparently contradictory nature, the foregoing problems show the importance of isolating their real origin, and piecing together a libertarian theory of immigration that clarifies the principles that should govern the processes of immigration and emigration in a free society.

The pure theory of movements of persons in a libertarian environment

Like Murray N. Rothbard, we shall begin our analysis assuming the pure anarcho-capitalist model, i.e. the model in which 'no land areas, no square footage in the world, shall remain "public"; every square foot of land area, be they streets, squares, or neighbourhoods, is privatized'.[3] It is obvious that none of the problems relating to immigration diagnosed in the preceding paragraph can arise here. The conditions, volume and duration of personal visits may be those accepted or decided by the parties involved. Thus, even mass movements of labour are conceivable, if the employers in question are willing to give work to the immigrants, make it possible for them to find accommodation, arrange and even pay for their journey, etc. In short, the possible contracts between the parties involved will vary greatly, and will admit all the richness that the special characteristics of each case allow.

Under these conditions, migratory flows, far from being harmful to economic and social development, become a driving force for civilization. The argument that an abundance of new labour is necessarily harmful to the working classes of the recipient country is untenable. Human beings are not a uniform production factor, and do not behave in exclusively biological terms in relation to scarce resources, as is the case with rats and other animals, whose population increases always tend to diminish the volume of resources available for each individual. On the contrary, human beings are endowed with – and in appropriate institutional settings make use of – an innate creative entrepreneurial capacity. In a dynamic environment, an increase in population allows the continual discovery and exploitation of new opportunities, and thus a growth without limit in the standard of living.

The human mind has a limited capacity to assimilate information (or knowledge), while the social process, driven by entrepreneurship, produces an ever-increasing volume of information. Thus, the advance of civilization requires a continual extension and deepening of the division of labour or, if one prefers, of knowledge. This simply means that the development process implies, from a vertical standpoint, an increasingly deep, specialized and detailed knowledge, which, in order to extend horizontally, requires an increasing number of human beings, i.e. a constant population growth. Worldwide, this population growth takes place in the long term when births are in excess of deaths. But in the short and medium terms, the only rapid and effective response to the continual adjustments required by economic and social changes is through emigration and immigration flows. These flows permit a quick deepening in the division of labour, thus overcoming the limited capacity of assimilation of each individual human mind by rapidly increasing the number of people involved in social processes.[4] As Hayek rightly says, 'we have become civilized by the increase of our numbers, just as civilisation made that increase possible: we can be few and savage, or many and civilised'.[5]

The development of cities as centres of wealth and civilization is a clear illustration of this process of the expansion of knowledge made possible by immigration. The continuous depopulation of countryside and the mass movement of workers toward urban centres, far from impoverishing the cities, promotes their development in a cumulative process that has been one of the most characteristic manifestations of human progress since the Industrial Revolution. Furthermore, emigration and immigration flows, in the libertarian environment we are considering at this point, tend to multiply the variety and diversity of possible solutions to the different problems that emerge. All this favours cultural selection and economic and social advance, since all movements take place as a result of voluntary agreements, and, whenever circumstances change, those concerned have the chance to emigrate or move to other enterprises in different geographical locations.[6]

Lastly, we should note the fact that, in a libertarian environment in which all resources and goods which are today considered 'public' have been privatized, neither of the negative effects identified above in relation to the cases of forced integration takes place. Anti-discrimination laws, affirmative action laws or simply the flood of immigrants in the streets or elsewhere would be reduced to a minimum. Movements would always be made using private means of transport, meeting the contractual conditions fixed by their owners and paying the corresponding market price. Different agencies would specialize in organizing the itineraries and guaranteeing beforehand the necessary access to each means of transport. Likewise, in their own interests, the respective owners would take care to ensure that the travellers passed through the successive means of transport without becoming unwanted guests. This process would continue, with a wealth of social arrangements and juridical and economic institutions that we cannot even imagine today, since the market and entrepreneurial creativity are not allowed to act upon the goods today considered public.

We may, therefore, conclude that emigration and immigration *per se*, subject to the general principles of law in an environment where all resources are private, not only do not pose any problems of forced integration or external costs but, on the contrary, are important leading forces of economic and social development and of the wealth and variety of culture and civilization.[7]

Problems posed by coercive state intervention

Our analysis allows us to isolate and identify the real origin of the problems regarding emigration and immigration we have noted. All of them originate from coercive state intervention at different levels. First of all, such intervention raises barriers which hinder or prevent movements which have been voluntarily agreed to. Second, states at the same time insist on imposing various measures of forced integration, either directly (through so-called anti-discrimination and affirmative action laws, etc.) or indirectly, by declaring important territorial areas (streets, squares, parks, etc.) to be public and, therefore, freely accessible to all. As it does not adequately define the relevant property rights of 'foreigners' and 'natives', state intervention is the cause of all the problems and conflicts that arise today in this whole area.

The coercive action of the state appears at two levels. First, within the borders of each nation-state, the typical problems of forced integration and negative externalities, which inevitably arise whenever privatization of 'public' resources is prevented, emerge in their most virulent form. In the second place, state interventionism also appears internationally, by regulating the migratory flows across borders. Here, interventionism has a dual and contradictory aspect. On the one hand, difficulties are put in the way of movements voluntarily agreed to by the parties (natives of a country and foreigners). On the other hand, mass international movements are artificially promoted by the subsidies and advantages offered by the welfare state.

Thus, today, there is often the paradox that those who wish to abide scrupulously by the law find that their movements are not permitted, even if desired by all the parties involved. At the same time, the existence of public goods and the free availability of welfare state benefits attract, like a magnet, a continuous tide of immigration, mostly illegal, which generates significant conflicts and external costs. All of this encourages xenophobia and promotes subsequent interventionist measures, which further aggravate the problems. Meanwhile, the citizens are unable to identify the true origin of the difficulty; in this climate of confusion, they easily become the victims of demagogy, and end up supporting measures which, in addition to being contradictory, are both inefficient and harmful.

Finally, we should not forget that, at least with regard to the immigration question, present problems are usually more serious at the international than at the intranational level. Within each nation-state, a greater economic, social and cultural homogenization usually takes place in the course of its historical evolution, which tends to decrease incentives for mass movements. In contrast, internationally, disparities in income are much greater, and the enormous development of communications and means of transport makes it much easier and cheaper to travel between different countries: today, in only a few hours, one can fly from New Delhi to New York, or from Latin America to Spain; in the case of emigration from North Africa to Europe, or from Mexico to the United States, the costs involved are even lower.

Solution of the problems posed today by emigration and immigration flows

The ideal solution to all these problems would come from the total privatization of the resources which are today considered public, and the disappearance of state intervention at all levels in the area of emigration and immigration. In other words, since the problems we have just identified originate from the harmful effects of coercive state intervention, rather than from emigration or immigration *per se*, the pure anarcho-capitalist system would eliminate the greater part of them.

However, as long as nation-states continue to exist, we must find 'procedural' solutions that allow the problems to be solved under present conditions. In this respect, several libertarian theorists have recently been developing a model of secession and decentralization which, since it tends to break down today's heavily centralized nation-states into increasingly smaller political units, favours a decline in state interventionism. This would result from competition among the various states to attract citizens and investments (or avoid their fleeing abroad). The dynamic inherent in this situation would oblige the states to adopt increasingly libertarian policies. In the competition among such ever-smaller and more decentralized states, emigration and immigration flows would play an essential role. Such movements constitute 'voting with one's feet'. They would oblige the states to dismantle larger and larger parts of the tax-and-interventionist apparatus of the current governments. As Hans-Hermann Hoppe writes,

> a world consisting of tens of thousands of distinct countries, regions, and cantons, and of hundreds of thousands of independent free cities such as the present-day 'oddities' of Monaco, Andorra, San Marino, Liechtenstein, Hong Kong, and Singapore, with the resulting greatly increased opportunities for economically motivated migration, would be one of small liberal governments economically integrated through free trade and an international commodity money such as gold. It would be a world of unprecedented economic growth and unheard prosperity.[8]

However, the identification of both ideal and procedural solutions to these problems does not relieve us of the obligation to study the principles which should govern migratory flows under present circumstances, where heavily interventionist nation-states exist. These principles should be compatible with libertarian ideals. At the same time, they should take into account the *real, existing* difficulties and contradictions caused by the existence of nation-states. The following section analyses what these principles should be.

Principles on which present immigration processes should be based

For several reasons, it is indispensable to establish a set of principles compatible with libertarian ideas that should act as guidelines today. Even if the process of state dismemberment proposed by Rothbard, Hoppe and many others were to get underway, that would not guarantee that the measures adopted in this area by each decentralized government were correct from a libertarian point of view. As Hoppe himself acknowledges, 'secession solves this problem by letting smaller territories each have their own admission standards and determine independently with whom they will associate on their own territory and with whom they prefer to cooperate from a distance'.[9] However, it is quite possible that these standards or regulations will also prove to be interventionist, preventing movements that were agreed upon voluntarily between natives and foreigners.

Furthermore, as long as states (however small they may be) continue to exist and, within them, 'public' streets, roads and land where property rights are not well defined or protected, there may continue to be forced integration or else mass-occupation phenomena like the *favelas* in Brazil, which generate significant external costs and seriously violate the property rights of the natives. Finally, the proposed solutions must not only lead in the right direction and be compatible with libertarian principles, they must also be 'operative', by providing a response to the most pressing problems posed today (for example emigration across the border between Mexico and the United States, or between North Africa and Europe). In short, a series of rules should be designed to prevent immigration being used for coercive and interventionist ends in conflict with free interaction between nations and individuals.

The first of these principles is that people who immigrate must do so at their own risk. This means that immigration must in no way be subsidized by the welfare state, i.e. by benefits provided by the government and financed through taxes. These benefits are not only the traditional ones (education, health care, social security, etc.), but the benefits of the free use of publicly owned goods. Such benefits – in the final analysis, compulsory transfers of income from one social group to another – will become a magnet, artificially attracting many immigrants. For the negative effects to materialize, it is sufficient for some (not necessarily all) groups of emigrants, in making their decisions, to take into account the welfare benefits they expect to receive. Our argument is, therefore, perfectly compatible with the thesis put forward by some authors, that immigrants contribute to the system a much larger amount than the total value of the welfare benefits they receive (above all in the first few years of their stay in the new country). It is sufficient that certain groups – even if they are in a minority – consider themselves to be subsidized for a perverse effect of artificial encouragement of immigration to occur, to the detriment of the citizens of the recipient country.

Thus, the first rule is that immigrants have no right to any of the largesse of the welfare state. This will prevent some groups from obtaining subsidies for their movements. In cases where it is considered that the contributions made by the immigrants are higher than the benefits they receive, in order to avoid subjecting them to exploitation by the system they should at most be obliged to maintain a certain level of coverage, although this should always be contracted, under their own responsibility, through private institutions. In this way, two libertarian objectives would be attained: avoidance of the artificial promotion of immigration through state redistribution policies, and a quicker dismantling of state social security programmes based on the 'pay as you go' principle. This would also encourage the development of private systems based on saving and the capitalization which immigrants would acquire as new clients.[10]

The second principle that should inspire current policy is that all immigrants must be able to demonstrate that they have independent means of support, and thus will not be a burden on the taxpayers. In other words, immigrants must be able to show that they are joining the new social group in order to contribute their labour, technical or entrepreneurial talents, or capital. There are ways to put this principle into practice, although none is perfect. Perhaps the most appropriate is for each immigrant to have, at all times, a native person or private institution that guarantees his financial competence, by giving him an employment contract, acting as the depository of a certain amount of money or investments, or assuming the legal responsibility for caring for him. Logically, market flexibility requires that, within a reasonable period of time, foreign workers who are dismissed or leave their employment voluntarily should have the chance to seek a new job before they are repatriated. Although this would require the employers to notify the state control body of the rescission of the relevant contracts, from an administrative point of view it would be no more cumbersome or costly than the immigration procedures which currently exist in almost all countries, including my own.

The third essential principle is that under no circumstance should the political vote be granted to immigrants quickly, since this would create the danger of political exploitation by various groups of immigrants. Those who move to a new country and cultural environment will, presumably, improve their living conditions. But they have no right to use the mechanism of political coercion – the democratic ballot – to promote policies of income redistribution or to intervene in the spontaneous processes of the national markets which they enter. It is true that, as dismemberment into increasingly smaller states progresses, the right to vote and political elections will lose importance and will, in practice, be replaced by 'voting with one's feet'. But it is no less true that, until this process of decentralization is complete, the automatic granting of political rights to immigrants may be a time-bomb that under certain circumstances can be used by a voting majority to destroy the market, culture and language of the recipient country. Only after a long period of time, when the immigrants may be assumed to have fully absorbed the cultural principles of their new society, should the granting of full citizenship, including voting rights, be considered. Apropos of this, the principle established in the European Union, whereby citizens of other EU countries may vote in the elections of the municipality where they reside, is highly questionable. Such a rule could completely distort the atmosphere and culture of many localities where there happens to be a majority of foreign residents, for example in parts of Spain, where elderly persons come to live from the United Kingdom, Germany, etc. Only when such residents have been living in the new area for a minimum number of years and have acquired property rights there (homes or other real estate) would it be justified to grant them the right to vote.

Finally, the most important principle is that all immigrants must at all times observe the law of the social group that receives them. Specifically, they must scrupulously respect all the property rights established in the society. Any violation of these rights should be punished not only by the penalties fixed in the criminal code but also by the expulsion (definitive in most cases) of the immigrant in question. Thus, the phenomena of mass occupation (as is the case already mentioned of the *favelas* in Brazil, which have generally been built on land belonging to other people) would be avoided.

We have already seen how the most visible problems posed by immigration arise from the fact that there is no clear definition or strict defence of the property rights of the natives, meaning that the immigrants often generate significant overall external costs for the native citizens. This leads to serious outbreaks of xenophobia and violence that themselves have a high social cost, and in turn produce juridical and political results the additional costs of which are often paid by the innocent. These conflicts would be minimized precisely to the extent that private property rights became effective and were extended to include resources at present considered to be publicly owned. Until total privatization can take place, the use of public goods must be regulated in order to avoid the mass occupation problems we have mentioned.[11]

Conclusion

The measures outlined here will not eliminate all the problems posed by migratory flows at present. They will, however, tend to reduce them and lead in the direction that all freedom lovers desire. In any event, the definitive solution of these problems will not come until the present-day states are dissolved into tiny political units and all their publicly owned goods fully privatized.

9 The crisis and reform of social security[1]

Introduction

The problems posed by public social security may be divided into two broad areas: first, the problem of *pensions* in the case of retirement, widowhood, orphaned children and disability, that is to say, the regular payment of benefits in the case of survival, disability or death; second, the problem posed by medical assistance, which is also of great importance. We are going to deal with these two problems separately, although we will pay special attention to the subject of pensions, as it probably constitutes the most significant problem in Western countries, in view of the importance of the liabilities which have been assumed and the difficulties stemming from any attempted reform process in this area.

Thus, we will devote the first section to the *diagnosis* of the problem posed by social security in the pensions field, from both the *technical* and *ethical* standpoints. We will then conclude that there is an *inherent contradiction* in all state social security systems and will present the *libertarian model of social security* which we consider most appropriate. Fourth, we will propose a *reform process* for the social security which, oriented towards the appropriate objective, minimizes the tensions arising from any reform. We will go on to analyse, from different points of view, what the most suitable *strategy* is for such a reform to meet with success. Lastly, we will devote a section exclusively to the problem arising from public health insurance.

Diagnosis of the problem

The crisis of public social security, which has been unanimously acknowledged, is of a twofold nature: on the one hand, it is a technical crisis, of an economic and actuarial nature; on the other, it is an ethical crisis.

Technical problems

First, technical problems are the easiest to recognize. Specifically, it should be observed how *the 'pay as you go' social security financial system tends to substantially decrease the overall savings of the country.* This occurs because the pensions paid each year are charged against taxes and social security contributions which are *coercively* taken from the contributors in each financial year. This makes it very difficult to save, not only because the pressure of taxation, in the form of taxes and social security contributions, in many cases is almost unbearable, but also because citizens in general subjectively trust (or, at least, have trusted up to now) that future generations will finance social security in the same way as we have done so far.[2] It is very difficult to minimize the prejudicial effect which this negative influence of social security on savings has had on the evolution of the domestic economy. For instance, the savings rate in Spain showed a percentage decrease, with respect to the gross national product, from nearly 27 per cent in 1975 to 19 per cent in 1992.[3] Furthermore, this drop in savings may be considered to play a leading role in the appearance and exacerbation of the current and past economic recessions which have become manifest, above all, in the emergence of numerous investment projects which have lost profitability due to a lack of the necessary supply, at favourable interest rates, of real financial resources previously saved. If this had been significantly higher, a large number of the investment projects which have had to be abandoned or restructured would have been able to be put into operation, thanks to the abundance of financial resources which any increase in real savings causes and which allows trade and industry to be financed at lower interest rates.[4]

Second, also from a technical and economic point of view, it is necessary to clarify that, regardless of how the system works from a legal or juridical standpoint, it is a fallacy to think that company contributions to social security are paid by the employers. In fact, although it apparently could not be the case according to the external legal requirements, *from an economic viewpoint, such contributions are, in the final analysis, always paid by the workers themselves,* given that they form part of the employer's *total labour cost* and it would make no difference to the employer to pay them directly to his workers instead of having to pay them to the state social security system. This key economic insight was first developed by Ludwig von Mises in 1922, when he stated that

> the insurance contributions are always at the expense of wages, immaterial of whether they are collected from the entrepreneur or from the workers. What the entrepreneur has to pay for the insurance is a charge of Labour's marginal productivity, it thus tends to reduce the wages of Labour.[5]

Third, moreover, now from a more *technical-actuarial* perspective, the burden which social security implies for the working generations is snowballing. This is the inevitable result of the gradual aging of the population that we are currently witnessing in most Western countries, which leads to a constant increase in the number of retired persons, in relative terms, with respect to the working population. For instance, in Spain in 1993 it could be roughly calculated that there was one pensioner (retired or widowed) for every two workers and it is estimated that, at the beginning of the twenty-first century, each worker will have to support one retired person if the current public social security system continues. Moreover, inflation leads to constant pressure to revalue the pensions which are being paid.[6]

All this explains that the burden on the working population implied by pensions is beginning to be unbearable for each country in general and for the taxpayer in particular, oppressed by a clear economic recession and a growing pressure of taxation. It is, therefore, increasingly doubtful whether the public social security systems will be able to pay the pensions to which they have committed themselves, and it is conceivable that we will reach a time when the working generations wash their hands, to a greater or lesser extent, of their 'obligations' towards those who are already retired, given the unbearable weight of the financial burden which they imply. It would, therefore, seem clear that it is necessary to carry out a profound reform of the present social security system, gradually establishing a new one, by virtue of which the non-working groups who retire will be able to look after themselves, without having to necessarily and coercively depend financially on the younger generations who continue working.

Fourth, and perhaps the most important argument of economic theory on social security, is, however, the argument derived from its *coercive* nature. In fact, public social security systems constitute one of the most important cases of generalized and indiscriminate institutional aggression against the citizens in Western countries.[7] It is impossible to minimize the perverse effects of this coercion, which massively prevents free, spontaneous human interaction and the creative development of entrepreneurship, in relation to all the actors affected by the system (companies, workers, retired persons, orphans, widows or widowers, disabled and sick people, insurance companies, financial institutions, hospitals, doctors, savers and investors).[8] This coercion not only causes a profound misdirection of the allocation of labour and capital, together with its bias against savings,[9] but also, and this is even more important, prevents the entrepreneurial discovery, creative generation and transmission of the information necessary to try out new and imaginative solutions to the innumerable problems to which the institution of public social security gives rise. In this way, social imbalances are continually aggravated and individual plans remain uncoordinated.[10]

Ethical problems

The technical, economic and actuarial problems discussed in the preceding section do not arise alone, but are accompanied by significant and serious problems of an ethical-political nature. Specifically, the social security system is based on an outdated paternalism, is unsupportive, as it encourages tension and conflict between the generations, is seriously prejudicial, in view of its inflexibility, to the possibilities of the human and professional development of senior citizens, and is based upon concepts of 'social justice' and 'redistribution of income' which libertarians cannot share. We will discuss each of these problems separately.

First, public social security systems are based on the *paternalist idea* that people, by nature, lack foresight and, therefore, that it is necessary to establish a compulsory and omni-comprehensive social security system. However, this idea is totally unfounded at the present time. And it is difficult to understand how, on the one hand, citizens are considered sufficiently mature and responsible to vote and freely elect their rulers, while, on the other, they are considered incapable of solving the problem of their retirement themselves. This means that the paternalist arguments in favour of social security, in a democratic environment such as the one we live in at present, *imply the clear paradox that 'public matters' are organized in accordance with the wish of voters whom the legislator itself considers incapable of organizing their own affairs.*[11]

Therefore, the role of the state could be limited at the utmost to the minimum level of social assistance considered necessary in relation to the minority of the population who, for various reasons (lack of foresight, bad luck, etc.) reach their old age without having covered their indispensable needs themselves. But what seems absurd is that, as happens at present, because a minority of the population have not been able to provide for their retirement in time, the coercive participation in a state system is imposed upon the whole population, preventing them from using a large part of their resources for their old age in the way which they consider most profitable and appropriate. Social security, therefore, *implies an attack against the freedom of each citizen*, equally serious as it would be if, due to the fact that a minority of the population had difficulties in obtaining food, a system were established which obliged the *whole* population to eat in canteens. The lack of ethics is especially serious, moreover, if we remember that, as mentioned previously, the whole amount of social security contributions are paid, in the final analysis, by the workers and, therefore, it may be said that they are being deprived of a significant part of their income, which they cannot, therefore, use to ensure their retirement in the way they consider most appropriate to their personal circumstances.[12]

Second, it must be remembered that whenever a free economy is intervened in by state regulations of a coercive nature, the appearance of conflicts and tension between different groups, which substitute, to a greater or lesser extent, the network of voluntary and pacific exchanges typical of any free society, is fomented. This is especially clear in the case of social security. In fact, before the appearance of public social security systems, based on the 'pay as you go' financial system and the idea that the young people who work should compulsorily finance the pensions of those who have retired, the problem of retirement was solved in various voluntary ways and it did not create tension and conflicts between the generations. These intergenerational conflicts are especially serious nowadays and, in fact, it seems very difficult to take any political decision on the social security system without the emergence of *tension and friction between the working generation and the generation which has already retired*. As the system, for financial and technical reasons, cannot be maintained, the pensioners, whom it is increasingly difficult to support financially, are implicitly blamed for the problem.[13]

The situation is very similar to that which is provoked when the labour market ceases to be free and, as a consequence of all kinds of institutional and trade union restrictions, unemployment appears. Conflicts and tensions between the different social groups then emerge, as the persons who are working feel their jobs to be threatened by young people and by people who do not wish to retire. There is constant pressure for rules to be made increasing the age at which people may start work and coercively reducing the retirement age, seriously prejudicing the social groups affected (young people, the unemployed and older people).

It may be concluded, therefore, that social security is a destabilizing instrument in modern societies, which endangers the harmonious and pacific progress thereof, leading to serious tension and conflicts which are impossible to solve.

Third, the situation of the people who, rigidly and inflexibly, are retired in accordance with the rules which govern social security is especially disturbing. One of the most negative aspects of the state social security system is its inflexible and uniform nature for the whole population. It is incomprehensible that each company, institution or individual is not allowed freedom to design the transition from working life to retirement in the way it or s/he considers most appropriate to the circumstances and least prejudicial to the parties involved. In a free society, the most varied retirement systems would *spontaneously* emerge and would permit each citizen to *choose* the most suitable way of spending his retirement. Institutions would appear, such as those of gradual retirement and part-time work for retired persons, which would minimize the serious psychological and physical traumas which the older people in our society suffer when they compulsorily retire under the public social security system. As Hayek has so clearly explained,

> significantly enough, in the two main fields which the state threatens to monopolize – the provision for old age and for medical care – we are witnessing the most rapid growth of new methods wherever the state has not yet taken complete control, a variety of experiments which are almost certain to produce new answers to current needs, answers which no advance planning can contemplate.[14]

Fourth and last, we must criticize the idea that social security is, at least, good for the ideal of 'social justice', as it redistributes income in favour of the least favoured social groups. First, it should be pointed out that, from an economic viewpoint, *the effects of the policies of redistributing income are very prejudicial precisely to the least favoured social groups.* This is the case because, in a free society, it is impossible to distinguish the production processes from the processes of distribution of income. In a market economy, production is carried out in accordance with the profits it is expected to obtain, meaning that it is impossible to modify the results through policies of redistribution of income without seriously affecting the production process itself. The policies of redistribution of income strongly discourage the energy of the country's production agents and, therefore, impoverish the whole country, particularly the least favoured classes. Moreover, there is nothing progressive about policies of redistribution of income which tend to prevent the people with the lowest incomes from rising to the highest levels on the social scale.

As Hayek has so rightly demonstrated, the ideal of 'social justice' is especially dangerous and must be criticized by libertarians. In the first place, the concept of social justice has no meaning and is incompatible with the principles which should govern a free society. As we have just mentioned, a free society gives rise to a harmonious and dynamic economic development, but causes an unequal and constantly changing distribution of income. Any effort to equalize the results of the process of freedom could only be carried out once, as it would destroy the process itself and the foundations of the free society which we should defend. Moreover, the ideal of 'social justice' implies granting the state enormous powers over the life of its citizens, which are incompatible with our idea of freedom. In a free society, there should be no more justice than that which is constituted by laws of a general nature which are applied abstractly to all the citizens and which prevent *a priori* knowledge of what the specific result of the interaction between them will be. The only equality which libertarians should defend is, therefore, the *equality in the eyes of the law* in the sense we have just defined it, but they should never defend an equality of results, which is fundamentally incompatible with freedom and is based on the spurious and false concept of 'social justice'.[15]

The inherent contradiction in social security[16]

The public system of social security has, since it began, shown an unresolvable contradiction which is the main cause of many of its problems. It has tried to work simultaneously as a system of 'insurance' and of 'social assistance' or welfare, which are radically incompatible with each other.

Social security works as 'insurance' when it pays out benefits in accordance with formulae which determine higher pensions for those who have paid higher contributions over a longer time period. Moreover, these payments are made to the beneficiaries regardless of whether they need them or not. These characteristics (benefits depending on the contributions and the payment of them regardless of the actual need) are common to the social security system and private insurance institutions, which, in this respect, are based on the same principles.

But, at the same time, social security aims to work as a welfare system. It carries out this function whenever it pays out benefits to groups which are considered to be most in need, regardless (or taking less account) of the amount of the contributions and the period over which they have been paid. Moreover, in accordance with this 'social' function, it is aimed to carry out a process of redistribution of income which is considered fair and which, as we have already seen, cannot be accepted from the libertarian standpoint.

Specialized works often call the two objectives which we have just described the objective of 'individual equity' (insurance) and the objective of 'social equity' (welfare).

However, these two functions are strictly and fundamentally incompatible with each other and the result of trying to put them into effect through the same institution of public social security means that, from the individual point of view, social security is a highly deficient 'insurance' and, from the social point of view, it is a very defective and unfair instrument of social welfare. This is because it is not possible to attain simultaneously objectives which belong to 'private insurance', based on the principle of granting benefits in accordance with the contributions made, regardless of the individual need of the beneficiary, and objectives of social justice and distribution of income, which imply the provision of benefits to persons in need, regardless of whether or not they have contributed to the system.

The wish to pursue the objective of social justice or social welfare using the social security system clearly affects the principle of 'individual equity' (insurance) as, as we have seen, the 'pay as you go' financing of social security has a very negative effect on the country's savings and economy and creates a dynamic which makes it impossible to meet the obligations acquired. And, in view of the weight of the increasing financial burden of the non-working persons, there will come a moment when social security will have to reduce its benefits, and the pensions which the beneficiaries expected in accordance with the contributions they had made to the system in the past will not be received. Moreover, the individual contributor to social security ceases to get the financial return which, in the case of a real private insurance system, he would obtain from the resources saved to assure his retirement.[17]

This lack of equality between what is contributed and what is obtained from the system means that such a system in unavoidably constructed on the basis of the concept of coercion and its compulsory nature for all citizens. This is because it could not be expected that a system like social security would work by people joining it voluntarily: the contributors who received a greater amount than their contributions in benefits would remain within the system, while those whose contributions were greater than the benefits received would leave it, meaning that the financial equilibrium thereof could not be maintained.

Moreover, the fact that the state social security system must be, by its own nature, *coercive* implies, for most people, that the only appropriate organism to manage it is the government. This subjects the system to a series of political influences which makes it *essentially unstable*: politicians are tempted to use the programme to attain their own ends, often at the expense of the participants in the system and the general economy of the country. The cases of buying votes in the short term by demagogic modifications, reforms or increases in social security benefits is normal practice in most Western democracies. It should be pointed out that this tendency affects both the political parties in power and the opposition.[18]

In addition, social security does not meet its objectives of social welfare, as payment of the benefits is made regardless of whether the beneficiaries need them or not. Thus, in many cases, young people in the lower income brackets, struggling to support their families, are obliged to lose a substantial part of their income to finance the pensions of older people who have less need of income or are receiving pensions from several sources at the same time.[19]

As a conclusion, it is clear that the 'insurance' elements of social security systematically abort and make ineffective the social welfare programme which social security aims to carry out, and vice versa.

The problems of social security cannot be understood, nor a serious reform undertaken, until the essential contradiction between the objectives social security is supposed to meet is understood. *And no serious reform of social security can be conceived of which is not founded on the basic principle of separating the two goals and attaining them through different institutions.*

The objective of social welfare could initially[20] be pursued through a state system of social welfare financed through the State Budget (that is to say, using the 'pay as you go' financing system), which provides the beneficiaries with benefits in accordance with their needs and guarantees that all *needy* citizens will receive a minimum pension.

On the contrary, the provision of pensions above the minimum level, in accordance with the wishes and the economic capacity of each citizen, together with the number of years over which s/he has contributed and the amount of the respective contributions, should be made through a system based on *individual and collective private pension schemes* and, therefore, on the traditional principles and techniques of the private life insurance sector.

Only in this way will these two goals, considered highly necessary in our society, be attained without contradictions or serious economic problems. And any partial reform of the public social security system must be carried out bearing in mind the key idea that the aforementioned contradiction is at the root of all the problems and, therefore, that the correct path for reform consists in the identification of this contradiction and gradually reducing and overcoming it.

The ideal model of social security from a libertarian perspective

The technical and ethical problems discussed in the previous section would be avoided if the financial resources for payment of the pensions for retirement, widowhood, loss of parents and disability came from three different sources: first, *social assistance*, at a minimum level, provided by individuals and subsidiarily by the state only to those who had not been able, for whatever reason, to make provisions for this minimum themselves. Second, and predominantly, there would be pensions coming from *private pension schemes* of an individual or collective nature and, third, we should mention the *individual savings* accumulated by each person in the course of his or her life.

Private pension schemes are private systems, mainly based on actuarial life insurance techniques and contracts, which emerge at the level of individuals, companies, groups of companies, professional associations, etc., by virtue of which a *financial fund* is created over the working life of the workers. This fund is able to afford payment of retirement pensions for life once said workers have retired. The fund also permits payment of the benefits which the scheme provides for in the case of death or disability (pensions for widowhood, loss of parents and disability).

This system, which is so easy to describe, has emerged spontaneously[21] and reached an important degree of development in the industrialized Western countries. It permits the simultaneous solution of two serious problems: first, it makes possible a significant increase in the country's overall savings, thus favouring the end of the crisis and economic development and, second, it solves the other aforementioned technical and ethical problems of social security, which are basically derived from the fact that one generation is responsible for another through the 'pay as you go' financing system.

The favourable effect on savings is produced because the contributions made to social security at present by the employers and workers, which are immediately used for the retired people, who receive them as pensions, would go into pension funds which would increase enormously the resources available to the domestic economy. This would stimulate investment, making possible companies and economic projects which are not viable today due to the lack of the necessary savings. The private pension scheme system would make possible, in the medium term: (1) *the financing of retirement pensions without tensions* or financial problems and without a negative effect on the country's overall savings which, to the contrary, the private system would foment; (2) *a reduction in labour costs*, decreasing the unemployment level in the country as, by the actuarial system of capitalization, making lower contributions than those which are currently made to the social security, the same level of pensions as that paid today could be guaranteed – this effect is very easy to understand, as at present no market interest is obtained from the social security contributions, while, by contrast, in a private pension scheme system the financial return on the contributions which constitute the funds is very important and significantly reduces the final total cost of the benefits; (3) *an increase in the real salary of the workers* as a result of the stimulation of the economy which would take place in the country and which would be the result of the greater capital accumulation produced by the abundance of financial funds for productive investment at lower interest rates.[22]

But, moreover, the private pension scheme system would solve the problem which currently arises from one generation supporting another, getting rid of the inevitable social tension and conflicts that arise from the present social security system, which we have already discussed.

The creation of pension funds during the working life of the employees would allow them, once they had retired, *not to depend on the younger generations*, but on the funds which they themselves had generated during their active period. It is simply the application, at a public level, of the elementary principle of cost auditing, by virtue of which costs must be recorded at the time they are incurred, not later. That is to say, the cost of the retirement pensions must be passed on to the products produced when people are working (private pension scheme system) and not to the goods and services which have been produced later by other people who have nothing to do with those who have retired (social security system based on 'pay as you go' financing). When each generation looks after itself, intergenerational conflicts, which have no solution and which have been artificially created by social security, are avoided.

Finally, private pension schemes give rise to a rich variety of solutions and alternatives in the area of the design of different formulae to determine the retirement pensions, age, systems, etc. Private pension schemes constitute a mechanism which allows the need for *flexibility*, felt by every company and individual, to be satisfied and makes it compatible with a much more flexible and *human* treatment of the retirement problem from the worker's point of view.

How would the market entirely solve the problem currently posed by social security? In principle, it is absurd to theorize *a priori* as to how the market would solve the problem of satisfying the demand for any new good or service in general.[23] However, we can benefit from the experience already spontaneously developed in the life insurance institutions, together with the development of the private pension schemes sector in many countries. We can distinguish two broad groups of instruments for financing private pension schemes, depending on whether or not a life insurance company is used. In the first system, the insurance policy or contract of the pension scheme includes the regulations of the plan, which set out in full detail the benefits and different aspects of the pension scheme. Second, a pension fund, which may or may not be a legal entity, may also be used. It would be managed by a professional manager and a financial institution would intervene for making and depositing the corresponding investments. These non-insured pension schemes are usually created in relation to groups of people sufficiently large to make the actuarial technical stability greater and in which, therefore, insurance is not so important.

The main advantages of the financing instruments offered by life insurance companies are of a technical and administrative nature. From the technical point of view, it should be remembered that life assurance companies have been solving, at an optimum level for almost two centuries, an identical problem to that which is now posed with the private pension schemes, that is to say, the guarantee of capital or pensions in the case of survival or death. The institution of life insurance has played its role to great perfection in economic and historical circumstances which have often been so adverse that other financial institutions have been unable to support them without the financial help of the government. This has been made possible thanks to a whole set of actuarial, financial and contract *principles* which have been developed and tested over many generations and that are still continually evolving in a spontaneous way.[24] From the administrative viewpoint, life insurance companies are accustomed to using uniform and computerized processes for a substantial number of policies which, together with the actuarial and financial services which pertain to them, make important economies of scale possible in the management of the pension schemes. Lastly, life insurance companies offer a very wide variety of private pension scheme contracts, which meet the different needs that exist on the market (deferred income contracts, deposit administration contracts, etc.).

Notwithstanding the foregoing, it is possible to conceive of many specific cases in which a fund separated from the corporation and not assured is considered most suitable. Above all, this would be the case of the large corporation in which the respective funds alone would be comparable to the strongest life assurance companies. However, it must be stressed that, although the fund is not contracted with a life assurance company, it is necessary to act as if it were, that is to say, using actuarial and financially conservative criteria, as well as the criterion of solvency, which pertain to this kind of institution.

Strategy for social security reform

It is necessary to begin with some consideration of the problems posed by the libertarian political strategy to achieve appropriate reforms, not only in the social security field, but also in any other field which forms part of the libertarian programme.

Some basic strategic principles

The most important danger of any libertarian strategy is to fall into *day-to-day political pragmatism*, forgetting the final objectives it is supposed to meet, because of the supposed political impossibility of achieving them in the short term. This strategy is very dangerous and, in the past, has had very prejudicial effects on libertarian ideology. Pragmatism has systematically meant that, in order to obtain or maintain political power, a consensus has been reached and political decisions have been adopted which have often been inconsistent with what should have been the ultimate goals from the libertarian viewpoint. Moreover, discussion focused exclusively on what was politically viable in the short term, relegating and completely forgetting the final objectives, has prevented the necessary detailed study and process of dissemination of such objectives, all of which has caused a continual loss of the contents of our ideology, which, in many cases, has become completely blurred and diluted by other programmes and ideologies.

The correct strategy for libertarian reform must be based, therefore, on a principle with a *dual* nature. This strategy consists, first, of constantly studying and *educating* the public about the final objectives which it is designed to meet in the medium and long term and, second, in carrying out a short-term policy which gets closer to these objectives and which is always *coherent* with them. Only this strategy will allow what may seem difficult to achieve today to become politically possible in the future.[25]

Returning now to our subject, social security, in the two following sections we are going to propose a process for the reform thereof which has been designed taking the strategy described into account.

Stages in the reform of the social security

Table 9.1 shows the four basic stages in social security reform. They will evolve naturally from right to left, that is to say, from less to more 'progressive' from the libertarian perspective. The first stage is characterized by the existence of a classic state social security system of the Bismarck kind.

Table 9.1 Stages in the Reform or the Social Security (SS)

4th Stage	3rd Stage	2nd Stage	1st Stage
1 Social assistance: (on the basis of demonstrated needs and charged to State Budget)	1 Minimum state pension (State Budget)	Levels: 1 Minimum state pension (State Budget)	Classic state Social Security
2 Private life insurance and pension funds (individual and collective and all of them voluntary)	2 Private pension schemes (Obligatory up to 50%–60% of salary, voluntary above this level)	2 Contributive SS pension (60%–70% of salary)	Single level (90%–100% of salary)
3 Individual savings	3 Individual savings	4 Private pension schemes (collective and voluntary) 5 Individual savings	

Table 9.2 Relative position of different countries

SWITZERLAND	UNITED KINGDOM	FRANCE	SPAIN	ITALY
Most progressive systems	(from the point of view of individual freedom)		*Least* progressive systems	

The second stage is characterized basically by the reduction of the benefits guaranteed by the state social security system and, as a consequence, by the appearance of a certain scope for the development of private pension schemes. Also, it may be considered that, in this second stage, there appears a dissociation from the point of view of the financing of the social security system, so that one begins to talk about a minimum pension for all citizens which is financed through the State Budget and upon which the pension guaranteed by the state social security system is superimposed. *The evolution from the first to the second stage appears to have been introduced very tentatively by some European socialist governments currently in power (Spain, Italy, etc.).*

In the third stage, although the system of compulsory inclusion in the public system of social provision is maintained, it is divided into two grades. The first grade is constituted, as in the second stage, by a minimum pension guaranteed by the state and financed through the State Budget. However, the second grade, although it is compulsory, may be managed through private pension schemes, with the public social security system playing only a subsidiary role (the case in England up to now) or none at all (the case in Switzerland).

The fourth stage corresponds to the final objective towards which we should be oriented and is based, as we have already explained, on reducing to the utmost the role of the state, i.e. the establishment of a system of welfare which grants minimum benefits only in the case of demonstrated need.[26] The rest of the provisions would be made *privately* through individual and collective private pension schemes.

In view of the above scheme, it is evident that the reform of social security from the libertarian viewpoint must have the following characteristics:

1 It must always mean an advance towards the left of the chart we are discussing. That is to say, it must always be directed towards the fourth stage.
2 In no case must political decisions which mean going completely or partially in an opposite direction be taken (criterion of coherence with the final objective).
3 In the short term, the model for social security reform must be clearly more daring than the one planned by many governments at present. That is to say, *we must establish a short term strategy for the reform of social security which permits a jump directly from stage one to stage three.* We will now establish the basic features of such a reform.

Basic lines of a short-term libertarian political project for the reform of social security

The proposed reform consists of passing from the first stage to the third stage, leaving for later, once the reform has been consolidated, the study of a necessary second chapter (the change from the third to the fourth stage).[27]

The reform of social security should be made in accordance with the following broad lines:

1 Private pension schemes should be permitted and supported, favouring their development and *incorporating all the young employees who are beginning their professional life*. In this way, the current group of retired and working persons becomes a group to be extinguished, thus placing a limit on the aggravation of the present problems.
2 At first, a minimum level of pension must be established (which could be fixed at around 50 per cent of the minimum wage), to be paid through the State Budget. The second level may, for now, continue to be obligatory, up to a determined level (not higher than 50 per cent of the final salary). However, *the management of this second level must be carried out through private pension schemes*, and only companies which do not voluntarily *contract out* their own fund will contribute to and continue to form part of the state social security system. As is logical, the private pension schemes can guarantee pensions above the minimum compulsory amount of this second level.
3 *Part of the contributions currently made to social security must be allowed to be paid into private pension schemes*. In accordance with the experience of other countries (United Kingdom and Chile), the companies who *opt* for the private management of the second level will have their contributions to social security lessened, but will continue to pay reduced public contributions in order to help finance the pensions which are currently being paid until they are extinguished.
4 Social security and the state must *continue to pay the pensions* of the pensioners who have already retired. These pensions must be financed through taxes and the remaining contributions which continue to be paid to social security.
5 It would be necessary to allow the people who are currently working complete freedom to decide whether to continue in the old social security system or to transfer to a new system based on private pension schemes. To do this, it would be necessary to recognize a *voucher equivalent to the actuarial value* of what had been paid to the state social security system, in relation to employees who, in the middle of their professional career, decide to be incorporated into the new private pension scheme system.
6 The present group of retired persons would be constituted by a group to be extinguished, which would disappear over one generation. This implies that the *financial cost of the transition to the new system would gradually decrease* over future years, freeing an increasing amount of social security contributions which could be used to increase the endowment of the private pension schemes, to decrease the overall cost to the companies and workers of maintaining the two systems (the new private pension scheme system and the old system in relation to the already retired pensioners, which will be extinguished), or to any combination of these two objectives.

7 In the proposed project, it is planned that the companies which do not opt to manage the problem of their employees' pensions through a private pension scheme continue participating and contributing to social security. However, it seems advisable to encourage the creation of private pension schemes (through their tax treatment[28] etc.) to such an extent that the state social security system really becomes a *system to be extinguished* over coming years, as it will be used by fewer and fewer companies and individuals (the case of Great Britain).

8 Lastly, it will be necessary to decide whether the transfer to the new system of private pension schemes will be the result of a *decision at company level* (as occurred in Great Britain, where the companies which decided to establish a private pension scheme had to cover all their employees, regardless of whether or not they are near retirement age) or *at an individual level* (as in Chile – or now in England – which is much more progressive in this respect). Both systems have their advantages and disadvantages and require a detailed analysis from the technical and political points of view which is clearly outside the scope of this work.[29]

Other strategic aspects

It evidently will not be possible to make a profound reform of social security, as we have proposed and as the economy and society demand, *until a series of social and political forces are mobilized in pursuit of it*. It is a process which it is necessary to design correctly.[30] The essential points of the specific strategy for a profound reform of social security must be, therefore, the following:

1 *A simple and clear scheme of where to go and why.* It is necessary, as we have already stated, to have a clear scheme as to what the ideal system of public and private provision should be. This scheme must be based on as many actuarial, statistical and economic studies as necessary, but, in the final analysis, it must crystallize into an elementary series of principles which we have already discussed, but from among which the following should be emphasized:
   - the problems of social security originate from the fact that it is aimed at achieving simultaneously the *contradictory* objectives of individual equity and social welfare;
   - the present social security system is not the most suitable system for achieving the desired objectives of social equity; these objectives must be pursued through a developed system of social welfare and private charity;
   - the best way of attaining the objectives of individual equity is through the private institutions which exist in the market and which are based on life insurance techniques, mutual benefits and individual and collective private pension funds;

The crisis and reform of social security   135

- the subsidiary system of social welfare must be financed through the State Budget;
- the system of individual provision must be financed by the participants in it (regardless of whether the corresponding contributions are legally paid by the companies or the workers);
- the reform should be undertaken as soon as possible: every step in the direction of any of these principles is positive;
- concession on any of these principles in return for other short-term advantages in political or collective negotiation must be avoided.

2 *The minds of the people who are currently retired must be set at rest.* This is a *sine qua non* condition for the success of any profound reform. Reassuring the people who are currently retired is indispensable, as it is a group of sufficient importance to be able to abort any democratic reform of the state social security system.[31]

3 *The public must be educated.* There must be a campaign which explains to the public how the social security system really works. People do not know that the contributions they pay in are spent every year on the pensions of those who are already retired and that, therefore, receipt of pensions in the future will depend, if social security is not reformed, solely and exclusively on the political circumstances of the moment and the supportive behaviour of younger generations.

Also, the working population must be made to see, numerically, the benefits which they could derive from the annual cost of social security if the corresponding contributions were paid into a private system based on capitalization.[32] Finally, it is necessary to explain how it is possible, over a period of adaptation, to transfer the necessary part of the present social security benefits to the private sector, while the acquired rights of the current pensioners are maintained.

Only if the general public know the truth of the situation and what is at stake, and the advantages or disadvantages of the alternative systems are explained, will it be willing to make the sacrifice implied by continuing to support those who are already retired while, at the same time, additional contributions are being transferred to the private system.

4 A *coalition of interests* must be gradually constructed.[33] It must be sufficiently broad and powerful to exert pressure for social security reform. The most significant groups which could form part of this coalition are the following: the business world, as it would be the first to benefit from the reform, as a result of the great increase in savings and, therefore, in the supply of financial resources, which would lead to the appearance of a system of private pension schemes and would make the financing of business projects easier and cheaper.

It must be stressed that the main interest of the business world is this, not the apparent reduction of costs which would arise from a reduction in the contributions. Moreover, the reduction in contributions seems almost impossible to achieve in the short term as, in any case, they would have to be raised to make possible the simultaneous financing of the current benefits and the constitution of the corresponding private pension funds. The only thing provided for, therefore, is a transfer of the current level of contributions, or of a part thereof, from public to private systems. In this respect, it is essential to assist in the identification of the true interests of businessmen and women in the social security field, as the understanding and present position of many of them on this matter is not encouraging. Within the business world, life insurance companies, financial institutions, etc., stand out as the main parties interested in the development of private pension schemes. It is not simply that the expansion of new markets is good for them, but that they are the institutions which, in view of their nature, should be able to respond to the new challenges.

Finally, the group which has the clearest interests in favour of the reform is made up of the great mass of workers who are young or still a long way away from retirement age. These are the people who, without doubt, will have to bear, often unfairly, the increasingly oppressive burden of financing social security if it is not reformed.

5 Lastly, *it is necessary to weaken the opposition.* There is no better way of weakening those who oppose the reform of the present social security system than taking steps along the correct path towards the privatization of its sphere of influence, explaining to the public the inexorable negative consequences of the current system and the advantages of the proposed one. Any reform of social security which takes the right direction, however modest it may be, reveals the great advantages that private pension schemes already have in countries where they have reached an appreciable degree of development and creates social interests in favour of maintaining and expanding them which are very difficult to resist. Moreover, the education of the public may lead to the initiation of social demands which take away the basis of the current system and weaken resistance.

In any case, it is necessary not to interrupt action even in the periods when parties of the left control the legislature. This is the case because even socialist governments are forced to adopt unpopular reform measures which, although timid, are oriented in the right direction. Moreover, it is precisely in the periods of opposition when it is necessary to establish strategies of resistance and to clarify concepts and objectives which may be carried out at a later date.[34]

The problem of medical assistance

It has normally been said that the main reasons which make it advisable that compulsory health insurance should exist are to maintain a high level of public health, to avoid the spread of infectious diseases and to minimize the possibility of a citizen becoming a public burden because of a precarious state of health. Although the analysis of these arguments is outside the scope of this work, it is important to recognize that the fact that compulsory health insurance should exist *does not in any way imply that this should be provided by the state under a monopoly*. On the contrary, there are powerful reasons against a state monopoly in the health insurance sphere and overwhelming arguments against the existence of universal medical assistance free of charge.

The arguments in favour of a free medical service usually contain two serious, fundamental errors. First, they are based on the assumption that the need for medical assistance can be established objectively and that it can and should be provided in all cases, regardless of economic considerations; second, they consider that this medical cover is, from the financial viewpoint, possible, as a complete medical service usually means the restoration of work efficiency or production capacity of the beneficiary workers and, therefore, it is believed that the system indubitably finances itself.

However, it should be emphasized that there is no objective yardstick to gauge the care and effort required in each specific case.[35] As medical science progresses, it becomes increasingly clear that *there are no limits* on the figure which it could be advantageous to spend in order to carry out as much as is objectively possible in the health field.

Moreover, it should be pointed out that, in the everyday individual valuation, it is not true that everything which can be done to ensure health and life has *absolute priority* over other needs. On the basis of different considerations, we constantly accept risks and decide whether a determined provision is profitable or not, weighing up whether it is better to cover the risk or attend to other needs. *Not even the richest man usually heeds all the demands which medical science makes in favour of health, as other tasks absorb his time, energy and resources.*

Someone must decide, therefore, in each specific case, whether the additional effort of the supplementary employment of resources in favour of health is worthwhile. The essential question is, therefore, whether the affected person is who should decide whether or not s/he is capacitated, by making an additional sacrifice, to receive greater attention, or whether this decision should be adopted by the state and its bureaucrats.[36]

The ideal solution in the medical assistance field is, from a libertarian viewpoint, very similar to the solution put forward with regard to the economic benefits of social security. The ideal objective would be that each person should, on his own account, establish the medical assistance system which he considered most suitable, comparing the economic costs of each possibility of cover and taking a decision in each case in accordance with his personal circumstances and valuations. The role of the state should, as always, be reduced to maintaining a level of public medical assistance for people who, due to a lack of resources, cannot ensure that they have the basic, minimum level of medical assistance which would be determined *a priori*.[37]

Experience in other countries indicates that the market is capable of providing, through health insurance companies, health maintenance organizations (HMOs) and private hospitals, private medicine which works freely and which reaches very high levels of medical assistance.

Along with the ideal scheme for medical assistance described, a practical reform project, politically possible to achieve in the short term, may be considered. In this project, the state could even continue to be the promoter, coordinator and controller of the health system in some of its different aspects and facets, but it would allow the *management* of medical assistance to be basically in private hands. *The state monopoly of medical assistance is not the best guarantee of efficiency, flexibility and speed.* The price to be paid in the long term will be certainly very high in terms of the efficiency, costs and quality of the benefits. It is, on the contrary, necessary to propitiate the emergence of non-monopolistic private organizations, the competition between which guarantees their efficiency, and where the efficiency of each system can be compared with that of the others.

Monopolistic medical assistance systems always constitute a threat to freedom, in view of the exclusive power to supply the benefits and make decisions regarding the health of individuals which such systems indubitably have, and always imply serious impositions on individuals by the persons who control them. It is evident that, in a democratic system, the capability of individuals to choose cannot be cast aside by submitting them to the iron tutelage of the state with regard to their health, without attacking the foundations of the democratic system itself. Moreover, it is a known fact that the state monopoly system in the health field is not more efficient in achieving the rapid advance of medicine, technical developments and research, which, in most cases, only achieve their successes as a result of private entrepreneurial initiatives.

In short, libertarian policy must be against the socialization of medicine and in favour of the management of what are considered to be the basic levels of medical assistance through private institutions which compete with each other in the market.

10 A critical analysis of central banks and fractional-reserve free banking from the Austrian School perspective[1]

The theory of money, bank credit and financial markets constitutes the most important theoretical challenge for economic science on the threshold of the twenty-first century. In fact, it is no exaggeration to say that, now that the 'theoretical gap' represented by the analysis of socialism has been covered, perhaps the least known and, moreover, most significant field is the monetary one. As Friedrich A. Hayek has rightly stated,[2] methodological errors, lack of theoretical knowledge and, as a result thereof, systematic coercion originating from the government prevail throughout this area. The fact is that social relations in which money is involved are by far the most abstract and difficult to understand, meaning that the social knowledge generated and implied thereby is the broadest, most complex and hardest to define. This explains why the systematic coercion practised by governments and central banks in this field is by far the most damaging and prejudicial. Moreover, this intellectual lag in monetary and banking theory has had serious effects on the evolution of the world economy. At present, in spite of all the sacrifices made to reorganize the Western economies after the crisis of the 1970s, the same errors of lack of financial and monetary control have unfailingly been committed, inexorably leading to the appearance of a new worldwide economic recession of considerable magnitude.

The fact that the recent monetary and financial abuses mainly originated in the second part of the decade of the 1980s in the policies applied by the supposedly conservative-libertarian administrations of the United States and United Kingdom dramatizes even more the importance of making theoretical advances in order to avoid, even in the libertarian field, political leaders such as Ronald Reagan and Margaret Thatcher committing the same errors. It is important to make such leaders capable of clearly identifying the only monetary and banking system truly compatible with a free society. In short, it is necessary to develop an entire research programme aimed at conceiving what the monetary and banking system of a non-interventionist society should be – a system which it is evident that many libertarians do not see at all clearly.

In the present article, we propose a new approach to the analysis of the problems of monetary and banking theory. We aim to provoke a renewal of the intellectual debate over some aspects of the doctrinal controversy between the advocates of free banking and those who defend central banking, particularly why the institution of central banking may not be a spontaneous and evolutionary result arising from the market. We also hope to throw some light on many specific problems of economic policy of great current importance, in particular the future evolution of the European monetary system.

The debate between the theorists of free banking and central banking

Beginning with the doctrinal controversy between the supporters of central banking and those who favour free banking, it is first necessary to state that our analysis does not entirely coincide with the nineteenth century controversy between the theorists of the banking and currency schools. In fact, many of those who defended free banking based their reasons on the fallacious and defective inflationist arguments of the banking school, while the majority of the currency school theorists aimed to attain their objectives of financial solvency and economic stability by the creation of a central bank to put a stop to monetary abuses.

From the beginning, however, some reputable currency school theorists considered it impossible and utopian to think that a central bank would not make the problems even worse. They were aware that the best way of putting a stop to the creation of fiduciary media and of achieving monetary stability was through a free banking system subject, like all other economic agents, to the traditional principles of civil and mercantile law. In addition, paradoxically, the majority of those who defended the tenets of the banking school were, in the end, pleased to accept the establishment of a central bank that, as last resort lender, guaranteed and perpetuated the expansionist privileges of private banking. The privileged bankers tried, in this way, to evade their commitments and devote themselves to the lucrative 'business' of creating fiduciary money through the expansion of credit, without having to worry excessively about liquidity problems, thanks to the support implied by the establishment of a central bank.

It is important to emphasize the fact that most of the currency school theorists, even though the heart of their theoretical contributions was correct, were incapable of appreciating that the same defects they rightly attributed to the freedom of the banks to issue fiduciary money in the form of notes were fully and identically reproduced, though in a more hidden, and therefore dangerous, way, in the 'business' of expansively granting credits against the banks' demand deposits. And, moreover, these theorists erred in proposing, as a more appropriate policy, the establishment of legislation which would merely put an end to the freedom to issue notes without backing and create a central bank to defend the most solvent monetary principles.

Only Ludwig von Mises, following the tradition of Cernuschi, Hübner and Michaelis, was capable of realizing that the currency school theorists' recommendation for a central bank was erroneous and that the best and only way of achieving the credible monetary principles of the school was through a free banking system subject, without any privileges, to private law. This failure on the part of the majority of the currency school theorists was fatal. It not only led to the fact that Peel's Act of 1844, in spite of its good intentions and its elimination of the free issue of bank notes, did not eliminate the creation of fiduciary credit. Instead, Peel's Act in effect led to the creation of a central banking system which, subsequently and above all due to the influence of banking school theorists like Marshall and Keynes, was used to justify and promote policies containing a lack of monetary control and financial abuses much worse than those it was originally intended to remedy.

The evolution of the banking system and the central bank

The central bank is not a natural product of the development of the banking system.[3] On the contrary, it is coercively imposed from outside the market as a result of governmental action. Such action, as a consequence of a series of historical accidents, gave rise to a monetary and financial system very different from that which would have emerged spontaneously under a free banking system subject, without privileges, to.private law and not coerced by government through the central bank. It is impossible to know what knowledge and institutions the banking entrepreneurs would have created freely if they had been subject to the general principles of law and not to any kind of state coercion.[4] Yet we may imagine a generalized system of investment funds in which current 'deposits' would be invested, and endowed with great liquidity, but without a guarantee of receiving the face value (which would be subject to evolution of the market value of the corresponding units); a network of entities providing payment and accounting services, etc., operating in free competition and charging fees for their services; and, separately, *without any connection with credit*, a series of private institutions devoted to the extraction, design and offer of different types of private money (also charging a small margin for their services).[5]

In fact, the current central banking system is merely the logical and inevitable result of the gradual and surreptitious introduction by private bankers, historically in complicity with the governments, of a banking system based on a fractional reserve. And it is here essential not to fall into the same intellectual trap as the majority of the theorists who have defended the free banking system. With the honourable exception of Mises and very few others,[6] they do not realize that the only way to achieve a truly free banking system is to re-establish the legal principle according to which it is necessary to keep a reserve of 100 per cent of the sums of money received as demand deposits.

In the final analysis, the question is the application in the monetary and banking field of Hayek's seminal idea according to which, whenever a traditional rule of conduct is violated, either through institutional coercion on the part of the government or by the latter's granting special privileges to certain persons or entities, damaging and undesired consequences will, sooner or later, appear, seriously prejudicing the spontaneous social process of cooperation.

The traditional rule of conduct violated in the case of the banking business is the principle of law according to which, in the contract for the deposit of fungible money (also called *irregular deposit*), the traditional obligation of *custody*, which is the essential element of all non-fungible deposits, requires that, at all times, a reserve of 100 per cent of the amount of fungible money received in deposit be maintained. This means that all acts which make use of that money, specifically the granting of credits against it, are a violation of that principle and, in short, an illegitimate act of undue appropriation.

In the continental European juridical tradition, there is a long-established principle that dates back to the old Roman Law according to which *custody, in irregular deposits, consists precisely of the obligation to always have an amount equal to that received at the depositor's disposal.* The custodian of a deposit must 'have always available a quantity and quality equal to that received of certain things', regardless of whether they are continually renewed or substituted. This requirement is the equivalent, for fungible goods like money, of the continued existence of the item *in individuo* for infungible goods.[7] This general legal principle which requires 100 per cent reserve banking has been upheld, even in this century, by French and Spanish jurisprudence.

A ruling of the Court of Paris of 12 June 1927 condemned a banker for the offence of undue appropriation because he had used, in accordance with common banking practice, the funds which he had received on deposit from his clients. Another decision of the same Court dated 4 January 1934 made the same ruling, and even more curious was the ruling of the Court of First Level which heard the case of the bankruptcy of the Bank of Barcelona, according to which the depositor's power to draw cheques implies for the depositee the obligation to *always* have funds at the disposal of the current account holder, making it unacceptable that a bank consider the funds deposited in a current account in cash as belonging exclusively to itself.[8] We should add that the 'undue appropriation' arises when the undue act (lending the amount deposited) is committed, and not when it is discovered a long time afterwards (generally by the depositor at the counter of a bank which cannot return his money to him). Moreover, the trite argument that the 'law of large numbers' allows the banks to act safely with a fractional reserve cannot be accepted, since the degree of probability of an untypical withdrawal of deposits is not, in view of its own nature, an insurable risk.

The Austrian theory of economic cycles has perfectly explained how the system of fractional reserve banking itself generates economic recessions *endogenously* and recurrently and, hence, generates the need to liquidate wrongly induced investment projects, to return bad loans and withdraw deposits on a massive scale. And, as all insurance theorists know, the consequences of an event (untypical withdrawal of deposits) which is not totally independent of the 'insurance' itself (fractional reserve) are not technically insurable, for reasons of *moral hazard*.[9]

In the course of history, bankers were soon tempted to violate the above-mentioned rule of conduct, using the money of their depositors to their own benefit.[10] This happened shamefacedly and secretly at first, since the bankers were still conscious of acting incorrectly. It occurred, for example, with the Bank of Amsterdam, when the activities of the bank were carried out, for the reasons mentioned, according to the words of Sir James Steuart, with the *maximum secrecy*.[11] It should be noted that the entire prestige of the Bank of Amsterdam was based on the belief that it held a reserve of 100 per cent, a principle which, only fifteen years previously, David Hume believed to be in force.[12] And in 1776, Adam Smith mentioned that, at that time, the Bank of Amsterdam *continued to say* that it held a cash ratio of 100 per cent.[13]

Only later did the bankers achieve the open and legal violation of the traditional legal principle, when they were fortunate enough to obtain from the government the *privilege* of using part of the money of their depositors to their own benefit (generally in the form of credits, often granted initially to the government itself). In this way the relationship of complicity and the coalition of interests which now traditionally exists between governments and banks commenced, explaining perfectly the relationship of intimate 'comprehension' and 'cooperation' which exist between both types of institutions and which, nowadays, may be observed, with slight differences of nuance, in all Western countries at all levels. Furthermore, the bankers soon realized that the violation of the traditional legal principle mentioned above gave rise to financial activity which was highly lucrative for them, but which always required the existence of a last resort lender, or central bank, to provide the necessary liquidity at the difficult moments which, as experience demonstrated, always recurred.[14]

The fractional-reserve banking system: the central bank and the theory of economic cycles

The inauspicious social consequences of this *privilege* granted to the bankers (but not to any other individual or entity) were not completely understood until the development, by Mises and Hayek, of the Austrian theory of economic cycles.[15] In short, what the Austrian School theorists have shown is that persistence in pursuing the theoretically impossible objective – from the legal, contractual and technical-economic viewpoints – of offering a contract that simultaneously tries to combine the best features of investment funds (especially the possibility of obtaining interest on the 'deposits') with the traditional deposit contract (which, by definition, must permit withdrawal of its face value at any moment) must inexorably, sooner or later, lead to uncontrolled expansion in the monetary supply, inflation and the generalized incorrect allocation of productive resources at a microeconomic level. In the final analysis, the result will be recession, the rectification of errors induced in the productive structure by prior credit expansion and massive unemployment.

It is necessary to realize that the privilege granted to the banks permitting them to carry on activity with a fractional reserve, implies an evident attack against a correct definition and defence of the property rights of the depositors by the governmental authorities. This inevitably generates, as is always the case when property rights are not appropriately defined, the typical effect of 'tragedy of the commons', by virtue of which the banks are inclined to try to get ahead and expand their corresponding credit base before, and more than, their competitors. Therefore, a banking system based on a fractional reserve will always tend towards more or less uncontrolled expansion, even if it is controlled by a central bank which, in contrast to what has normally been the case, is seriously concerned about controlling it and establishing limits. In this respect, Anna J. Schwartz reaches the conclusion that many modern theorists of the free banking system do not completely understand: that the system of interbank clearing houses which they propose does not act as a brake on credit expansion if all the banks decide to expand their credit simultaneously, to a greater or lesser extent.[16] This phenomenon, which had already been set out by Ludwig von Mises in his brilliant explanation of the free banking system,[17] drove us to seek its explanation in the typical process of the 'tragedy of the commons': the entire expansive process originates, as we have seen, from *a privilege* that contravenes property rights. Each bank internalizes all the profits obtained from expanding its credit, making the corresponding costs fall, dilutedly, upon the entire banking system. For this reason, it is easy to understand that a mechanism of interbank compensation or clearing houses may put a stop to individual, isolated expansion initiatives in a free banking system with fractional reserves, but is useless if all the banks, to a greater or lesser extent, are carried away by 'optimism' in the granting of credits.

The proposal to establish a banking system with a 100 per cent reserve was already included in the first edition of *The Theory of Money and Credit*, published by Mises in 1912, in which the author reached the conclusion that

> it is obvious that the only way of eliminating human influence on the credit system is to suppress all further issue of fiduciary media. The basic conception of Peel's Act ought to be restated and more completely implemented than it was in the England of his time by including the issue of credit in the form of bank balances within the legislative prohibition.[18]

Subsequently, Mises again dealt with the matter, even more explicitly, in 1928[19] and especially in the appendix on *Monetary Reconstruction* which he incorporated into the English edition of *The Theory of Money and Credit* in 1953, where he expressly states that the main thing is that the government should no longer be in a position to increase the quantity of money in circulation and the amount of cheque book money not fully – that is, 100 per cent – covered by deposits paid in by the public.[20]

Hayek already referred to this proposal in 1937[21] and it is evident that Hayek, like Mises, proposes the free choice of currency and banking system as a means to achieve, in the final analysis, a banking system based on a 100 per cent cash ratio.[22] After Mises, the writer who has, in modern times, defended the elimination of the banking system as we know it today with the greatest determination and brilliance is, without doubt, Murray N. Rothbard.[23]

Also in modern times, Maurice Allais has defended the principle of the 100 per cent reserve, although it is true that he defends it as a means to facilitate the monetary policies of governments, preventing their elastic and distortive expansion through the fractional reserve banking system.[24] Maurice Allais, in this respect, merely follows the now abandoned Chicago School tradition in favour of the 100 per cent cash ratio in order to make the monetary policies of the governments more effective and predictable.[25] Although monetary policy would be more predictable with a 100 per cent cash ratio, all the Chicago theorists are ingenuous if they think that the government can and will want to carry out a stable monetary policy. This ingenuousness is parallel and similar to that shown by the modern fractional-reserve free banking theorists, when they trust that spontaneous clearing house mechanisms can put a brake on a simultaneous and agreed expansion by a majority of banks. *The only correct solution for a society free of privileges and economic cycles is, therefore, banking which is free but subject to the law, i.e. with a reserve ratio of 100 per cent.*

The monetary and banking system in a free society

In short, the main defect of the majority of the theorists who defend free banking is their failure to realize that the demand for a 100 per cent reserve requirement is theoretically inseparable from their proposal. Specifically, they have not appreciated that all the defects which advocates of the central bank see in the free banking system lose their potential and completely disappear if it is put into practice on the basis of traditional legal principles. Or, to put it another way, using Mises' words, the issue is to subject the banks to the traditional principles of civil and mercantile law, according to which each individual and each enterprise must meet its obligations in strict accordance with what is literally established in each contract.[26]

This error is very generalized and affects, in particular, the interesting and broad literature which has been developed as a result of the great echo arising from the publication of Hayek's book on the *Denationalization of Money*, together with the important economic and financial crisis which took place at the end of the 1970s. The most important comment I have on all this literature is that, apart from a few exceptions, it uses the defence of a free banking system to put forward whims typical of the old 'banking school', the erroneous principles of which were demonstrated long ago. Moreover, all this literature, which is headed by the works of White, Selgin and Dowd,[27] among others, forgets that, as we have argued, the only way of getting rid of the central bank and its excesses is by eliminating the fractional-reserve privilege which private bankers currently exploit.

If one wishes to defend a truly stable financial and monetary system for the next century, one which immunizes our economies against crises and recessions as much as is humanly possible, it will be necessary to establish three conditions: (1) complete freedom of choice of currency; (2) a free banking system; and (3), most importantly, that all the agents involved in the free banking system are subject to and follow, in general, traditional legal rules and principles. In particular, the principle according to which nobody, not even the bankers, should enjoy the privilege of lending something which has been deposited with him as a demand deposit (i.e. to maintain a banking system with a reserve of 100 per cent).

The modern free banking theorists erroneously consider (due, among other things, to their lack of a juridical background) that the 100 per cent reserve requirement would be an inadmissible *administrative* interference with individual freedom. They do not realize that, far from implying systematic administrative coercion by the government, as we have seen, this precept is merely the application of the traditional principle of *property rights*. In other words, they do not realize that the famous anonymous phrase of an American quoted by Tooke, according to which 'free banking is equivalent to free swindling',[28] is applicable to free banking not subject to law (and which therefore has fractional reserves). In the final analysis, the defence of free banking must be made, not as a means to exploit the lucrative possibilities of credit expansion, but as an *indirect* means to get closer to the ideal model of free banking with a 100 per cent reserve requirement, which, additionally, must be *directly* pursued by all the legal means available in each historical circumstance.[29]

Although the foregoing economic policy recommendations may appear *utopian* and very distant from the practical problems we have to deal with, especially with regard to the design and management of a European monetary system, they indicate, at all times, at least the appropriate direction which reform should take and dangers that must be avoided. Thus, it seems clear that we should reject both a system of monopolistic national currencies which compete among themselves in a chaotic environment of flexible exchange rates and the move towards the creation of a central European bank.

This proposed central European bank would prevent competition among currencies over a wide economic area, would not confront the challenges of banking reform, would not guarantee a monetary stability which is at least as great as that of the most stable national currency at each moment and would set up, in short, a definitive obstacle to making subsequent reforms in the right direction.

Perhaps the most practicable and appropriate model in the short and medium terms is, therefore, to introduce throughout Europe the complete freedom of choice of public and private currencies inside and outside the Community, linking the national currencies which, for reasons of historical tradition, continue in use to a system of fixed exchange rates. These rates would discipline the monetary policy of each country in accordance with the policy of that country which, at each historical moment, is carrying out the most solvent and stable monetary policy. In this way, at least the door would remain open for some nation-state of the EEC to have the possibility of advancing along the three lines of monetary and banking reform already indicated,[30] forcing its partners in the Community to follow its monetary leadership along the right lines. (This, and nothing else, appears to have been the essence of the project defended by Margaret Thatcher and the incorrectly named group of 'Eurosceptics' who follow her, among whom this author is included, for the monetary future of the EEC).

It is evident that the definitive work on monetary and banking theory, in the light of the historic controversy taking place between those who favour free banking and those who support a central bank, has not yet been written. Therefore, we are afraid that it is not unrealistic to think that the world will continue to suffer, recurrently, very dangerous economic recessions as long as the central banks maintain their monopoly on currency issue while the privilege granted to the bankers by the governments is not abolished. And, in the same way as we began this article, we would dare to say that, after the historic, theoretical and actual fall of socialism, the main theoretical challenge faced by both professional economists and lovers of freedom well into this century will consist in fighting with all their strength against both the institution of central banking and the maintenance of the privilege currently enjoyed by those who practise private banking activities.

11 A critical note on fractional-reserve free banking[1]

Introduction

Over the last fifteen years, there has been a revival of some of the economic doctrines of the old Free-Banking School under the auspices of a group of theorists who defend the idea that fractional-reserve free banking would not only lead to fewer distortions and financial crises than those generated by the current central banking system, but also tend to eliminate economic recessions. We will group these theorists together under the name of the 'Fractional-Reserve Free Banking School'.[2] This school is formed by a coalition of theorists with heterogeneous origins.[3] Thus, its components include distinguished members of the Austrian School, such as Lawrence White,[4] George A. Selgin[5] and, more recently, Steven Horwitz;[6] members of the English Subjectivist School, like Kevin Dowd;[7] and, lastly, monetarists like David Glasner,[8] Leland B. Yeager[9] and Richard Timberlake.[10] Even Milton Friedman, although he cannot be considered to form part of this new school, has gradually leant towards it, above all after his disappointment on seeing the failure of the central banks when putting his well-known monetary rule proposal into practice.[11]

Furthermore, some modern theorists of the Fractional-Reserve Free Banking School, led by George Selgin, have proposed a theory of money supply under free banking that, using the analytical framework of monetary equilibrium–disequilibrium developed by the Monetarist and Keynesian Schools during the first third of the last century,[12] aims to show that fractional-reserve free banking would merely adjust the creation of fiduciary media (bank notes and deposits) to public demand for them. Thus, they argue that fractional-reserve free banking would tend to achieve 'monetary equilibrium' better than other alternative systems, as it would adapt the supply of money to its demand more efficiently.

In very simplified terms, this argument is based on considering what happens if there is an increase in the demand for fiduciary media by the economic agents, assuming an unchanging supply of bank reserves of commodity money.[13] The reasoning is that, if this occurs, the flow of the exchange of fiduciary media for the reserves of the banks will decrease, meaning that the latter will increase and the banks, anxious to obtain higher profits and aware that they now need less 'prudential' reserves, will expand credit and the issue of bank notes, giving rise to an increase in the issue of fiduciary media that will tend to respond and adapt itself to the *previous* increase in the demand for them. The contrary occurs in the event of a decrease in the demand for fiduciary media: the economic agents will increase the flow of the exchange of fiduciary media for bank reserves, meaning that the banks will feel their solvency to be endangered and will be forced to reduce credit and decrease the issue of deposits and bank notes. Thus, the decrease in the supply of fiduciary media will follow the *previous* decrease in the demand for them.

This analysis of 'monetary equilibrium' is reminiscent of some arguments of the old Banking School concerning the 'needs of trade'. According to these arguments, the creation of fiduciary media by private banks would not be harmful if it responded to an increase in the 'needs' of the traders.[14] According to the new theory of 'monetary equilibrium' in free banking, the creation of fiduciary media (bank notes and deposits) by private banks will not generate economic cycles because *it will only tend to respond to an increase in the demand for such instruments on the part of the public*. Although the embryo of this new and refined version of the 'needs of trade' theory had already been set forth in Lawrence H. White's book on *Free Banking in Britain*,[15] it was nevertheless not developed by this author, but by one of his most distinguished students, George A. Selgin. We will now make a critical study of Selgin's theory of 'monetary equilibrium' under free banking in more detail and, in general, of fractional-reserve free banking.

Consideration of the changes in the demand for fiduciary media as an exogenous variable

Modern fractional-reserve free banking theorists base their analysis on considering that the demand for money in the form of fiduciary media is a variable which is exogenous to the system and increases or decreases at the will of the economic agents. Therefore, for White and Selgin, the main virtue of the free banking system is that it adapts the issue of deposits and bank notes to the increases and decreases in the demand for them.[16] *However, this demand would not always be exogenous to the free banking system, but could be determined endogenously by the system itself.*

It is understandable that the theorists of the Fractional-Reserve Free Banking School usually begin their monetary equilibrium analysis by assuming that there have been sudden variations in the demand for fiduciary media, the origin and etiology of which they rarely explain.[17] It is as if they were aware that, on the supply side, the Austrian analysis has demonstrated that credit expansion causes important distortions of the economy which seem to justify a rigid monetary system[18] that prevents the monetary expansions and contractions generated by their fractional-reserve free banking system. On the monetary supply side, therefore, it seems that the theoretical arguments of the Austrians support the establishment of a relatively inelastic monetary system such as the pure gold standard with a 100 per cent reserve requirement for bank demand deposits.[19] Consequently, it is easy to understand that anyone who wants to justify theoretically a fractional-reserve free banking system, that may give rise to significant increases and decreases in the supply of fiduciary media, must inevitably resort to the monetary demand side of the problem, in the hope of being able to show that when these modifications in the fiduciary media supply occur (and they will, in a fractional-reserve free banking system) it is because they always satisfy *prior* and entirely independent variations in the demand for them. Thus, a hypothetical 'monetary equilibrium', which existed previously and had been altered by an exogenous variation in the demand for fiduciary media, would be re-established.

However, the evolution of events may often be different to what these theorists indicate. It could start, not with autonomous or original movements in the demand for fiduciary media, but rather in the manipulation of the monetary supply (credit expansion) which, to a variable extent, all fractional-reserve free banking systems can generate autonomously and exogenously. These increases in credit expansion will distort the productive structure and provoke an economic cycle which leads to sudden variations in the demand for money and fiduciary media, especially during the last stages of each boom and during periods of crisis and recession.

It is true that, if there exist many free banks that are not supported by a central bank, credit expansion will stop much earlier than in an environment in which the central bank orchestrated and drove it, and also used its liquidity to support any banks which might be in danger. This is the main argument in favour of fractional-reserve free banking originally developed by Parnell and also later considered as a *second-best* by Mises.[20] However, it is one thing to affirm that completely free banking will find its limits to the credit expansion *earlier*, and quite a different one to say that in no case will the credit expansion generated by a fractional-reserve free banking system distort the productive structure because it will only tend to re-establish a hypothetical 'monetary equilibrium'. In fact, Ludwig von Mises himself makes it very clear that *all* credit expansion distorts the productive system, thus rejecting the essence of the modern theory of monetary equilibrium. Mises states that 'the notion of "normal" credit expansion is absurd. *Issue of additional fiduciary media, no matter what its quantity may be, always sets in motion those changes in the price structure the description of which is the task of the theory of the trade cycle*'.[21]

The theory of 'monetary equilibrium' under fractional-reserve free banking does not recognize that the *supply of fiduciary media can generate, to a large extent, its own demand*. In other words, modern free banking theory shares the essential error of the old Banking School which stems, as Ludwig von Mises showed, from not having realized that the credit demand from the public is a magnitude which depends precisely on the banks' willingness to lend. Thus, banks which are not too concerned about their future solvency are in a situation where they can expand credit and place new fiduciary media in the market simply by reducing the interest they ask on the new loans they create and making easier the other contractual conditions they normally require for granting their new credits.[22] Moreover, the increase in money to which the credit expansion gives rise tends, at least during an initial period, to increase the demand for fiduciary media. In fact, those economic agents who are not entirely aware that an inflationary process of expansion has commenced will see how the prices of certain goods and services start to grow relatively faster and, maintaining the hope that these prices will have to return to their 'normal' level, will probably decide to increase their demand for fiduciary media. To quote Mises again, while the first stage of this inflationary process lasts,

> the prices of many goods and services are not yet adjusted to the altered money relation. There are still people in the country who have not yet become aware of the fact that they are confronted with a price revolution which will finally result in a considerable rise of all prices, although the extent of this rise will not be the same in the various commodities and services. These people still believe that prices one day will drop. Waiting for this day, they restrict their purchases and concomitantly increase their cash holdings.[23]

Therefore, it is not only that the banks of a real fractional-reserve free banking system can initiate credit expansion *unilaterally*; also, over significant periods of time, the increase in the supply of fiduciary media can produce an increase in its own demand, which will last until the public understands and begins to distrust the economic boom situation and realizes that there is going to be a general price rise. Afterwards, during the last stages of the boom and when confidence is shaken during the recession, people can also tend to increase their demand for bank money.

We may conclude that if the origin of the mutations in the demand for money is in the free banking supply of fiduciary media, the essential foundation of the theory of monetary equilibrium under fractional-reserve free banking, according to which the supply of fiduciary media simply adjusts itself to the demand for them, disappears. In fact, it could be the demand for fiduciary media which, at least for significant time periods, tends to adjust itself to the greater monetary supply generated by the banks in the form of credits.

Possible sources of unilateral credit expansions in real fractional-reserve free banking systems

There are several reasons that may make it possible for a real fractional-reserve free banking system to generate credit expansions that do not correspond to previous variations in the demand for fiduciary media.

First, the analysis of monetary equilibrium in a free banking system shares many of the limitations of the traditional neoclassical analysis which, in both microeconomic and macroeconomic fields, merely explains how a hypothetical final state of rest of the social processes (monetary equilibrium) is reached as a result of the strictly maximizing behaviour of the economic agents (private bankers). The Austrian economic analysis, on the other hand, places the emphasis on the dynamic entrepreneurial process that is continually taking place in the market, rather than on equilibrium. Each entrepreneurial act serves to coordinate and establish a *trend* towards equilibrium which, however, is never reached because, during this process, new information is continually generated by the entrepreneurs and other changes in market circumstances occur, making it impossible to attain. Applying this well-known theoretical scheme of the dynamic entrepreneurial process studied by the Austrians to the model of monetary equilibrium, it is clear that, in a real fractional-reserve free banking system, a perfect adjustment between the issue of fiduciary media and the demand for them, included so mechanically in the model, cannot be accepted, except in a very imperfect and, at most, approximate way.

In real life, many banking entrepreneurs, each of whom has his or her own personal alertness, subjective interpretation of the information from the external world (including the evaluation, optimistic or otherwise, of the evolution of economic events, of what may be considered to be a 'prudential' level of reserves and of his or her own solvency) and entrepreneurial creativity, will take day-to-day decisions on the volume of fiduciary media to be issued in an environment of ineradicable uncertainty. It is obvious that many errors will be committed during this entrepreneurial process in the form of unilateral issues of fiduciary media that distort the real productive economy. The truth is that errors will tend to be discovered and eliminated, but only over a prolonged process, which may last a longer or shorter time, during which certain volumes of fiduciary media will be produced by error and will cause *real* damage to the productive structure. If to this we add the intimate relations that exist between the supply of fiduciary media and the demand for them by the public, mentioned under the preceding heading, we can understand the great problem posed in order to reach monetary equilibrium in the real world of fractional-reserve free banking: the banking entrepreneurs, through a trial and error process, will try to adapt their issue of fiduciary media to a demand that, first, they do not know and, second, tends, in turn, to vary as a consequence of the inevitable errors committed by the bankers is the form of 'undue issues' of fiduciary media during the adjustment process. It is debatable, and will depend, above all, on the historical circumstances in each particular case, whether, in fact, the bankers' entrepreneurial process of coordination will converge in the direction of some 'equilibrium', but what cannot, in our opinion, be denied is that, at least during the coordination process, errors will be committed, fiduciary media will be unduly issued in the form of a credit expansion and the productive structure will be distorted, as shown by the Austrian theory of economic cycles.[24]

The same may be said, in the second place, with regard to the possibilities of the 'in-concert' expansion of fiduciary media arranged *simultaneously* by a larger or more reduced group of bankers, or with regard to the chances that mergers or acquisitions take place among the free banks, in order to 'pool' and better manage the 'prudential' reserves they hold, thus increasing their capacity to create fiduciary media in order to raise their profits.[25] Unless the advocates of a free banking system wish to avoid the adoption of these types of entrepreneurial strategies by applying strict antitrust legislation in the banking industry (which we doubt), it seems possible that this kind of phenomenon will often occur in a fractional-reserve free banking system. In relation to the pre-arranged expansion, George A. Selgin argues that the 'spontaneous in-concert expansions will be self-correcting' because the growth in total clearings will increase the *variance* of clearing debits and credits.[26] However, apart from the fact that, in his model, Selgin always assumes a fixed amount of banking reserves and that a number of authors doubt that this mechanism is effective,[27] even if, for dialectical purposes, we suppose that Selgin is right, it may again be argued that the adjustment would never be perfect or immediate and that, during their readjustment and coordination process, in-concert expansions and mergers may facilitate the unilateral issue of significant volumes of new fiduciary media which may give rise to an economic cycle.

Finally, in the third place, a fractional-reserve free banking system leads to unilateral increases in the issue of fiduciary media that do not correspond to previous increases in demand when an increase in the global stock of commodity money (gold) used by the banks as prudential reserves takes place. If we remember that, historically, the worldwide stock of gold has increased at an annual rate of between 1 and 5 per cent,[28] it is clear that a free banking system could permit, even if it were only as a consequence of annual worldwide gold production, a significant growth (also between 1 and 5 per cent annually) in the issue of fiduciary media that does not originate from an increase in demand.[29]

We may, therefore, conclude that, even in a fractional-reserve free banking system, significant inflationary processes[30] and serious economic crises[31] may take place.

The theory of 'monetary equilibrium' in fractional-reserve free banking is based on an exclusively macroeconomic analysis

Attention should be drawn to the fact that modern analysis of monetary equilibrium in a fractional-reserve free banking system ignores the *microeconomic* effects which arise from the increases and decreases in the supply of fiduciary media generated by the banking system. In other words, even accepting, for dialectic purposes, that the origin of all evils is, as the fractional-reserve free banking theorists assume, unexpected mutations in the demand for bank money by the economic agents, it is evident that the fiduciary media supply generated by the banking system to accommodate these changes in the money demand do not arrive instantaneously at the precise economic agents whose valuations in respect of holding new fiduciary media have been modified. They rather flow into the market through very specific points and in a very precise way: step by step in a temporal process and in the form of credits granted by reducing interest rates and received, in the first place, by certain entrepreneurs and investors who thus tend to initiate new investment projects which distort the structure of production.

It is not surprising, therefore, that the modern theorists of the Fractional-Reserve Free Banking School tend to ignore some essential elements of the Austrian theory of economic cycles. This Austrian theory is difficult to fit in with their analysis of the issue of fiduciary media in a fractional-reserve free banking system. This is because they normally take refuge in an exclusively macroeconomic analysis and use instruments which, like the equation of exchange or the concept of 'price level', tend precisely to conceal the important microeconomic phenomena which take place in an economy when there is credit expansion and the amount of fiduciary media changes (variation in relative prices and intertemporal discoordination).

In normal market processes, the supply of consumer goods and services tends to vary in accordance with the demand for them and the new production of this type of goods tends to reach precisely the consumers whose subjective valuation of them has increased. However, the situation in relation to fiduciary media is very different: the supply of fiduciary media does not generally go immediately and *directly* into the pockets of the economic agents whose demand for them may have increased, but reaches them after a long and sinuous process, passing previously through the pockets of many other economic agents and distorting the whole productive structure during this long transitional phase.

When the fractional-reserve free bankers create new fiduciary media, they do not hand them directly to the economic agents that feel a greater demand for bank money. They grant credits to entrepreneurs, who receive and *entirely invest* them without taking any account at all of the proportion at which the final holders of the new fiduciary media desire to consume and invest. And thus it is very possible that, if social preferences in consumption and investment have not changed, the new fiduciary media created by the banks to offset the already increased demand for bank money will at least partially be *used to increase consumer goods* expenditure, forcing the relative prices of this type of goods to rise. As Hayek says,

> so long as any part of the additional income thus created is spent on consumer's goods (i.e. unless all of it is saved), the prices of consumer's goods must rise permanently in relation to those of various kinds of input. And this, as will by now be evident, cannot be lastingly without

A critical note on fractional-reserve free banking 155

effect on the relative prices of the various kinds of input and on the methods of production that will appear profitable.[32]

Hayek clarifies even more our position when he concludes that:

> All that is required to make our analysis applicable is that, when incomes are increased by investment, the share of the additional income spent on consumer's goods during every period of time should be larger than the proportion by which the new investment adds to the output of consumer's goods during the same period of time. And there is of course no reason to expect that more than a fraction of the new income [created by credit expansion], and certainly not as much as has been newly invested, will be saved, because this would mean that practically all the income earned from the new investment would have to be saved.[33]

In order to illustrate our argument, we will assume that there is an increase in the demand for fiduciary media without any variation in the proportion in which the economic agents wish to consume or invest.[34] If these conditions exist, the economic agents will be forced to reduce their monetary demand for consumer goods, to sell bonds and investment assets and, above all, to decrease their reinvestment in the different stages of the process of production, until they are able to accumulate the higher volume of bank money desired. As we assume that the time preference has not varied, using Hayek's well-known triangular diagrams[35] to describe the changes that have taken place in the productive structure, we see, in Figure 11.1, how the increase in

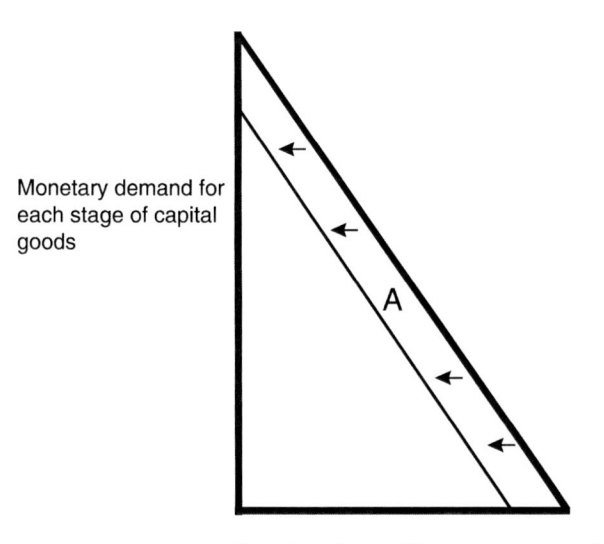

Figure 11.1

the demand for fiduciary media causes the hypotenuse of the triangle to move to the left, which indicates that there is a lower monetary demand for consumption and investment, although the proportion between them remains intact. In this figure, surface A represents the new 'hoarding' of fiduciary media by individuals:

The essential conclusion of the theory of monetary equilibrium in a fractional-reserve free banking system is that the banks will respond to the increase that takes place in the demand for fiduciary media by expanding them by an identical volume (represented by surface A) to that which will leave the productive structure intact, as shown in Figure 11.2. However, it should be remembered that the new volume of fiduciary media created by the banks is not delivered directly to its final users (the economic agents who increased their stock of bank money by the amount of A in Figure 11.1), but is, at first, granted as loans to the entrepreneurs who spend the whole of the volume represented by surface A on investment goods, giving rise, at the beginning, to a productive structure like the one shown in Figure 11.3. However, this more capital intensive structure cannot be maintained in the long term since, once the newly created fiduciary media reach their final users (who already accumulated the new banking money they wanted from the beginning, shown in Figure 11.1), they spend them, under our hypothesis, on consumer and investment goods in a proportion identical to that shown in Figures 11.1 and 11.2. If we place Figure 11.3 on top of Figure 11.2, it is easy to observe the distortion that takes place in the productive structure.

In Figure 11.4, the shaded area B represents the investment projects undertaken erroneously as a consequence of the fact that the whole new

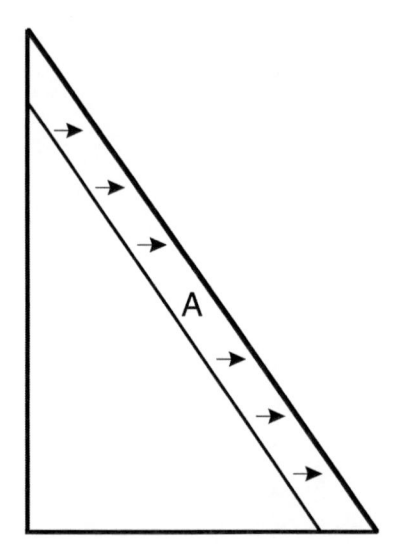

Figure 11.2

A critical note on fractional-reserve free banking 157

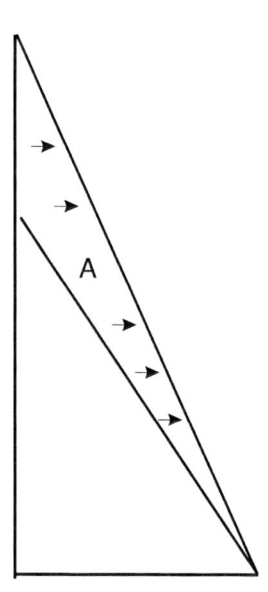

Figure 11.3

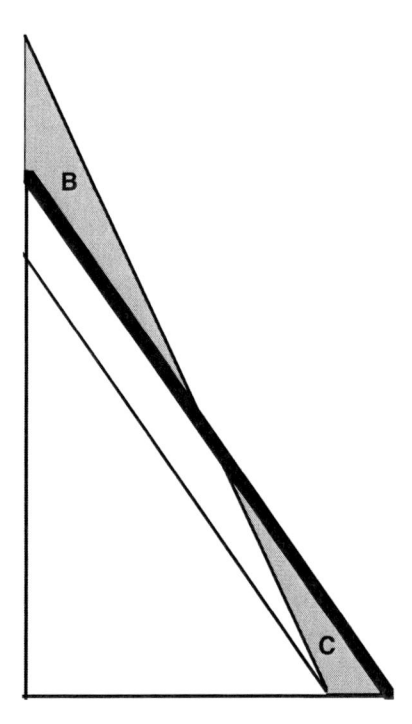

Figure 11.4

credit issue made by free banking in order to offset the previous increase in demand for fiduciary media is used for investment.[36] The shaded area C (with a surface equal to B) represents the part that the final holders of fiduciary media spend on the goods closest to consumption, leaving the productive structure in the same proportions as in Figure 11.1, but only after the painful and inevitable readjustment indicated in the Austrian theory of economic cycles, which the fractional-reserve free banking system has been unable to avoid, has taken place. We may conclude that, in this case, to the contrary of what Selgin and White suggest,[37] even though the increase in fiduciary media is exactly matched by a previous increase in the holdings of fiduciary media by the economic agents, it sets in motion the Austrian business cycle.

The possible confusion between the concept of saving and the concept of demand for money

The attempt to recover at least the essence of the doctrine of the 'needs of trade' and demonstrate that fractional-reserve free banking will not give rise to economic cycles has led George A. Selgin to defend a somewhat similar thesis to that set forth by John Maynard Keynes when he discussed bank deposits. We should remember how, for Keynes, the man who holds the additional money corresponding to the new bank credit is said to be *saving*:

> Moreover, the savings which result from this decision are just as genuine as any other savings. No one can be compelled to own the additional money corresponding to the new bank-credit, unless he deliberately prefers to hold more money rather than some other form of wealth.[38]

George Selgin's position seems to be parallel to that of Keynes when he considers that the public demand to hold cash balances in the form of bank notes and deposit accounts simultaneously reflects the desire to offer short-term 'loans' for an identical amount through the banking system. The only difference between the two authors on this matter is that Selgin seems to limit his conclusion to 'adjustments in the supply of loanable funds, meant to preserve monetary equilibrium'.[39] In fact, Selgin affirms that

> to hold inside money is to engage in voluntary saving. ... Whenever a bank expands its liabilities in the process of making new loans and investments, it is the holders of the liabilities who are the ultimate lenders of credit, and what they lend are the real resources they could acquire if, instead of holding money, they spent it. When the expansion or contraction of bank liabilities proceeds in such a way as to be at all times in agreement with changing demands for inside money, the quantity of real capital funds supplied to borrowers by the banks is equal to the quantity voluntarily offered to the banks by the public. Under these conditions, banks are simply intermediaries of loanable funds.[40]

However, an increase in the balances of fiduciary media that the public wishes to hold is perfectly compatible with a simultaneous increase in the demand for consumer goods and services if the public decides to decrease its investment expenditure. The truth is that any economic agent may use his money balances in any of the following three ways: he may spend them on consumer goods and services; he may spend them on investments; or he may hold them in the form of cash balances or fiduciary media. There is no other alternative. The decision as to the proportion that will be spent on consumption or investment is different to and independent of the decision taken on the fiduciary media and cash balances one wishes to hold. Thus, it cannot be concluded that all money balances are equivalent to 'savings' which the corresponding bank credits and investment should match, as it is perfectly possible, as we have seen before, that part of the new fiduciary media created by the banks is not invested but consumed by their final holders.

To say that 'every holder of demand liabilities issued by a free bank grants that bank a loan for the value of his holdings'[41] is the same as saying that any creation of bank money in response to an increase in the demand for fiduciary media implies, ultimately, the *a posteriori* grant of a loan for the same amount to the bank. However, the bank generates credits from nowhere and offers purchasing power to entrepreneurs, who receive it without taking any account at all of the real desires on consumption and investment of the economic agents who, in the final analysis, will become the ultimate holders of the fiduciary media it creates. And thus it is very possible, as we have already seen, that if social preferences on consumption and investment have not changed, at least part of the new fiduciary media created by the banks will ultimately be used to increase consumer goods expenditure, forcing the relative prices of this type of goods to rise.

Normally, the fractional-reserve free banking theorist considers that all notes or deposits issued by a bank are 'financial assets' which instrument a 'loan'. Juridically, there are serious problems with this idea, which we will explain later. Economically, this conception implies considering that bank money is a 'financial asset' that represents the voluntary saving of an economic agent who 'lends' present goods (generally money) in exchange for future goods (generally also money).[42] However, *money is in itself a present good* that is perfectly liquid[43] and holding fiduciary media balances gives no indication of the behaviour of the economic agent who owns the money in relation to the proportion in which s/he wishes to consume or invest. For the overall banking system, the total stocks of fiduciary media are not 'financial assets', as *they are not normally withdrawn* from the system, but rather circulate indefinitely, passing from hand to hand, since they are money (or, better, a perfect 'money substitute'). On the contrary, a financial asset represents the delivery of present goods in exchange for future goods which must always be returned on a *certain future date* (even if it is after a short time period) and its creation results from a real and previous increase in saving by the economic agents. Furthermore, the financial asset is generally a certificate which represents that, today, present money has been renounced in exchange for obtaining a higher amount of money tomorrow. If the financial asset itself is, in turn, considered to be converted into money, an inflationary duplication of payment means would be being created from nowhere without the need for any actual saving.

New savings always require a decrease in the rate of real consumption that has existed (i.e. a sacrifice). They are not the difference between real consumption and the hypothetical 'potential' consumption which could be enjoyed if all the fiduciary media balances were spent on consumer goods. Selgin appears to uphold this second conception when he proposes to change Machlup's definition of 'created credit' because the latter considers, in our opinion correctly, that there is 'created credit' whenever the expansionary granting of credits can provide a purchasing power that has not previously been sacrificed from consumption (i.e. saved) by anybody, even if, as we have shown, the creation of credit tends to compensate a previous increase in the demand for fiduciary media. Credit should always come from *previous* saving if it is not to distort the productive structure. If this consumption sacrifice has not taken place, but rather the investment is financed by a newly created credit, the structure of production can, as we know, become distorted.[44]

Some comments on the historical illustrations of fractional-reserve free banking systems

Fractional-reserve free banking theorists have been putting significant intellectual effort into illustrating the essential elements of their theory with real historical cases. So far, some sixty specific historical cases, in which a fractional-reserve banking system was developed with a considerable amount of freedom, have been identified and studied in a variable degree of depth.[45] The general conclusion usually drawn from these historical studies is that 'bank failure rates were lower in systems free of restrictions on capital, branching and diversification (e.g. Scotland and Canada), than in systems restricted in these respects (England and the United States)',[46] and, in fact, even if it is accepted that a free banking system may give rise, *in relative terms*, to less banking crises than those which have arisen in some central bank systems, for the purposes of the present 'Critical Note', this conclusion is practically irrelevant for the following reasons.

In the first place, the historical studies carried out to date, instead of concentrating on an analysis of whether the free banking system avoided unilateral credit expansions, artificial booms and economic recessions, have, in practice, been limited to studying whether bank panics were more or less frequent and serious than in a central bank system (which is, obviously, a very different matter). We have already explained the theoretical reasons why we believe that a real fractional-reserve free banking system may give rise to significant processes of unilateral expansion of fiduciary media, and how the fact that the creation of new bank money is always injected into the market in the form of credits, regardless of the desires of the economic agents to consume and invest, distorts the productive structure and gives rise to cycles of boom and recession. Although there is still a long way to go in the field of historical research into the cyclical impact of fractional-reserve free banking, there are a number of studies that analyse real fractional-reserve free banking systems with no (or very few) legal restrictions, central bank or institutional barriers. All of them seem to confirm the thesis that fractional-reserve free banking systems can generate important credit expansions capable of provoking economic recessions. Thus, Carlo M. Cipolla has made a study that interprets the economic crisis of the second half of sixteenth century Italy, in which the expansion of bank money played a leading role.[47] And even the Scottish fractional-reserve free banking system was subject to recurrent phases of credit expansion and contraction, which led to the corresponding economic cycles of boom and recession, at least over the years 1770, 1772, 1778, 1793, 1797, 1802–1803, 1809–1810, 1818–1819, 1825–1826, 1836–1837, 1839 and 1847.[48] Likewise, there are traces of similar phenomena in the remaining cases of fractional-reserve free banking systems which have existed historically.[49]

In the second place, the fact that the historical studies seem to indicate that in fractional-reserve free banking systems there were less bank panics than in the systems with a central bank does not mean that the former were totally free from bank crises. Selgin himself gives at least three significant cases: those which took place in Scotland in 1797, in Canada in 1837 and in Australia in 1893.[50] And although, as we have already say, the relevant issue for our purposes is the volume of credit expansion and the general cycles of boom and recession induced by the banks in the economic system, rather than bank crises and panics *per se*, there are a number of institutional reasons that, in addition to the 'lower' expansionary capacity of a free banking system in comparison with a central bank system, may help to explain this result. Thus, Murray N. Rothbard indicates how, in the case of Scotland, the banks had 'promoted' the use of their notes in economic transactions to such an extent that almost nobody demanded they be paid in gold and anyone who occasionally requested cash at the cash desk of their bank received general disapproval and all kinds of pressures from the bankers, who usually described this behaviour as 'disloyal' and threatened to make it more difficult for the customer to obtain credits in the future.[51]

In any case, I do not think that the elimination of bank crises is the definitive historical criterion for evaluating which banking system is the best. If this were the case, even the fractional-reserve free banking theorists would have to admit that the ideal banking system is a 100 per cent gold reserve free banking system, since George A. Selgin himself recognizes that 'a 100 per cent reserve banking crisis is an impossibility'.[52]

Finally, in the third place, there is an unquestionable historical fact: *none* of the sixty cases of fractional-reserve free banking have survived. All of them have been replaced by central bank systems, most of them during the period (from the second half of the nineteenth century to the beginning of the twentieth century) in which the world lived in a situation of relative *laissez-faire* and had not yet inclined towards the high level of economic interventionism characteristic of the present century. The fact is that knowledge of *human nature* allows us to explain, to a great extent, the reasons why fractional-reserve free banking has given rise to the central bank systems with heavy interventionism that we know today. Once the 100 per cent reserve free banking principle was violated and abandoned, the systematic *temptations* to which the different economic, social and political agents were submitted were practically irresistible. Some of these economic agents, bankers, succumbed by abusing their capacity to issue fiduciary media, even though this endangered their own solvency; others, depositors, by making deposits 'with interest' with an enthusiasm and energy that is only comparable to that which they show if their bank goes bankrupt, when they make a tremendous fuss and demand the help and intervention of the government; also, above all, governments, always trying to obtain easy and painless funding, who found the mythical 'philosopher's stone' that they had so longed looked for in the control and manipulation of fractional-reserve banking; and, finally, businessmen, economic theorists and general public who, for centuries, have succumbed to the expansionary and inflationary ideology. In an interesting summary chart, Kevin Dowd describes the *dominant* reasons (bank crisis, theory-ideology and seigniorage) that finished with each of the known fractional-reserve free banking systems and concludes that 'of course, free banking was not perfect; in a world populated by imperfect people, no institution can be'.[53] I would say, rather, that, given the imperfection of human beings and their abandonment of the most elementary moral and legal principles which should guide their actions (among which I include the need to practise free banking with a 100 per cent reserve ratio for demand deposits), the evolution of historical events to date in the banking field should not come as a surprise to anyone.

The juridical arguments

The analysis of banking issues must be essentially multidisciplinary because there is an intimate theoretical and practical connection between the juridical and economic aspects of all social processes in general, and those related to banking in particular.[54] According to the juridical tradition of continental Europe which originates from Roman Law, the task of the classical jurist is a true *art*, aimed at seeking and finding the essence (*das Wesen*) of the juridical institutions that emerge from the network of social interactions. In this task, jurists never entertain the intention of being 'original', 'imaginative' or having 'bright ideas', but rather of 'serving a certain number of *fundamental principles,* which is, as Savigny pointed out, the merit of their greatness'.[55] Their basic undertaking is to *discover* the universal legal principles which are inherent to the logic of human relations and immutable, although it is true that, as a consequence of social evolution itself, the need often arises to apply these intrinsically immutable principles to new situations and problems created by such evolution. In this continual task of exegesis and refinement of general legal principles, the jurists not only apply the logic of their discipline to the different cases they analyse, but also often receive important aid from other disciplines which, like economic theory and history, can show the fields of social interaction that are functioning with an imperfect or contradictory juridical foundation.

One of the most relevant cases which shows how a confused and contradictory juridical foundation can give rise to serious historical cases of discoordination and social damage is fractional-reserve banking. This originates and develops as a result of the wish to merge two contracts, the deposit contract and the loan contract, which, like water and oil, are essentially incompatible with each other. Whenever it is attempted to violate or force general legal principles which are incompatible, many harmful consequences arise that were not initially foreseen, some of which have been discussed from the economic point of view on the preceding pages.[56] The essential differences between the contracts (which differ radically) of the irregular deposit of money (as a fungible good) and the loan of money are summarized in Table 11.1, which helps us to understand the juridical issues and problems which may arise from the contracts on which fractional-reserve banking is based.[57]

Thus, in the first place, it should be noted that the practice of banking with a fractional reserve involves a logical impossibility from the juridical point of view. In fact, whenever a bank grants loans against money which has been deposited with it *at demand*, an ownership of money that did not previously exist is created from nowhere for an amount identical to that which has been lent by the bank. In fact, the depositor *holds* his money in the form of a deposit and it forms part of his money balances. Simultaneously, the person receiving the loan from the bank receives an amount of money which, in turn, becomes part of his cash balances. This result shows an extremely serious juridical irregularity as contracts, at best, can only be the materialization of a cross-transfer of properties (*do ut des*) but cannot create a property which did not exist before *ex nihilo*. In fact, a new amount of physical money (e.g. gold) has not been created, but both actors (the depositor and the borrower) think and act as if they owned the same physical gold. This result, at least in the initial stages of the formation of the modern banking system, arose as a consequence of the undue appropriation and fraud committed by many bankers that used money that had given to them as deposits to make loans.[58]

Once the bankers obtained from the government the *privilege* of acting on the base of a fractional reserve, their criminal status disappeared, at least from the standpoint of positive law. But this privilege in no way endows the monetary bank deposit contract with an adequate juridical foundation. On the contrary, this contract appears, on most occasions, as a contract which is null and void, from the point of view of general legal principles, since the *predominant purpose* of one of the parties, the depositor, is to make a deposit, while the other party, the depositary banker, receives it as a loan. And, according to the most standard legal principles, when each of the participants in an exchange believes that they are making a different contract, that contract is null and void. If this juridical theory of the *predominant subjective purpose*[59] of the contract (main *causa* of the contract in Roman Law) is applied to the millions of bank contracts currently in force, it will be very easy to see how the immense majority of the depositors think that they have, in fact, made a contract in which the nature of a deposit predominates, in order for such a deposit to form part of their money balances which can be transformed into currency at any time. On the contrary, the bankers receive the money as a 'loan', as demonstrated by the fact that they, in turn, hand it over to their borrowers, who thus increase their money balances. I think that nobody can deny the serious juridical ambiguity of the bank demand deposit contracts which have been made to date.[60] They are called 'deposits' commercially and contractually and, in fact, this name corresponds to the real main purpose which the banks' clients intend to attain. However, the bankers receive the deposits and use them as if they were loans which, as we have seen in Table 11.1, are radically different contracts.[61] Furthermore, it is clear that, if the majority of depositors cheat themselves (or are cheated) with regard to the true nature of the contract they make and, moreover, are tempted by the promise of interest[62] or the provision of free banking services, it cannot be accepted that the fact that this type of transaction is carried out massively is a *prima facie* demonstration that

Table 11.1 Essential differences between two radically different contracts

Irregular deposit of money	*Loan of money*
Economic differences	
1 Present goods are not exchanged for future goods	1 Present goods are exchanged for future goods
2 There is complete and continual availability in favour of the depositor	2 Availability is fully transferred to the borrower and lost by the lender
3 There is no interest, since present goods are not exchanged for future goods	3 There is interest, since present goods are exchanged for future goods
Legal differences	
1 The essential element that prevails is the *custody* or holding of the *tantundem* that constitutes the depositor's basic motivation	1 The essential element is the transfer of the availability of the present goods in favour of the borrower
2 There is no term for returning the deposit and the contract is, rather, 'on demand'	2 The contract requires a *term* be fixed for return of the loan and the calculation and payment of interest
3 The depositary's obligation is to keep the *tantundem* available to the depositor at all times (100% reserve ratio)	3 The borrower's obligation is to return the *tantundem* when the term expires, also paying the agreed interest

shows or reveals the public's real preference for this type of contract, or much less that it is socially necessary.

Third, even if the two parties, the depositors and the bankers, coincided exactly in the belief that the predominant purpose of the transaction was a loan (which is not certain to have been the case for the majority of people up to now), the juridical nature of the monetary bank deposit contract would not be resolved. This is because, from a juridical point of view, it is impossible that the banks can comply with the obligation to return the deposits they have received for an amount in excess of the reserves they hold. This impossibility is, furthermore, aggravated to the extent that the practice of fractional-reserve banking can generate banking crises and economic recessions which endanger the public's confidence in the banks. And contracts which are *impossible* to put into practice under certain circumstances are also null, according to general legal principles. Only by maintaining a 100 per cent reserve which guarantees that the supposed 'loans' granted (by the depositors) may be repurchased (by the banks) at any moment, or through the existence and support of a central bank which provided all the liquidity necessary in moments of difficulty, could these hypothetical 'loan' contracts with a covenant for the repayment of their *nominal* value at any moment be made *possible* and, therefore, valid.

In the fourth place, even if it is argued that the impossibility of compliance with bank deposit contracts of money only occurs every certain number of years for some specific banks, their legal nature would still not be solved, because the practice of fractional-reserve banking is a *breach of public order* and is damaging to third parties.[63] In fact, fractional-reserve banking, as it generates expansionary credits without the support of real savings, distorts the structure of production and leads the entrepreneurs who receive the loans, deceived by the greater ease of the credit conditions, to undertake investments which, in the final analysis, will not be profitable. When the inevitable economic recession arrives, their investment projects will have to be interrupted and liquidated, with a high cost from the economic, social and personal points of view, not only for the entrepreneurs and investors themselves, but also for the rest of the economic agents involved in the market process (workers, suppliers, consumers, depositors, bankers, etc.). We cannot, therefore, accept the argument that, in a free society, the banks and their clients should be free to establish the contractual covenants they consider most fitting.[64] Actually, when mutually satisfactory agreements between two parties are made with damages to third parties and which, therefore, constitute a breach of public order, the corresponding 'contracts' are entirely null and void.

Hans-Hermann Hoppe[65] explains how this type of 'contract' damages third parties in three different ways: first, to the extent that the credit expansion increases the monetary supply and decreases the purchasing power of the monetary units of the other holders of money balances, who are, thus, expropriated of that part of the value their monetary units would have had if the credit expansion had not occurred; second, the depositors in general are damaged because, as a consequence of the credit expansion process, the probability that, in the absence of a central bank, they will be able to recover their monetary units intact decreases; and, if a central bank exists, to the extent that, although the return of their nominal deposits could be guaranteed, the purchasing power of their monetary units will be significantly reduced; and, third, the greatest harm is done to the rest of the borrowers and economic agents in the form of generalized malinvestment, financial crisis, unemployment and significant unrest, stress and human suffering.

Any manipulation of money, which is the *generalized* means of exchange accepted in society, always implies, in accordance with the very definition of the concept of money, that unidentified third-party participants are affected. We are, of course, not talking about the so-called 'pecuniary externalities' which are transferred in the market through the price system as a result of changes in subjective valuations and in human actions subject to general legal principles. On the contrary, we refer to serious social interferences which originate from the irregular juridical foundation of some bank demand deposit contracts which make possible the anomaly of multiplying the amount of money, regardless of the wishes of the parties, without any saving taking place or anything new having occurred.[66] In fact, economically speaking, the effects of the credit expansion are, from a *qualitative* point of view, identical to those of the criminal forgery of coins and bank notes which are dealt with, for example, in articles 283–290 of the Spanish Criminal Code.[67] Both of them imply the creation of money, the redistribution of income in favour of a few people to the detriment of the other citizens, and the overall distortion of the productive system. However, from a *quantitative* point of view, only a credit expansion is able to expand the monetary supply by a sufficient volume and at a rate capable of feeding an artificial boom and causing a recession. In comparison with the credit expansion of fractional-reserve free banking and the monetary manipulation of governments and central banks, the criminal forgery of money is child's play and almost imperceptible.

The above considerations have had their influence on some modern fractional-reserve free banking theorists, who have proposed, in order to guarantee the stability of the system, that the banks should establish a 'safeguard' clause on their notes and deposits, 'informing' their clients that the bank may decide, at any time, to suspend or defer the return of the deposits or the payment of the corresponding notes in cash.[68] It is clear that the introduction of this 'option clause' goes against the nature of the concept of money, the essence of which is precisely the availability of perfect, i.e. immediate, complete and totally unconditional, liquidity at any moment. The 'option clause' means that the depositors and note-holders, in crisis conditions, can be converted into compulsory lenders, rather than continuing as depositors holding perfectly liquid monetary units or perfect money substitutes. Thus, the traditional deposit contract would be converted into a peculiar form of 'random contract' or lottery, in which recovery of the corresponding deposits would depend on luck, influence and other specific circumstances at any moment. No objection can be raised to the fact that certain parties decide to make such an irregular random contract. But, to the extent that, in spite of the existence of this clause and the 'perfect' knowledge of its implications by all the participants (bankers and their clients), they and the rest of the economic agents would behave as if they considered, from the subjective point of view, that for practical purposes their demand deposits are perfectly liquid, then the banking system could identically create credit expansions. 'Option clauses', therefore, would not avoid the reproduction of the processes of expansion, crisis and economic recession which the practice of fractional-reserve free banking can create. Option clauses at most can protect the banks, but not society or the economic system, from the damage produced by the successive phases of credit expansion, boom and recession. Thus, the 'option clauses' argument is only a 'last line of defence' that in no way solves the fact that fractional-reserve free banking can produce very serious systematic damage to third parties, which constitute a breach of public order.

It is surprising that, in spite of all the foregoing arguments, most of the Fractional-Reserve Free Banking School theorists, instead of proposing the abolition of fractional-reserve banking, only propose the elimination of central banks and the complete privatization of the banking system, without making any reference to what would be the best solution to all the economic and juridical problems discussed in this article: a free banking system with a 100 per cent reserve requirement. It is true that this privatization would tend to put an earlier stop to the almost unlimited abuses that the monetary authorities commit today in the financial field, but it does not prevent the possibility that abuses also be committed (on a smaller scale) in the private field. This is similar to the situation that would arise if governments were allowed to systematically kill, steal or commit any other crime. The social damage that this would generate would be tremendous, in view of the enormous power and monopolistic nature of the state. And, without any doubt, the privatization of these criminal activities (eliminating the systematic practice of them by the government) would tend to 'improve' the situation appreciably: at least the great criminal power of the state would disappear and private economic agents would be allowed to develop prevention and defence procedures against these crimes. However, the privatization of criminal activities is not the final solution to the problem they pose and they would only be completely eliminated if they were put down by all possible legal means, even if they were committed by private agents in an entirely private environment. In fact, all central banks, all the present tangle of banking legislation and all the economic problems which may be generated by fractional-reserve free banking could be solved through a simple article in the Criminal Code of the future Libertarian Society saying: 'Any banker who appropriates the money deposited with him at demand for his own benefit, and does not maintain a 100 per cent reserve in relation thereto at all times, shall be punished by imprisonment and obliged to indemnify the victims'.[69]

Conclusion

The traditional form in which the controversy between the supporters of central banks and those of fractional-reserve free banking is posed is essentially erroneous. In fact, the advocates of fractional-reserve free banking do not realize that their proposal unleashes an almost unavoidable trend towards the emergence, development and consolidation of a central bank. The credit expansion that can be generated by any fractional-reserve banking system gives rise to reversion processes, in the form of possible banking crises and economic recessions, which almost inevitably cause the affected citizens and bankers to demand the intervention of the government, as well as the state regulation of the activity. Furthermore, the bankers themselves soon discover that they reduce the risk of insolvency if they reach agreements among themselves, merge and even demand the creation of a last resort lender (central bank), which provides them with the necessary liquidity in times of adversity and institutionalizes and officially orchestrates and coordinates the growth of credit expansion. Finally, governments cannot avoid the temptation to use for their own benefit the enormous power to create money permitted by fractional-reserve banking.

We can, therefore, conclude that the practice of fractional-reserve banking is the main factor responsible for the emergence and development of the central bank. For this reason, the theoretical and practical discussion should be raised, not in traditional terms, but between the only two feasible alternatives, radically opposed to each other, which are: either a free banking system subject to traditional legal principles (i.e. with a 100 per cent reserve ratio for demand deposits), in which, therefore, all transactions in which a fractional reserve is established, be they 'voluntary' or otherwise, are considered illegal and a breach of public order; or a system which allows the practice of fractional-reserve banking, from which a central bank will inevitably emerge as a last resort lender and controller of the whole financial system. These are the only two theoretically and practically viable alternatives.

12 The ethics of capitalism[1]

Introduction

Traditional studies on natural law and justice have been eclipsed by the development of a conception of economic science which, clumsily and mechanically, has tried to apply a methodology originally formed for the natural sciences and the world of physics to the social sciences. According to this conception, the 'differentiating' characteristic of economic theory would consist of the systematic application of a narrow criterion of 'rationality', so that both individual human action and economic policy at a general level would be considered to be determined by calculations and valuations of costs and benefits through a maximization criterion which supposedly made it possible to 'optimize' the attainment of the ends pursued on the basis of given means. According to this approach, it seemed obvious that considerations relative to ethical principles as guides for human behaviour lost relevance and significance. In effect, it seemed that a universal guide for human behaviour had been found and, at its different levels (individual and social), it could be put into practice by applying a simple criterion of maximization of the beneficial *consequences* derived from each action, without the need, therefore, to adapt any kind of behaviour to pre-fixed ethical rules. Science had apparently thus managed to eliminate considerations related to justice and make them obsolete.

The failure of consequentialism

However, the *consequentialist* ideal, consisting of believing that it is possible to act by taking decisions to maximize the forecast positive consequences on the basis of given means and costs which are also known, has ostensibly failed.[2] First, the evolution of economic theory itself has shown that it is theoretically impossible to obtain the necessary information on the benefits and costs arising from each human action. This theorem of modern economics is based on the innate creative capacity of the human being, who is continually discovering new ends and means, giving rise, therefore, to a flow of new information or knowledge which makes it impossible to predict the specific future consequences of the different human actions and/or political decisions adopted at any given moment.[3] In addition, the failure of real socialism, understood as the most ambitious social engineering experiment carried out by the human race throughout its history, has meant a shattering blow for consequentialist doctrine. In effect, the immense resources devoted, over a period of more than seventy years, to trying to evaluate different political options in terms of costs and benefits, imposing them by force on citizens in order to 'optimally' attain the ends pursued, have been seen to be incapable of meeting the expectations that had been placed on them, leading to significant economic underdevelopment and, above all, to great human suffering.

Although, due to lack of the necessary historical perspective, we are not yet fully aware of the far-reaching consequences that the fall of real socialism will have on the evolution of science and human thought, some very significant effects can now begin to be appreciated. First, attention should be drawn to the development of a new economic theory, much more human and realistic, which, based on the study of the human being as a creative actor, aims to analyse the dynamic processes of social coordination which really take place in the market. This approach, the predominant driving force of which comes from the Austrian School of Economics, is much less ambitious than the scientistic paradigm that, to date, has filled the economics textbooks and deformed generations of students, generating expectations among citizens regarding the possibilities of our science which, logically, it has been unable to meet.

Another important consequence has been the formation of an evolutionist theory of social processes, also developed by the Austrian School of Economics. This has shown how the most important institutions for life in society (linguistic, economic, juridical and moral) arise spontaneously, over a very extended time period, on the basis of custom, as a consequence of the participation of a very large number of human beings who act in very varied specific circumstances of time and place. Thus, a series of institutions appear which involve an enormous volume of information and which are far in excess of the capacity of comprehension and design of the human mind.

Lastly, the third effect which should be highlighted is the significant re-emergence of ethics and the analysis of justice as one of the most important social studies research fields. In fact, the theoretical and historical failure of scientistic consequentialism has returned a leading role to rules of behaviour based on dogmatic ethical principles, the important function of which as irreplaceable 'automatic pilots' for behaviour and human freedom is again beginning to be fully appreciated.

The importance of an ethical foundation for freedom

Perhaps one of the most important contributions of the theory of freedom in this century has been to show that the consequentialist analysis of costs and benefits is not sufficient to justify a market economy. It is not only that a large part of the economic science developed to date was based on the intellectual error of presupposing a static framework of given ends and means, but also that even the much more realistic and fruitful analytical point of view of the Austrian School, based on the creative capacity of the human being and the theoretical study of the dynamic processes of social coordination is, *alone*, insufficient to serve as a categorical foundation for libertarian ideology. Even if we abandon the static criterion of Paretian efficiency and replace it by another more dynamic criterion based on coordination, the considerations of 'efficiency' will never be enough, alone, to convince all those who put considerations related to justice before those related to the different ideas of 'efficiency'. In addition, neither does recognition of the effects of social discoordination ('inefficiencies'), which arise, in the long term, from any systematic attempt to coerce the spontaneous processes of human interaction, guarantee the automatic agreement of all those whose *time preference* is so intense that, despite the negative effects of intervention in the medium and long term, they place a higher value on its short-term benefits.[4]

In short, the development of ethical foundations for the theory of freedom is indispensable for the following reasons: (1) because of the failure of 'social engineering' and, especially, of the consequentialism derived from the neoclassical-Walrasian paradigm which has been the mainstream paradigm in economic science to date; (2) because the theoretical analysis of the market processes based on the entrepreneurial capacity of the human being, even though it is much more powerful than the analysis derived from the neoclassical paradigm, is not, alone, *sufficient* to justify the market economy; (3) because, given the situation of ineradicable ignorance of human beings and their constant capacity to create new information, they need a moral framework of principles of behaviour that automatically indicates the guided behaviours they should follow; and (4) because, from a strategic point of view, it is basically moral considerations that drive the reformist behaviour of human beings, who are often willing to make significant sacrifices in order to pursue what they consider good and just from the moral point of view. It is much more difficult to ensure this behaviour on the grounds of cold calculations of costs and benefits which, moreover, are of very doubtful scientific potential.

On the possibility of building a theory of social ethics

A significant number of scientists still consider that it is not possible to achieve an objective theory of justice and moral principles. The development of this opinion has been strongly influenced by the evolution of scientistic economics, which, obsessed by the maximization criterion, considers that, not only are the ends and means of each actor subjective, but moral principles of behaviour also depend on the subjective autonomy of the decision-maker. If, under any circumstance, an *ad hoc* decision may be made on the basis of a pure cost–benefit analysis, the existence of morality understood as a scheme containing previously fixed behaviour guidelines is not necessary, meaning that any such scheme becomes completely blurred and may be considered to be limited to the particular scope of the subjective autonomy of each individual. Against this position, which has been prevalent to date, we consider that one thing is for valuations, utilities and costs to be subjective, as shown by economic science, and a completely different thing is for no objectively valid moral principles to exist.[5]

Furthermore, we consider that the development of a whole scientific theory on the moral principles which should guide human behaviour in social interaction is not only advisable, but also possible. In fact, over recent years, several very significant works in this field have appeared. Among them, Israel M. Kirzner's contribution suggesting a new concept of distributive justice in capitalism should be highlighted. Attention should be drawn to the fact that this contribution has been developed by one of the most distinguished theorists of the Austrian School of Economics, which shows that the field of correctly developed economic theory is significantly interrelated to that of social ethics. The fact is that economic science, even if it is *wertfrei* or free from value judgements, is not only able to help to adopt clearer ethical positions but can, furthermore, as Kirzner illustrates, make logical-deductive reasoning easier and surer in the social ethics field, avoiding the many errors and dangers that would arise from a badly proposed static analysis of economic theory under unreal assumptions of complete information.[6]

According to this conception, the considerations of 'efficiency' and 'justice', far from being a *trade-off* which would allow different combinations in varying proportions, would appear to be two sides of the same coin. In effect, from our point of view, only justice leads to efficiency; and, *vice versa*, what is efficient cannot be unjust. Thus, both considerations, those relative to moral principles and those on economic efficiency, far from being in opposition to each other, mutually strengthen and support each other.[7]

Morality and efficiency

The idea that efficiency and justice are two different dimensions which can be combined in varying proportions is one of the negative consequences which arise naturally from the neoclassical paradigm which has dominated economic science to date. In effect, if one believes that it is possible to decide on the basis of a cost–benefit analysis because one assumes that the required information is given in a static context, not only is it unnecessary for individual actors to follow any prior scheme of guided moral behaviour to direct them in their action (other than merely 'maximizing its utility *ad hoc*'), but it is also easy to reach the conclusion (included, for example, in the 'second fundamental theorem of welfare economics') that any scheme of equity imposed by force is compatible with the static criteria of Paretian efficiency.

However, the consideration of the social process as a dynamic reality constituted by the interaction of thousands of human beings, each of which is endowed with an innate and constant creative capacity, makes it impossible to know the costs and benefits that will arise from any given action in detail, meaning that the human being has to use a series of guides, or moral principles of action, as an automatic pilot. These moral principles tend, furthermore, to make coordinated interaction between different human beings possible and, therefore, generate a coordination process that, in a certain sense, could be described as dynamically efficient. Seen from the conception of the market as a dynamic process, efficiency, understood as coordination, arises from the behaviour of human beings when the latter act following specific moral guidelines and, *vice versa*, human action performed in accordance with these ethical principles gives rise to dynamic efficiency understood as the coordinating trend in processes of social interaction. Therefore, we may conclude that, from a dynamic point of view, efficiency is not compatible with different schemes of equity or justice, but rather arises solely and exclusively from a single scheme.

As we have already said, neither is it admissible to affirm that criteria of efficiency and those of equity are opposed to each other. The polemic between these two dimensions is false and erroneous. What is just cannot be inefficient, nor can what is efficient be unjust. The fact is that, under the perspective of dynamic analysis, equity or justice and efficiency are simply two sides of the same coin which, moreover, confirm the integrated and consistent order that exists in the social universe. The supposed opposition between these two dimensions originates from the erroneous conception of static efficiency developed by the neoclassical paradigm of 'welfare economics', together with the erroneous idea of equity or 'social justice', according to which the results of the social process can be judged regardless of the individual behaviour of those who participate in it. The theoretical developments of welfare economics based on static criteria of Paretian efficiency arose with the vain hope of avoiding the need to explicitly enter the ethics field and have made it impossible to appreciate the serious problems of dynamic inefficiency that emerge when the entrepreneurial process is institutionally coerced to a greater or lesser extent. The consideration of economics as a process not only allows efficiency to be appropriately redefined in dynamic terms, but also throws a great deal of light on the criterion of justice which should prevail in social relations. This criterion is based on the traditional principles of morality which allow individual behaviour to be judged as just or unjust in accordance with general and abstract juridical rules regulating, basically, the property rights that make it possible for human beings to appropriate everything that results from their own innate entrepreneurial creativity. Furthermore, this point of view shows how alternative criteria of justice are essentially immoral. Among them, and particularly open to criticism, is the concept of 'social justice' that aims to judge as just or unjust the specific results of the social process at determined historical moments *regardless of whether or not the behaviour of its artifices has been in line with general juridical and moral rules*. 'Social justice' only makes sense in a phantasmagoric static world where the goods and services are given and the only problem that can arise is their distribution. However, in the real world, where the production and distribution processes take place *simultaneously* as a consequence of entrepreneurial impetus, there is no analytical sense to the concept of 'social justice', which may be considered essentially immoral in three different ways: (1) from the evolutionary point of view, to the extent that the principles derived from the idea of 'social justice' violate the traditional principles of property rights which have been formed by common law and have made modern civilization possible; (2) from the theoretical point of view, since it is impossible to organize society on the basis of 'social justice', as the systematic coercion required in order to impose the objective of the redistribution of income prevents the free practice of entrepreneurship and, therefore, the creativity and coordination that make the development of civilization possible; and (3) from the ethical point of view, to the extent that the moral principle that all human beings have a natural right to the results of their own entrepreneurial creativity is violated. It is foreseeable that, as citizens realize the serious errors and essential immorality derived from this spurious concept of 'social justice', institutional coercion on the part of the state which this is considered to justify will gradually disappear.[8]

Israel Kirzner's contribution to ethics

Kirzner's great contribution consists, precisely, of having shown that a large part of the thinking about distributive justice, which has constituted the majority position to date and has formed the 'ethical foundation' of important political and social movements (of socialists and social democrats), has its origin and fundaments in the erroneous static conception of economics.[9] In effect, the neoclassical paradigm is based, to a greater or less extent, on the assumption that information is objective and given (either in certain or probabilistic terms) and, therefore, it is possible to make cost–benefit analyses on the basis thereof. If this is the case, it seems logical that utility maximization considerations are completely independent of moral aspects and that these two factors can be combined in different proportions. Furthermore, the static conception inexorably leads to the presupposition that, in a certain sense, the resources are given and known, meaning that the economic problem of their distribution is different and separate from the problem posed by their production. In effect, if the resources are given, how both the means of production and the result of the different productive processes are to be distributed among the different human beings acquires an exceptional importance.

This whole idea has been made obsolete by the dynamic conception of market processes developed by the Austrian School of Economics in general and, specifically, by the analysis of entrepreneurship and its ethical implications carried out by Israel M. Kirzner. For Kirzner, entrepreneurship consists of the innate capacity of all human beings to appreciate or discover the opportunities for gain that arise in their surroundings and act in consequence in order to take advantage of them. Entrepreneurship consists, therefore, of the typically human capacity continually to create and discover new ends and means. Under this conception, resources are not given, but rather both the ends and the means are continually thought up and conceived *ex novo* by entrepreneurs, who are always anxious to attain new objectives which they *discover* to have a higher value. If the ends, the means and the resources are not given, but are continually being created from nothing by the entrepreneurship of human beings, it is clear that the fundamental ethical approach is no longer how to distribute 'what exists' on an equitable basis, but should rather be conceived as the way to stimulate creativity most adapted to human nature. It is here where Kirzner's contribution to social ethics reaches its full force: the conception of the human being as a creative actor makes it inevitable to accept, as an axiom, that *all human beings have a natural right to the fruits of their own entrepreneurial creativity*. This is not only because, if it were not the case, such fruits would not act as an incentive capable of stimulating the entrepreneurial and creative alertness of the human being, but also because it is a universal principle which may be applied to all human beings in all conceivable circumstances.

The ethical principle we have just explained also has other significant advantages. First, its great intuitive attraction should be highlighted: it seems evident that if somebody creates something from nothing, s/he has the right to appropriate it, since nobody is prejudiced (before it was created, what was created did not exist and, therefore, its creation does not prejudice anyone and, at least, benefits the creative actor and may well also benefit many other human beings). In the second place, it is a universally valid ethical principle, closely related to the principle of Roman Law concerning the original appropriation of resources that do not belong to anyone (*ocupatio rei nullius*), allowing the resolution of the paradoxical problem posed by what is known as 'Locke's proviso', according to which the limit on the original appropriation of resources is based on leaving a 'sufficient' amount thereof for other human beings. As Kirzner shows in what is perhaps one of the most original contributions of his work on social ethics, his principle based on creativity resolves the existence of 'Locke's proviso' and makes it unnecessary, since any result of human creativity did not exist before it was discovered or created entrepreneurially and, therefore, the appropriation thereof cannot prejudice anyone. Locke's conception only makes sense in a static environment in which it is assumed that the resources already exist (or are 'given') and are fixed, and that they should be distributed among a predetermined number of human beings.

Kirzner also shows us, in the third place, how most of the alternative theories on justice, particularly the theory developed by John Rawls, contain the underlying paradigm of full information, which presupposes a static environment of pre-existing resources. Although Rawls considers a 'veil of ignorance' in his analysis, he reaches the conclusion that the most just system is the one in which, without knowing the exact place that s/he will occupy in the social scale, each human being may nevertheless be sure that, if the most unfavourable situation corresponds to him or her, s/he will have a maximum of resources.[10] It is clear that, if economics is considered as a dynamic entrepreneurial process, the ethical principle has to be very different: the most just society will be the society that most forcefully promotes the entrepreneurial creativity of all the human beings who compose it. In order to do this, it is indispensable for each human being to be certain, *a priori*, that s/he will be able to appropriate the results of his or her entrepreneurial creativity (which would not exist in the social body before being discovered or created by each individual actor) and that nobody will expropriate them.

In the fourth place, another advantage of Kirzner's analysis is that it makes obvious the immoral nature of socialism, understood as any system of institutional aggression carried out by the state against the free practice of human action or entrepreneurship. In effect, coercion against the actor prevents the latter from developing what is most natural to him, that is, his innate capacity to create and conceive new ends and means and to act in consequence to attain them. To the extent that state coercion prevents entrepreneurial human action, the human being's creative capacity will be restricted and neither the information nor the knowledge necessary to coordinate society will emerge. Precisely for this reason, socialism is an intellectual error, since it makes it impossible for human beings to generate the information required by the governing body in order to coordinate society through coercive commands. Furthermore, Kirzner's analysis has the potential to demonstrate that the socialist system is immoral because it is based on preventing, by force, human beings from appropriating the results of their own entrepreneurial creativity. Thus, socialism is not only seen as something that is theoretically erroneous or economically impossible (i.e. *inefficient*), but also, simultaneously, as an essentially *immoral* system, since it violates the most intimate entrepreneurial nature of human beings and prevents us from freely appropriating the results of our entrepreneurial creativity.[11]

The social doctrine of the Catholic Church and Kirzner's contribution

Perhaps one of the most significant aspects of the latest formulations of the social doctrine of the Catholic Church in favour of a market economy stems from the great influence that the thinking of the Austrian School of Economics has had, particularly that of Hayek and Kirzner, the former of whom was a non-practising Catholic agnostic, while the latter is a profoundly religious practising Jew. In effect, the Catholic thinker Michael Novak surprised the world when he made public the long personal conversation between Pope John Paul II and Hayek which took place before the latter's death.[12] Subsequently, in his book *The Catholic Ethic and the Spirit of Capitalism*, Novak points out the great parallelism that exists between the conception of creative human action developed by the pope in his doctoral thesis entitled *The Acting Person* and the conception of entrepreneurship we owe to Kirzner.[13]

This concept was refined by John Paul II in his encyclical *Centesimus Annus*, where he expressly refers to entrepreneurial capacity or creative human action as the decisive factor in society or, in his own words, '*man himself*, that is his knowledge', in its two embodiments of scientific knowledge and practical knowledge, which John Paul II defines as what is necessary in order to 'perceive the needs of others and to satisfy them'. According to John Paul II, this knowledge allows human beings 'to express their creativity and develop their potential' and to introduce themselves into 'the network of knowledge and intercommunication' that constitutes the market and society. Thus, for John Paul II, 'the *role* of disciplined and creative *human work* [I would prefer to say 'human action'] and, as an essential part of that work, *initiative and entrepreneurial ability* becomes increasing evident and decisive'.[14] Without any doubt, the encyclical *Centesimus Annus* shows how its author's conception of economic science has been enormously modernized and taken a significant leap from the scientific point of view, rendering a great deal of the Church's former social doctrine obsolete. It even surmounts significant sectors of economic science itself which have, to date, been anchored in the mechanism of the neoclassical–Keynesian paradigm and been unable to include the eminently creative and dynamic nature of entrepreneurship in their 'models'. For the first time in history, thanks to the positive influence of the Austrian School of Economics, the social doctrine of the Catholic Church has overtaken the mainstream paradigm of economic science, which has, so far, ignored the creative human being and continues anchored in a static conception of market and society.

Some critical comments

An objection can be raised to the best of books, and small defects contribute to a good book – as to a good man – to the same extent as virtues. I would not, therefore, like to conclude this comment on Kirzner's work on social ethics without referring to two specific aspects in which I think his position could be improved.

Kirzner and the supposed relativism of ethical principles according to historical circumstances

The first objection we would raise to Kirzner's analysis refers to the concession – unjustified, in our opinion – that he makes on pages 126–127 and 176–177 of his book *Discovery, Capitalism and Distributive Justice* when he affirms that it will be in circumstances where the levels of disequilibrium, uncertainty and creativity are greatest that the principle of justice he proposes, based on the appropriation of the goods and services discovered by the entrepreneurs, will be most relevant.[15] However, he then states that, in relatively more stable markets and in particular circumstances, his rule of justice will be less relevant. In our opinion, the dynamic rule of justice proposed by Kirzner has, on the contrary, universal validity, regardless of what the particular circumstances appear to be at any given moment. Whenever institutional coercion is used in order to redistribute the social product, the use of a creative capacity which originates from the most intimate and essential nature of the human being is being impeded to a greater or lesser extent, thus harming the possibilities of creating information and coordinating the social process. Furthermore, there is no analytical possibility of distinguishing situations in which the relatively more 'stable' nature of the social process supposedly permits application of alternative criteria, based on 'social' or distributive justice, from situations where the relative social stagnation is, precisely, a direct result of the systematic practice of state coercion with which such alternative criteria always manifest themselves. However, Kirzner himself acknowledges that 'the extent to which discovery insights need to be introduced into both the economics and moral philosophy of capitalism seems to be greater and greater as capitalism itself develops and becomes more intricate and "open-ended"'.[16] Our disagreement with Kirzner, therefore, stems from the fact that we consider that there are no exceptions to the principle of justice based on entrepreneurship that he proposes. The principle is universally applicable to all conceivable historical circumstances in which a human being, intrinsically endowed with an innate entrepreneurial and creative capacity, is involved.

The application of the Kirznerian theory of entrepreneurship to the emergence of institutions and moral behaviour

Recently, in two somewhat disconcerting articles, Israel Kirzner has upheld the thesis that the theory of entrepreneurship, which he has developed so brilliantly and with so much perseverance throughout his academic life, is not directly applicable in order to justify the existence of a spontaneous trend towards the formation and improvement of social institutions.[17] The main (and only) argument put forward by Kirzner in support of this thesis, is the supposed existence of an 'externality' that prevents the institutional improvements relevant to society from materializing in the form of opportunities for explicit gain that may be exploited and appropriated by entrepreneurs. Thus, according to Kirzner, the process of entrepreneurial creativity and discovery would not take place in the field of institutions, since the entrepreneurs would be unable to appropriate for themselves the profits arising from their entrepreneurial activity in the institutional field. In addition, Kirzner correctly maintains that, in a market context, the existence of a situation of 'public good' cannot be considered a defect if the state prevents an adequate definition and/or defence of property rights by force, since it is absurd to classify the non-existence of a Utopian situation resulting from institutional insufficiencies as a 'market defect'. Kirzner goes on to say, and this is where we disagree, that these institutional insufficiencies may also emerge and be maintained as the result of a supposed situation of 'public good', which, as we have already mentioned, prevents, according to Kirzner, entrepreneurial activity from discovering and driving forward the necessary institutional improvements.[18]

We cannot share this paradoxical and restrictive position that Kirzner has recently adopted in relation to the application of his own theory of entrepreneurship to the emergence of institutions. First, within the dynamic context of the market process, we do not consider that public good problems are not a market defect simply because they emerge as the result of an institutional 'inefficiency'. In our opinion, the public good 'problem' is never a market defect, since whenever an apparent situation of joint supply and the impossibility of exclusion of *free riders* arises, in the absence of the coercive intervention of the state, the incentives necessary for entrepreneurial activity to come into operation emerge and, appropriating the results thereof, it discovers the technical, juridical and institutional innovations required to conclude the supposed public good situation. This is, for example, what occurred in relation to the commons in the American West, where, until it was possible to adequately define the property rights over the land that belonged to the different users (farmers and stockbreeders), there were significant conflicts and difficulties in social coordination. However, this situation created precisely the incentive for the entrepreneurs finally to discover and introduce an important technological innovation: barbed wire, which, from then onwards, allowed the property rights over large extensions of land to be separated and defined at a reasonable cost. This resolved the public good problems. Another example refers to lighthouses as an aid to navigation. At many times in history, they have been run privately, various technical and institutional procedures having been found through entrepreneurship in order to force preferences to be revealed and the beneficiaries to assume the cost thereof (social boycott of *free riders*, associations of fishermen and ship-owners, etc.). We do not even need to mention many other technological innovations, such as cable television, that have solved, thanks to entrepreneurial creativity, the public good problems that existed up to now in their respective fields. Therefore, from a dynamic point of view, if the state does not intervene, the set of public goods tends to become empty as a result of the creative capacity of entrepreneurship.

It is true that, in the field of social institutions (juridical, moral, economic and linguistic), the problems arising from the individual appropriation of the results of entrepreneurial creativity are more arduous and difficult. However, this does not mean that it cannot be done and that, therefore, improvements are not constantly being introduced. Moreover, without the creative capacity of entrepreneurship, neither the process of generation nor that of development and improvement of the most important social institutions can even be conceived. This is precisely what Menger showed in his analysis of the evolutionary emergence of social institutions, which he applied specifically to money and which can only be understood as the result of the initial leadership of a few relatively more alert human beings, who realized before the others that they could attain their ends more easily if, in exchange for their goods and services, they asked for goods that were more easy to commercialize on the market, which thus became known as 'means of exchange'. This behaviour, through a learning process, was extended throughout the market until the means of exchange became generally used and, therefore, were converted into money.[19] In addition, it is clear that languages are constantly evolving and that, thanks to the creativity of a large number of actors, new terms are introduced, old ones are improved, grammatical rules and rules of pronunciation are simplified and modified, etc., in such a way that, if we compare documents written in the same language at different times, we note important and very significant details. None of these could be explained without the entrepreneurial capacity and alertness of the users of each language and each moment of history.

Finally, it is evident that there is no objective criterion that allows us to establish that a 'rationally' conceived institution is more efficient from the point of view of the dynamic social processes moved by the impetus of entrepreneurship than one which has been formed through evolution. Is, perhaps, Esperanto a more perfect and 'efficient' language than English or Spanish? Using what criteria can we establish that a metric system is more efficient from the point of view of dynamic coordination processes than any other? And, with regard to the very few essential juridical principles that make social coordination and the practice of entrepreneurship possible, they have clearly emerged through an evolutionary process and could be reduced to: respect for life, for property, for peacefully acquired possession and fulfilment of contracts.

The idea that the theory of entrepreneurship developed by Kirzner is precisely, in spite of its author's opinion, the missing link that was required in order to improve and provide adequate foundations for the Austrian theory on the emergence and development of social institutions, does not mean that it is not possible to theorize on the possibilities of 'improving' currently existing social institutions.[20] However, it is a work of immanent 'criticism', in other words, of exegesis, refinement of logical defects and application of the principles formed through evolution to new areas and challenges which arise as a consequence of entrepreneurial creativity (for example the application of the body of traditional principles of contract law to new privatized areas of the sea or to the 'rental' of mothers, etc., etc.). We can, therefore, conclude that, curiously, Kirzner does not appear to be sufficiently Kirznerian with regard to the recognition of the possibilities of applying his own theory of entrepreneurial analysis to the emergence, development and improvement of social institutions.

Conclusion

The above objections in no way diminish the great merit of Kirzner's work in the field of entrepreneurial theory and its application to the development and provision of foundations for a whole theory of social ethics, which has been capable of setting aside the demands of 'social' or redistributive justice based on the analytical error of presupposing a static economy with given resources and information. The dynamic conception of the market makes it easier to take up a position in the ethical field and strengthens the consideration that free markets driven by entrepreneurship not only are more efficient from the dynamic point of view, but are the only just markets. Therefore, there is no justification for any actors who act entrepreneurially and meet the traditional principles of property law feeling any sense of guilt when they appropriate the results of their creative capacity. Understanding how the entrepreneurial market process functions in dynamic terms makes it obvious that the essential principles of social justice and ethics should be based on appropriation of the results of the entrepreneurial creativity of each actor, and, as is logical, it is perfectly compatible for this entrepreneurial creativity and spirit also to be used voluntarily, to seek, discover and alleviate any situations of urgent need into which other human beings may have fallen.

13 A Hayekian strategy to implement free market reforms[1]

In his lifelong battle for liberty in the field of ideas, F. A. Hayek never forgot the great importance of following an effective and consistent strategy to implement free market reforms. Now, we also need to continue and improve Hayek's insights and leadership in this practical effort if we want to see the success of libertarian ideals in the future. Is with this goal in mind that the present article in honour of Dr Gerrit Meijer has been written.

Introduction

The theory of liberty has advanced considerably in the second half of the last century. Today, it may be said, without any doubt, that, at least within the field of economic *theory*, the triumph of free market principles has been complete. Not only has it become obvious that real socialism is, as had been demonstrated by Mises, Hayek and other members of the Austrian School of Economics, theoretically impossible,[2] but, in addition, the most reliable analyses are likewise showing that the interventionist economic policy followed in 'mixed' economies is also doomed to failure. Moreover, works which place in evidence the crisis of the so-called 'welfare state' are continually appearing. We can, therefore, conclude that, today, at the start of the new century, the theoretical debate has been won by those who defend the free market economy.

However, with regard to the *practical* application of libertarian principles, there is still a long way to go. Even though the historic fall of real socialism in Eastern Europe has shown the impossibility of communism and certain liberalizing reforms are being made in the rest of the interventionist countries (incorrectly called 'market economy' countries), there are still many difficulties to overcome. In fact, it seems as if, although the final objective pursued has become clear from a theoretical point of view, it is very difficult to begin the necessary reforms and put them into practice. Specifically, although free market reforms have been shown to be advisable from a theoretical and even moral point of view, the argument that 'their political impossibility is obvious' is often heard. In the present article, therefore, we propose to confront the objection relative to the supposed impossibility of going forward in libertarian ideology. In order to do this, we must analyse the most adequate strategy and tactics to stimulate and bring about free market reforms and the relations which should exist between the libertarian economic theorist and those politicians who wish to advance in the right direction day by day.

We will study below, first, the reasons which are usually alleged to justify the supposed political impossibility of any advance in putting free market theory into practice, reviewing a number of recent historical examples which, to a greater or lesser extent clearly refute the pessimism which exists in this field. Subsequently, we will present the strategy that we consider most fitting to surmount the barrier of what is considered 'politically impossible' from three points of view: theoretical, ethical and historical. After proposing an inventory of activities that can and should be promoted in order to bring about a change in the right direction in public opinion, we will highlight the important role of politicians in general and libertarian politicians in particular. A classification of professional politicians into four different types in accordance with their commitment to the theory and practice of liberty and an analysis of the most important circumstances that influence their behaviour, together with a list of recommended practices which we consider important for all libertarians who decide to enter politics, will bring the present work to an end.

Reasons usually alleged for considering free market reforms politically impossible

There are various reasons which are usually put forward to argue that many libertarian reforms are not politically possible and thereby justify the maintenance of the *status quo*. Thus, for example, it is alleged that the theoretical reasons which support free market policies are, in general, very abstract and difficult to explain. It is also argued that people are very reluctant to change, especially when the changes are based on abstract theories and the attainment of medium- and long-term results which, although it is understood that they will be favourable, are nevertheless felt to require 'important sacrifices' at the beginning. All this means that politicians normally tend to err on the side of timidity and lack of conviction when presenting reforms which lead in the right direction: it is felt that libertarian arguments leave too many flanks open to facile criticism, particularly with a socialist opposition which, in general, has shown itself to be unscrupulous and ready to have recourse to the most demagogic reasoning.

These and other arguments, which are those most commonly used by the politicians who consider making free market reforms, appear to have found, moreover, theoretical support in the contributions of the 'Public Choice School'. In fact, several analyses made by the Public Choice School, led by James M. Buchanan, provide a theoretical explanation of the difficulties in undertaking and bringing about the appropriate reforms. Thus, among other aspects, they talk about what they call the 'effect of the rationality of ignorance', according to which, given the reduced probability that the single vote of an individual voter can influence the final result of the elections, the current democratic system encourages citizens, consciously or unconsciously, to spare themselves the great effort implied by studying in the necessary depth the multiple complex issues which are discussed and debated at the political level.[3] In contrast to this generalized omission on the part of citizens, lobbies and 'pressure groups' appear. These identify a strong interest in a specific area and successfully mobilize their forces to exert pressure and influence over public authorities in order to obtain privileges at the cost of the silent majority' that nobody bothers to defend. Likewise, there have been theories about the effect of the 'governmental short-sightedness' which tends to arise from the fact that the priority of the politicians is to get into power and stay there at any cost, which explains that they take their decisions thinking only of the very short-term future (the next elections), making it almost inevitable that they often end up sacrificing the community's long-term welfare in the interests of obtaining short-term 'political advantages'. Lastly, it has been shown that bureaucratic bodies have a tendency to constantly over-expand and seek justification of the need for their existence and growth, as they do not depend on a profit and loss account and are not forced to ratify their services every day in the marketplace as any private company must, since their existence, funded through the State Budget, is guaranteed if they obtain sufficient political support (generally encouraged by a pressure group).

Leaving aside its evident scientific potential, which we are not going to discuss here, it is obvious that there is also a grave risk that the Public Choice School's theoretical analysis tends to foment *nihilism* among those who want to devote their efforts to providing an impetus for short-term practical reforms in the right direction. In fact, it seems that the Public Choice theory explains and confirms that, in the political field, there exists a 'vicious circle' which is very difficult to break. It shows that the politician, to a great extent, merely harvests an already existing state of public opinion which is felt to be very difficult to mobilize in the right direction in the short term, as a result of the combined effects of the 'rationality of ignorance' and the activities of the privileged pressure groups themselves (to which the 'effect of governmental short-sightedness' and the bureaucratic bodies' tendency to over-expand with hardly any limit should be added). If the numerous frustrating experiences encountered by many politicians when trying to put free market reforms into practice are added to this vicious circle, for which there is, apparently, a theoretical explanation, it is understandable that it is very easy for somebody to become sceptical or discouraged if he reaches the conclusion that the barrier of the 'politically impossible' is very difficult, or even impossible, to cross.

Historical examples which refute pessimism

However, there are several historical examples which illustrate how it is possible to promote radical reforms, even when circumstances are very adverse. Thus, referring almost exclusively to the best-known cases since World War II,[4] we should mention, in the first place, the liberalizing reform put into practice by Ludwig Erhard in Federal Germany after the Second World War, which constituted head-on defiance of the interventionist 'recommendations' of the economic advisors (Galbraith etc.) whom the victorious powers in the conflict had sent. Erhard's liberalizing decrees were issued at one stroke, by surprise, in 1948 and led to the spectacular *Wirtschaftswunder*, or 'German economic miracle'.[5]

Thirty years later, the 'conservative revolution' in the United States, promoted by Ronald Reagan in his two presidential mandates (1980–1988) also had a great impact. During this period, Reagan carried out an important fiscal reform which reduced the marginal income tax rate to 28 per cent and dismantled, to a great extent, the governmental regulation of the economy and the weight that the Federal Administration had acquired in the United States, resulting in an economic upsurge that materialized in the creation of more that 12 million jobs.[6]

Closer to us, we can mention the conservative revolution which Margaret Thatcher carried out in the United Kingdom, which stimulated, over a period of almost twelve years, the most ambitious programme for the privatization of nationalized corporations carried out in the world to date. Thatcher sold millions of council houses to their tenants, thus converting extensive social classes into small proprietors. Likewise, she carried out a profound reform of the tax system, reducing the marginal income tax rate to 40 per cent, and initiated a programme of moral regeneration which provided a strong impetus to the country's economy, which had been affected by the decades of interventionist policies applied since the Second World War, not only by Labour governments, but also, in particular, by several Conservative governments that committed the strategic error of 'pragmatism'.[7]

Finally, in view of its great historical importance, we must refer to the fall of real socialism in the Eastern European countries which, as a result of a series of, in general, bloodless revolutions, took place from 1989 onwards, to the astonishment of the Western world and the surprise of its main intellectuals and political leaders. The reforms carried out in Latin America, particularly in countries such as Chile, Argentina, Mexico, and Peru, led by 'populist' politicians who, however, have been able to promote measures in the right direction, will, in the long run, acquire a similar level of importance.[8]

It is clear, therefore, that, as opposed to the abovementioned nihilist temptation, these and other historical examples illustrate how it is perfectly possible, even in very adverse historical circumstances, to surmount the barrier of the 'politically impossible' which apparently always arises when an attempt is made to undertake free market reforms and put them successfully into practice. We will now study the strategies and measures it is necessary to adopt and execute in order to make what today seems very difficult, or even politically impossible, viable from a political standpoint.

The three levels of action required by the reforms: theoretical, historical and ethical

Elsewhere, I have developed the thesis that there are three different levels of approach to each political, economic and social situation: a theoretical level, a historical level and an ethical level.[9] According to this conception, the analysis and interpretation of social phenomena can and should be made from these three points of view.

Thus, following this model, it is easy to understand how any erroneous policy always arises as the result of a chain of factors which correspond to each of these three levels. In fact, behind any policy which is harmful to society, there are usually, at a strictly *theoretical* level, serious scientific errors and fallacies. Effectively, false theories are continually being used to justify the most harmful interventionist policies. Sometimes, these theories emerge independently, by chance, and policies are subsequently adopted as a consequence of the theoretical and methodological errors committed. On many other occasions, however, erroneous theories are constructed *ad hoc* in order to justify certain policies which have been decided previously.[10]

At a *historical* level – in other words, the level of the practical everyday situation – one of the most important factors which stimulates mistaken policies is the intervention of the pressure groups or privileged lobbies which benefit from them. Thus, the existence of certain persons or social groups who are to be specially privileged or favoured as a consequence of the harmful political measure taken must be added to the errors in the theoretical foundations.

Finally, at an *ethical* level, it should be noted that the harmful policies that result from theoretical errors and the malicious support of certain privileged pressure groups are practically inevitable when the moral principles of the social body – in other words, the basic behavioural rules which guide it – go into crisis. Put in another way, the only line of defence left for any society in which theoretical errors and privileged pressure groups arise is for its leaders and citizens to uphold a series of guided behaviours of a moral nature. If this last barrier or moral brake disappears, the society will be lost and will fall victim to the demagogic, interventionist and harmful politicians who will always find an erroneous theoretical justification and the support of some privileged lobby.

The above considerations will enable us to undertake, as a contrast, a parallel analysis of the *strategy* necessary to ensure that what we today feel to be impossible to achieve will be politically viable in the future, that is to say, the elimination of interventionist policies, replacing them with others more consistent with free market ideals. Thus, we will propose a series of specific measures and actions which should be undertaken at each of the three levels (theoretical, historical and ethical) in order to break through what today seems to be the insurmountable barrier of the politically impossible in relation to reforms with libertarian content.

Actions in the theoretical field

The part played by the pure theorist is essential in the battle for freedom. His role consists basically of a radical search for scientific truth, without any prior commitments. In order to make it possible to break the vicious circle of the politically impossible, the pure theorist plays, in the long term, the most important role. There is no doubt that ideas make the world go round or that, one way or another, their influence always filters through to the social body in the end and leaves its mark.

Moreover, it is precisely in the field of libertarian theory where most advances have been made. Today, we may say that, in this field, there has been a runaway victory over the theories which have been used to justify socialism or interventionism to date. It is sufficient to mention, for example, how the analysis of the Austrian School of Economics (Mises and Hayek) on the impossibility of socialism has been fully confirmed after several decades of controversy, not only by the fall of real socialism in Eastern Europe, but also by the apparently insoluble crisis into which the interventionist or 'welfare' state has fallen all over the Western world.[11]

At the theoretical level, perhaps the most important principle of action consists of continuing the search for the scientific truth, without making any concessions aimed at achieving short-term advantages or political influence in return. As Hayek said,

> I don't think the work of the politician and the true student of society are compatible. Indeed it seems to me that in order to be successful as a politician, to become a political leader, it is almost essential that you have no original ideas on social matters but just express what the majority feel. ... I think [the economist] ought to avoid committing himself to a party – or even devoting himself predominantly to some one good cause. That not only warps his judgement – but the influence it gives him is almost certainly bought at the price of intellectual independence. Too much anxiety to get a particular thing done, or to keep one's influence over a particular group, is almost certain to be an obstacle to his saying many unpopular things he ought to say – and leads to his compromising with 'dominant views' which have to be accepted, and even accepting views which would not stand serious examination.[12]

In short, Hayek places us on guard against the activity of, for example, some distinguished libertarian members of the School of Chicago when they present what are merely 'compromise solutions' as scientific conclusions in their studies. This has been the case, for example, of many of their prescriptions, like the monetary growth rule, flexible exchange rates, 'negative income tax', school vouchers, immigration reform and others, which have been widely debated at a scientific level and even among the population in general. The presentation and defence of these positions without making the final theoretical objectives explicit or explaining that, to a great extent, they were only intended to achieve a politically acceptable compromise has been to the detriment of the prestige of their role as theorists of liberty.[13] Thus, the leading role in the theoretical defence of free market principles, little by little, has been taken over by the Austrian School, much purer in its theory of liberty and much less committed to the search for short-term political 'solutions'.

In order to avoid this and other risks, the most appropriate strategy which should be planned in the theoretical field is what, following William H. Hutt, we will call *dual strategy* and consists basically of the following.[14] First, the essential principles of free market theory and its consequences should be studied, defining the final goals which it is intended to attain in the long term and their essential theoretical implications without any kind of prior commitment. At the same time, in the shorter term, a policy to bring us closer to these goals can and should be designed, remembering that this policy must always be *consistent* with them.

'Compromise solutions' which lead in the opposite direction of the prefixed goals or which conceal or confuse the citizens as to the final objectives and their implications must be avoided. Only this strategy may make it possible to attain, in the medium and long term, the political ends which today seem, perhaps, difficult to achieve.

The essential points of the *dual strategy* to be developed by all libertarian theorists should be, therefore, the following:

1. To study the theoretical principles and the ultimate consequences derived from them with tenacity and persistence, making no concessions to short-term political demands.
2. Never to give up the above activity; to carry out a labour of education and dissemination of the essential theoretical principles and their implications among the citizens.
3. Without losing sight of the ultimate goals and their implications or abandoning the labour of education and dissemination, to work on the theoretical design of *alternative transition processes* which, without ever violating the theoretical principles, always lead in the right direction.
4. If acceptance of a short-term political commitment is unavoidable, it must always pass the test of not violating the essential principles (i.e. the commitment must never imply moving further away from them). Moreover, it will be necessary to explain to the citizens that it is a short-term concession or commitment, due to political circumstances rather than to a theoretical principle which is the logical and inevitable consequence of libertarian ideas.

In the theoretical field, only activity which always strictly follows these principles can avoid the most dangerous risk for any free market strategist, which is to commit the error of *day-to-day political pragmatism*, forgetting, when faced with the exertion and difficulties which overwhelm the person who has to take short-term political decisions, the ultimate objectives pursued, in view of the supposed political impossibility of attaining them. *Pragmatism* is the most dangerous vice for the libertarian and, in the past, has had devastating effects on its ideology. It has systematically led to the agreement and adoption of political decisions aimed at getting into power or remaining there which, in many cases, were essentially inconsistent with (i.e. leading in the opposite direction from) those which should have been the ultimate objectives to be pursued from the libertarian standpoint. Moreover, the discussion exclusively of what was politically viable in the very short term and the fact that the scientists themselves relegated the final goals to second place, or even forgot them completely, has often prevented detailed study of the theoretical principles and of the necessary process for disseminating them. All this has, in the past, meant a continual loss of the content of free market ideology which, in many cases, has become totally blurred and diluted with other programmes, interests and ideologies.

Fortunately, at the present time, circumstances have changed and libertarian theorists are again on the offensive, studying the purest theoretical principles and disseminating their contents and implications among the population. This explains the great revival and renewed impetus of the market economy and libertarianism all over the world.

Actions in the ethical field

The field of ethics has been, up to now, cast into oblivion in the strategies to defend and promote libertarianism in general and the free market economy in particular. The reason for this regrettable omission should be sought in the prevalence of the narrow 'scientistic' conception in economics. This conception has tried to develop our discipline following the methodology and scientific procedures which belong to physics and other natural sciences. Thus, the neoclassical models which have prevailed in economics to date are based on a reductionist concept of human rationality, which presupposes a closed environment of ends and means or, in other words, of complete information (either in certain or probabilistic terms), in which human beings are supposed merely to make *ad hoc* decisions in terms of constrained maximization. According to this approach, it seems that it is not necessary for human beings to adapt their behaviour to any moral guidelines, as the correct decision in each case will stem from a mere criterion of optimization of the known ends it is intended to reach (presented, moreover, with the scientific halo which mathematical formalism enjoys today), using means that are also supposedly known and within the reach of the person making the decision. This scientific conception of economics is the idea developed tirelessly by most libertarians of the Neoclassical School. However the defence of the market made by these authors is based exclusively on reasons of narrow utilitarian efficiency and, therefore, they tend to give theoretical weapons and arguments to those who, to the contrary, advocate state intervention and even socialism. In fact, if it is presupposed that the information is given and that it is only possible to act following a narrow maximization criterion, it is almost inevitable to take the small additional theoretical step of assuming that such information and operational criteria may be used, with even greater efficiency, by the government or state planning body itself in order to 'adequately' organize society in general or any of its specific areas via coercive commands.[15]

As opposed to this reductionist conception of economics, Mises, Hayek and their followers of the Austrian School have shown that it is impossible for either the human actor or the scientist or members of any government or planning board to obtain the information which the neoclassical models presuppose to be available. The reason for this impossibility stems from the *entrepreneurial creativity* of the human being, which is constantly discovering new ends, means and opportunities for gain. Therefore, the reductionist and static concept of 'rationality' handled by the neoclassical theorists, which nips the creative capacity of the human being in the bud, cannot be accepted.[16]

Moreover, the impossibility of narrow maximization criteria providing an exclusive guide to human action makes it inevitable for the latter to be developed within a framework of guided juridical and moral behaviours which evolve as the representation of human nature in the multiple processes of social interaction that have unfolded in the course of history. These moral and legal institutions cannot be deliberately created by human beings, as they incorporate a volume of information so vast and variable that it greatly exceeds the capacity of foresight, analysis and comprehension of the mind of each individual. However, these juridical, moral, economic and linguistic institutions are precisely the most important ones for the evolution of life in society and, therefore, of civilization. All these teachings, which have been refined by Mises, Hayek and other Austrian School theorists, mainly in the course of the debate they have maintained during the past century on the theoretical impossibility of socialism, show that market and economic freedom must be defended, not only for reasons strictly of 'dynamic efficiency'[17] (in other words, because they promote greater creativity and more effective coordination between human behaviours), but also, above all, because capitalism is the only moral economic system, from an ethical point of view.[18]

If ethics entered into crisis during the twentieth century, this was the result of the deification of reason which is typical of exaggerated scientism and according to which it is assumed that every human being can and should decide *ad hoc* following his or her subjective impulses on the basis of constrained maximization criteria, without the need to subject him- or herself to moral behaviours with pre-established guidelines. This erroneous scientistic conception of economics so much criticized by Hayek has become one of the essential foundations of socialism, which can, in fact, be defined as the economic system in which it is intended for the government to coordinate civil society through commands without the need to submit itself to any dogmatic moral principles, as it is assumed that it has the necessary information to take any decision based on a cost–benefit analysis. Therefore, Mises and Hayek's theoretical demonstration[19] that it is impossible to act in this way, mainly due to lack of information, has returned the leading role in social cooperation to the ethical principles of traditional morality on which the market economy is based and which had been cast into oblivion by politicians, scientists and a large part of the public. Among these principles, we can highlight the right to ownership and pacifically acquired possession of the fruits of one's own entrepreneurial creativity; individual responsibility, taken as each actor's assumption of the costs derived from his or her action; the consideration that forced 'solidarity' is immoral, as it loses the ethical component which should never be given up and which comes only from voluntarism and freedom; and, in short, the fact that state coercion applied to achieve specific goals in the social field is immoral, since it contravenes human nature and the principles of respect for the freedom of individual human action and equality before the law upon which the true rule of law is based.

The ethical and moral defence of the market economy is indispensable in order to ensure the political success of libertarian reforms. It should put an end to the monopoly of the 'moral' arguments enjoyed, up to now, by interventionist politicians (from the left and the right) mainly due to the absence of ethical criteria, which derives from the narrow utilitarian rationalism of the Neoclassical School of economics. One of the most recent and important contributions to the theory of liberty in this century has been, precisely, to show that the merely consequentialist cost–benefit analysis developed to date by economic science in terms of strict utilitarian efficiency *is insufficient* to justify, alone, a market economy. Thus, the development of the ethical foundations of the theory of liberty is indispensable for the following basic reasons: (1) the failure of 'social engineering' and, specifically, the consequentialism derived from the neoclassical-Walrasian paradigm which has dominated economic science to date; (2) the theoretical analysis of market processes made by the Austrian School on the basis of the theory of entrepreneurship and the concept of 'dynamic efficiency' is also, alone, insufficient to justify a market economy, particularly in respect of the privileged pressure groups which always reap short-term benefits from the coercive intervention of the state and whose time preference in favour of the *present* subsidies, privileges and advantages they always obtain prevails over the subjective value they may place on the negative consequences that the interventionism of which they are now taking advantage may have in the future;[20] and (3), above all, from a strategic point of view, it is basically moral considerations that drive the reformist behaviour of human beings, who are often willing to make important sacrifices in pursuit of what they consider good and just from a moral viewpoint, while it is much more difficult to ensure such behaviour on the basis of narrow criteria of efficiency, which consist only of cold calculations of cost–benefit analysis the scientific potentiality and foundation of which are, moreover, more than doubtful. In view of all the foregoing, we should conclude that no free market reform will be successful in the long run if its promoters do not argue to their fellow citizens, with full knowledge and vigour, that, not only is the market economic more efficient, but also, above all, it is the only economic system consistent with morality; and, simultaneously, that state interventionism and the action of the pressure groups which support it are, in essence, immoral.

Actions at a historical level

The third and last level at which action should be taken in order to break the vicious circle of political impossibility is in practical everyday life, which we will call the 'historical level'. It is clear that political decisions depend on the public opinion at any given moment and on the way in which it influences the political processes.[21] Moreover, public opinion is the result of a series of ideologies, beliefs and principles which, although they are often false and contradictory, slowly filter into the social network through a constellation of *ideological intermediaries*, which Hayek calls *second-hand dealers of ideas*. Among these, what are generally called 'intellectuals' may be highlighted: novelists,[22] historians, cinema scriptwriters and those professional disseminators of other people's ideas who undertake to communicate and interpret the most topical news every day (journalists).

The main and most urgent need at this everyday reality level is to modify public opinion and provide it with an appropriate theory and morality in accordance with libertarian principles. In order to do this, great effort and perseverance are necessary, aimed, in the first place, at educating the 'intellectuals' and disseminators of other people's ideas, winning them over to the scientific and ethical cause of freedom, which has already been formulated at the theoretical and ethical levels we have already discussed. Thus, the libertarian ideal may ferment in the social body, thanks to the effective labour of an 'army' of disseminators and intellectuals who act applying the established principles of the pure theory of freedom to the everyday reality.

What kind of specific activities can and should be carried out in this field? Although it is not an exhaustive list, as examples we can identify the following activities that should be promoted and performed every day in this field, without respite:

1 Teaching and educational activities: these include organizing educational seminars in university environments and, in general, promoting meetings, congresses, conferences and talks at which intellectuals and disseminators may receive first-hand information on the essential principles and arguments upon which the free market economy is based. These meetings also serve to interchange experiences and propose new forms of explaining the practical application of libertarian principles to the citizens.
2 Activities of dissemination and publication of books, works and studies related to the libertarian ideal: here, we should mention, for example, the

great editorial effort made by several publishing companies and institutions to publish the most important classics in libertarian theory. There is also a numerous group of institutes, business organizations, foundations, etc., which promote, to a greater or lesser extent, studies and research intended to apply free market ideas to the most pressing social problems.

3 Activities related to the media, such as the promotion of journals and magazines specialized in the study and application of free market ideas; having prestigious newspapers adopt an editorial line committed to the free market economy; seeking good and sustained relations with mass media professionals, especially those who are most sympathetic to libertarian ideas; and, finally, obtaining influence over the mass media which, like the radio and television, have the broadest impact on society today.

4 The creation of institutes and *think tanks* with a libertarian leaning; in other words, to reproduce the successfully tried and tested method consisting of the creation, promotion and development of free market institutes and foundations devoted to the analysis of social problems from a libertarian point of view, together with the award of scholarships and grants for the study, development and articulation of the specific political measures for libertarian reform.[23]

5 Finally, an adequate *international coordination* of all these activities is indispensable. Thus, for example, the interchange of experiences among institutes in different countries and mutual assistance internationally among the theorists and disseminators of libertarian ideas have been found to be extremely useful. Here, in the academic field, the Mont Pèlerin Society, created by Hayek after the Second World War, has played a leading role. Today, its members include more than 400 libertarian intellectuals, seven of whom have won the Nobel Prize for Economics.[24] The role of the Atlas Research Foundation, founded by Anthony Fisher, in promoting the creation of institutes in Latin America, Asia and Eastern Europe has also been of great importance in spreading libertarianism into areas which, until recently, were a closed shop of Marxism and international socialism. Finally, the labour of organizing academic seminars and publications, carried out at an international level by Liberty Fund, the Institute for Humane Studies, the Cato Institute, the Ludwig von Mises Institute and many others, should be highlighted.

As is logical, all these types of activities must be carried out following the principle of specialization and division of labour. The same person or institution cannot and should not dilute his efforts over all of them. On the contrary, it is necessary for the different activities to be carried out on a specialized and professional basis, although it is true that an adequate coordination and organization of functions tends to reinforce the success of each initiative. Thus, little by little, sustained and combined action in all these fields finally not only reveals to the citizens the errors of interventionism, its profound immorality and the egoism of the privileged pressure groups that take short-term advantage of the mechanisms of political power, but also makes possible the irreversible erosion of the *establishment* of interventionist ideologies, generating a situation where the presence of public opinion favourable to the free market and libertarianism slowly grows and is finally consolidated, becoming inexorable and irresistible from the social and political point of view.

The role of the politician in libertarian reform

It is usually said that a good politician is one who gets on best with the voters and, therefore, that, in general, politicians merely *reap the harvest* of existing public opinion. According to this approach, politicians are simply a melting pot of the society from which they emerge and, in fact, there is a great deal of truth in this idea.[25] Thus, for example, Goldwater and Reagan, in their respective campaigns for the presidency of the United States, set forth very similar free market ideas. However, one of them, Goldwater, lost the elections because American society in 1964 was imbued with the mythical culture of the welfare state, whereas Reagan won two elections by absolute majority from 1980 onwards, basically because the centre of gravity of public opinion in the United States had shifted massively toward the moral and theoretical principles of the capitalist system. Therefore, to the extent that it is true that politicians merely reap the harvest of a certain climate of public opinion, the need to take action in respect of intellectuals and those who spread ideas takes on a special relevance in accordance with the recommendations we make in the preceding section, since they are the people who, in the final analysis, guarantee the change of public opinion in the right direction which the politicians tend to follow.

However, the thesis that the politician simply harvests a climate of opinion does not tell the *whole* truth. We think that, actually, politicians, in spite of the evident restrictions imposed on them by the environment and public opinion, often have significant *room for manoeuvre*, not only to take action in order to achieve the appropriate reforms, but even to mobilize public opinion in favour of them. We therefore find what is now the classic definition of political activity given by the Spanish politician Cánovas del Castillo to be very appropriate: 'politics is the art of bringing about, at each historical moment, the part of the ideal the circumstances make possible'.[26] It should be noted that this definition talks about trying to bring about the greatest amount possible of the ideal and, therefore, in accordance with this concept, a clear sense of libertarian belligerence should be given to all political activity. The cases of Thatcher and Reagan driving the libertarian-conservative revolution of the 1980s in the United Kingdom and United States and the case of the Argentinian president Menem, who, in spite of winning his elections with a populist message, has carried out a free market transformation in the political, social and economic structures of his country, are paradigmatic and demonstrate how much can be done by charismatic politicians who, due to conviction or circumstances, decide to promote free market reforms in their countries.

It is therefore very important to place the greatest number possible of 'professional politicians' with a libertarian education and commitment among our public servants. They should know the principles upon which the free market reforms are based and the main consequences, implications and arguments that favour them, so that they become capable of explaining libertarian ideology in a way that can be understood and is attractive to the majority of citizens. The capacity of a professional politician to explain these principles to the people, making the libertarian project convincing and exciting for the masses, has an incalculable value. From this point of view, it is very useful to classify professional politicians into four large groups, which could be as follows:

1 Professional politicians who are clearly and exclusively *pragmatic*: these are those who do not know the free market principles or their implications. They neither know nor want to know anything about libertarian ideology, as their sole interest is to achieve and maintain political power, and their personal abilities are sufficient to do this. Unfortunately, this group of ignorant and pragmatic politicians has been, to date, the most numerous of the groups that comprise the professional politicians, mainly composed of lawyers, teachers, intellectuals or journalists, whose main political experience or skill is their ability to spread unfounded ideas.[27]
2 Pragmatic politicians who, however, *have learnt something* about the essential principles and implications of free market theory: these politicians have an intuition and some knowledge of the correct functioning of the processes of social interaction that they have acquired either by education or through the experience of spending a number of years in power. Thanks to this greater knowledge, they are, therefore, at least aware of the great damage they do when they sponsor interventionist measures in their societies, although, in view of their lack of conviction and highly pragmatic nature, it would be illusory to think that they might acquire some kind of guilt complex as a result of their responsibility for the harmful effects generated by the interventionist measures they sponsor at a political level.
3 Politicians who are well educated in free market ideals and who try, at least diffidently, to point their political action in the *right direction*: this group of professional politicians are imbued with libertarian ideology and do their best to reduce the damage that their activity naturally generates to a minimum, although it is true that, on most occasions, they become disconcerted by the serious difficulties and restrictions of everyday problems and can take little effective action to promote libertarian reforms in practice.[28]
4 Politicians who are familiar with libertarian theory and are able to control the progress of political events towards the final goals: their main

characteristics are: their capacity to *formulate* libertarian ideology optimistically, in a way that is attractive to the voters *en masse*; their capacity to *convince* the citizens of the need for the reforms; and their capacity to *excite* the majority of the electorate with their project. This fourth and last group is formed by a handful of *exceptional politicians*. The nations in which, at some time in history, a 'thoroughbred' politician with all these characteristics emerges should consider themselves to be very lucky. This is the case, although not throughout their whole political activity, of Erhard in Germany, Reagan in the United States, Thatcher in England and Vaclav Klaus in Czechoslovakia, among those who have been successful in promoting, developing and culminating important free market reforms, and of Vargas Llosa in Peru and Antonio Martino in Italy, among those who tried and, for one reason or another, were unable to succeed. All of them are a noble example, which any professional politician who wishes to triumph when putting his free market beliefs into practice should follow.[29]

It is obvious that the activities described in the preceding section should give priority to educating and influencing the largest and best qualified group of current or future politicians possible, so as to enable them to be classified in the third and fourth of the groups described above. In order to attain this ambitious goal, the most varied combination possible of ideas and activities should be used, among which the libertarian institutions should play a leading role, above all in connecting the principles of libertarian ethics and theory with their practical application as real political measures that lead in the right direction towards the final goals and are well articulated in political terms and attractive to wide areas of society. The reforms, moreover, should be conceived in such a way that they contain elements which make them irreversible *de facto*, since they favour important and very numerous groups of citizens who, having benefited from them, are definitively won over to the free market cause.[30] It is, therefore, indispensable to creatively introduce all possible elements that will make the libertarian reforms irreversible.

How much should politicians lie?

In spite of the above considerations, we should not deceive ourselves: there are many constraints on politicians and they often have very little room for manoeuvre. What is more, there are so many difficulties that arise in daily political work that it has become generally accepted that one of the typical characteristics of a politician is his ability to deceive and lie to the electorate. Is this inevitable? Where are the limits which, from our point of view, a politician should never exceed?

The recognition of the limits and restrictions to which the libertarian politician is subject should never allow him to forget the unavoidable necessity to follow the *dual strategy* that we explained earlier. The libertarian politician, therefore, should never lose his point of reference (the final goals and their essential theoretical and ethical implications) and, at most, it is acceptable that he should adapt his behaviour to the difficulties and pitfalls that arise at any given moment. Thus, he may be excused if, on certain occasions, he *keeps quiet* above some of the reforms he intends to carry out when circumstances so permit, or even that he should not mention some of the consequences and implications of his political decisions. Some calculatedly *ambiguous* lines of action may be accepted, above all in election periods, in order to avoid arguments on issues that, in view of their complexity, may be very tricky to explain to the public or leave flanks unnecessarily exposed to the facile demagoguery of the opposition. Finally, it is acceptable that the libertarian politician 'knows how to tell the truth' when convenient and should even use a *healthy demagoguery* when, for example, measures which are both popular and have a great libertarian content are defended, like those relative to indiscriminate tax reductions or the abolishment of conscription.[31]

However, the following conduct may in no case be admitted from a libertarian standpoint: (1) lying deliberately in relation to any specific aspect of political activity by telling the public the exact opposite of what it is intended to do; (2) accepting modifications to the programme that distort the whole free market ideology; and (3), the most serious one, taking measures that lead in the opposite direction to the long-term goals that should be pursued, betraying the essential ethical or theoretical principles of libertarian ideology.

Never exceeding the above limits, we could even accept a 'Leninist-type' strategy,[32] aimed at obtaining as much support as necessary in order to carry out the libertarian reforms which, depending on the specific scope and circumstances, will require allies to be sought among other social groups or institutions. Moreover, as we have already seen, it is necessary for free market reforms to be consolidated and carried out in such a way that they finally become irreversible. In short, our libertarian strategy should always be directed towards winning support and weakening and inhibiting the interventionist opposition. In addition, with regard to the design and impetus of libertarian reforms, it is better to do too much than too little. There is nothing more regrettable than the frequent case of the politician who gets into power with a free market programme supported by the public who, when the crunch comes, due to his lack of tenacity or belief in his own ideas, or to diffidence when putting them into practice, does not come anywhere near the expectations created, losing all his own prestige and, what is worse, the prestige of the libertarian ideals he claims to defend.[33]

However, the actual political result depends on the specific circumstances at any given historical moment, upon which it is not possible to theorize. Notwithstanding, a series of rules of thumb may be drawn up in order to facilitate the politician's line of action when understanding and trying to handle the relationship between the world of public opinion and the specific field of political action in which he moves. Thus, it may be said that, all other things being equal, the more educated public opinion is, the more radical the libertarian politician's message may be. And *vice versa*, the more unschooled public opinion is, the more difficult it is for the libertarian content of the political message to be understood and shared by the citizens. Another rule is that the more traumatic the social starting situation, the more radical the message may be. In fact, it is in situations of real social crisis that the citizens are more willing to accept sacrifices and *shock* policies.[34] Furthermore, *ceteris paribus*, the more professional politicians there are belonging to the third and fourth groups (made up, we should remember, of the politicians who are best educated in libertarian ideology, with the greatest capacity to get their message across and make it attractive), the more radical the libertarian policy they recommend may be. And *vice versa*, less educated professional politicians – in other words, those belonging to groups 1 and 2 – will find that their own limitations and lack of theoretical and ethical knowledge make it impossible for them to correctly express and defend a libertarian message the contents of which they neither know nor share. Finally, in election periods, the more certain somebody may be of winning for ancillary reasons, the less need they have to employ a radical libertarian message. And, *vice versa*, under circumstances where an electoral triumph is more distant, a more radical message against the interventionist *status quo* may be launched.

Conclusion

Finally, we will conclude by making some recommendations for any libertarian politician for whom the final goal of preparing, promoting and culminating a generalized reform to liberalize the economy and society prevails over his wishes to get into power and remain there.

First, we should reiterate the fact that, in any case, it is always better to do too much than too little. In other words, the message should be radicalized to the point where it puts both the members of his or her own party and the rest of the citizens to the test. Only in this way is it possible to find out whether, in fact, a politician meets the requirements to belong to group 4, that is to say, whether s/he is able to excite and stimulate the electorate in favour of a correctly expressed libertarian reform policy. The worst that can happen is that, as a consequence of taking up a relatively more radical position, s/he does not succeed in his or her own party and is left on the sideline by his more 'pragmatic' colleagues. Nevertheless, precisely the acceptance or otherwise of his or her person and his or her message is the irrefutable and final proof of whether or not s/he should continue to devote his efforts to political activity. If s/he is not accepted, it could be better for him or her to allow other professional politicians with less commitment (belonging to groups 3 and 2) to temporarily take the lead, in order not to burn himself and squander his efforts, which will possibly be much more fruitful in the long term in other (non-political) activities related to the study and dissemination of libertarianism.

In this way, he will not waste time or exhaust himself with activities that, in view of restrictions imposed by the environment, make it very difficult to pursue his ideal and which, in any case, may be carried out by other, less committed, politicians. However, it is always advisable that the necessary number of libertarian politicians should be kept 'in reserve' in case circumstances change in the future and, in the light of more pressing needs, s/he is called upon to occupy greater political responsibilities in an environment where s/he can develop his or her libertarian programme without being unnecessarily shackled by his own party.[35]

There is, therefore, an obvious relationship between what the political environment allows one to do and the advisability of the personal involvement of a politician with strong libertarian convictions. The greater the restrictions, the more difficult s/he will find it to act in that environment and the more possible it is that other colleagues, with fewer ideological convictions (belonging to groups 2 and 3), will be able to carry out their work adequately. On the contrary, in circumstances where it is possible to drive forward a more radical programme, his or her personal participation and involvement will be more difficult to substitute, since other colleagues with less education and ideological commitment cannot be expected to recognize and take advantage of the historical opportunity which emerges to implement profoundly libertarian reforms. As is logical, the evaluation of whether the existing circumstances are of one type or the other depends on the discernment and intelligence of each free market politician.

In any case, the main risk of the recommended strategy is that the group 4 politician may finally be accepted by his or her party and, after presenting his or her programme and steadfastly defending it, fail to win the elections or fall from power. Nevertheless, even in such adverse circumstances, which have repeatedly occurred throughout history,[36] the negative result should not be considered a failure in the strict sense of the term. From the libertarian point of view, it would only be a real failure either to betray the principles or to have fallen short by encouraging only diffident liberalizing policies when the circumstances would have allowed things to go much further. Outside these two cases, failure to win elections in certain historical circumstances should merely be considered a tactical defeat in the long and difficult struggle to win over the future for liberty.

14 The future of liberalism
The deconstruction of the state through direct democracy[1]

I am fully in sympathy with Bruno Frey's plea for more direct democracy through the use of referenda following the model of the Swiss political system. However, a careful libertarian reader of his paper could easily get the impression that, for Bruno Frey, democracy is an end in itself and that, for this reason, it is important to improve the direct democratic participation of the citizens. Although it is true that the Swiss system of referenda has interesting advantages, which Bruno Frey correctly explains, vs the more widely extended systems of indirect democracy, I will argue that our main goal as libertarians should be, in the future, to strengthen free market liberalism, and not democracy *per se*. Or, in other words, if direct democracy has any merits, they are precisely to allow a (still imperfect) approximation to our ideal of free market and limited government.

Politicians against the voters

It is true that politicians in general dislike referenda. A paradigmatic case would be the elite of Spanish politicians who agreed and wrote the 1978 Spanish Constitution currently in force in my country. Article 92 of our Constitution only allows referenda that are not binding on the government in Spain (i.e. only purely advisory ones). The Spanish Constitution (probably together with the Swedish one) is the most restrictive in Europe regarding the conditions, scope and effects of referenda. As a result, following Frey's analysis, in Spain it is almost impossible to break the politicians' cartel in the way that it was broken, for instance, in Switzerland when the Swiss people rejected joining the European Economic Space in the Referendum of 6 December 1992 (although it is true that this result was at least partially reversed in the Referendum of 22 May 2000, when 67.2 per cent of Swiss voters approved the bilateral agreements of Switzerland with the European Union). The lack of Referendum Democracy in Spain also gives a continual pretext to the Stalinist assassins belonging to the Basque terrorist gang ETA, who call themselves 'separatists' and would very probably lose their implicit sociological support (which we could estimate at around 10 per cent of the Basque population) if a referendum on the separation of the Basque country from Spain could be organized with full democratic guarantees. Although such a referendum is politically impossible for the time being, I am sure: first, that the majority of the Basque Country citizens (around 2 million people) would reject separation; and, second, that, irrespective of the final result, such a referendum could be an important element toward the final solution of the Basque country terrorist problems. So, in this matter I also agree with Bruno Frey when he concludes in his paper (Section IV, 4) that direct democracy can settle separatist matters with 'less strife and bloodshed than normally occurs in democracies in which referenda are uncommon, or used only in the form of a plebiscite'.

However, it is true that, in the final analysis, for a libertarian, the libertarian content of the political decision taken is much more important than the specific democratic procedure followed to reach that decision. In fact, none of us would be comfortable, for example, with an independent Basque country converted into a kind of Albanian socialist state separated from the rest of Spain and the European Union, relatively much more libertarian. This principle forces us to search for the political procedures that will most effectively limit government and enhance a true free market. Direct democracy can be one of these procedures, provided it is always combined with the right of any social group to self-determination and *secession* from the political organization in which it is included.

The necessary condition of direct democracy: the right of secession

Bruno Frey devotes the shortest section of his paper (Section III 'Referendum and Federalism') to what I consider to be the most important matter: the connections between direct democracy and the decentralization of political decision-making. For direct democracy 'small is beautiful and efficient',[2] and Bruno Frey clearly explains how the knowledge needed for informed political decision-making is more easily obtained in smaller political communities (in fact, it is not merely a coincidence that the tradition of referenda is much greater in cantonal Switzerland, with 7 million citizens, than in traditionally centralized countries like Spain or France, with 40 and 60 million inhabitants, respectively). In this respect, we should remember the following economic law: other things being equal, the smaller the state to which a political community is affiliated, the more difficult it will be for that state to impose interventionist policies and protectionism and the more it will be forced to accept free trade and libertarianism. This is the case because, the smaller the state in question, the more its inhabitants will suffer and perceive the costs of regulation and barriers to foreign markets and resources if there is not complete economic and trade freedom. Furthermore, Bruno Frey mentions (following Tiebout, Buchanan and others) how the increased possibilities of voting with one's feet among small political units 'tend to undermine regional cartels by politicians', so that we can conclude that, in a political environment based on the libertarian principles of self-determination, free trade and freedom of emigration and immigration (subjected to private property laws), a constellation of small states will greatly enhance freedom and prosperity.[3]

From a libertarian point of view there is, however, a key point I miss in Frey's paper. This refers to the actual possibility that, through an act of direct democracy (i.e. a referendum), a majority could enact a regulation to exploit a minority. Direct democracy is, in the best case, an improved form of democracy, but gives no guarantee of avoiding the use of political power and institutionalized coercion against minorities. For this reason, for a libertarian it is of the utmost importance to combine the political procedures of direct democracy with the effective existence of the right of secession of any minority that feels itself exploited by the result of any referendum. Thus, my conclusion is more radical than Bruno Frey's: more than considering simple federalism as a *prerequisite* for making direct democracy effective (Section III of Frey's paper), our libertarian ideals should demand democracy be limited (even 'direct' democracy) through the effective use of the right of secession, which means that any group or association of individuals should be free to decide at any moment whether or not to be included in a state or political unit, to create a new one or to be included in a previously existing one.

The deconstruction of the State through direct democracy and secession

The explosion of the technological revolution and the global economy is creating new possibilities for direct democracy and secession, which, even now, are unimaginable. In an integrated world of online elections through the Internet using, for instance, cryptographic individual keys, practically all matters could be subject to direct democracy at very low cost. In the world today, the traditional nation-states are becoming more and more anachronistic. A political process based on combined direct democracy and effective secession could create in the twenty-first century

> a world consisting of tens of thousands of distinct countries, regions, and cantons, and of hundreds of thousands of independent free cities such as the present-day 'oddities' of Monaco, Andorra, San Marino, Liechtenstein, Hong Kong and Singapore, with the resulting greatly increased opportunities for economically motivated migration.[4]

This world would be one of small liberal governments economically integrated through free trade and an international commodity private money, such as gold, and would be a world of unprecedented economic growth and unheard-of prosperity. In this new world that many libertarians are envisioning for the century that is now beginning, it would not even be necessary to vote in every case with one's feet to guarantee freedom (for instance to avoid any 'island' of tyranny or oppression) if a system of Functional Overlapping

Competing Jurisdictions (FOCJs), based on direct democracy and referenda, more or less spontaneously develops. These Jurisdictions, which would overlap and have a governmental nature, although they would not be restricted to any historically determined geographical area, could compete with each other, and were imagined and explained in a very brilliant paper presented by Professor Bruno Frey at the 1997 Regional Meeting of the Mont Pèlerin Society held in Barcelona (Spain),[5] which I recommend to all of you.

Private property anarchism in a free market: the asymptotical ideal of direct 'democracy'

We cannot, of course, go into any detail in explaining Frey's Functional Overlapping Competing Jurisdictions here. My main criticism of them (and also of Hoppe's minimal states and free cities) is that these Jurisdictions would, at all events, be governmental, i.e. they could still coerce their citizens by collecting taxes etc. So my main question is the following: why not improve direct democracy even more by making these Jurisdictions entirely voluntary? If this were the case, we would have reached the most perfect 'direct democracy' conceivable, a state of affairs already described by Frank Albert Fetter in 1913, when he called the market a kind of democracy in which every penny gives the right to cast a ballot, [6] or by our former distinguished member William Hutt, when he used for the first time the concept 'consumer's sovereignty'.[7] It is true that these expressions and comparisons are not entirely perfect because, instead of comparing the market with the so called 'democratic ideal', the comparison should, at all events, be the other way round: it would be much more correct to say that direct democracy is a scheme to assign to citizens the same supremacy in the political sphere as the market economy gives them in other areas.[8] If this is so, the most perfect direct democracy only will be reached once the free market is also extended to the areas currently covered by governments through a constellation of overlapping voluntary and competing private agencies, associations and corporations.[9] In this way we would have found the way to entirely eliminate politicians and their cartels against the ordinary citizens, reaching the most perfect 'democracy' conceivable for the twenty-first century: that constituted by the process of private property and free market anarchism.

15 Juan de Mariana and the Spanish scholastics[1]

One of the main contributions of Professor Murray N. Rothbard has been to show that the prehistory of the Austrian School of Economics should be sought in the works of the Spanish scholastics of what is known as the 'Siglo de Oro Español' (in English, the 'Spanish Golden Century'), which ran from the mid-sixteenth century through the seventeenth century. Rothbard first developed this thesis in 1974[2] and, more recently, in chapter 4, volume I, of his monumental *History of Economic Thought from the Austrian Perspective*, entitled 'The Late Spanish Scholastics'.[3]

However, Rothbard was not the only important Austrian economist to show the Spanish origins of the Austrian School of Economics. Friedrich Hayek himself also had the same point of view, especially after meeting Bruno Leoni, the great Italian scholar, author of the book *Freedom and the Law*.[4] Leoni met Hayek in the 1950s and was able to convince him that the intellectual roots of classical economic liberalism were of continental and Catholic origins and should be sought in Mediterranean Europe, not in Scotland.[5]

Who were these Spanish intellectual forerunners of the Austrian School of Economics? Most of them were scholastics teaching morals and theology at the University of Salamanca, a wonderful Spanish medieval city located 150 miles to the north-west of Madrid, close to the border of Spain with Portugal. These scholastics were mainly either Dominicans or Jesuits and were able to articulate the subjectivist, dynamic and libertarian tradition on which, 250 years later, Carl Menger and his followers of the Austrian School would place so much importance.[6] Perhaps the most libertarian of all the scholastics, particularly in his later works, was the Jesuit father Juan de Mariana.

Mariana was born in 1536 in the city of Talavera de la Reina, near Toledo in Spain. He appears to have been the illegitimate son of a canon of Talavera and, when he was 16, joined the Society of Jesus, which had just been created. At the age of 24, he was summoned to Rome to teach theology, then transferred to the school the Jesuits ran in Sicily and from there to the University of Paris. In 1574, he returned to Spain and lived and studied in the city of Toledo until his death in 1623, at the age of 87.

Juan de Mariana and the Spanish scholastics 205

Although Father Juan de Mariana wrote many books, the first one with a libertarian content was, perhaps, the book entitled *De rege et regis institutione* ('On the king and the Royal Institution') published in 1598, in which he set forth his famous defence of tyrannicide. According to Mariana any individual citizen can justly assassinate a king who imposes taxes without the people's consent, seizes the property of individuals and squanders it, or prevents a meeting of a democratic parliament.[7] The doctrines contained in this book were apparently used to justify the assassination of the French tyrant kings Henry III and Henry IV and the book was burned in Paris by the executioner as a result of a decree issued by the Parliament of Paris on 4 July 1610.[8]

In Spain, although the authorities were not enthusiastic about it, the book was respected. In fact, all Mariana did was to take to its logical conclusion the idea that natural law is morally superior to the might of the state. This idea had previously been developed in detail by the great founder of international law, the Dominican Francisco de Vitoria (1485–1546), who began the Spanish scholastic tradition of denouncing the conquest and particularly the enslavement of the Indians by the Spaniards in the New World.

But perhaps Mariana's most important book was the work published in 1605 with the title *De monetae mutatione* ('On the alteration of money').[9] In this book, Mariana began to question whether the king or governor was the owner of the private property of his vassals or citizens and reached the clear conclusion that he was not. The author then applied his distinction between a king and a tyrant and concluded that 'the tyrant is he who tramples everything underfoot and believes everything to belong to him; the king restricts or limits his covetousness within the terms of reason and justice'.

From this, Mariana deduces that the king cannot demand tax without the people's consent, since taxes are simply an appropriation of part of the subjects' wealth. In order for such an appropriation to be legitimate, the subjects must be in agreement. Neither may the king create state monopolies, since they would simply be a disguised means of collecting taxes.

And neither may the king – this is the most important part of the book's contents – obtain fiscal revenue by lowering the metal content of coins. De Mariana realized that the reduction of the precious metal content in coins and the increase in the number of coins in circulation is simply a form of inflation (although he does not use this word, which was unknown at the time) and that inflation inevitably leads to a rise in prices because, 'if money falls from the legal value, all goods increase unavoidably, in the same proportion as the money fell, and all the accounts break down'.

Mariana describes the serious economic consequences to which the debasement and government tampering with the market value of money lead as follows:

> Only a fool would try to separate these values in such a way that the legal price should differ from the natural. Foolish, nay, wicked the ruler

who orders that a thing the common people value, let us say, at five should be sold from ten. Men are guided in this matter by common estimation founded on considerations of the quality of things, and of their abundance or scarcity. It would be vain for a Prince to seek to undermine these principles of commerce. 'Tis best to leave them intact instead of assailing them by force to the public detriment.[10]

We should note how de Mariana refers to the fact that the 'common estimation' of men is the origin of the value of things, thus following the traditional subjectivist doctrine of the scholastics, which was initially proposed by Diego de Covarrubias y Leyva. Covarrubias was born in 1512 and died in 1577. The son of a famous architect, he became bishop of the city of Segovia and a minister of King Philip II. Thus, in 1554, he set forth better than anyone before the subjectivist theory of value, stating that 'the value of an article does not depend on its essential nature but on the subjective estimation of men, even if that estimation is foolish', illustrating his thesis with the example that 'in the Indies wheat is dearer than in Spain because men esteem it more highly, though the nature of the wheat is the same in both places'.[11] Covarrubias' subjectivist conception was completed by another of his scholastic contemporaries Luis Saravia de la Calle, who was the first to demonstrate that prices determine costs, not *vice versa*. Saravia de la Calle also had the special merit of writing his main book in Spanish, not in Latin. Its title was *Instrucción de mercaderes* (in English, 'Instructions to merchants') and there we can read that 'those who measure the just price by the labour, costs and risk incurred by the person who deals in the merchandise are greatly in error. The just price is found not by counting the cost but by common estimation'.[12]

The subjectivist conception initiated by Covarrubias also allowed other Spanish scholastics to get a clear insight into the true nature of market prices and the impossibility of attaining an economic equilibrium. Thus, the Jesuit Cardinal Juan de Lugo, wondering what the price of equilibrium was, as early as 1643 reached the conclusion that equilibrium depended on such a large number of specific circumstances that only God was able to know it (*'Pretium iustum mathematicum licet soli Deo notum'*).[13] Another Jesuit, Juan de Salas, referring to the possibilities of knowing the specific market information, reached the very Hayekian conclusion that it was so complex that *'quas exacte comprehendere et ponderare Dei est non hominum'* (in English, 'only God, not men, can understand it exactly').[14]

Furthermore, the Spanish scholastics were the first to introduce the dynamic concept of competition (in Latin *concurrentium*), understood as a process of rivalry among entrepreneurs. For instance, Jerónimo Castillo de Bovadilla (1547–) wrote that 'prices will go down as a result of abundance, rivalry (*emulación*) and competition (*concurrencia*) among the sellers'.[15]

This same idea is closely followed by Luis de Molina.[16] Covarrubias also anticipated many of the conclusions of Father Juan de Mariana in his empirical study on the history of the devaluation of the main coin of that time, the Castilian Maravedí. This study contained a compilation of a large number of statistics on the evolution of prices in the previous century and was published in Latin in his book *Veterum collatio numismatum* (in plain English, 'Compilation of old monies').[17] This book was highly praised in Italy by Davanzaty and Galiani and was also quoted by the founder of the Austrian School of Economics Carl Menger in his *Principles of Economics.*[18]

We should also note how Father de Mariana, when explaining the effects of inflation, listed the basic elements of the quantitative theory of money, which had previously been explained in full detail by another notable scholastic, Martín Azpilcueta Navarro, also known as Dr Navarro, who was born in Navarra (north-east Spain, near France) the year after the discovery of America (1493). Azpilcueta lived 94 years and is specially famous for explaining for the first time, in 1556, the quantitative theory of money, in his book *Resolutory Commentary on Exchanges*. Observing the effects on Spanish prices of the massive inflow of precious metals coming from America, Azpilcueta declared that,

> as can be seen from experience, in France, where there is less money than in Spain, bread, wine, clothing, labor and work cost much less; and even in Spain, at the time when there was less money, the things which could be sold and the labor and work of men were given for much less than after the Indies were discovered and covered her with gold and silver. The cause of which is that money is worth more where and when it is lacking than where and when it is in abundance.[19]

Returning to Father Juan de Mariana, it is clear that his most important contribution was to see that inflation was a tax that 'taxes those who had money before and, as a consequence thereof, are forced to buy things more dearly'. Furthermore, Mariana argues that the effects of inflation cannot be solved by fixing maximum rates or prices, since experience shows that these have always been ineffective. In addition, given that inflation is a tax, according to his theory of tyranny, the people's consent would, in any event, be required but, even if such consent existed, it would always be a very damaging tax that disorganized economic life: 'this new levy or tax of the alloyed metal, which is illicit and bad if it is done without the agreement of the kingdom and, if it is done therewith, I take it as erroneous and harmful in many ways'.

How could resorting to the comfortable expedient of inflation be avoided? By balancing the budget, for which purpose Mariana basically proposed spending less on the royal family because 'a moderate amount, spent with order, glitters more and represents greater majesty than a superfluous amount without order'.

Second, he proposed that 'the king should reduce his favours'; in other words, he should not reward the real or supposed services of his vassals so generously:

there is no kingdom in the world with so many prizes, commissions, pensions, benefits and posts; if they were well distributed in an orderly fashion, less would need to be taken from the public treasury or from other taxes from which money contributions can be got.

As we can see, the lack of control over public spending and the purchase of political support with subsidies date from a very long time ago. Mariana also proposed that 'the king should avoid and excuse unnecessary undertakings and wars, cut off the cancerous limbs that cannot be healed'.

In short, as we can see, he set forth a whole programme for a reduction in public spending and keeping the budget balanced which would, even today, serve as a model.

It is obvious that, if Father Juan de Mariana had known the economic mechanisms that lead to the credit expansion process generated by banks and the effects of this process, he would have condemned as robbery not only the government debasement of coins, but also the even more disturbing credit inflation created by banks. However, other Spanish scholastics were able to analyse the credit expansion of banks. Thus, Luis Saravia de la Calle was very critical of fractional-reserve banking. He maintained that receiving interest was incompatible with the nature of a demand deposit and that, in any case, a fee should be paid to the banker for keeping the money under his custody. A similar conclusion is reached by the more famous Martín Azpilcueta Navarro.[20]

The Jesuit Luis de Molina was sympathetic to fractional reserve-banking and confused the nature of two different contracts, loans and deposits, which Azpilcueta and Saravia de la Calle had clearly differentiated from each other previously. A more relevant aspect is that Molina was the first theorist to discover, in 1597, therefore much earlier than Pennington in 1826, that bank deposits are part of the monetary supply. He even proposed the name 'written money' (*chirographis pecuniarium* in Latin) to refer to the written documents that were accepted in trade as bank money.[21] Our scholastics included, therefore, two incipient schools, a kind of 'Currency School', formed by Saravia de la Calle, Azpilcueta Navarro and Tomás de Mercado, who were very distrustful of banking activities, for which they implicitly demanded a 100 per cent reserve should be held; and a kind of 'Banking School' headed by the Jesuits Luis de Molina and Juan de Lugo, who were much more tolerant of fractional-reserve banking.[22] Both groups were to a certain extent the forerunners of some of the theoretical developments which were to arise three centuries later in England, as a result of the debate between the Currency School and the Banking School.

Murray Rothbard stresses how another important contribution of the Spanish scholastics, especially of Azpilcueta, was to revive the vital concept of time preference, originally developed by one of the most brilliant pupils of Saint Thomas Aquinas, Giles Lessines, who, as early as 1285, wrote that future goods are not valued so highly as the same goods available at an immediate moment of time, nor do they allow their owners to achieve the same utility. For this reason, it must be considered that they have a more reduced value in accordance with justice.[23]

Father Juan de Mariana wrote another important book, *Discurso de las enfermedades de la Compañía* ('A discourse on the sicknesses of the Jesuit order'), which was published posthumously. In this book Mariana criticized the military hierarchy established in the Jesuit order, but also developed the pure Austrian insight that it is impossible to endow state commands with a coordinating content due to lack of information. In the words of Mariana himself,

> power and command is mad. ... Rome is far away, the general does not know the people or the facts, at least, with all the circumstances that surround them, on which success depends ... it is unavoidable that many serious errors will be committed and the people are displeased thereby and despise such a blind government ... it is a great mistake for the blind to wish to guide the sighted.

Mariana concludes that, when there are many laws, 'as not all of them may be kept or known, respect for all of them is lost'.[24]

In summary, Father Juan de Mariana and the Spanish scholastics were capable of developing the essential elements of what would later be the theoretical basis of the Austrian School of Economics, specifically the following: first, the subjective theory of value (Diego de Covarrubias y Leyva); second, the proper relationship between prices and costs (Luis Saravia de la Calle); third, the dynamic nature of the market and the impossibility of the model of equilibrium (Juan de Lugo and Juan de Salas); fourth, the dynamic concept of competition understood as a process of rivalry among sellers (Castillo de Bovadilla and Luis de Molina); fifth, the rediscovery of the time preference principle (Azpilcueta Navarro); sixth, the distorting influence of the inflationary growth of money on prices (Juan de Mariana, Diego de Covarrubias and Azpilcueta Navarro); seventh, the negative economic effects of fractional-reserve banking (Luis Saravia de la Calle and Azpilcueta Navarro); eighth, that bank deposits form part of the monetary supply (Luis de Molina and Juan de Lugo); ninth, the impossibility of organizing society by coercive commands due to lack of information (Juan de Mariana); and, tenth, the libertarian tradition that any unjustified intervention on the part of the state violates natural law (Juan de Mariana).

In order to understand the influence of the Spanish scholastics on the later development of the Austrian School of Economics, we should remember that in the sixteenth century the Emperor Charles V, who was the king of Spain, sent his brother Ferdinand I to be king of Austria. 'Austria' means, etymologically, 'eastern part of the Empire' and the Empire in those days comprised almost all continental Europe, with the sole exception of France, which remained an isolated island surrounded by Spanish forces. So it is easy to understand the origin of the intellectual influence of the Spanish scholastics on the Austrian School. It is not a pure coincidence or a mere whim of history, but originated from the intimate historical, political and cultural relations which existed between Spain and Austria from the sixteenth century onwards and were to continue for several centuries. In addition, Italy also played an important role in these relations, acting as an authentic cultural, economic and financial bridge over which the relations between the two furthest points of the Empire in Europe (Spain and Vienna) flowed. So there are very important arguments to defend the thesis that, at least at its roots, the Austrian School is truly a Spanish school.

Indeed, we could say that the greatest merit of Carl Menger was to rediscover and take up this continental Catholic tradition of Spanish scholastic thought that was almost forgotten and cut short as a consequence of the black legend against Spain and the very negative influence on the history of economic thought of Adam Smith and his followers of the British Classical School.[25]

Fortunately, and despite the overwhelming intellectual imperialism of the British Classical School of Economics, the continental tradition was never totally forgotten. Several economists like Cantillon, Turgot and Say kept the torch of subjectivism burning. Even in Spain, in the years of decadence in the eighteenth and nineteenth centuries, the old scholastic tradition survived in spite of the inferiority complex toward the British intellectual world that was so typical of those years. Proof of this is how another Spanish Catholic writer solved the 'paradox of value' and clearly set forth the theory of marginal utility twenty-seven years earlier than Carl Menger. This was Jaime Balmes, who was born in Catalonia in 1810 and died in 1848. During his short life, he became the most important Spanish Thomistic philosopher of his time. A few years before his death, on 7 September 1844, he published an article entitled 'True idea of value or thoughts on the origin, nature and variety of prices', in which he solves the paradox of value and clearly sets forth the idea of marginal utility. Balmes wondered, 'Why is a precious stone worth more than a piece of bread?', and he answered:

> It is not difficult to explain. Being the value of a thing its utility ... if the number of units of this means increases, decreases the need of anyone of them in particular; because being possible to choose among many units, none of them is indispensable. For this reason there is a necessary relation between the increase or decrease in value, and the shortage or abundance of a thing.[26]

In this way Balmes was able to close the circle of the continental tradition, which was ready to be taken up, completed and enhanced a few years later by Carl Menger and his followers from the Austrian School of Economics.

16 New light on the prehistory of the theory of banking and the School of Salamanca[1]

Introduction

As is known, Murray N. Rothbard was one of the theorists who defended with the most creativity and coherence the need for free banking subject to general legal principles, in other words, banking with a cash ratio of 100 per cent of demand deposits. Likewise, he was one of the first theorists to stress the great influence which the theoretical contributions of the Spanish scholastics related to the University of Salamanca in the sixteenth and seventeenth centuries were to have as the direct predecessors of the Austrian School of Economics.[2]

We feel that perhaps one of the greatest tributes which can be paid to Murray N. Rothbard is to show how the theorists of the School of Salamanca, whose intellectual activity took place from the reign of Charles V in the sixteenth century onwards, developed an incipient theory on the legitimate practice of banking which coincides, to a great extent, with the later contributions on this subject by the Austrian School in general and, particularly, by Murray N. Rothbard.

The analysis of banking during the reign of Charles V is paradigmatic for several reasons: first, because the massive inflow of precious metals from America caused the economic centre of gravity to move, at least temporarily, from the mercantile cities in the north of Italy towards Spain, specifically Seville, and the other Spanish markets; second, because Charles V's constant need for cash, which was the result of his extravagant imperial policy, led him to continually finance himself through the banking system, taking advantage of the liquidity with which it provided him without any kind of scruples. The traditional complicity between bankers and governors which, although there was some degree of dissimulation, had already become a general rule was thus taken to its utmost limit by Charles V. Moreover, he could not avoid the bankruptcy of the royal treasury, which, logically, had pernicious consequences for the Spanish economy in general and, in particular, for the bankers who had financed him. All these events led the sharpest minds of the era, the theorists of the School of Salamanca, to begin to reflect on financial and banking activities and, as a result, we have a series of

The development of the banks in Seville

Thanks to the work of Ramón Carande,[3] we know about the development of private banking in Seville during the reign of Charles V in some detail. Carande explains that he was able to carry out his research as a result of the list of bankers drawn up in relation to the confiscation of precious metals by the *Casa de Contratación* (Trade House) of Seville in 1545. The unsatisfactory situation of the treasury meant that Charles V, violating the most elementary legal principles, resorted to appropriating money from where it was most readily available: deposits in the safes of the bankers of Seville. It is true that these bankers, as we will see later, also violated legal principles in relation to the demand deposit contract (i.e. deposit of fungible money) and used a large part of the deposits received for their own business. However, it is no less true that the inauspicious imperial policy, by transgressing the most elementary principles of property rights and directly confiscating the stocks of money kept in the vaults, merely provided an even bigger incentive for the bankers to invest the greater part of the deposits received in loans, which became a habitual practice: if, in the final analysis, there was no guarantee that the public authorities would respect the part of the cash reserve which was kept in the bank (and experience showed that, when times were difficult, the emperor did not hesitate to confiscate this reserve and substitute it by compulsory loans to the Crown), it was preferable to devote the greater part of the deposits to loans to private industry and commerce, thus avoiding expropriation and obtaining greater profitability.

In any case, this policy of confiscation is perhaps the most extreme manifestation of public authorities' traditional policy of taking advantage of illegitimate banking profits by expropriating the assets of those who, by legal obligation, should best guard and preserve the deposits of third parties. It is understandable, therefore, that the governors, as the main beneficiaries of this illegitimate activity, ended up by justifying it and granting it all kinds of privileges so that it could continue to act, with a fractional cash ratio, outside the framework of general legal principles.

In his *magnum opus Carlos V y sus Banqueros* ('Charles V and his bankers'), Ramón Carande lists the most important bankers in the Seville of Charles V, specifically the Espinosas, Domingo de Lizarrazas and Pedro de Morga, together with other, less important, bankers, such as Cristóbal Francisquín, Diego Martínez, Juan Íñiguez and Octavio de Negrón. All of them inexorably went bankrupt, basically due to their having insufficient liquidity to meet the withdrawal of the demand deposits which had been placed with them. This shows that they worked with a fractional cash ratio, thanks to the licence or privilege in this respect which they had obtained from the Municipality of Seville and from Charles V himself. We have no information on the percentage of reserves they held, but we do know that, on many occasions, they invested in their own businesses related to shipping fleets which traded with America, the collection of taxes, etc., which were always a tremendous temptation, as if the results were favourable, the profits were very significant. Moreover, the successive confiscations of precious metals deposited with the bankers merely provided a greater incentive to the illegitimate behaviour of the latter. Thus, the Espinosas went bankrupt in 1579 and the main partners were imprisoned. The bankruptcy of Domingo de Lizarrazas occurred on 11 March 1553, when he could not meet a payment of more than 6.5 million maravedis. Pedro de Morga, who began operations in 1553, went bankrupt in 1575, during the second bankruptcy of King Felipe II. The rest of the less important bankers met the same fate and, in this respect, it is interesting to note the presence and comment of Thomas Gresham, who travelled to Seville with instructions to withdraw 320,000 ducats in cash, for which he had obtained the necessary licence from the emperor and from Queen María. Gresham was astounded to find that, precisely in the city which received the treasures of the Indies, money was very scarce, as it was in the trade markets, and he feared that, upon withdrawal of the funds to which the orders he was bearing referred, all the banks of the city would suspend payments.[4] It is regrettable that Ramón Carande's theoretical analysis leaves so much to be desired and that his study interpreting the bankruptcy of these banks is based solely on anecdotal 'explanations', such as the 'greed' for metals, which constantly placed the solvency of the bankers in a situation of crisis; the fact that the bankers carried out risky personal business deals, which continually implied heavy obligations (the chartering of vessels, overseas maritime trade, insurance transactions and various speculative types of business, etc.); and the royal treasury's repeated confiscations and need for liquidity. Nowhere is the true cause of the phenomenon mentioned: the inevitable recession and economic crisis resulting from the artificial boom caused by the inflation of precious metals from America and the artificial credit expansion without an adequate base of real saving, derived from the practice of banking with a fractional cash ratio.

Fortunately, Carlo M. Cipolla has covered this gap in the theory of Ramón Carande, at least partially, and has made a study interpreting the banking and economic crisis of the second half of the sixteenth century which, although it refers strictly to the Italian banks, is also directly applicable to the Spanish financial system, as the trading and financial circuits and flows between the two nations were, at that time, intimately related.[5] Cipolla explains that the monetary supply (what is today called M1 or M2) in the second half of the sixteenth century included a large amount of 'bank money' or deposits created out of nowhere by the bankers who did not keep a 100 per cent reserve ratio of the cash which had been deposited with them at demand by their clients. This led to a tremendous artificial thriving of the economy, which inexorably reverted from the second half of the sixteenth century onwards, when the depositors began to undergo and fear growing economic difficulties and the succession of bankruptcies of the most important bankers in Florence commenced.

This expansionary phase was started in Italy, according to Cipolla, by the managers of the Ricci Bank, who used a significant part of the bank's newly created deposits to purchase public funds and grant credits. This policy of credit expansion dragged the other private banks along with it, if they wanted to be competitive and maintain their profits and market share. A state of credit euphoria was thus created, which gave rise to a great artificial expansion that soon began to revert. Thus, we can read an edict of 1574 in which accusations are made against the bankers who refuse to return the deposits in cash and which proclaims the fact that they only 'paid with ink'. They had increasing difficulties in returning the deposits in ready money and a significant money shortage began to be perceived in the Venetian cities. The artisans could not withdraw their money or pay their debts and there was a heavy credit contraction (in other words, deflation) and a deep economic crisis, which Cipolla analyses in detail in his brilliant book. Cipolla's analysis is, therefore, much more solid from a theoretical point of view than that of Ramón Carande, although it cannot be considered perfect, as it places the emphasis more on the crisis and the period of credit contraction than on the preceding phase of artificial credit expansion, which was the true origin of the evils and of which, in turn, the most intimate cause was the bankers' violation of the obligation to guard and conserve intact 100 per cent of the *tantundem* or equivalent of the original deposits.[6]

The School of Salamanca and the banking business: the initial contribution of Dr Saravia de la Calle

The financial and banking phenomena that we are discussing made an impression on the outstanding minds of the members of the School of Salamanca, who, according to the most reliable research carried out, are the forerunners of the subjectivist conception developed by the Austrian School of Economics.[7]

Chronologically, the first work we should mention, which is also, perhaps, the most relevant to our purpose, is *Instrucción de Mercaderes* ('Instruction of merchants') by Doctor Saravia de la Calle, which was published in Medina del Campo in 1544.[8] Saravia de la Calle is extraordinarily hard on bankers, whom he describes as 'hungry gluttons, who swallow everything, destroy everything, confuse everything, steal and dirty everything, like the harpies of Pineo'.[9] He tells us how the bankers 'come out into the square and road with their table and chair and cashbox and book, like the whores to the brothel with their chair', and, having obtained the corresponding licence and guarantee ordered by the laws of the kingdom, they devote themselves to obtaining deposits from the clients, to whom they offer bookkeeping and cashier services, paying by order and for account of them and even paying interest on such deposits.

The theory of banking and the School of Salamanca 215

With sound legal criteria, Saravia de la Calle says that receiving interest is incompatible with the nature of a demand deposit and that, in any case, a fee should be paid to the banker for keeping or guarding the money under his custody. He even reprehends harshly the clients of the banks who agree to enter into such deals with the bankers. In this respect he states:

> And if you say, merchant, that you do not lend it, but that you place it (or deposit it), that is a greater mockery; who ever saw the depositary pay? He is usually paid for the safekeeping and the work of the deposit; much more than that, if you now place your money with the money-lender as a loan or as a deposit, in the same way as you take your part of the profit that the moneylender takes, you also take part of the blame, and even the greatest part.[10]

In Chapter XII of his book, Saravia de la Calle also correctly distinguishes between the two radically different transactions which the banks carry out. On the one hand, demand deposits, which the clients give, without any interest, to the bankers

> to have them safer and to have them more at hand in order to deliver them to whom they are owed, and to free themselves from the burden and the work of reckoning and safekeeping, and also because, as thanks for this good deed which they do to the moneylenders in giving them their money, if it occurs that they have no money in the hands of the moneylender, the moneylender accepts some overdrafts from them also without interest.[11]

On the other hand, very different from these contracts are the term 'deposits', which are true loans and are characterized because they are given over a time period in exchange for interest. Saravia de la Calle, following the traditional canon law doctrine, deeply condemns this practice. Moreover, he clearly indicates that, in the case of the first type of demand deposit contracts, the clients should pay the banker 'because if they place monies on deposit, they must give for their safekeeping, not receive the profits given to them when they deposit monies or goods which must be safely kept'.[12] Saravia de la Calle therefore criticizes those clients who selfishly try to take advantage of the illegitimate activity of the bankers, entrusting them with their money on demand deposit and trying to obtain interest on it. He adds the following illustrative words:

> he is not free from sin, at least venial sin, because he entrusted the deposit of his money to whom he knows will not keep his deposit, but will spend his money, like he who entrusts the maiden to the lecher or the delicacy to the glutton.[13]

Neither may the depositor clear his conscience by thinking that the banker will lend or use the money of others, but not his own, as if it is believed of him that he will probably keep that money of the deposit and will not lend it; and this probability cannot be thought of any of these moneylenders, but the contrary, that he will immediately lend it and deal and obtain earnings with it, because how can those who give seven and ten per cent to those who give them monies leave the monies which are thus placed with them in deposit idle? And even if it were very certain that you do not sin (which it is not, but the contrary), it is very sure that the moneylender sins lending your monies, and that he steals the patrimony of your neighbours with your money.[14]

The doctrine of Saravia de la Calle is, therefore, quite clear: the bankers' use of demand deposit money in their own interest by granting loans is illegitimate and implies a grave sin. This doctrine fully coincides with the doctrine which was established by the classical authors on Roman Law and arises naturally from the essence, purpose and legal nature of the contract for the demand deposit of money.[15]

Saravia de la Calle is also very descriptive when talking about the enormous profits that bankers obtain from their illegitimate behaviour when they appropriate the deposits of their depositors, instead of being content with the much more reduced remuneration which they would receive for the simple safekeeping or custody of the deposits, like good fathers of families. Let us see how vividly he expresses this:

> And if you receive wages, they should be moderate, for you to support yourselves, and not such excessive robberies that you build superb houses and purchase rich property, have excessive costs of family and servants, and hold great banquets and dress in such a costly fashion, especially when you were poor when you began to lend and left poor trades.[16]

Saravia de la Calle indicates how the bankers have a great tendency to go bankrupt, even making a brief theoretical analysis which shows that, after the expansionary phase resulting from the artificial expansion of the credits which these *logreros* ('moneylenders') grant, there inevitably comes a phase of recession in which the bad debts cause a chain of bankruptcies among the banks. And he adds that,

> if the merchant does not pay the moneylender, it makes him bankrupt, and thus he suspends payments and all is lost, of all which, as is notorious, these moneylenders are the beginning, occasion and cause, *because if they did not exist, each person would trade with his money as he could and no more, and thus things would cost their fair price and more than the price in cash would not be charged.* And, therefore, it would be a great advantage if the princes did not consent to them in Spain, as no other nation in the world consents to them, and banished them from their court and kingdom.[17]

As we know, it is not true that the governors of other nations had had more success in controlling the activity of the bankers or lenders than in Spain, as more or less the same was occurring everywhere and the kings ended up by granting privileges for the bankers to carry on their activities using the money of their depositors in their own interests, in return for also being able to take full or partial advantage of a banking system from which they obtained funds much more easily and rapidly than from taxes.

As a conclusion to his whole analysis, Saravia de la Calle states that

> under no circumstance should the Christian give his monies to these lenders because, if he sins in giving them, as he always sins, he should cease it because it is his own sin; and if he does not sin, he should cease it in order to avoid the sin of the moneylender.

Moreover, Saravia de la Calle adds that, if the bankers are not used, there will be the additional advantage that the depositors 'will not be startled if the lender suspends payments; if he becomes bankrupt, as we see so commonly and our Lord God permits, they and their owners will be lost like an ill-gained thing'.[18] As we can see, Saravia de la Calle's analysis, in addition to its ingenuity and humour, is impeccable and has no contradictions, except, perhaps, that it puts too much emphasis on the criticism of the bankers for charging interest, which violated the canonical prohibition of usury, rather than for their undue appropriation of the demand deposits placed with them by their clients.

Martín de Azpilcueta Navarro

Another writer who made a correct analysis of the contract for the demand deposit of money is Martín de Azpilcueta, better known as 'Doctor Navarro', in his book *Comentario Resolutorio de Cambios* ('Resolutory commentary on exchanges'), first published in Salamanca at the end of 1556. Martín de Azpilcueta expressly refers to 'banking for safekeeping', which is the monetary demand deposit transaction performed by the banks. For Martín de Azpilcueta, banking for safekeeping or the demand deposit contract is completely fair and consists of the banker being the

> warden, depositary and guarantor of the monies, which those who give him or send to him give to him or bank with him for what may be necessary; and that he is obliged to pay to the merchants, or to the persons whom the depositors wish in such or such a way, for which he may licitly take his fair wage, either from the republic or from the depositors; because this trade and duty is useful to the republic and does not contain any iniquity, as it is fair that he who works earns his wage. And the banker works in receiving, holding in deposit and ready the money of so many merchants, and in writing, giving and keeping accounts with all of

them, with great difficulty, and sometimes danger of errors in reckoning and other things. The same could be done with a contract with which a person committed himself to the others to receive and hold their money in deposit, give, pay and keep the accounts of all of them, as they tell him, etc., because this contract is of hire to another and from another of his works and employment, which is a designated, just and holy contract.[19]

As we can see, for Martín de Azpilcueta, the contract of demand deposit is a fully legitimate contract, which consists of entrusting the safekeeping, custody or deposit of money to a professional, the banker, who should care for it like the good father of a family, always keeping it at the depositor's disposal and performing the cashier services requested by the latter on his behalf. In return, he will have the right to receive the appropriate remuneration of his services from the depositors. In effect, for Martín de Azpilcueta, *the depositors should pay the depositary or banker, never vice versa*, so that the depositors 'pay the former for the work and care of the banker in receiving and keeping their money and doing his work', and, therefore, the bankers should perform 'their trade cleanly and be content with a just wage, receiving it from those who owe it to them and whose money they safeguard and accounts they keep and not from those who do not owe it to them'.[20] Moreover, in order to avoid confusion and make things totally clear, Martín de Azpilcueta, along the same lines as Doctor Saravia de la Calle which we have seen, expressly condemns the clients who do not wish to pay for the services of custody of their deposits or even try to receive interest on them. Thus, Doctor Navarro concludes that,

> in this type of exchange, not only the bankers sin, but, even with the obligation to restore, those who give them monies for them to keep, and do the same. And afterwards they do not want to pay them anything, saying that that which they earn with their money, and will receive from those to whom they pay in cash, suffices for their wages. And if the bankers ask them for anything, they leave them and go to deal with others, and so that they do not leave them, the bankers renounce the wage owed to them and take it from who does not owe it.[21]

The contribution of Tomás de Mercado

Tomás de Mercado, in his *Suma de Tratos y Contratos* ('Compilation of deals and contracts'), Seville, 1571, makes an analysis of the banking business which follows a very similar line to the two above authors. First, he points out, following the correct doctrine, that the depositors should pay the bankers for the work of keeping their monetary demand deposits, concluding that

> for all of them it is a common and general rule to be able to take wages from those who place money in their bank, either a certain amount each

year or a certain amount for each thousand, as they serve them and keep their patrimony.[22]

However, Tomás de Mercado ironically mentions that the bankers of Seville are so 'generous' that they do not make any charge for the custody of the deposits, using the following words: 'those of this city, it is true, are so regal and noble that they do not ask for or take any wage'. And Tomás de Mercado remarks how the bankers of Seville do not need to charge anything as, with the large amount of money they obtain from the deposits, they carry out their private businesses, which are very lucrative. We should stress the fact that, in our opinion, the analysis made by Tomás de Mercado in this respect refers simply to the observation of a fact, and does not imply any acceptance of its legitimacy, as several modern critics appear to suggest. To the contrary, following the purest classical Roman doctrine and the essence of the legal nature of the contract for the demand deposit of money, Tomás de Mercado is the scholastic writer who most clearly shows that the transfer of property which occurs in the monetary bank deposit does not imply a parallel transfer of availability and, therefore, for practical purposes, a *full* transfer of property does not take place. Let us see how clearly he expresses this: '(the bankers) must understand that the money is not theirs but belongs to someone else, and that is not all, when they have it serve them, it ceases to serve its owner'. Tomás de Mercado adds that the bankers should be subject to two basic principles:

> [The first:] not to leave the bank so bare that they cannot then pay the drafts which come, because, if they make it impossible to pay them, spending and employing money in investments and speculative earnings or other deals, it is certain that they sin. ... The second: they should not enter dangerous businesses, because they sin, even if they result favourably, due to the danger of behaving wrongly and doing grave damage to those who trusted them.[23]

Although it is true that, with these recommendations, it seems as if Tomás de Mercado would admit the use of a certain fractional-reserve ratio, the fact is that he is very forthright when he expresses his legal opinion that, in the final analysis, the money of the deposits does not belong to the bankers but to the depositors and when he says, moreover, that no banker heeds his two recommendations: 'but in the case of earning, when it is comfortable, it is very difficult to restrain avarice, none of them heeds these two warnings, nor meets these conditions'.[24] Therefore, he considers very favourably the enactment of a rule prohibiting the bankers from doing private business, in order to remove the temptation implied by financing them indefinitely with the money obtained from demand deposits.

In addition, elsewhere in *Suma de Tratos y Contratos*, at the end of chapter IV, Tomás de Mercado tells us how the bankers of Seville act as depositaries for the money and precious metals of the merchants from the fleet of the Indies and how, with such substantial deposits, 'they make great investments' and obtain lucrative profits, now without expressly condemning this type of activity, although it is true that the passage in question is rather a description of a state of affairs than an analysis of the legitimacy of the situation. This analysis is made in much more depth in chapter XIV, which we have already discussed. Tomás de Mercado concludes, moreover, that the bankers

> also become involved in giving and taking in exchange and in collecting, and a banker in this republic covers a whole world and embraces more than the ocean, although sometimes he leaves so many loose ends that everything goes to ruin.[25]

The cases of Domingo de Soto, Luis de Molina and Juan de Lugo

The scholastics who are most confused on the doctrinal treatment of the contract for the monetary bank deposit are Domingo de Soto and, above all, Luis de Molina and Juan de Lugo. In fact, these theorists allowed themselves to be influenced by the wrong medieval tradition of the glossators and, especially, by the doctrinal confusion which developed due to the concept of *depositum confessatum*. This was simply a loan which was disguised as a deposit in order to elude the canonical prohibition on charging interest, as this practice was considered acceptable if there was a (fictitious) delay on the part of the depositary. In fact, de Soto and, above all, Molina wrongly considered that the demand deposit was merely a 'loan' which transferred not only the property, but also the full availability of the deposits to the banker and, therefore, it could be considered legitimate to use them as loans, provided that these were made 'prudently'. It may be interpreted that Domingo de Soto was the first to uphold this thesis, although very indirectly. In fact, in Book VI, Question XI of his work on *La Justicia y el Derecho* ('Justice and law') (1556), we read that, among the bankers, there was

> the custom, it is said, that if a merchant makes a bank deposit in cash, as a result thereof the banker answers for a higher amount. I delivered ten thousand to the moneychanger, then he will answer for me for twelve, perhaps fifteen; because it is very good earning for the banker to have money in cash. Neither is any vice found therein.[26]

Another case of typical credit creation which seems to be admitted by Domingo de Soto is that of a loan in the form of the discount of bills financed against the demand deposits of the clients.

But perhaps the member of the School of Salamanca who upheld the most erroneous doctrine in relation to the contract for the demand deposit of money made by the bankers was Luis de Molina.[27] In fact, Luis de Molina, in his *Tratado sobre los Cambios* ('Treaty on exchanges'), upholds the medieval doctrine that the demand deposit is merely a 'loan' contract in favour of the banker, which transfers not only the property, but also the full availability of the thing, and, therefore, the banker can legitimately use it in his own interests, in the form of loans or in any other way. Let us see how he expresses his argument:

> because these bankers, like all the rest, are the true owners of the money which is deposited in their banks, in which they are greatly differentiated from the other depositaries ... in such a way that they receive it as a loan with no rights attached and, therefore, at their own risk.

Further on, he again repeats that 'such a deposit is really a loan, as has been said, and the property of the money deposited passes to the banker and, therefore, in the event that it perishes, it perishes for the banker'.[28] This doctrinal position, apart from the fact that it is not very rigorous, is a clear lapse and contradicts what the writer himself says in his other work, *Tratado sobre los Préstamos y la Usura* ('Treaty on loans and usury'), where he warns that the *term* is an essential element of any loan contract and that, if the time for which a loan may be held is not expressly stated (as happens in a demand deposit) and no date has been fixed for its repayment, 'it will be necessary to abide by what the judge judges as to the time for which it may be held'.[29] In addition, Luis de Molina ignores the fact that the nature and legal essence of the demand deposit contract has nothing to do with the loan contract and, therefore, his doctrine which tries to identify the one with the other is a clear regression, not only in relation to the much more coherent positions of Saravia de la Calle and Azpilcueta Navarro, but also in relation to the true legal nature of the contract as it had been developed by the old Roman legal tradition. It is, therefore, surprising that so clear and profound a mind as that of Luis de Molina did not realize how extremely dangerous it was to accept the violation of the general legal principles on the bank deposit and to say that 'it never occurs that all the depositors need their money in such a way that they do not leave many thousands of ducats in deposit with which the bankers may do business to obtain profits or losses'.[30] Molina did not realize that not only the objective or essential purpose of the contract, which is safekeeping and custody, is thus violated, but all kinds of illicit businesses and abuses are encouraged, which inexorably generate an economic recession and the bankruptcy of the bankers. If the traditional legal principle which requires the continual safekeeping of 100 per cent of the *tantundem* in favour of the depositor is not met, there is no clear guideline for avoiding the bankruptcy of the bankers. And it is evident that such superficial and vague suggestions as to 'try to act with prudence' or 'not get involved in dangerous business' are insufficient to avoid the very prejudicial economic and social effects of fractional-reserve banking. However, Luis de Molina does at least take the trouble to point out that

> a warning should be given that (the bankers) are in mortal sin if they commit the money they hold in deposit in their businesses to such an extent that they then find themselves unable to deliver, at the appropriate moment, the amounts which the depositors request or order to be paid against the money which they hold in deposit. ... Likewise, they are in mortal sin if they engage in such businesses that they are in danger of reaching a situation in which they cannot pay the deposits. For example, if they send so much merchandise overseas that, if the ship is wrecked, or if it is captured by pirates, it is not possible for them to pay the deposits, even if they sell their patrimony. *And not only are they in mortal sin when the business ends badly, but even if the outcome is favourable. And this is due to the danger to which they expose themselves of causing damage to the depositors and guarantors which they themselves contributed for the deposits.*[31]

We consider this warning by Luis de Molina to be commendable, but we also consider it extraordinary that it seems that he did not realize that it is, in the final analysis, intimately contradictory to his express acceptance of fractional-reserve banking, provided that the bankers practise it with 'prudence'. And it does not matter how prudent the bankers are, the only way to avoid risks and to guarantee that the depositors' money is always at their disposal is by maintaining a cash ratio of 100 per cent of all the demand deposits received.

After Molina, the only author who upheld an analogous position on banking is Juan de Lugo,[32] also a Jesuit. In our opinion, this can lead us to consider that, in relation to banking, there were two schools of thought within the School of Salamanca: one, well-founded and doctrinally correct (close to the future 'Currency School'), to which Saravia de la Calle, Azpilcueta Navarro and Tomás de Mercado belonged; and another, more inclined towards the capriciousness of the inflationist doctrine and the fractional reserve (close to the future 'Banking School'), represented by Luis de Molina, Juan de Lugo and, to a much lesser extent, Domingo de Soto. We will study these two points of view in more detail in the next section.

The banking and currency points of view in the School of Salamanca

The contributions of the theorists of the School of Salamanca in the monetary field are important and have been the subject of detailed studies.[33]

The first scholastic treaty which dealt with money was written by Diego de Covarrubias y Leyva and published in 1550 under the title *Veterum Collatio Numismatum* ('Compilation on old moneys'). In this work, the famous Bishop of Segovia studied the history of the devaluation of the Castilian maravedi and compiled a large amount of statistics on the evolution of prices. Although the essential ideas of the quantitative theory of money are already implicit in Covarrubias' treaty, he does not put forward an explicitly articulated monetary theory.[34] Some years were to pass before, in 1556,

Azpilcueta Navarro expressed, for the first time, clearly and convincingly that the increase in prices, or, if one prefers, the decrease in the purchasing power of money, was the result of the increase in the monetary supply which was taking place in Castile as a result of the massive inflow of precious metals from America.

In fact, the relationship between the amount of money in circulation and prices is impeccably expressed by Martín de Azpilcueta, for whom,

> in the lands where there is a great shortage of money, all the other things which may be sold, even the labour and work of men, are given for less money than in places where there is an abundance; as can be seen from experience, in France, where there is less money than in Spain, bread, wine, clothing, labour and work cost much less; and even in Spain, at the time when there was less money, the things which could be sold and the labour and work of men were given for much less than after the Indies were discovered and covered her with gold and silver. *The cause of which is that money is worth more where and when it is lacking than where and when it is in abundance.*[35]

However, in contrast to the deep and detailed studies which have been made of the monetary theory of the School of Salamanca, up to now there has been practically no effort to analyse the position of the scholastics in relation to banking.[36] And nevertheless, as we have seen in preceding sections, the theorists of the School of Salamanca made a very acute analysis of banking practices and, to a great extent, were the forerunners of the different positions which, more than two centuries later, were reproduced in England in the controversy between the members of the *Banking School* and those of the *Currency School*.

In fact, we have already set out the profoundly critical treatment of fractional-reserve banking which we owe, mainly, to Doctor Saravia de la Calle and which is included in the final chapters of his *Instrucción de Mercaderes*. Martín de Azpilcueta and Tomás de Mercado also developed a rigorous and very demanding critical analysis of banking activities which, although it did not reach the degree of criticism of Saravia de la Calle, included an impeccable treatment of the demands which, in accordance with justice, should be observed in the monetary bank deposit contract. For this reason, and due to their rigorous critical analysis of banking, we may consider this first group of authors (most of them Dominicans) to form part of an incipient *Currency School*, which had been developed from the start within the School of Salamanca and which was characterized by upholding coherent and rigorous positions in respect of the legal demands of the monetary bank deposit contract and by being, in general, very critical and distrustful of the practice of banking activities.

In opposition to this first group of theorists, a second group of 'members' (most of them Jesuits) of the School of Salamanca can be clearly distinguished.

This group would be led by Luis de Molina and also included Juan de Lugo and, to a lesser extent, Lessius and Domingo de Soto. These authors followed the leadership of Molina and, as we have already explained, are characterized by the wrong legal foundations which they give to the monetary bank deposit contract and by admitting that a fractional reserve be maintained, arguing that, more than a deposit, it is a 'loan' contract. This is not the place to reproduce all the arguments against the position of Molina in respect of the monetary bank deposit contract which merely refer to an error that, very much influenced by the *depositum confessatum*, had been upheld throughout the Middle Ages by the glossators. What we wish to emphasize here is that this second group of authors of the School of Salamanca was much more 'understanding' of banking activities and even fully justified the practice thereof outside the framework of traditional legal principles. It is not, therefore, inappropriate to consider this second group of authors to form part of an incipient *Banking School* within the School of Salamanca who, like their successors of the English and continental Banking School several centuries later, not only justified the practice of banking based on a fractional reserve – that is to say, violating basic legal principles – but also believed that this had very beneficial effects on the economy.

Although Luis de Molina's theoretical arguments on the bank deposit contract are a clear regression and cannot be upheld on the basis of traditional legal principles, it is, however, *curious to draw attention to the fact that this author is the first member of the Banking School tradition who was capable of realizing that cheques and documents ordering payment on sight of specific amounts charged against the deposits fulfilled exactly the same function as cash*. The appreciation that it was the theorists of the English Banking School who, in the nineteenth century, first showed that the demand deposits of the banks formed an integral part of the monetary supply and thus had the same effect on the economy as bank notes is, therefore, not correct. More than two centuries earlier, Luis de Molina had already shown this idea clearly in Disp. 409 of his *Tratado sobre los Cambios*. In effect, Luis de Molina tells us that

> the money is paid to the bankers in two ways: one, in cash, handing over the coins to them; and the other, by trade bills or any other bills which are given to them, by virtue of which he who has to pay a bill becomes a debtor to the bank for the amount which the bill indicates will be paid into the account of he who presents the bill at the bank.[37]

Specifically, Luis de Molina refers to the written documents, which he calls in Latin *chirographis pecuniarum*, which were used as payment in the majority of the transactions carried out at the markets. Thus, 'although many transactions are made in cash, the majority are made by written documents which evidence either that the bank owes to them or that it agrees to pay, and the money remains in the bank'. Molina also says that these cheques are drawn with 'sight' or demand value and adds that 'these payments are usually called 'sight' because the money must be paid at the moment the bill is presented and read'.[38]

But the most important aspect is that Molina expressed, much earlier than Pennington in 1826,[39] the essential idea that the total volume of monetary transactions carried out at a market could not be paid with the amount of cash which changed hands there, if it were not for the use of the money which the banks *generate* by their deposit entries and the issue of *cheques* against them by the depositors. So that, thanks to the financial activity of the banks, a new amount of money is created from nowhere in the form of deposits, and is used in the transactions. In fact, Molina expressly tells us that

> the majority of the transactions are previously carried out (are formalized) by signed documents; *as money is not so abundant as to be able to buy in cash the enormous quantity of merchandise which is taken there to sell, if they must be paid for in cash, nor to be able to carry out so much business.*[40]

Lastly, Molina distinguishes very clearly between those operations which imply the grant of credit, as payment of a debt is temporarily postponed, and those which are carried out by paying by cheque or by charging the amount to a bank account, concluding that

> it should be observed that it is not considered that credit is bought if the price is charged to the bank account itself, even if at the time cash is not paid; as the banker will pay in cash the debit balance which exists, at least at the end of the market.[41]

Juan de Lugo follows firmly and absolutely the doctrine of Molina and erroneously considers, in the same way as the latter, that the monetary bank deposit is a 'loan' which permits that, until the depositors require it, it may be used for the banker's private business.[42]

Molina and Lugo uphold such a confused position in respect of their legal foundations for the bank deposit contract that they even admit that the contract may simultaneously (!) have a different legal nature, depending on the party under consideration (in other words, it may be a deposit for the depositor and a loan contract for the depositary banker). Apparently, they do not see any incongruence in this position and, as we know, in respect of the bankers' activity, they fix only one limit: that they should act with 'prudence' so that, by virtue of the law of large numbers, they always have sufficient liquidity to allow the return of the deposits which are 'normally' demanded from them. They do not realize that the criterion of *prudence* which they declare is not an objective criterion that can guide the banker's actions. It evidently does not coincide with the capacity to return the deposits held at any given moment and they themselves take great care to emphasize that the bankers are in 'mortal sin' when they employ the funds of their depositors in imprudent and speculative activities, *even if they have a favourable result and they are able to return the money to the depositors on time.*[43] Moreover, the criterion of prudence is not, in itself, sufficient: one can be very prudent and, however, not be very shrewd or even have bad luck in business, so that, when the moment arrives, sufficient liquidity is not available and the deposits cannot be returned.[44] What, then, does the criterion of prudence consist of? It is clear that there is no objective reply to this question which could serve as a guide for the bankers' activities. Particularly when the law of large numbers is not applicable to fractional-reserve banking, as the credit expansion which it causes leads to the generation of recurrent cycles of boom and depression which, inevitably, place the bankers in difficult situations. And the fact is that fractional-reserve banking itself, as shown by the Austrian theory of the economic cycles, generates liquidity crises and, therefore, the generalized insolvency of the banks. In any case, at the moment of the crisis, it is very possible that the bank cannot pay – in other words, that it suspend payments – and, even if all its creditors are lucky enough to finally collect their money, this will only happen, in the best of circumstances, after a long period of liquidation during which the role of the depositors will change, as they will lose the immediate availability of their money and become *compulsory lenders*, who will be obliged to postpone collection of their deposits until the moment when the orderly liquidation of the bank culminates.

The above considerations are those which, without any doubt, lead Tomás de Mercado to indicate that the principles of prudence declared by Molina and Juan de Lugo constitute an objective which, in practice, *no* banker can meet. It seems as if Tomás de Mercado was aware that such principles did not serve as a practical guide in order to guarantee the solvency of the banks. And, if such principles are not efficient in permanently attaining the objective of solvency and liquidity, it is evident that the fractional-reserve banking system will not be able to meet its commitments under all conceivable circumstances.

Conclusion: the contemporary positions of the Jesuits Bernard W. Dempsey and Francisco Belda

Recently, in the previous century, two Jesuit economists have again studied the doctrine of the scholastics concerning banking, one from the standpoint of the Banking School and the other from the position of the Currency School. The former is the Spanish Jesuit Francisco Belda, author of an interesting work entitled 'Ética de la creación de créditos según la doctrina de Molina, Lesio y Lugo' ('Ethics of the creation of credits according to the doctrine of Molina, Lessius and Lugo').[45] In fact, for Father Belda it is evident that,

> from Molina's description, it may be deduced that, in the case of the bankers, there is authentic credit creation. Thanks to the intervention of

the banks, a new purchasing power has been created, which did not exist previously. The same money is used simultaneously twice; the bank uses it for its business and so does the depositor. The overall result is that the payment means in circulation are several times greater than the real amount of money in cash which originated them and the bank benefits from all these transactions.

Moreover, Belda considers that, for Molina, 'it is licit to do business with the clients' deposits, provided this is done prudently, not risking being unable to meet one's obligations on a timely basis'.[46]

With regard to Juan de Lugo, Belda indicates that he gives

a meticulous description of the bankers' practices. Here, there is explicit approval of credit creation, although not with the formal appearance of *created* credit. The banks do business with the deposits of their clients who, in turn, are not denied the use of their own money. There is an expansion of the payment means, produced by the banks through credits, the discount of trade bills and other economic activities carried on with the money of others. The final result is an increase in the purchasing power in the market very much greater than the amount represented by the cash deposits from which it originates.[47]

It is evident that Belda is correct in indicating how the doctrines of Molina and Lugo are, from among those of the scholastics, the most favourable towards the banking business. However, we are obliged to criticize Father Belda for not even mentioning the positions of the other members of the School of Salamanca, specifically those of Tomás de Mercado and, above all, of Martín de Azpilcueta and Saravia de la Calle, which are much more rigorous and critical when analysing banking institutions. Moreover, Belda's analysis of the contributions of Molina and Lugo is based on a Keynesian conception of the economy, which not only ignores all the negative effects which the credit expansion provokes in the structure of production, but also considers it to be highly beneficial to the extent that it increases the 'effective demand' and national income. Belda's analysis is, therefore, a study of the contributions of the members of the School of Salamanca from the point of view of the Keynesian and Banking Schools and is very confused in respect of the legal justification of the institution of the monetary bank deposit, tending, therefore, to consider fractional-reserve banking to be legitimate.

There is, however, an economic treaty by another notable Jesuit, Father Bernard W. Dempsey, entitled *Interest and Usury*,[48] in which he analyses the position of the members of the School of Salamanca on the banking business, employing a profound knowledge of monetary and capital theory, very much superior to that of Father Belda.[49]

Curiously enough, Dempsey develops his thesis, not by analysing the positions of the theorists of the School of Salamanca who are most unfavourable to banking activity (Saravia de la Calle, Martín de Azpilcueta Navarro and Tomás de Mercado), but by concentrating on the works of the representatives who are closest to the Banking School, Luis de Molina, Juan de Lugo and Lessius, making an interpretative study of the works of these authors which leads him to conclude that, *from the point of view of their own doctrines, banking activity based on a fractional reserve would not be legitimate.* Dempsey's conclusion is based on the application of the traditional principles on usury, defended by these authors of Salamanca, to banking institutions and the economic effects thereof, which, although they were unknown at the time the School of Salamanca was writing, had, however, already been theoretically revealed by Mises and Hayek when Dempsey wrote his book. In fact, although Molina and Lugo's more favourable treatment of banking must be acknowledged, Dempsey expressly indicates that the loans which are created from nowhere by the banks, as a result of practising their activity with a fractional reserve, mean the generation of a purchasing power which does not require any prior saving or sacrifice and gives rise to important damage to a large number of third parties, who see how the purchasing power of their monetary units decreases as a consequence of the inflationary credit expansion of the banks.[50] According to Dempsey, this creation of purchasing power from nowhere, which does not imply any prior loss of other people's purchasing power, is contrary to essential legal principles, as constructed by Molina and Lugo themselves, and, in this respect, should be condemned. Specifically, Dempsey affirms that

> we may conclude from this that a Scholastic of the seventeenth century viewing the modern monetary problems would readily favour a 100 per cent reserve plan, or a time limit on the validity of money. A fixed money supply, or a supply altered only in accord with objective and calculated criteria, is a necessary condition to a meaningful just price of money.[51]

Dempsey states that the credit expansion generated by the banking industry tends to depreciate the purchasing power of money, so that the banks tend to return the monetary deposits claimed from them in monetary units with an increasingly reduced purchasing power.[52] He therefore correctly concludes that, if the members of the School of Salamanca had had a detailed theoretical knowledge of the functioning and implications of the economic process to which fractional-reserve banking gives rise, it would have been described as a perverse, vast and illegitimate process of *institutional usury*, even by Molina, Lessius and Lugo themselves.

17 Ludwig von Mises' *Human Action* as a textbook of economics[1]

Introduction

The fortieth anniversary of the publication of the revised third English edition of Ludwig von Mises' most important work, his economic treatise entitled *Human Action*, is, without doubt, a magnificent opportunity to make a series of reflections which place the work in the correct context, explain its scientific importance and manifest its great comparative advantages in the university, academic and intellectual world. In addition, a new eighth Spanish edition of Mises' work at the present time acquires a deep significance, due not only to the full confirmation of Mises' analysis in all areas by the historic collapse of real socialism in the Eastern European countries, but also to the grave crisis of the neoclassical Walrasian paradigm which, although it has dominated Economic Science to date, has now come to an obscure dead-end.[2] Moreover, from the strictly academic point of view, it is now twenty years since we began to recommend *Human Action* as a basic textbook for courses on political economy at the Complutense and King Juan Carlos Universities of Madrid and, in this time, it has been used as a study and work instrument by more than 3,000 students, who have been capable of generating a great wealth of academic and intellectual experiences which should by now be known.

We will, therefore, discuss below the main contributions contained in Mises' *Human Action* and its comparative advantages in respect of most of the economics manuals and textbooks which could be used as alternatives. Subsequently, after a brief intellectual biography of the author, we will explain the evolution of the successive editions of *Human Action* all over the world, together with the stimulus it is providing for the development of Economic Science. Our study will conclude with a series of practical educational recommendations, for both students and teachers, relating to the use of this book as a key instrument for work at university.

Main comparative advantages of human action

Typical shortcomings of current economics textbooks

Most of the introductory textbooks or manuals on political economy, which are today appearing on the market in ever-increasing numbers, contain significant defects, the majority of which have not, to date, been fully appreciated. However, their consequences for the education of future economists are very negative. First, almost all modern manuals are obsessed by the idea of novelty. It is assumed that the best textbook is the most modern one – in other words, the one which includes the latest fashions which have appeared in the academic world and reflects the novelties which have become widely known through publications in what are considered to be the most prestigious specialized economic journals. This attitude is simply a regrettable manifestation of the old myth of 'scientific meliorism', according to which everything recent includes and improves upon previous theoretical developments. This conception, which could have some foundation in the natural science field or in the technical disciplines related to engineering, does not, however, have any justification in the social science field in general or, in particular, in political economy. In fact, our science is based on principles and characteristics essential to the nature of human beings, which cannot be moulded in accordance with the whim of scientific fashion and/or technical stimuli and which, therefore, are very enduring, or even completely unchanging. This means that the construction of the theoretical edifice to be used by our future economists requires our discipline to be built on solid foundations, avoiding, above all at the beginning of their education, any distraction towards aspects which, although they are in fashion or appear attractive in view of their novelty, are really relatively incidental or hide, or tend to hide, the essential principles upon which Economic Science is based and constructed.[3]

This obsession with novelty explains, second, the fact that many textbook authors believe that their work is fully completed by preparing a simple compendium of fashionable doctrines, which may be more or less heterogeneous and well conceived, without making any effort to reflect profoundly on their foundations or taking the trouble to explain in detail or clarify their consistency for future students and/or readers. Normally, an attempt is made to disguise this lack of reflection and consistency by including mathematical formulae (which always give the layman the impression of a 'high' scientific level) and by the use of a large number of visual and statistical elements. This method of compiling manuals is, in spite of appearances, much easier and requires less commitment than preparing a volume on real, consistent economic principles which forces the students (and teachers) to reflect and, above all, reconsider critically, at each step, the foundations of the analytical tools they are using. Very few people engage in a rigorous study of the foundations of economics and those who at least mention them gloss quickly over the subject on the pretext that it is preferable not to 'confuse' the students by the study of the 'difficult' questions related to the principles, foundations and method of our science.

Third, the above considerations also explain that, on many occasions, writers frivolously simplify the presentation and contents of their works in order to make them 'attractive' and comprehensible to the students. Likewise, this objective explains the obsession with including topical examples, numerical charts and detailed statistics in many manuals. The continual decrease in the academic level of the students who enter university, together with the triumph of 'light culture', which is taking over our society, is leading many introductory economics books to be closer to manuals explaining the terminology for use in economic journalism than to true scientific works on economics devoted to the basic principles and foundations of our discipline and, above all, to teaching the students who come into contact with our science for the first time to think in terms of economic logic. The fact that one of the most prestigious current introductory economics manuals categorically states that 'price *measures* scarcity',[4] or that another indicates that applying the rule of making prices equal to marginal costs can make a socialist economy achieve and exceed the 'optimum', which is difficult to achieve in a capitalist economy,[5] are only two examples which show the extent to which lack of rigour and the obsessive desire to simplify are damaging the education of our students and creating an intellectual handicap for them which it will take many years to overcome, if it does not become completely irreversible.

It would be erroneous to think that the abovementioned defects are due solely to a transient fashion or to the mere whim or lack of criteria of the authors of the manuals in question. On the contrary, the greatest cause for concern is that, to a great extent, these defects are the natural results of the prevalent extension in our science of a narrow scientistic and positivist conception of economics. In fact, fourth, the image the majority of the manuals present of our science is usually the image of a discipline which it is hoped will develop and proceed in exactly the same way as the natural sciences and engineering. Its developments are based on the assumption that the necessary information on the ends and means of human beings is available or 'given', in either certain or probabilistic terms, and that this knowledge or information is *constant* and does not vary, thus reducing economic problems to mere technical exercises of optimization or maximization. This conception has the implicit objective of developing a whole discipline of 'social engineering', which aims to reduce the content of our science to a set of practical prescriptions for intervention which, profusely accompanied by functions or graphs (of supply, demand, costs, indifference–preference, production possibilities, etc., etc.), lead the student, without any kind of critical analysis, to the false conviction that there exists an intervention technique which is capable of directing the steps of the 'analyst' in respect of any economic problem. The damage to the students' education which results from this approach is enormous. They follow the first introductory economics courses without learning the essential principles and foundations, acquiring the erroneous impression that there is one true answer to each problem which can be found by simply making the correct 'diagnosis' and automatically applying the corresponding 'prescription'. The students' aspirations are reduced to mechanically formulating and finding the solution to the equations that supposedly contain the constant and unchanging information relative to, for example, demand, supply and 'elasticity'[6] of the corresponding functions. This means that the centres of economic education which apply these criteria are closer to mediocre academies engaged in training (social) 'engineers' than to what they should be: *true* university centres engaged in research into, and the study of, the principles and foundations of economic science.[7]

Fifth, the above considerations also clarify the reasons why modern manuals usually have, at best, a very ephemeral lifespan. In fact, the obsession with novelties and excessive simplification mean that, in the successive editions, (which are quickly sold out as they are avidly consumed by whole cohorts of young economists, whose teachers always 'recommend' they acquire the latest editions), theories and explanations which, in earlier editions, supposedly constituted very important parts of the book are abandoned with no kind of explanation from the author. Thus, for example, in one of the most popular textbooks, the treatment which the first thirteen editions gave to the so-called 'paradox of saving or frugality' has (fortunately, in our opinion) disappeared and the fourteenth edition silently eliminates the corresponding section with no explanation from the author. We do not, therefore, know whether the teaching provided to previous generations of students was erroneous or whether, on the contrary, readers of the latest edition are missing an important element in their education.[8]

The mirage of novelty and, therefore, the vice of superficiality are not only detrimental to the rigour and consistency of the manuals and the education of the students, but also usually provoke, sixth, the presentation of a partial vision of Economic Science, where the different approaches and treatments, perhaps with the incorrectly understood objective of not 'confusing' the student, are presented without setting forth all the alternative theoretical positions or making an appropriate and complete critical analysis of these. Thus, theoretical positions and developments which, although they are rigorous, reach conclusions other than those explained are concealed by applying the 'law of silence', giving the new intake of students the impression that there is a greater degree of consensus among authors than is, in fact the case. Alternatively, a clumsy 'democratic' criterion is applied whereby a supposed 'majority' of followers makes it legitimate to cast what are considered to be minority positions into oblivion. References to other schools of thought and doctrines are, at best, relegated to brief comments on the history of economic thought, often included in boxes outside the main text, which always give the impression that the parts of them that were correct have been included in the explanation given, that the rest has been left behind by later theoretical developments, and that it is not worth wasting time on things which have gone out of fashion or are no longer applicable. How many economics textbooks mention the existence of rigorous analyses demonstrating, for example, that the law of the equality of weighted (by prices) marginal utilities makes no theoretical sense? How many express even a remote doubt on the indiscriminate use of functional analysis in our science or on such generalized tools as, for example, indifference–preference curves?[9] How many submit the axiomatic hypotheses of the so-called theory of revealed preference to criticism due to the fact that is it based on the assumption of *constancy* in subjective valuations, which is never the case in real life, rather than on indisputable criteria of 'consistency' and 'rationality'?[10] In short, how may we explain that there are important schools of thought in our discipline which develop it aprioristically and deductively, without resorting to the old hypotheses of methodological positivism?[11]

The importance of treatises on the foundations or principles of Economic Science

The only way in which the insufficiencies we summarize in the preceding section can be avoided consists of returning to the tradition of writing real treatises on the principles or foundations of Economic Science for our students. Instead of preparing simple manuals or textbooks which summarize the latest fashions and scientific novelties, real treatises should be written which, as the fruit of long scientific reflection and academic experience, bring coherently together the essential principles which constitute the foundations and bases of economics. Thus, students will be provided with analytical tools of an incalculable value with which they will be able to continue to construct the whole theoretical edifice of economics and which will serve as a guide for them throughout their future professional career. The stability and the durability of treatises on economic principles should be much greater than those of the manuals and textbooks published today. They should be written, therefore, using criteria which are much more timeless and abstract (i.e. avoiding the use of highly topical or quasi-journalistic examples), always providing an integral vision of Economic Science in which all its areas are conveniently inter-related. In any case, the objective of any treatise on principles or foundations should consist of teaching the students to think in terms of the essential elements of the discipline. Moreover, as the preparation and theoretical justification of essential principles must be carried out with great care, detail and analytical rigour, it is necessary to refer to the different approaches and alternative viewpoints, always avoiding a pernicious partiality and providing adequate justification of the theoretical position adopted in comparison with the different alternatives analysed. This means that, in real treatises on economic principles, far from concealing the different options, these are openly explained to the reader and are analytically dissected in all the detail necessary to reach what is considered to be the most appropriate theoretical conclusion.

As is logical, this typical approach of the treatises on economic principles or foundations is not in any way incompatible with the theoretical analysis of more specific problems which it is felt may have an important practical relevance. On the contrary, a good theoretical and abstract basis is the *sine qua non* requirement, not only for an accurate understanding and interpretation of what occurs in the historical economic reality of any given moment, but also, to correctly guide the theoretical analysis and practical recommendations considered most appropriate in each circumstance.[12]

From this point of view, Mises *Human Action* constitutes the most important treatise on the essential principles and foundations of Economic Science written in the last century. Its most characteristic features are its profound analytical rigour and the constant consistency and total logical concatenation which overflow from each of its thirty-nine chapters, in which almost all economic problems are discussed. In short, Mises, in this book, systematically constructs the edifice of economic theory which is integrated into a consistent and unified whole.[13] The Treatise, moreover, is written in a very clear and flowing style. It does not only analyse and reach conclusions on the most varied schools which have arisen during the history of economic thought, but also, as is the case with the very few works which, like this one, have rapidly become classic reference points for any economist, shows, in every paragraph, great wisdom and originality and constitutes a real intellectual treasury of ideas and suggestions, each of which, if studied and analysed in greater depth, easily becomes an entire research topic for a doctoral thesis or even for a new treatise or book.[14]

The author and his work: Mises' main contributions to Economic Science

Although, logically, it is not possible to make even a brief and succinct summary here of all the theoretical contributions of *Human Action*, it is nevertheless necessary to place it in its correct intellectual context, explaining, above all, the evolution of the author's thought which was finally set forth in his Treatise.

Mises' contributions to the field of Economic Science cover the first two-thirds of the last century. In fact, as he himself confesses, Mises became an economist after reading Carl Menger's *Principles of Economics* over Christmas 1903.[15] It was, therefore, from that moment onwards that a very long and fruitful academic life dedicated to economic research and teaching commenced, continuing until 1969, when Mises retired as professor of economics at the University of New York.

Menger's book, which had so much influence on Mises, represented a milestone in the history of economic thought. For the first time, an attempt was made to construct the whole of Economic Science on the basis of the human being, considered as a creative actor with the leading role in every social process. Menger believed it was indispensable to abandon the sterile 'objectivity' of the classical Anglo-Saxon School and, following a continental tradition of thought which dated from much earlier, going back as far as the Spanish scholastics of the sixteenth and seventeenth centuries,[16] considered that the scientist should always adopt the subjective viewpoint of the human being who acts, in such a way that this viewpoint would have a determining and inevitable influence on the way in which all economic theories were developed and on their conclusions and practical results. It is, therefore, understandable that Menger considered it indispensable to abandon the sterile objectivity of the Classical Anglo-Saxon School, which was always obsessed by the supposed existence of objective external factors (social classes, aggregates, material production factors, etc.). A natural consequence of the 'subjectivist'[17] conception, which has been re-adopted thanks to Menger, is not only the development of the subjective theory of value and of its corollary, the law of marginal utility, but also the idea of cost as a subjective valuation of the alternatives which are renounced on acting (opportunity cost).

Menger's seminal contribution was continued by his most brilliant student, Eugen von Böhm-Bawerk (1851–1914),[18] who was professor of economics first at Innsbruck and then at Vienna. He was also finance minister in the government of the Austro-Hungarian Empire on three different occasions. Böhm-Bawerk not only contributed to the dissemination of the subjectivist conception which was originally owed to Menger, but also made a notable extension to its application, especially in the sphere of the theory of capital and interest. Böhm-Bawerk criticized all the theories which had existed prior to the appearance of his work on the emergence of interest (and was especially correct in his critical analysis of the Marxist theory of exploitation and the theories which consider that interest originates from the marginal productivity of capital). He also drew up a whole new theory on the emergence of interest, based on the subjective reality of time preference. Böhm-Bawerk's most brilliant student was, without doubt, Ludwig von Mises, who very soon drew attention for being the most outstanding participant in the seminar run by Böhm-Bawerk at the University of Vienna until just before the First World War. In this seminar, in which theorists of the standing of J. A. Schumpeter also participated, Mises proposed extending the application of the traditional subjectivist conception of economics, which had been re-adopted by Menger, to the sphere of money and credit. In 1912, he published the first edition of his first important book on economics under the title of *The Theory of Money and Credit*.[19]

Ludwig von Mises and the theory of money, credit and economic cycles

This first seminal contribution of Mises in the monetary sphere implied a great step forward and led to the advance of the subjectivism of the Austrian School by applying it to the field of money and basing the value of the latter on the theory of marginal utility. Moreover, Mises solved, for the first time, the apparently insoluble problem of circular reasoning which was until then considered to exist in relation to the application of the theory of marginal utility to money. In fact, the price or purchasing power of money is determined by its supply and demand. The demand for money, in turn, is made by human beings, not on the basis of the direct utility provided by money, but in accordance with its purchasing power. Mises resolved this apparent circular reasoning with his regression theorem of purchasing power, which he analyses and explains in detail in point 4 of Chapter XVII of *Human Action*. According to this theorem, the demand for money is determined, not by its purchasing power *today* (which would give rise to the abovementioned circular reasoning), but by the knowledge of the purchasing power that it had *yesterday*, formed by the actor on the basis of his experience. In turn, yesterday's purchasing power had been determined by a demand for money formed on the basis of knowledge of its purchasing power the day before yesterday. This sequence continues until the moment of history is reached when, for the first time, a certain commodity (gold or silver) began to be demanded as a means of exchange.

The Theory of Money and Credit soon became the standard work in the monetary field[20] and also included the incipient development of an outstanding theory of trade cycles. With time, this theory would become known as the Austrian theory of the economic cycles. In fact, Mises, by applying the monetary theories of the Currency School to Böhm-Bawerk's subjectivist theories of capital and interest, realized that the expansive creation of credits without the support of effective saving (fiduciary media), to which the banking system based on a fractional reserve and organized by a central bank gave rise, not only generated a cyclical and uncontrolled growth of the monetary supply. In addition, as it resulted in the *ex nihilo* creation of credits at artificially reduced interest rates, it inexorably led to a fictitious and untenable 'lengthening' of the productive processes, which thus tended unduly to become excessively capital intensive. Sooner or later, the amplification of any inflationary process by credit expansion will, spontaneously and inexorably, have to revert, giving rise to an economic crisis or recession in which the investment errors induced will produce their results and there will be massive unemployment and the need to liquidate and reassign all the erroneously invested resources. Mises' development of the theory of the cycle, which is studied in detail in Chapters XX and XXXI of *Human Action*, led, for the first time, to the full integration of the 'micro' and 'macro' aspects of economic theory[21] and to the availability of analytical tools able to explain the recurrent phenomena of boom and depression which affect impeded markets. It is not surprising, therefore, that Mises was the main driving force behind the creation of the Austrian Institute of Economic Research, at the head of which he placed F. A. Hayek (winner of the Nobel Prize for Economics in 1974) as the first director. This Institute was the only one able to predict the coming of the Great Depression of 1929 as the inevitable result of the monetary and credit excesses of the artificially 'prosperous' 1920s which followed the First World War.[22] We should also highlight how Mises and his disciples refined their theory of cycles at the same time as their analysis on the impossibility of socialism which we discuss below. In fact, the Austrian theory of crises is simply a specific application of the discoordinating effects of the systematic coercion of governments in the tax, credit and monetary fields (within and between time periods) on the productive structure.

The Misesian analysis of the impossibility of socialism

Mises' third great contribution consists of his theory on the impossibility of socialism. For Mises, from the viewpoint of Austrian subjectivism, this impossibility is evident.[23] In fact, if the source of all volition, valuation and knowledge is to be found in the creative capacity of the human being as an actor, all systems based on the use of violent coercion against free human action, as is the case of socialism and, to a lesser extent, of interventionism, will prevent the emergence of the information necessary to coordinate society in the minds of the individual actors. Mises realized that *economic calculation*, understood as any estimated judgement on the result of alternative courses of action which are open to the actor, requires first-hand information and becomes impossible in a system which, like socialism, is based on coercion and impedes, to a greater or lesser extent, voluntary exchange (in which individual valuations are set forth, discovered and created) and the free use of money as a voluntary, commonly accepted means of exchange.[24] Mises therefore concludes that where there is no free market, free market monetary prices and/or money, no 'rational' economic calculation is possible, if we understand 'rational' to refer to a calculation made when the necessary information (not merely arbitrary information) is available in order to carry it out. Mises' first essential ideas were systematized and included in his great critical treatise on this social system, the first edition of which was published in German in 1922 under the title *Die Gemeinwirtschaft: Untersuchungen über den Sozialismus* and subsequently translated into English, French and Spanish.[25] Mises' *Socialism* was a work which achieved extraordinary popularity in continental Europe and had, among other consequences, the result of making theorists of the standing of F. A. Hayek, initially a Fabian socialist, Wilhelm Röpke and Lionel Robbins change their opinions after reading it and become converted to libertarianism.[26]

Moreover, this book marked the beginning of one of the four great controversies in which the Austrian School theorists have been involved: the controversy on the impossibility of socialist economic calculation.[27] Recently, I have had the opportunity to study and re-evaluate in detail, in an extensive work,[28] all the aspects of this controversy which, without doubt, as has today finally been generally acknowledged even by the former socialist theorists,[29] was won by the members of the Austrian School and is one of the most interesting controversies, with some of the most significant consequences, in the history of economic thought.[30]

The theory of entrepreneurship

The consideration of the human being as the essential and inevitable protagonist of all social processes constitutes the essence of Mises' fourth contribution to the field of economic science. In fact, Mises realizes that economics, which had first arisen centred around a historical ideal type in Max Weber's sense of the term, the *homo oeconomicus*, thanks to the subjectivist conception of Menger, becomes generalized and is converted into a whole general theory on human action and interaction (praxeology, in Mises' terminology). The essential characteristics and implications of human action and interaction are studied in detail and constitute the basic research matter of the Treatise on Economics which Mises, for this precise reason, entitled *Human Action*.[31] Mises considers that any action has an entrepreneurial and speculative component and develops a theory of entrepreneurship, understood as the human being's ability to create the subjective opportunities for gain or profit which arise in his environment and to realize that they exist, acting in consequence to take advantage of them.[32] The Misesian theory of entrepreneurship has been very much developed over recent years by one of Mises' most brilliant students, Israel M. Kirzner (b.1930), professor of economics at the University of New York.[33] The entrepreneurial capacity of the human being not only explains his or her constant search for and creation of new information on ends and means,[34] but is also the key to understanding the coordinating tendency which emerges spontaneously and continuously on the market when it is not coercively intervened in. This coordinating capacity of entrepreneurship is precisely what makes it possible to draw up a logical *corpus* of economic theory without the need to fall into the vices of scientistic (mathematical and statistical) analysis, which, based on hypotheses of constancy, comes from and is a bad copy of the alien world of physics and the rest of the natural sciences.

Aprioristic-deductive methodology and the criticism of scientistic positivism

Since Menger, methodological and epistemological problems have been treated at length and in depth by the Austrian theorists, particularly by Mises himself, whose contribution in this field is among the most essential contributions made by the great twentieth century Austrian economist. Effectively, the fact that the 'observing' scientist cannot obtain the practical information which is being constantly created and discovered in a decentralized way by the 'observed' actors-entrepreneurs explains the theoretical impossibility of any type of empirical verification in our field. In fact, from this point of view, it may be considered that the same reasons that determine the theoretical impossibility of socialism explain that both empiricism and the cost–benefit analysis, or utilitarianism in its strictest interpretation, are not viable in our science. It is irrelevant whether it is a scientist or a governor who vainly tries to obtain the practical information that is relevant to each case in order to verify theories or endow his commands with a coordinating nature. If this were possible, it would be viable to use this information either to coordinate society through coercive commands (socialism and interventionism) or to empirically verify economic theories. However, for the same reasons, first, in view of the immense volume of information in question; second, due to the nature of the relevant information (disseminated, subjective and tacit); third, because of the dynamic nature of the entrepreneurial process (information which has not yet been generated by the entrepreneurs in their process of constant innovatory creation cannot be transmitted); and, fourth, due to the effect of coercion and of scientific 'observation' itself (which distorts, corrupts, impedes or simply makes the entrepreneurial creation of information impossible), both the socialist ideal and the positive or strictly utilitarian ideal are impossible from the point of view of economic theory.[35]

These same arguments are also applicable in order to justify the theoretical impossibility of making specific predictions (i.e. referring to determined coordinates of time and place) in economics. What will happen tomorrow can never be scientifically known today, as it largely depends on knowledge and information which have not yet been entrepreneurially generated and which, therefore, cannot yet be known. In economics, therefore, only general 'trend predictions' can be made (what Hayek calls 'pattern predictions'), which are of an essentially theoretical nature and relative, at most, to the qualitative forecast of the disorders and effects of social discoordination produced by institutional coercion (socialism and interventionism) on the market.

Moreover, the non-existence of objective facts which may be directly observed in the external world, derived from the circumstance that, according to the subjectivist conception, economic research 'facts' are simply ideas that others have on what they pursue and do,[36] which may never be observed directly, but only interpreted in historical terms, together with the constantly variable and very complex nature of social processes and events, in which there are no 'parameters' or 'constants', but in which everything is a 'variable', makes the traditional objective of econometrics impossible and leads to the non-viability of any of the versions of the positivist methodological programme (from the most ingenuous verificationism to the most sophisticated Popperian falsificationism).

As opposed to the positivist ideal, in *Human Action* Mises shows that the whole of Economic Science can be constructed through apriorism and deduction. The question is, in brief, to prepare an entire logical-deductive arsenal on the basis of self-evident knowledge (axioms such as the subjective concept of human action itself with its essential elements) with which nobody can argue without contradicting himself.[37] This theoretical arsenal is indispensable for an adequate interpretation of the apparently unrelated mass of complex historical phenomena which constitute the social world, and for drawing up a history of the past, or to predict events in the future (which is the typical mission of the entrepreneur) with a minimum degree of consistency, guarantees and chances of success. It is now possible to understand the great importance which Mises places in his work on history as a discipline, on its relation to theory and on the role of the historian, together with the fact that he defines the entrepreneur as an 'acting man [who] looks, as it were, with the eyes of a historian into the future'.[38]

Economics as a theory of dynamic social processes: criticism of the analysis of the equilibrium (general and partial) and of the conception of economics as a mere maximizing technique

Finally, in the sixth place, Mises' work gives a great impetus to the theory of dynamic processes. In fact, for Mises, the mathematical construction of an Economic Science based on the model of equilibrium (general or partial),[39] in which all the information relevant, for example, to the construction of the corresponding functions of supply and demand is considered constant and 'given' (even though it may be in probabilistic terms), makes no sense.

The basic economic problem for Mises is a completely different one: to study the dynamic process of social coordination in which different individuals are continuously entrepreneurially generating new information (which is never 'given' or constant) when they seek the ends and means they consider relevant under each specific circumstance, thus establishing, without realizing it, a spontaneous process of coordination. In contrast to the world of physics and the natural sciences, functional relations (and, therefore, functions of supply, demand, costs or of any other type) do not exist in economics. Let us remember that, mathematically, according to set theory, a function is merely a correspondence between the elements or points of two sets which are called the 'initial set' and the 'final set'. Given the innate creative capacity of the human being, who is continuously generating and discovering new information in each specific circumstance in which s/he acts in respect of the ends s/he aims to pursue and the means to attain them s/he considers to be within his or her reach, it is evident that there is none of the three elements necessary for a functional relationship to exist: (1) the elements of the initial set are not given or constant; (2) the elements which constitute the final set are not given or constant; and (3), and this is the most important point, *neither are the correspondences between the elements of the two sets given or constant, but rather they vary continuously as a result of the action and creative capacity of the human being.*[40] Thus, in our science, the use of functions requires that a *presupposition of constancy* be introduced into the information, eliminating the protagonist of the whole social process: the human being endowed with an innate creative entrepreneurial capacity. Mises' great merit consists in having shown that it is perfectly possible to create Economic Science in its entirety logically, without any need to use functions and, therefore, to establish hypotheses of constancy which are contrary to the nature of the human being, that is, of the protagonist of the whole of the social process which it is aimed to study.[41]

It has, therefore, been demonstrated that the basic economic problem is not of a technical or technological nature, as it is usually set out by the mathematical economists of the neoclassical paradigm, when they assume that the ends and means are 'given' and that the rest of the information necessary is constant, thus considering the economic problem as if it were a mere technical problem of optimization or maximization.[42] In other words, the basic economic problem is neither technical nor a problem of maximization of an objective function which is 'known' and constant, subject to constraints which are also 'known' and constant. It is, on the contrary, strictly economic: *it emerges when there are many ends and means competing among themselves, when knowledge of them is neither given nor constant, but is dispersed over the minds of innumerable human beings who are continuously creating and generating it ex novo and, therefore, all the possible alternatives which exist, all those which will be created in the future, and the relative intensity with which each of them will be pursued cannot ever be known.* Perhaps Mises' most important and fruitful contribution to Economic Science consists precisely in the definitive eradication of this erroneous conception of our science as a mere maximization technique.[43]

Brief summary of the biography of Ludwig von Mises

Ludwig Edler von Mises was born on 29 September 1881 in the city of Lemberg, located, at the time, within the Austro-Hungarian Empire. Today, this city is called Lvov and forms part of the new Independent Republic of the Ukraine. Ludwig's father studied at the Zurich Polytechnic College and became an important engineer who specialized in the construction of railways. Ludwig was the eldest of three brothers, one of whom died when he was a child. The other, Richard, became a well-known mathematician and logical positivist. Throughout his life, Ludwig maintained a cold personal relationship with his brother.

Ludwig von Mises obtained a doctorate in law on 20 February 1906 and, until 1914, was one of the most outstanding participants in the economics seminar held by Eugen von Böhm-Bawerk at the University of Vienna. Another participant in this seminar was J. A. Schumpeter, whom Mises considered to be an excessively confused and frivolous theorist who had fallen into the trap of neoclassical scientism and whose constant desire was to astonish.

In 1906, Mises commenced his teaching activities, first, for six years, teaching economics at the *Wiener Handelsakademie für Mädchen* (Vienna School of Mercantile Studies for Young Ladies) and, later, for twenty years, from 1913 on, as a professor at the University of Vienna. In 1934, he was appointed professor of International Economics at the *Institut des Hautes Études Internationales* in Geneva, Switzerland, and at the outbreak of the Second World War he fled from Hitler to the United States, where he acquired American nationality and was appointed professor at the University of New York, where he remained until his retirement in 1969. Between 1920 and 1934, Mises organized, directed and held a famous economics seminar (*Privatseminar*) in his official office at the Vienna Chamber of Commerce, where he was head of the Economics Department and through which he acquired great influence over his country's economic policy. Not only the students who were preparing their doctoral theses under the direction of Mises attended this seminar, which took place on Friday evenings, but also, by invitation, very prestigious economists from all over the world. Among the German speakers who regularly attended were Friedrich A. Hayek, Fritz Machlup, Gottfried von Haberler, Oskar Morgensten, Paul N. Rosenstein-Rodan, Felix Kaufman, Alfred Schutz, Richard von Strigl, Karl Menger (the mathematician, son of Carl Menger, the founder of the Austrian School) and Erich Voegelin. From the United Kingdom and United States came Lionel Robbins, Hugh Gaitskell, Ragnar Nurske and Albert G. Hart, among others. Subsequently, in the United States, Mises recreated his seminar at the University of New York and the meetings took place on Thursday evenings from autumn 1948 until spring 1969. Murray N. Rothbard and Israel Kirzner, who would later become professors, stand out among the numerous participants in this second stage. Ludwig von Mises was awarded doctorates *honoris causa* by the University of New York and, at the request of F. A. Hayek, the University of Freiburg (Brisgovia, Germany). In 1962, he received the Medal of Honour for Sciences and Arts of the Republic of Austria and, in 1969, was appointed a Distinguished Fellow of the American Economic Association. He died in New York on 10 October 1973, having published twenty-two books and hundreds of articles and papers on economic matters.[44]

Mises had the good fortune to be able to lead a long academic life which covered almost seven decades of the last century and was acknowledged, during his lifetime, as an economist of universal fame. Thus, as early as 1944, Henry C. Simons described him as 'the greatest living teacher of economics'.[45] Nobel Prizewinner Milton Friedman, a positivist economist of the School of Chicago, who cannot be suspected of any sympathy with Mises' theoretical positions, spoke of him shortly after his death in 1973 as 'one of the greatest economists of all time'.[46] Another winner of the Nobel Prize for Economics, Maurice Allais, has written that Mises was 'un homme d'une intelligence exceptionnelle dont les contributions à la science économique ont été de tout premier ordre'.[47] Finally, Lord Robbins, remembering Mises in his intellectual autobiography, concluded: 'I fail to comprehend how anyone not blinded by political prejudice can read his main contributions and the magisterial general treatise *Human Action*, without experiencing at once a sense of rare quality and an intellectual stimulus of a high order.'[48]

The successive editions of *Human Action*

Although Mises' *Human Action* is not an easy book to read, being a lengthy and profound treatise on political economy, it has been one of the most notable publishing successes for a book of this nature. Up to the date of writing this article, there have been a total of twenty-five editions of the book and nearly as many reprints, corresponding to the four successive editions corrected and revised by the author during his lifetime. It may be estimated that over 150,000 copies of *Human Action* have been sold to date.[49] The book has been published in eleven different languages, English, German,

Italian, French, Spanish, Portuguese, Russian, Japanese, Chinese, Czech and Korean, and is one of the most widely quoted treatises, above all in monographic works, in specialized articles on economic matters in general, on the methodology of Economic Science and, particularly, in those on the economic analysis of socialism. We will describe briefly in what follows the main editions of *Human Action* published to date and how they have evolved.

Nationalökonomie: *an immediate forerunner of* Human Action *written in German*

Nationalökonomie: Theorie des Handelns und Wirtschaftens[50] ('Economics: theory of action and change') is the first systematic economic treatise written by Mises and may be considered as the immediate forerunner of *Human Action*. It was written during the happy years that Mises spent teaching in Geneva and was published in May 1940. Due to the outbreak of the Second World War, its publication had little influence on the academic world. When he wrote this first version of his Treatise, Mises aimed to cover, systematically and comprehensively, all the economic theory of human behaviour using a language which could be understood by any educated person.[51]

To date, no English translation of *Nationalökonomie* has been published. This is a pity from the academic point of view, because it does not fully coincide with *Human Action* in many important aspects. In fact, *Nationalökonomie* may provide the researcher with better guidelines, as there are more and fuller footnotes which give more profuse details on the sources which had most influence on the author. Moreover, entire sections of *Nationalökonomie* of great interest were not included in the English edition of *Human Action*, such as those which refer, for example, to the criticism of Böhm-Bawerk's theory of interest.[52]

The need to make Mises' treatise available again in the German-speaking world led to a further publication of *Nationalökonomie* in 1980, this time in Germany, under the auspices of the International Carl Menger Library.[53] Many very favourable reviews of this second edition were published in Austria and Germany.[54] Finally a de luxe facsimile edition was published by Klassiker der Nationalökonomie, with a *Vademecum* written by Peter J. Boetke, Kurt R. Leube and Enrico Colombato.

English editions of Human Action

The first edition of *Human Action* in English was published under the title *Human Action: A Treatise on Economics* by Yale University Press in 1949. It is, without any doubt, the *magnum opus* which crowned the whole of Ludwig von Mises' academic life. As stated above, it is not merely an English translation of *Nationalökonomie*. On reaching the United States, Mises, over a five-year period, completely revised and almost rewrote a whole new book. *Human Action* immediately became an important publishing success and the first edition, which was published simultaneously in the United States and England,[55] was reprinted six times in the following ten years.

In 1963 Yale University Press published the second edition of *Human Action*, revised and expanded by Mises himself. The most notable modifications and additions refer to the treatment of the concept of freedom and government included under heading 6 of Chapter XV; to the theory of monopoly developed under heading 6 of Chapter XVI; and, finally, to the analysis of corruption which is included as heading 6 of Chapter XXVII. Mises was very annoyed by the number of errata and typographical mistakes in this edition and, in general, by the negligent (if not fraudulent) behaviour of his publisher (Yale University Press)[56] and, therefore, reached an agreement for the publication of a third edition in which all the errors committed in the previous one would be corrected. This was published in 1966 by the publisher Henry Regnery and was to become the definitive edition of this *magnum opus*.[57] To date, three reprints of the third English edition of *Human Action* have been issued: the first in 1978; the second in a luxury edition of 1985; and the third, for the first time in paperback, in 1990. We should also mention that a taped version of *Human Action* in English, on thirty cassettes, was also issued in 1990, read by Bernard Mayes.[58]

Finally, three important new editions of *Human Action* have recently been published in English: first Bettina Bien Greaves' carefully revised fourth edition in 1996;[59] second, the magnificent Scholar's Edition prepared in 1998 from the original 1949 edition by Professors Jeffrey H. Herbener, Hans-Hermann Hoppe and Joseph T. Salerno;[60] and third the four volume edition published by Liberty Fund in 2007.

Translations of Human Action *into languages other than Spanish*

The success of *Human Action* soon led to the publication of translations of the book into other languages. Apart from the successive editions of the Spanish translation, to which we will refer in the following section, we mention below, in strict chronological order, each of the translations published to date.

The first version of *Human Action* outside the United States and England was published in 1959 in Italy under the title *L'Azione Umana: Trattato di Economia*. This edition was translated and published in Italian due to the efforts of Tullio Bagiotti, professor of Political Economy at the Bocconi University of Milan, who also wrote a 'Presentazione' which included a brief biographical note on Mises and reference to his different works.[61]

The first translation of *Human Action* into Chinese appeared in 1976. It was translated by Professor Tao-Ping Hsia from the third English edition of 1966 and published in two volumes. This translation, revised by Professor Hui-Lin Wu, was later published in Taiwan in 1991, also in two volumes.[62]

The French translation of *Human Action* was published in 1985 under the title *L'Action humaine: Traité d'économie*. This edition was translated from the third English edition of 1966 by Raoul Audouin and was published in the prestigious collection 'Libre Échange' of Presses Universitaires de France, directed by Florin Aftalion.⁶³

In the course of 1987–8, a Korean translation of *Human Action*, also based on the English edition, was published in two volumes with a foreword by Professor Toshio Murata.⁶⁴

In 1990, the Portuguese translation of the third edition of *Human Action* was published in Brazil under the title *Açào humana: um tratado de economia*. Donald Stewart, Jr was responsible for the translation and it was published by the Instituto Liberal of Rio de Janeiro.⁶⁵ The high standard of Stewart's Portuguese translation should be emphasized, although his edition, unlike the others, is more difficult to read, as he transfers the footnotes to the end of each chapter.

In 1991, the Japanese translation of the third English edition of *Human Action* was published under the title of *Ningen-Kōi-Gaku*. This Japanese version was meticulously prepared over many years by Toshio Murata, who was one of Ludwig von Mises' students in New York before becoming professor of economics at the University of Yokohama.⁶⁶ Murata, who learnt Spanish from a Jesuit priest, was stationed with the General Staff of the 13th Japanese Army which occupied Shanghai during the Second World War. There, he was a first-hand witness of the impossibility of coercively organizing the flourishing market economy which then prevailed in that part of China and of the serious hyperinflation provoked by the monetary policy of the occupiers. These problems put him in touch with the economic theories of Mises, the study and popularization of which he has not ceased to foment in Japan throughout his academic career.

Finally, the first Russian translation of *Human Action* was published at Christmastime in 2000, thanks to A. B. Kuriaev (Economic Publishers, Moscow, 2000), and the first Czech edition appeared thanks to Professor Josef Sima in 2007.

The eight Spanish editions of Human Action

The history of the Spanish editions of *Human Action* cannot be understood without reference to their translator, Joaquín Reig Albiol. Joaquín Reig obtained his doctorate in Law on 15 February 1958 reading a doctoral thesis the title of which was 'Los modernos problemas sociales a la luz del ideario económico de Ludwig von Mises' ('Modern social problems from the point of view of Ludwig von Mises' economic thought'). This thesis (directed by Jesús Prados Arrarte, professor of Political Economy in the Law Faculty of the Madrid Complutense University), was the first monographic work written in Spanish on the first English edition of *Human Action*, which had appeared in the United States a few years earlier.⁶⁷

Two years later, the first Spanish version appeared, translated by Joaquín Reig Albiol from the first English edition of *Human Action* published in

1949. The Spanish edition was published in two volumes by the Fundación Ignacio Villalonga of Valencia (Spain).[68] Joaquín Reig also included an extensive preliminary study, which appears on pages 26–62 of Volume I, introducing Mises' work to Spanish-speaking readers.

Eight years later, the second Spanish edition of *Human Action* appeared, published by Editorial Sopec in a single volume. This was the first Spanish translation of the third English edition of 1966. Like the first, this new Spanish edition included a foreword 'for Spanish-speaking readers', also written by Joaquín Reig (pp. 17–19), but much briefer and more concise than that in the first edition.[69]

From the 1970s onwards, Unión Editorial took over the Spanish reprints of the works of Mises and the third edition of *Human Action* was published in 1980.[70] This was a very high quality edition with excellent typographical presentation, which, as well as a brief foreword by the translator, included a series of footnotes in which Joaquín Reig, basically following the guideline of the glossary prepared and published in English by Percy Greaves in 1978, explained to the reader the concepts in the book which are most complex or difficult to understand. The 1980 edition sold out rapidly and was followed by a fourth edition, also published by Unión Editorial, in 1985.[71]

Ten years later, in November 1995, Unión Editorial brought out the fifth Spanish edition of *Human Action*, with a carefully revised, corrected and updated translation. As the original translator, Joaquín Reig Albiol, died in 1986, he was not able to collaborate in this important revision, which, respecting the original translation to the greatest possible extent, consisted basically of the modernization and simplification of certain expressions and the introduction of terms which have now come into common use in Economic Science. Likewise, the most important notes of those prepared by Joaquín Reig for the previous editions have been maintained, the bibliography has been completed with the corresponding bibliographical references published in Spanish and an extensive Preliminary Study, written by the author of the present article, has been included. The sixth and seventh revised and corrected editions were published in 2001 and 2004. Finally, readers may now acquire the eighth (2007) and latest Spanish edition of *Human Action*, which again has been revised and updated.

In order to complete this section, it is necessary to note that Ludwig von Mises always enjoyed a high prestige in Spanish-speaking countries. In the first place, not only is the number of editions of *Human Action* published in Spanish far higher than in any country outside the United States, but also, moreover, Mises himself made several academic tours to different Latin-American countries (Mexico, Peru and Argentina), where he expounded his ideas at the most important universities and created a very significant number of disciples and students of his works. It is also interesting to emphasize how, in the 'Preface' to the third English edition, the only Spanish-speaking person whose help in preparing his Treatise is acknowledged by Mises is precisely Dr Joaquín Reig Albiol.[72]

The impetus given by *Human Action* to the development of Economic Science

If anything is characteristic of Mises' Treatise on Economics, it is its profound seminal nature. As we have said, practically every paragraph of the book is full of ideas and suggestions which could serve as a basis for the research for a doctoral thesis. It is not, therefore, surprising that, over the years which have elapsed since it was first published, *Human Action* has contributed to important advances in the edifice of Economic Science. We will discuss briefly in what follows the fields in which the most interesting improvements have taken place.

Mises and the theory of evolution

Although it cannot be doubted that Mises fully accepted the evolutionary theory on the emergence of the institutions which we owe to Carl Menger and, in fact, expressly states his agreement, without any reservations, at several points of his Treatise,[73] it should be acknowledged that *Human Action* contains a series of affirmations which could induce an error and be incorrectly interpreted in terms of an exaggerated and strictly utilitarian rationalism. Thus, for example, on page 175 of *Human Action*, Mises excessively praises Bentham and his utilitarian doctrine, and, on pages 188 and 500, we read that 'Any given social order was thought out and designed before it could be realized', and that 'Laws were not an outgrowth of chance, historical accidents and geographical environment. They were the product of reason'. Although it is clear that these statements by Mises cannot be taken out of context, it is obvious that *Human Action* was not able to incorporate fully the important impetus which was subsequently given to the theory of the evolutionary emergence of institutions by his most brilliant student, F. A. Hayek, winner of the Nobel Prize for Economics in 1974. Hayek, continuing the research programme initiated in this field by Carl Menger, showed how institutions in general, understood as repetitive patterns of behaviour, and laws in particular, far from being a result which was expressly designed by human reason, developed spontaneously through evolution over a very prolonged process in which many generations of human beings participated. Therefore, we consider it advisable to combine the study of *Human Action* with a careful reading of the most important works written by Hayek on the theoretical analysis of social institutions, among which, for example, his *Law, Legislation and Liberty* and the last work he published before his death in 1992, *The Fatal Conceit: The Errors of Socialism*, stand out.[74]

The theory of Natural Law

In the different critical references to the doctrine of Natural Law which Mises makes in *Human Action*, his position is even clearer. First, he expresses the opinion that the principles of moral behaviour are purely subjective (p. 95) and, second, he does not only defend a strictly utilitarian position on moral principles,[75] but is also very critical of the doctrine of Natural Law (p. 175 and Chapter XXVII, heading 3). However, economics scholars have been placing increasing importance on the analysis of moral principles in general and, in particular, of Natural Law. Thus, for example, one of Mises' most brilliant students, Murray N. Rothbard, adopted a position clearly favourable to Natural Law, defending the idea that moral principles have an objective validity which is determined by the essence of human nature and, therefore, they are the only principles which make the social process of coordination possible.[76] Along the same lines, Hans-Hermann Hoppe, following Rothbard and using the Habermasian axiom of interpersonal argument as a starting point, logically deduces the moral need for property rights and the capitalist system.[77] Lastly, Israel M. Kirzner has set forth a whole new concept of distributive justice under capitalism based on the principle that every human being has the natural right to take possession of the results of his entrepreneurial creativity.[78] In any case, we consider that it is both possible and advisable to make a synthesis between the three points of view, the rational-utilitarian viewpoint defended by Mises, the evolutionary viewpoint developed by Hayek, and the Natural Law position which defends the existence of an objective theory of social morality and is fomented by Rothbard and Hoppe. Each of the three levels has its own scope of application and enriches and complements the other two, offsetting their possible excesses.[79]

The distinction between practical knowledge and scientific knowledge

Perhaps one of the most important seminal ideas contained in *Human Action* is the introduction of the concept of practical knowledge[80] of an entrepreneurial nature which is essentially different from scientific knowledge. However, the detailed analysis of the differences between the two types of knowledge and of their implications for economic science has been made by other authors who have continued in greater depth with this seminal idea of Mises'. Thus, we have integrated Mises' idea on the development of the market on the basis of the 'division of intellectual labor' (p. 709), which we interpret in terms of the division of the information or practical knowledge which is expansively generated by the open society.[81]

The theory of monopoly

One of the fields of economics in which advances have been made as a result of the impetus provided by Mises' *Human Action* is, precisely, the theory of monopoly. Even though Mises, in *Human Action*, pioneers the attempt to abandon the strictly static framework which, to date, has dominated the analysis of competition and monopoly, some of his considerations are still too much influenced by this framework. Fortunately, two of Mises' most brilliant students in the United States, Israel M. Kirzner and Murray N. Rothbard,[82] have given a great thrust forward to the theory of monopoly, concentrating their analysis on the study of the dynamic process of competition and, therefore, on whether the free practice of entrepreneurship is prevented by force in any part of the market, rather than on the number of enterprises 'existing' in each 'sector' and on the form or 'elasticity' of their supposed demand curves. Rothbard, moreover, hit the weak point of the neoclassical theory of monopoly, stating that its whole analysis is based on the static comparison between the 'monopoly price' and the 'price of perfect competition', which, as it is a price of equilibrium which never exists in the real market, cannot be known or, therefore, serve as a reference point to decide, in practice, whether or not there is a 'situation of monopoly'. It is important to highlight the fact that Mises, during his own lifetime, had the opportunity to see these studies on the theory of monopoly flourish, studies which in some way completed his own work, and fortunately we have direct testimony which indicates that he was in complete agreement with these new theoretical developments.[83]

Socialism and the theory of interventionism

Another of the characteristics of Misesian thought is the clear theoretical separation between the socialist economic system and the interventionist system (for example on pp. 258–259). For Mises, socialism is any system of social organization based on the public ownership of the means of production, while interventionism aims to be a compromise system, characterized by coercive state intervention in different economic fields but which, according to Mises, permits at least the most indispensable rudiments of economic calculation to be maintained. Theoretical research into socialism over recent years has shown that the differences which exist between an interventionist economic regime and a socialist one are far fewer than Mises thought. Both are characterized by coercive state intervention which impedes, to a greater or lesser extent, the free practice of entrepreneurship, although it is true that there are important differences in degree between the two systems. However, in the areas in which the state intervenes coercively, the entrepreneurial generation of information and, therefore, the estimation of the value of the different alternative courses of action (i.e. economic calculation) are made more difficult. The result is that important social disorders and discoordinations arise in the market. From this point of view, there is a current trend towards treating institutional coercion as a whole (regardless of whether it is all-embracing, as in the case of 'real' socialism, or only relates to specific areas, as occurs in the case of interventionism), as it has been shown that the perverse effects of discoordination of both of them are the same from a qualitative viewpoint.[84]

The theory of credit and the banking system

In *Human Action*, Mises affirms that he is in favour of a completely free banking system as the best possible procedure for achieving a stable monetary system which frees market economies from economic crises. He makes no detailed express reference in *Human Action* to the proposal of re-establishing the 100 per cent cash ratio for demand deposits in banks which, however, he explicitly defends in the rest of his works.[85] The position that Mises upholds in *Human Action* has led to the division of the later Austrian School theorists into two large groups. On the one hand, there are those who defend a system of complete free banking, even with a fractional reserve. This group includes Lawrence White, George Selgin and Kevin Dowd, among others. A second group, led by Murray N. Rothbard, Hans-Hermann Hoppe, Joseph T. Salerno and the author of the present article, considers that the most appropriate solution would consist of the defence of the traditional legal principles of banking (that is, the requirement of a 100 per cent cash ratio for demand deposits) as a necessary condition for the correct functioning of the whole system of free banking.[86]

The theory of population

Another aspect which has undergone an important theoretical development is the theory of population. In this field, although Mises' analysis in *Human Action* (Chapter XXV, heading 2) is still too much influenced by Malthusian doctrines, he nevertheless expressly states that, if a market economy system exists, the growth in the population, far from implying a drawback for economic development, increases wealth and provides an enormous impetus to the development of civilization.[87] This seminal idea was developed by Friedrich A. Hayek, especially in his last book, *The Fatal Conceit: The Errors of Socialism*, where he argues that, as the human being is not a homogenous production factor and is endowed with an innate entrepreneurial creative capacity, the growth of the population, far from placing a brake on economic development, is both the engine and the necessary condition for it to take place. Moreover, it has been shown that the development of civilization implies a constantly growing horizontal and vertical division of practical knowledge, which is only possible if, at the same time as civilization advances, there is an increase in the number of human beings able to support the growing volume of practical information used at a social level.[88] Hayek's ideas have been, in turn, developed by other scholars who, like Julian L. Simon, have applied them to the theory of demographic growth of third-world countries and the analysis of the beneficial economic effects of immigration.[89]

Human Action *as a forerunner of the Public Choice School*

Ludwig von Mises was one of the most important forerunners of the School of Public Choice, which studies, using economic analysis, the combined behaviour of politicians, bureaucrats and voters. This approach, which today has reached a high level of development under the auspices of theorists like James M. Buchanan (winner of the Nobel Prize for Economics in 1986), fits in perfectly with the broad praxeological conception of economics developed by Mises, who considered that the goal of our science was to build a general theory of human action in all its varieties and contexts (including, therefore, political actions).

Thus, Mises is one of the first authors to criticize the traditional assumption of political and economic analysis which considers that the governors are always 'wise and impartial' and that their servants, the civil servants or bureaucrats, are almost angelic creatures. On the contrary, for Mises, 'the politician is always selfish, no matter whether he supports a popular programme in order to achieve office or whether he firmly clings to his own convictions', and 'unfortunately the office-holders and their staffs are not angelic' (p. 735).[90] In contrast to the idyllic image of the governor as a 'man no less benevolent than wise, sincerely dedicated to the promotion of his subjects' lasting welfare', Mises puts forward the figure of the real governor, who 'turns out to be a mortal man who first of all aims at the perpetration of his own supremacy and that of his kin, his friends and his party' (p. 850).

Mises' reference to pressure groups should also be highlighted. He defines them as the 'alliance of people eager to promote their own material well-being by the employment of all means', always 'anxious to justify its demands as beneficial to the general public welfare' (p. 318).

The combined action of the behaviour of the bureaucrats, politicians and pressure groups disturbs the functioning of democracy and prevents many majority decisions from being correct and fitting, as public opinion is debased by erroneous and demagogic ideas.[91] The existence of institutions which, like the gold standard, eliminate decisions relative to monetary issues from the political arena is, therefore, of so much importance to Mises.[92]

It is not surprising, therefore, that James Buchanan, in homage to Mises and the Austrian School, which have so much influenced his thought, has said that 'I have often argued that the Austrians seem to be more successful in conveying the central principles of economics to students than alternative schools or approaches'.[93]

Method for the study and teaching of *Human Action*

Potential readership for this treatise

We have mentioned above that Mises, when conceiving his work *Human Action*, set himself the fundamental objective of writing an all-embracing Treatise on Economics for any educated person interested in the analysis of the most pressing problems of our time. In effect, according to Mises,

> Economics must not be relegated to classrooms and statistical offices and must not be left to esoteric circles. It is the philosophy of human

life and action and concerns everybody and everything. It is the pith of civilization and of man's human existence. (p. 878).

Therefore, if Mises is right, his Treatise on Economics is a tool for intellectual work that should be present in the libraries of all educated men in the modern world.

However, there is no doubt that the most important mission which Mises' *Human Action* can and should fulfil is related to university education. In this respect, it may be considered that the work is addressed to two large groups of students. First, the students of political economy within the schools of social studies and law schools, who need to receive a general education in Economic Science using a conception and methodology which are both rigorous and strongly humanist. In this respect, we should highlight the very positive experience of the last twenty academic years, during which *Human Action* has been the main textbook for my students of political economy first at the Law School of the Complutense University of Madrid, and afterwards at the School of Social Studies of King Juan Carlos University also in Madrid. The students understand the concatenation which exists between the knowledge of economics and the rest of the disciplines, which they study for their degree, more clearly from Mises, acquiring knowledge of the essential principles and foundations of our science which is invaluable for the future of their professional career. The situation of students in the schools of economics is different and, given the current circumstances of the academic world, they receive an education which is strongly conditioned by the positivist and scientistic methodology of which Mises was so critical. In our opinion, it is indispensable, in order to provide these students with a balanced education and provide them with an alternative viewpoint, different from the one they have traditionally received, that all economic science students should study Mises' Treatise on Economics in depth. In this way they will enrich their knowledge of the subject and will be able to compare and enter into contact with new points of view which they will find challenging, new and original. All of this will lead to a better and more complete professional education that will allow them to take up a healthier, more informed and critical intellectual position in respect of the different alternative theories.[94]

The fourth and last group of readers who may make good use of *Human Action* are specialized researchers in Economic Science, who are showing an increasing interest in the theories of the Austrian School of Economics, especially after the fall of real socialism and the crisis of the welfare state have shown that the interventionist theories upheld to date lack a solid theoretical basis. Moreover, the crisis of the neoclassical-Walrasian paradigm makes it inevitable that the theoretical *corpus* should be enriched by a much more humanist and dynamic conception, such as that which has always been developed by the Austrian theorists in general and, in particular, by Ludwig von Mises.

The course of political economy taught using **Human Action**

According to our teaching experience, *Human Action* may be studied without any great problem over a period of one academic year. Thus, assuming three classes of forty-five minutes each a week from October to June, which is how political economy courses have been organized to date at Spanish universities, there is no great difficulty in explaining the thirty-nine chapters contained in *Human Action*. In this respect, it is advisable to recommend that the student read the corresponding chapter of *Human Action* with effort, dedication and constancy before the teacher explains each subject, even though s/he may have some comprehension difficulties. Experience has shown that this makes the teacher's explanation much more fruitful and subsequently leads to an easier assimilation of the most important ideas contained in each chapter by the student.

The teaching of the book may also be organized over two four-month periods, dividing it into two parts: the first, up to Chapter XVII, inclusive, and the second, from Chapter XVIII until the end. This division does not correspond, as is usual in economics textbooks, to the separation of 'microeconomics' and 'macroeconomics' into two watertight compartments since, as we have already said, for Mises there was no sense in making a radical distinction between the two areas. However, it does seem advisable to leave the analysis of the theory of capital, interest and trade cycles for the second part as, to a certain extent, from the standpoint of the subtle subjectivist conception based on methodological individualism which is traditional in Mises, this second part includes the most practical and general problems related to the economy. In addition, it is also possible, if only four months are available, to make a sufficiently extensive study of *Human Action*, although the degree of detail and depth which can be achieved will obviously have to be less than in longer courses.[95]

With regard to the complementary bibliography required for the reading of *Human Action*, it should be pointed out that, in relation to two specific areas (the genetic-causal theory of the determination of market prices and the analysis of the formation of the price of production factors), Mises takes it for granted that the students have prior knowledge of its most elementary development. Thus, in the case of the theory of price determination, Mises expressly states (p. 201, note 1) that the elementary knowledge that he is assuming is developed by Böhm-Bawerk in Volume II of his economic treatise entitled *Capital and Interest*,[96] although he provides no guideline at all with reference to the theory of the formation of the prices of production factors.[97] In order to provide students with prior knowledge of these areas, I have published *Lecturas de Economía Política*, which completes the teaching of *Human Action* and which should be read at the same time as the latter is studied.[98]

Lastly, in respect of the complementary bibliography, not only the works of F.A. Hayek should be recommended, especially the previously quoted

Law, Legislation and Liberty and *The Fatal Conceit: The Errors of Socialism*, but also my own books on *Socialismo, cálculo económico y función empresarial* and *Money, Bank Credit, and Economic Cycles*. Finally, we should mention that the recent work on the history of economic thought published posthumously by Murray N. Rothbard has been translated into Spanish. In view of its approach and breadth, it should also become a very valuable complement to the study of *Human Action*.[99]

Conclusion

Mises' *Human Action* will continue to have an important influence on economic thought and will be considered in years to come as one of the most important classics of our science. We hope that its readers all over the world will continue to get the most out of this extraordinary intellectual tool and will continue to popularize Mises' ideas with the same enthusiasm as has been the case up to now. Thus, the edifice of Economic Science will become increasingly consolidated and will continue to advance, thus being able to fulfil its momentous mission of serving as theoretical support for the development of civilization, avoiding the crises and conflicts which may place the latter in danger. Moreover, the evolution of economic thought itself will make it inevitable that, in what we hope will be a not too distant future, there will appear a new treatise on the principles and foundations of Economic Science which covers and, as far as possible, exceeds and improves on, the contributions made by Mises in *Human Action*. We are certain that this very ambitious intellectual project which, in any case, will have to be carried out on the basis of the solid foundations laid by Ludwig von Mises, will be the best monument to this magnificent researcher which can be built in the future.[100]

18 In memoriam of Murray N. Rothbard[1]

I first heard of Murray N. Rothbard in autumn 1973, in the seminar on Austrian Economics which Luis Reig held at his Madrid home every Thursday evening. At that time, Rothbard's ideas raised heated controversies which took up a good part of our meetings. Specifically, there were detailed discussions on both Rothbard's contributions and those of his master Ludwig von Mises and the rest of the Austrian School theorists, comparing them with 'orthodox' economic theory. The theory of the monopoly which, thanks to Rothbard, had been purged of the imperfections and inconsistencies which it still displayed in Mises *Human Action* also attracted a great deal of attention. Finally, in the field of political philosophy, there was also a divergence between Rothbard and his master, as the former defended a Natural Law position which was in acute contrast with the clear utilitarianism of Mises. These reasons, among others, led me to undertake a detailed study of two key works which Murray Rothbard had written some years earlier: his treatise *Man, Economy, and State*[2] and his book *Power and Market*,[3] which served as a complement to the former. The fact that Rothbard was able to complete the almost 1,000 pages of his treatise at the age of 36 is admirable. The clearness, depth and acuteness of the analysis, critical spirit and originality are characteristics which exude from every page of *Man, Economy, and State*. It is not surprising, therefore, that this book had a profound influence on my university years of education in economics, which has also been felt by a whole generation of Austrian economists all over the world.

Eight years were to elapse, however, before my first personal encounter with Murray N. Rothbard, whom I met at his home in Palo Alto in 1980. I had this opportunity due to the happy coincidence that Rothbard was working under the auspices of the Institute for Human Studies, very close to Stanford University, where I had just arrived with a scholarship from the Bank of Spain to complete my studies in Political Economy. Although I already knew Rothbard's main works and theoretical contributions, my personal contact with him was a memorable experience. His extraordinary personal charm, tireless enthusiasm and surprising erudition made it an indescribable intellectual pleasure to debate and discuss with him not only the most topical, polemic and interesting issues of Economic Science, but also a multitude of other directly or indirectly related topics, concerning political science, philosophy, history, ethics and even theology.[4]

It was an extraordinary experience to converse with Murray N. Rothbard, sometimes until the early hours of the morning,[5] in an informal atmosphere where open expression of all conceivable positions was admitted, although Rothbard was an acute critic and made a theoretical dissection of each of the opinions formulated. However, it was even more extraordinary, if this is possible, to observe and enjoy the vast culture and almost unsurpassable erudition which Rothbard showed in all these discussion groups. He had an amazing knowledge of Spanish history[6] and of the role played by the *fueros* and the whole associated movement in the formation of our law and in our political history. He was also familiar with the Spanish libertarian tradition, which he always judged with great sympathy from the viewpoint of the consistent anarcho-capitalist position he upheld throughout his life. Moreover, Rothbard had a deep knowledge of the contributions of the theorists of the School of Salamanca of the Spanish Golden Age, which he summarized in his article 'New Light on the Prehistory of the Austrian School'.[7] According to Rothbard, the foundations of modern Austrian economics date from the Spanish scholastics of the sixteenth and seventeenth centuries, who not only developed the subjective theory of value, but also applied it to money and to the study of social institutions. Within this framework, moreover, it may be seen that the development of economics by the Classical Anglo-Saxon School based on the objective labour theory of value and the analysis of static equilibrium, may be interpreted as deviationism, of a Protestant origin, from the continental Thomist tradition based on the creative human being and not obsessed by the dogmas of predestination and redemption on the basis of work.[8]

Upon my return to Spain in 1982, I continued to maintain close correspondence with Murray N. Rothbard and I met him again on several occasions. The highlights of this period are not only the appearance of his seminal work on ethics, *The Ethics of Liberty*,[9] the manuscript of which he was kind enough to send to me and allow me to read and comment on prior to its publication, but also the foundation of the Ludwig von Mises Institute in 1985 and the appearance of the *Review of Austrian Economics* as a scientific journal devoted exclusively to the analysis and discussion of the main research fields of the Austrian School.

One of the most typical characteristics of the correspondence with Murray N. Rothbard was that he would reply to a brief comment or mention of any interesting issue with long letters of several pages typed in small, single-spaced writing, which were often really seminal articles given the breadth of knowledge and erudition, the suggestive and attractive ideas, and the theoretical solutions which they contained.

The last time I met Murray N. Rothbard was at the Regional Meeting of the Mont-Pèlerin Society which took place in Rio de Janeiro in September

1993. At this congress, Rothbard presented a work on the privatization of nations which has been published, with minor changes, in the *Journal of Libertarian Studies*.[10] This meeting of the Mont-Pèlerin Society was notable because it brought together the most significant theorists of the current Austrian School of Economics, led by Murray N. Rothbard and Israel M. Kirzner. It was a curious and interesting experience to observe the personal relationship between these two giants of the Austrian School whose personalities and characters were so different: Murray Rothbard, with his great warmth and congeniality; Israel M. Kirzner, serious, circumspect and always very correct. At all events, personal relations were always much more fluid and direct with Rothbard than with Kirzner, although Kirzner is more courteous in his critical comments and, unlike Rothbard, never offends personal susceptibilities.

Finally, I should add that, in Rio de Janeiro, Rothbard told me of his great desire to visit the University of Salamanca, which, he considered, was the origin of the foundations of the modern Austrian School of Economics. Moreover, Rothbard's interest in the Spanish scholastics increased when he found out that, as a result of my research on monetary theory, I had reached the conclusion that the opposing positions of the Banking and Currency Schools had emerged, not in nineteenth century England, but rather almost three centuries earlier, thanks to the Spanish scholastics. Rothbard encouraged me to write a summary of the main conclusions of my work to be published in the *Review of Austrian Economics*.[11] Together, we organized a lecture tour of Spain and Portugal, which would take place in the second half of 1995, culminating at the University of Salamanca. Sadly, in January this year, I received the proofs of my work, personally corrected by hand by Rothbard himself, together with a note from the editor informing me that the great master of Austrian economists had died of a heart attack on 7 January 1995. Unhappily, Rothbard will now never be able to visit Spain or his beloved University of Salamanca. Nevertheless, his twenty-five books and thousands of articles remain with us, and will continue to be an inexhaustible source of intellectual enrichment and suggestions for the future research of all his disciples.

19 Hayek's best test of a good economist[1]

A careful reading of the quotations that Hayek left us upon his death on hundreds of cards explains what is, in his opinion, the ultimate and definitive test of whether or not someone is a true economist. It is curious to draw attention to the fact that Hayek had already referred to this matter in Appendix III to his *Pure Theory of Capital*, which he wrote in 1941 and which ends with the following words: 'More than ever it seems to me to be true that the complete apprehension of the doctrine that "demand of commodities is not demand for labour" is "the best test of an economist"'.[2] Here, Hayek wishes to highlight one of the key points of the theory of capital: the real productive structure is very complex and is formed by many stages, in such a way that an increase in the demand for consumer commodities will always be detrimental to employment in the stages furthest away from consumption (which is precisely where most of the workers are employed). Or, in other words, the employers can perfectly well earn money, even if their revenue (or 'aggregate demand') drops, if they reduce their costs by replacing labour by capital equipment, thus indirectly generating a significant demand for employment in the stages of capital goods production furthest away from consumption.[3]

It is more than illustrative how Hayek, in the select group of quotations on economic theory that he has left us almost fifty years later that we are now discussing, wished to refer, once again, to these key ideas of the theory of capital. Effectively, Hayek now tells us that 'Investment is more discouraged than stimulated by a high demand for consumer goods, and so is employment *because in an advancing economy more workers are employed to work for the distant future than for the present*' (emphasis added). And he also says that 'In the end is the *decrease* of final demand at current prices that leads to new investment to reduce costs'. Therefore, Hayek concludes that 'employment is not determined by aggregate demand'. In short, for Hayek, the best test for an economist is to understand the implicit fallacy contained in underconsumption theories and in what is called the shrift paradox or paradox of saving: 'It is not consumers' demand that secures the generation of incomes. It is investment of the excess of incomes over consumers' expenditures which keeps incomes up'. A large number of economists are unable to understand these principles because they adopt the macroeconomic aggregate approach that Hayek considers to be a serious error and which leads, in the final analysis, to social engineering and socialism ('Socialism is based on macroeconomics – a scientific error'). The only way of understanding what happens at 'macro' level is by using microeconomics: 'We can understand the macrosociety only by microeconomics'. Furthermore, even the Chicago School monetarists are victims of this error: 'Even Milton Friedman is reported to have once said "we are all Keynesians now"'. The approach based on the model of equilibrium and macroeconomics is erroneous because 'a science which starts with the conceit that it possesses information which it cannot obtain is not a science'. The same may be said of Welfare Economics, which, for Hayek, is 'the spurious scientific foundation of socialist policies'.

The test of the economist is broadened to include the understanding of the essential role of economic calculation and the estimation of opportunity costs that are made possible by market prices, in the extended order of social cooperation. In fact, 'not before the understanding of opportunity costs (i.e. alternative forgone) was there an adequate science of economics'. This essential idea was never understood by the classical economists and is still today 'obscured by the Marshallian compromise' or, as is even better expressed by Hayek in another quotation, 'by the long dominance of the wishy-washy Marshallian compromise'. For Hayek, furthermore, 'economics is the science that can demonstrate that rationalism is wrong because rational knowledge of facts is not sufficient' and that allows us to conclude that 'the destroyers of western civilisation were some of the great rationalist thinkers of the nineteenth century, Bentham, Mill, Russell and Keynes'. Thus, 'The powerful seducers are no longer Marx and Engels, Proudhon or Lenin but Keynes, Tinbergen, Galbraith and Myrdal, Leontieff and Dworkin, etc., etc. They are to me the enemies of the great extended society'. All of them share, to a greater or lesser extent,

> The idea that without the existence of a market men would know as much as they do within a market system (which) is the fundamental error of those who, like Oskar Lange, assert the possibility of an effective economic calculation in a socialist economy.

In short, for Hayek, 'The fools are those who believe they know more than they do, that is the rationalists'.

On one occasion, Ludwig von Mises wrote that 'what distinguishes the Austrian School and will lend it immortal fame is precisely the fact that it created a theory of economic action and not of economic equilibrium or non-action'.[4] Hayek, in turn, takes Mises' idea to a general level and writes, on one of his cards, that

The main achievement of the Austrian School is that it has decidedly helped to clear up the differences which inevitably must exist between science dealing with relatively simple phenomena [macroeconomics, model of equilibrium] and science of highly complex phenomena [the true market process].

And perhaps, today, the best test of an economist is his full understanding of this essential difference.

20 The Ricardo effect[1]

This is one of the main microeconomic explanations for additional savings tending to be invested in more roundabout and capital-intensive production processes. Increases in voluntary savings exert a particularly important, immediate effect on the level of real wages. The monetary demand for consumer goods tends to fall whenever savings rise. Hence it is easy to understand why increases in savings *ceteris paribus* are followed by decreases in the relative prices of final consumer goods. If, as generally occurs, the wages or rents of the original factor labour are initially held constant in nominal terms, a decline in the prices of final consumer goods will be followed by a rise in the real wages of workers employed in all stages of the productive structure. With the same money incomes in nominal terms, workers will be able to acquire a greater quantity and quality of final consumer goods and services at consumer goods' new, more reduced prices. This increase in real wages, which arises from the growth in voluntary savings, means that, in relative terms, it is in the interests of entrepreneurs of all stages in the production process to replace labour with capital goods. Via an increase in real wages, the rise in voluntary savings sets a trend throughout the economic system towards longer and more capital-intensive productive stages. In other words, entrepreneurs now find it more attractive to use capital goods than labour. This constitutes a powerful effect tending toward the lengthening of the stages in the productive structure.

According to Friedrich A. Hayek, David Ricardo was the first person to analyse explicitly this effect. Ricardo concludes in his *Principles* (1817), that:

> Every rise of wages, therefore, or, which is the same thing, every fall of profits, would lower the value of those commodities which were produced with a capital of a durable nature, and would proportionally elevate those which were produced with a capital more perishable. A fall of wages would have precisely the contrary effect.

And in the well-known chapter 'On Machinery', which was added in the third edition, published in 1821, Ricardo adds that 'machinery and labour are in constant competition and the former can frequently not be employed until labour rises'.

This idea was later recovered by Hayek, who, beginning in 1939, applied it extensively to his writings on business cycles. Hayek explains the consequences that an upsurge in voluntary savings has on the productive structure to detract from theories on the so-called 'paradox of thrift' and the supposedly negative influence of saving on effective demand. According to Hayek,

> with high real wages and a low rate of profit, investment will take highly capitalistic forms: entrepreneurs will try to meet the high costs of labour by introducing very labour-saving machinery – the kind of machinery which it will be profitable to use only at a very low rate of profit and interest.

Hence the Ricardo effect is a pure microeconomic explanation for the behaviour of entrepreneurs, who react to an upsurge in voluntary saving by boosting their demand for capital goods and by investing in new stages further from consumption. It is important to remember that all increases in voluntary saving and investment initially bring about a decline in the production of new consumer goods and services with respect to the short-term maximum which could be achieved if inputs were not diverted from the stages closest to final consumption. This decline performs the function of freeing productive factors necessary to lengthen the stages furthest from consumption. In a modern economy, consumer goods and services which remain unsold when saving increases fulfil the important function of making it possible for the different economic agents (workers, owners of natural resources and capitalists) to sustain themselves during the time periods that follow. During these periods the recently initiated lengthening of the productive structure causes an inevitable slowdown in the arrival of new consumer goods and services at the market. This slowdown lasts until all the new, more capital-intensive processes have been culminated. If it were not for the consumer goods and services that remain unsold as a result of saving, the temporary drop in the supply of new consumer goods would trigger a substantial rise in the relative price of these goods and considerable difficulties in their provision.

Appendix
Interview: the Spanish roots of the Austrian School[1]

AEN: You made an extraordinary announcement today at the Austrian Scholars Conference. Can you share it with *AEN* readers?

Huerta de Soto: First, I'd like to thank the Mises Institute for sponsoring this great conference. It is gratifying to see so many countries and disciplines represented, and I look forward to reading all the papers that are being presented.

My announcement was this: beginning this October, we are publishing *The Collected Works of Ludwig von Mises*. We have support from 300 private subscribers, as well as some help from free market institutes in Spanish-speaking countries.

The *Collected Works* will total seven volumes, each one of them as thick as *Human Action*. The first volume, already in preparation, will be titled *Monetary Theory and Economic Cycles*. It will include *The Theory of Money and Credit* and other books and writings on the subject of money and business cycles.

The project is without precedent in the world, and it will be completed in four or five years. We are sure the *Collected Works* will be received favourably in the intellectual world, not only in Spain but also in Latin America. It is the best tribute we can pay to our master.

AEN: How does it happen that there is a ready market for these books?

Huerta de Soto: The publication of Spanish translations of Mises' books began very early. In 1936, *The Theory of Money and Credit* and Hayek's *Monetary Theory and the Trade Cycle* appeared. But the influence of them was small due to the outbreak of the Spanish Civil War that same year.

Real strides weren't made until twenty years later, when a young scholar named Joaquín Reig wrote his PhD thesis at the University of Madrid. Its title was 'Modern Social Problems From the Point of View of Ludwig von Mises' Economic Thought'. It was the first work written in Spain on *Human Action*, which had been published in the US only eight years earlier.

Reig had met Mises and became one of his best friends and admirers. In fact, Mises acknowledges Dr Reig's help in the 'Preface' to the third edition of *Human Action*. Reig used to tell the story of how he asked Mises what he thought of Murray Rothbard's treatment of monopoly theory in *Man, Economy, and State*. The question was important considering the disorganized treatment of the subject in *Human Action*. Mises told Reig that 'I agree with every word Professor Rothbard has written on the subject'.

AEN: When did *Human Action* finally appear in Spain?

Huerta de Soto: Reig's very good translation was published in 1960, but only with a great deal of difficulty. The censorship authorities deleted several paragraphs of the book which were considered politically dangerous for the regime of General Franco, who was then the Spanish dictator.

Starting in the 1970s, Joaquín Reig and his brother Luis organized a weekly Austrian seminar that met every Thursday in their home. This seminar, which I attended, was responsible for the spread of Austrian ideas. Hayek even attended it several times. During those years, Reig also translated *Bureaucracy*, *Liberalism*, *The Anticapitalistic Mentality* and *Theory and History*.

I received a chair in political economy at the Complutense University of Madrid in 1985. That's when the seminar left the Reig home and began to meet at the university. The most important Spanish universities are owned by the government. All professors are civil servants, who hold their chairs for life. But according to our Constitution, they can teach what they want with almost unlimited freedom. This system was used and abused by Marxists and socialists for many years. But since the early 1980s, it has also been used by free market economists.

The Complutense University is one of the oldest in Spain, founded in 1293. Today it has more than 100,000 students, and the Law School where I teach has 17,000. I have been teaching the same course for twelve years with increasing success and popularity among the students. *Human Action* is the required textbook, and up to now more than 2,000 students have passed examinations on the book. All told, more than 15,000 copies of Reig's Spanish edition have been sold.

AEN: Does your department accept the Austrian School as a legitimate alternative?

Huerta de Soto: At one time, no. But this has changed in the last twelve years. We now have a PhD seminar on Austrian economics, we participate in outside programmes on law and economics, and every year we provide guidance on research topics to foreign students who come to Spain. We recently had a two-day conference on Mises sponsored by the city of Madrid and the minister of education, Esperanza Aguirre. It attracted 300 professors and students and received generous media coverage.

In the US, you have debates among Austrians, with different people emphasizing different aspects of Mises Hayek, and Rothbard. For example,

I've been following the debate on economic calculation under socialism very closely. I have not reached a final conclusion. But I do tend to believe that Mises' and Hayek's arguments are two sides of the same coin.

For our part, we are trying to forge a synthesis between the rationalism and utilitarianism of Mises, the Aristotelian Natural Law position of Rothbard, and the evolutionary approach of Hayek. In my banking courses, I emphasize the 100 per cent reserve ratio, consistent with an old tradition of Spanish law on fungible demand deposits which is still in force.

AEN: Judging from the many books you've brought here, publishing has been crucial to the spread of the Austrian School in Spain.

Huerta de Soto: Apart from the collected works of Mises and Hayek, I edit a separate series called the New Collection of Liberty. Up to March of this year, twenty volumes have been published, the last of which was a Spanish translation of Raimondo Cubeddu's important book *The Philosophy of the Austrian School*.

Among the books are titles by Rothbard, Kirzner, Mises, Hayek, Bruno Leoni, Wilhelm Röpke, and a fiftieth anniversary edition of Hazlitt's *Economics in One Lesson*, which has an introduction by Llewellyn H. Rockwell, Jr. Future projects include Hans-Hermann Hoppe's *The Economics and Ethics of Private Property* and Bruce Benson's *The Enterprise of Law*. Most important, we are publishing a translation of Rothbard's *Austrian Perspective on the History of Economic Thought*. It will appear with my introduction in one large volume in 1998.

AEN: Did you ever meet Rothbard?

Huerta de Soto: Before I completed my PhD in Spain, I received a grant to come to the United States to study. Hayek wrote a letter of recommendation for me to Stanford University, which admitted me to its MBA programme. To my delight, Rothbard was there on fellowship with the Institute for Humane Studies, and we spent many wonderful days together, discussing, among other things, his manuscript for *The Ethics of Liberty*. I will always treasure the early draft he gave me.

He knew everything about Spain, all the details of the geography and the history, and especially the ideological factions in the Spanish Civil War. He was opposed to Franco, of course, but even more opposed to the Republican Communist Party. I agreed entirely. One of the worst things the communists did was kill all the anarchists. My grandfather used to say, 'those anarchists are fine people'. In a way, they were more sympathetic to market and private business than were the socialists and conservatives, who really hated the classical liberals.

The last time I saw Rothbard was at the Mont Pèlerin Society meetings in Rio de Janeiro in 1993. We organized a lecture tour for him in Spain and Portugal, which was to take place in the second half of 1995. It was to culminate at the University of Salamanca, the birthplace of the Austrian

School. Sadly, Rothbard was not able to visit Spain, nor his beloved Salamanca. However, I am sure he would be very happy about the size of this gathering here today, and would be even happier about the growing ties between Austrians on both sides of the Atlantic.

AEN: It still seems somewhat revisionist to describe Spain as the birthplace of the Austrian School.

Huerta de Soto: Yes, but it is accurate. To focus solely on Vienna is far too narrow. We tend to think, like all moderns, that only the new has value. To study the old is mere archaeology. But in economics and philosophy, it's the other way around. Most great ideas have already been thought by someone else in the past, including the most fundamental Austrian ideas.

One of the main contributions of Rothbard was to show that the prehistory of the Austrian School could be sought in the works of the Spanish scholastics during the '*Siglo de Oro Español*', the Spanish Golden Century, which ran from the reign of Carlos V in the sixteenth century through the seventeenth century. Rothbard first developed this theory in his 1974 paper delivered at the South Royalton Conference, published two years later in *The Foundations of Modern Austrian Economics*.

AEN: Yet even this insight has a prehistory.

Huerta de Soto: Of course. Joseph Schumpeter argued this point in his 1954 *History of Economic Analysis*. Also in the 1950s, Hayek had met the great Italian scholar Bruno Leoni, author of *Freedom and the Law*, who convinced Hayek that the intellectual origins of classical liberalism should be sought in Mediterranean Europe, not Scotland. This led Hayek to change his research programme dating back to his first legal studies at the London School of Economics. Later, one of Hayek's pupils, Marjorie Grice-Hutchinson (now Baroness Marjorie von Schlippenbach), translated the main texts of the scholastics.

There is a quotation in Bruno Leoni's book from Cicero, in which Cato says Roman law is the most perfect law of all because it hasn't been created by any one mind. It has not been constructed. It is a result of a process to which many minds have contributed their wisdom. The lawyers don't make the law; they discover it and can improve it only slowly.

Leoni convinced Hayek of his thesis. You can see this by comparing Hayek's more Scottish-oriented *Constitution of Liberty* with his Mediterranean-oriented series *Law, Legislation, and Liberty*. In this series, Hayek freely quotes the scholastics on economics.

And I have a letter from Hayek dated 7 January 1979, in which Hayek asks us to read Rothbard's article. He says that Rothbard and Marjorie Grice-Hutchinson 'demonstrate that the basic principles of the theory of the competitive market were worked out by the Spanish scholastics of the sixteenth century and that economic liberalism was not designed by the Calvinists but by the Spanish Jesuits'.

AEN: Who were these Spanish ancestors of the Austrian School?

Huerta de Soto: Most of them taught morals and theology at the University of Salamanca, a medieval city located 150 miles to the northwest of Madrid, close to the border with Portugal. They were mainly Dominicans or Jesuits, and their view on economics closely parallels that stressed by Carl Menger more than 300 years later.

One of my favourites is Diego de Covarrubias y Leyva, who set forth the subjective theory of value. He wrote that 'the value of an article does not depend on its essential nature, but on the subjective estimation of men, even if that estimation is foolish'. He was born in 1512, and served as bishop of Segovia and minister of King Philip II. Today, in the museum of the Spanish painter El Greco in Toledo, there is a stunning portrait of him. Carl Menger quotes Covarrubias' 1560 treatise on monetary depreciation.

Another important Salamancan is Luis Saravia de la Calle, the first thinker to demonstrate that prices determine costs, not the other way around. He wrote that 'those who measure the just price by the labour, costs, and risk incurred by the person who deals in the merchandise are greatly in error. The just price is found not by counting the cost but by common estimation'. He was also a fierce critic of fractional-reserve banking, arguing that fees should be paid to bankers for keeping gold under custody.

AEN: Now we can get to your article in the *Review of Austrian Economics* (vol. 9, no. 2) on this subject.

Huerta de Soto: The banking theories of the Salamancans are not something that Rothbard considered at great length in his history of thought. But there is quite a lot of material here. In fact, in their internal debates, they prefigured the nineteenth century British banking debates. The Salamancans were led to study banking by observing the corrupt relationship between banking and government, which depended most fundamentally on the legal protection of fractional reserves.

The Salamancans were opposed to all forms of inflation. For example there was Martín Azpilcueta Navarro. He was born in 1493, lived for ninety-four years, and is specially famous for explaining the quantity theory of money in his 1556 book *Commentary of Exchanges* (I own a first edition!), writing that 'money is worth more where and when it is lacking than where and when it is in abundance'.

Navarro opposed fractional reserves and made a clear distinction between loan banking and deposit banking. The banker, he said, should be the 'warden, depositor, and guarantor' of monies in his possession. He said there can be no valid contract between the depositor and the banker that allows for fractional reserves. If such a contract were made, all parties would be guilty of fraud.

More sympathetic to fractional reserve money was Luis de Molina, who was the first to argue that bank deposits should be considered part of the money supply. But he confused loans and deposits, and didn't understand how fractional reserves are inherently destabilizing. So Navarro and de la Calle were a kind of Currency School, and very distrustful of banking and anything less than 100 per cent reserves, while de Molina and Juan de Lugo, like the Banking School, were more tolerant of fractional reserves.

AEN: Beyond history of thought, do you plan to enter the debate among Austrians about reserve ratios?

Huerta de Soto: I've written a long paper defending the 100 per cent reserve position against George Selgin's theory of monetary equilibrium. His theory is that when the demand for fiduciary media increases or decreases, banks should be free to respond by expanding or contracting credit. These actions don't create investment distortions because banks are responding to prior changes in demand. With this theory, Selgin seems to be reviving the old 'needs of trade' doctrine of the Banking School. And, like Keynesians, free bankers seem fixated on short-term unilateral mutations in the demand for money.

But they don't deal with the prospect that the changes in money demand are not always exogenous to the free banking system, but can be determined endogenously as well. Banks themselves may manipulate the supply of money because it's in their interest to do so, so long as they can avoid runs. And this new supply can create its own demand and provoke economic cycles. History bears this out. Free banking theory doesn't take account of this because it is exclusively a macroeconomic theory.

AEN: As with banking, was the Salamancan political position generally pro-free market?

Huerta de Soto: They tended to defend libertarian positions across the board. For example, Francisco de Victoria is widely seen as the founder of international law. He revived the idea that Natural Law is morally superior to the might of the state. Then Juan de Mariana condemned any government debasement of coins as sheer robbery, and suggested that any individual citizen may assassinate a ruler who imposes taxes without the people's consent. The only place Mariana erred was in his condemnation of bullfighting, but since I am the grandson of a famous bullfighter, I'm not impartial.

AEN: Is the Spanish–Austrian link anything beyond an accident of history?

Huerta de Soto: Let's remember that in the sixteenth century, Emperor Charles V, the king of Spain, sent his brother Ferdinand I to be the king of 'Austria', which etymologically means 'Eastern Part of the Empire', which comprised most of Continental Europe. The only exception was France, then an isolated island surrounded by Spanish forces.

The economic, political and cultural relations between Austria and Spain continued for several centuries. Carl Menger rediscovered and took up this continental Catholic tradition of Spanish scholastic thought that was by then almost forgotten.

AEN: Well, what happened to this tradition that it *had* to be rediscovered?

Huerta de Soto: Adam Smith and his followers came to dominate economic thought, ending the development of the Subjectivist School, which not only supported the free market consistently, but also understood it theoretically. The tradition was kept alive in France in the writings of Cantillon, Turgot and Say, and some knowledge made it to England via the writings of Protestant Natural Law theorists Samuel Pufendorf and Hugo Grotius.

But in Spain, we experienced the years of decadence in the eighteenth and nineteenth centuries, with the last of the Habsburgs and the beginnings of the Bourbons from France. The statism of Philip IV led him to attempt to organize a vast empire and control it from Madrid, an inherently unviable project.

The scholastics were against this statism, of course, but they were disregarded and their tradition was lost. There was also the problem that they wrote in Latin, so there was a language barrier. In addition, there is the British-promoted Black Legend, which tended to discredit anything Catholic and Spanish for two centuries. Ironically, the Reformation actually set back the cause of free market economics. The Church had long been a vital equilibrating power to the state. As the Church declined, so did the wisdom of its best economic theorists, while the power of the state and the influence of its apologists grew.

AEN: Why did it take an Austrian to rediscover Spanish economics?

Huerta de Soto: The books of the scholastics were typically published in Brussels and in Italy, and they were sent to Spain and to Vienna. So they made inroads this way. There is also a scholastic tradition of thought in Austria which is, after all, 90 per cent Catholic.

Even so, a Spanish Catholic writer *did* solve the 'paradox of value' twenty-seven years before Carl Menger. His name was Jaime Balmes. He was born in Catalonia in 1810 and died in 1848. During his short life, he became the most important Thomist philosopher in Spain. In 1844, he published an article called 'The True Idea of Value; or Thoughts on the Origin, Nature, and Variety of Prices'.

Balmes asks, why is a precious stone worth more than bread? And he answers that the value of a thing is in its utility so that 'there is a necessary relation between the increase or decrease in value, and the shortage or abundance of a thing'.

AEN: In what way can Austrians use the writings of the Salamancans today?

Huerta de Soto: A few years ago, a group of scholars took it upon themselves to translate all the main works of the Salamancans into Spanish. They are making these writings widely available, and many scholars are now aware that these great thinkers were libertarians. And this has begun to change the status of the Austrian School in Spain. It has helped root it in history and thereby has given it a more substantial intellectual foundation.

Not too many years ago, I was just one guy in a university teaching unfamiliar literature. Now I am seen as representing a school that foretold the failure of socialism, and as a spokesman for the greatest thinkers from Spain's past. And this is happening at the same time that Spain is struggling to free its own markets from the welfare morass.

AEN: To assist that effort, you've produced a plan to reform Spain's system of social security.

Huerta de Soto: This problem of guaranteed old-age pensions is significant in all Western countries. In every case, the liabilities are enormous but demographics have made them essentially unpayable except through intolerably high taxes. Before we can know what to do about these systems, we have to understand their inherent contradictions.

First, these systems purport to be about saving money, but in fact they discourage savings. The taxes they require take the place of what would otherwise be private savings. And they encourage people to believe they will be taken care of in the future and therefore they don't need to save. Empirically, then, the rise of social security has paradoxically coincided with huge declines in savings. This fall in savings then drives up interest rates and reduces overall investment in ways we cannot account for.

Second, no matter what the law says about how employees and employers share the burden of contributing to the system, from an economic point of view the worker pays the whole tax. Mises first developed this insight in *Socialism*, where he said social insurance contributions always come at the expense of wages.

Third, the system is based on general and indiscriminate institutional aggression against the citizenry and thereby attacks freedom itself. This in turn inhibits the creative development of entrepreneurial discovery, new financial modes of savings and the efficient use of property. The resulting misdirection of labour and capital is incalculably huge.

Fourth, the system cannot work as both insurance and welfare, because these are incompatible concepts. Private insurance is based on the principle that benefits are linked with contributions. Welfare is based on need. With ever-declining returns, the 'insurance' element of the system is aborting the 'welfare' element, and *vice versa*.

And why do we have these systems? Supposedly because some people would not be able to provide for themselves. But this is like saying that because a small number of people can't get food, everyone in the whole population should be forced to eat in government canteens.

AEN: Is your reform plan based on the Chilean experience?

Huerta de Soto: We have to remember that the liabilities in Chile's system were very small as compared with Spain's and the US's. They had been largely inflated away and what remained were paid out of budget surpluses. So the Chile analogy only takes us so far. Our problems are much more difficult to solve.

In the transition period, the present working payers pay for present beneficiaries as well as save for their own retirement. The key is that the new savings should be entirely private and be controlled completely by the individual. It cannot be a forced programme.

We must allow those who want to go outside the system to do so, paying no taxes into it and taking no benefits out of it. That must be the long-term goal, and I expect most people would take this option. In my plan, our transition period allows for a 50 per cent tax cut today in exchange for forgoing all claims on future benefits. Also, taxes must never be raised to pay for the transition. It's too tempting for politicians to use the language of privatization to mask what is essentially a tax-funded bailout of an already failed system.

AEN: Can a similar transition strategy be used to dismantle medical socialism?

Huerta de Soto: Spain's system is more statist than the US's. Almost the whole of the medical sector is government controlled. I'm advocating a plan that would encourage the further development of a private system by use of tax cuts. Anyone who spends his own money on medical services can deduct that from his tax liability. This prevents people from paying health care twice.

AEN: And these ideas are getting a hearing?

Huerta de Soto: Last year we had elections, and the socialist candidate lost out in favour of 44-year-old José María Aznar. He is surrounded by a new wave of politicians and advisers who have been reading authors like Mises, Hayek and Rothbard. They are classical liberals. I have been advising Aznar's Popular Party for twelve years, always defending the most hardcore libertarian position. Though Aznar's libertarian people are still a minority in the parliament, tremendous progress is being made. Capital gains taxes have been reduced from 56 per cent to 20 per cent. Corporate taxes and income taxes are down as well.

The next big challenge will be in the labour sector. When the socialist government took charge fourteen years ago, none of General Franco's socialistic labour legislation was touched. The law requires that any business that lets an employee go must pay a very high lump sum to the employee totalling wages for 1,260 days. As a result, business does not want to hire. It can't afford to speculate that way. In addition, unemployment benefits are 90 per cent of salaries, so there is little incentive to seek new employment.

AEN: What's a reasonable change that is politically possible right now?

Huerta de Soto: For starters, we are attempting to reduce the required lump-sum payment for firing by half, and, when valid cause can be established, by more than half. The mandatory lump sum should never be beyond one year's salary. Of course that's far too high. I've suggested that all these details should be strictly a matter of contract. If an employee wants a large pension or lump sum in case of being fired, he accepts smaller wages now, or *vice versa*. It should be up to those parties to make the exchange, not the government.

This idea, like much of what we free marketeers want, will be a long time coming. But we look for progress where we can make it. The centre of gravity continues to shift in our direction, so that is an encouraging sign.

For example, military service is going to be made voluntary. Up to now it has been compulsory and it lasted one year. Young men would waste time, use drugs, chauffeur the generals or whatever. More than 200,000 young people were losing one year of productive time. So by regaining this time, the overall wealth of the country will increase.

AEN: Do you think these kids should be in school instead?

Huerta de Soto: Not necessarily because that could be an intellectual malinvestment, which often happens when education is subsidized by the state. The 'human capital' theory of Gary Becker would seem to imply that the more you learn in school the more valuable you are to society. The obvious conclusion is that government should pay for everyone's schooling to make society richer.

I entirely disagree with Becker. Because it's government money involved, there is no way to calculate economically whether education is a good investment or not. Most probably it is not. People spend years studying things that have no use for them. Neoclassical theory tends to treat capital in general this way: there is no good or bad capital investment; it's all just capital. And in some ways, the malinvestment of intellectual capital is even worse than the waste brought about through other resource misallocation.

AEN: Do you see a contradiction between your theoretical ideals and modest reform proposals?

Huerta de Soto: The biggest danger of libertarian strategy is to fall into day-to-day political pragmatism. It is easy to forget the final objectives because of the supposed political impossibility of achieving them in the short run. Our programmes and goals become blurred and our intellectuals are co-opted by the government.

The way to prevent this from happening is to adopt a dual strategy. On one hand, we must be open and honest about our goals and constantly educate the public about why our final objective is best for society. On the other, we should support any short-term policies which get us closer to our goals. That way, when our short-term goals are accomplished, there is no retreat. We can march on with full confidence that people understand that more needs to be done.

AEN: How did you come in contact with the Austrian School?

Huerta de Soto: When I was 16 years old, I took a very strong liking to economics generally. I would comb the bookstores for every economics text I could find. I thought I had read them all until I went to a book fair one day and saw one I didn't know about. It was *Human Action*. I like books the thicker the better, so I immediately bought a copy. I was amazed at its power from the outset.

One of my father's friends found me reading Mises one day, and invited me to join the Reig seminar I mentioned earlier. They were surprised that I knew the book as well or better than the other members. Next I read *Man, Economy, and State*. Then over the years I steadily increased my knowledge.

AEN: It would seem surprising that economics would be so intensely attractive to you at such a young age.

Huerta de Soto: My family business is life insurance, which is the only trait I have in common with John Maynard Keynes, who in the 1930s chaired the National Mutual Life Assurance Society of London. This is a very traditional business, having evolved spontaneously for 200 years. Working with my father I naturally became interested in money, finance and economic institutions. I wanted to be an actuary. I was very good at mathematics.

But I soon began to realize that what works for actuaries, which deals with life and death probabilities, cannot work in economic theory because there are no constants in human action. There is creativity, change, choice and discovery, but there are no fixed correspondents that allow the creation of functions.

Hans Mayer made a very interesting argument, which has appeared in Israel Kirzner's collection of Austrian writings. Mayer argued that supply and demand curves cannot reflect reality because the information necessary to construct them can only be provided over time by the entrepreneurial process. That information never appears at the same time, as the mathematics require that we assume. It was an argument he took from Mises and further developed. But Mayer was a political chameleon, especially during those crucial years before the Second World War, and as a consequence he was not highly regarded by Mises.

AEN: Keynes apparently did not draw the same lessons about human action from working in the insurance business.

Huerta de Soto: It turns out that Keynes not only corrupted economics, he also corrupted the practices of life insurance. He broke with the traditional policies of his company by valuing assets at market value instead of historical value. In the short term, it gave him an enormous competitive advantage. Keynes was able to distribute dividends to his clients against unrealized capital gains.

When the stock market was going up, it was wonderful. But when the Great Depression arrived, his company nearly went bankrupt. Both the British and the American insurance industries are suffering from his disastrous departure from tradition. On the continent it is still the practice to value assets at historical cost and only pay dividends against realized capital gains.

AEN: You have given the Mises Institute a picture of King Juan Carlos holding a book by Mises. Is he a Misesian?

Huerta de Soto: I wouldn't say that, but he likes free markets and understands that we have radical opinions on the subject. Every year we invite him to a fair that commemorates new books, and he is kind enough to come. Considering that he didn't study at the University of Chicago, he is more pro-Austrian than one might expect. You never know what individuals or types of groups are going to be attracted to the Austrian School.

AEN: For example, the influence of the Austrians via the Salamancans on the modern Catholic Church.

Huerta de Soto: The Catholic Church is like a huge transatlantic ocean liner. If you turn the wheel to the right, the boat moves slowly, slowly, and eventually begins to change direction.

There is a powerful Catholic group in Spain called Opus Dei. It is very close to the pope and it is very pro-business. Someone in the order read the works of Hayek, saw him as very pro business and sent out a message to the entire organization: Opus Dei should back the Austrians.

All of a sudden, all my books were being read by everyone in the order, and I began to lecture to their priests and members. In fact, I recently read a PhD thesis written on Mises and Hayek by a leading member of Opus Dei.

AEN: The pope seems to be correct on many economic issues, but labour unions seem to be a sticking point with him.

Huerta de Soto: In his writings, the pope often uses the word 'labour' when he really means 'human action'. When he says labour is creative, labour is entrepreneurial, labour is productive, he is not talking about unions. He is referring to the idea of economic action in exchange.

Of course, the Church can be wrong, as it was for many years on the question of interest, as Rothbard shows in his *History of Thought*.

The opinions of the Church on economic issues should be taken seriously, but they do not impact on matters of the faith. By the way, on my wall, I have a nice picture of Hayek with the current pope.

AEN: Do you think economists should take religion more seriously than they have?

Huerta de Soto: Certainly. Religion plays an important role in the life of an economy. It transmits from generation to generation certain patterns of behaviour and moral traditions that are essential for the rule of law, which makes economic exchange possible. For example, if contracts are not kept, society can fall apart. Religion, not the state, is the primary means for imparting to us a sense of our obligations to keep our promises and to respect the property of others.

AEN: Have any economists ever been declared saints?

Huerta de Soto: Two scholastics, in fact. Two economists among the scholastics became saints: San Bernardino of Siena and his great student San Antonino of Florence. Let's hope they will not be the last.

Notes

1 The theory of dynamic efficiency

1 See J. Huerta de Soto, *La Escuela Austriaca: mercado y creatividad empresarial*, Madrid, Editorial Síntesis, 2001 (English edition *The Austrian Schoool: Market order and Entrepreneurial Creativity*, Cheltenham: Edward Elgar, 2008); *Dinero, crédito bancario y ciclos económicos*, third edition, Madrid, Unión Editorial, 2002 (English edition *Money, Bank Credit, and Economic Cycles*, Auburn, AL: Ludwig von Mises Institute, 2006).
2 A. Blánquez, *Diccionario Latino-Español, Español-Latino*, vol. 1, Barcelona: Editorial Ramón Sopeña, 1998, p. 567, meaning 2.
3 Xenophon, *Xenophon in Seven Volumes*, translated by O. J. Todd, vol. 4, Cambridge, MA: Harvard University Press; London: William Heinemann, Ltd., 1979, Ec. 6.4, http://www.perseus.tufts.edu/cgi-bin/ptext?lookup=Xen.+Ec.+1.1 (21 September 2003).
4 'My dear, there is nothing so convenient or so good for human beings as order' (ibid., Ec. 8.3).
5 Ibid., Ec. 12.18.
6 'On the other hand, to a careful man, who works strenuously at agriculture, no business gives quicker returns than farming. My father taught me that and proved it by his own practice. For he never allowed me to buy a piece of land that was well farmed; but pressed me to buy any that was uncultivated and unplanted owing to the owner's neglect or incapacity. "Well farmed land," he would say, "costs a large sum and can't be improved." ... Now nothing improves more than a farm that is being transformed from a wilderness into fruitful fields. I assure you, Socrates, that we have often added a hundredfold to the value of a farm' (ibid., Ec. 20.22–24).
7 'So deep is their love of corn that on receiving reports that it is abundant anywhere, merchants will voyage in quest of it: they will cross the Aegean, the Euxine, the Sicilian sea; and when they have got as much as possible, they carry it over the sea, and they actually stow it in the very ship in which they sail themselves. And when they want money, they don't throw the corn away anywhere at haphazard, but they carry it to the place where they hear that corn is most valued and the people prize it most highly, and deliver it to them there' (ibid., Ec. 20.27–28).
8 M. Rothbard, *Economic Thought before Adam Smith*, vol. 1 of *An Austrian Perspective on the History of Economic Thought*, Aldershot: Edward Elgar, 1995.
9 In fact, the term 'energy' also derives etymologically from Greek and means 'vigorous action'.
10 *Webster's Third New International Dictionary*, 1981, Chicago, IL and London: Encyclopedia Britannica, 1:725 (italics added).

11 '*Proporción entre el producto o resultado obtenido y los medios utilizados*'. Diccionario de la Lengua Española, 1992, Madrid: Real Academia Española, Espasa Calpe, 559, 1254.
12 H. Mayer, 'The Cognitive Value of Functional Theories of Price: Critical and Positive Investigations Concerning the Price Problem', chapter 16 in *Classics in Austrian Economics: A Sampling in the History of a Tradition*, I. M. Kirzner (ed.), vol. 2, London: William Pickering, 1994.
13 P. Mirowski, *More Heat than Light: Economics as Social Physics, Physics as Nature's Economics*, Cambridge: Cambridge University Press, 1989. Mirowski later (*Machine Dreams*, Cambridge: Cambridge University Press, 2002) refined even further his critical analysis of the mechanicism of the Neoclassical School, which he refers to as 'the Cyborg incursion into economics'.
14 'Aussi a-t'on déjà signalé celles des *forces* et des *raretés* comme *vecteurs*, d'une part, et celles des *énergies* et des *utilités* comme *quantités scalaires*, d'autre part' (L. Walras, 'Economique et mécanique', *Bulletin de la Société Vaudoise des Sciences Naturelles*, no. 45 (1909), p. 318 ; quoted by Mirowski, op. cit., 220).
15 *The New Palgrave Dictionary of Economics*, 1987, edited by John Eatwell, Murray Milgate and Peter Newman, London: Macmillan, vol. 2, p. 107.
16 F. W. Taylor, *The Principles of Scientific Management*, New York and London: W. W. Norton and Company, 1967, p. 69. (First edition published in 1911.)
17 J. Keynes, *Collected Writings*, London: Macmillan, 1973, vol. 7, p. 26, vol. 28, pp. 333–334. Keynes also echoed the assertions of those intellectuals whose thinking was clouded by the economic 'victories' of the Soviet Union ('I have seen the future and it works'). See also Ralph Raico, 'Keynes and the Reds', *The Free Market* (April 1997).
18 See the following section (pp. 6–8).
19 On the practical impossibility, in any case, of applying the criterion of Kaldor–Hicks, see the article by E. Stringham, 'Kaldor–Hicks Efficiency and the Problem of Central Planning', *Quarterly Journal of Austrian Economics* 4, no. 2 (summer) (2001), pp. 41–50.
20 For a summarized update on the issue, see L. Gámir, *La economía del bienestar*, Grandes Cuestiones de la Economía no. 8, Madrid: Fundación Argentaria, 1996.
21 L. Robbins, *An Essay on the Nature and Significance of Economic Science*, London: Macmillan and St Martin's Press, 1972, pp. 36–37; R. G. Lipsey, *An Introduction to Positive Economics*, second edition, London: Weidenfeld and Nicolson, 1966; A. Alchian and W. R. Allen, *University Economics*, Belmont, CA: Wadsworth Publishing Co., 1964, pp. 435–437.
22 After writing this article, I noticed Buchanan suggests the same idea in J. M. Buchanan, *What Should Economists Do?*, Indianapolis, IN: Liberty Fund, 1979, p. 25.
23 *Webster's New World Dictionary and Thesaurus*, New York: Simon and Schuster, 1996.
24 On the theory of entrepreneurship and its essential elements and characteristics, see J. Huerta de Soto, *Socialismo, cálculo económico y función empresarial*, third edition, Madrid: Unión Editorial, 2005, chapter 2 (English edition forthcoming).
25 *Webster's Revised Unabridged Dictionary*, 1913, http://www.bennetyee.org// http_webster.cgi?compete&method = exact (8 October 2003).
26 J. Huerta de Soto, *La Escuela Austriaca*, op. cit., chapters 5 and 6.
27 I. Kirzner, *How Markets Work: Disequilibrium, Entrepreneurship and Discovery*, Hobart Paper, no. 133, London: Institute of Economic Affairs (IEA), 1997, p. 67.
28 I. Kirzner, 'Austrian Economics, the Coordination Criterion and Classical Liberalism', *Journal des économistes et des études humaines* 8, no. 2/3 (June–September 1998), pp. 187–200.
29 Kirzner, *How Markets Work*, op. cit., p. 64.

30 M. Rothbard, 'Comment: The Myth of Efficiency', in *Time, Uncertainty and Disequilibrium*, Mario J. Rizzo (ed.), 1979, p. 95; 'Toward a Reconstruction of Utility and Welfare Economics', in *The Logic of Action One: Method, Money and the Austrian School*, Cheltenham: Edward Elgar, 1997, pp. 211–254.
31 R. E. Cordato, *Welfare Economics in an Open Ended World: A Modern Austrian Perspective*, Dordrecht, Holland: Kluwer Academic Publishers, 1992.
32 J. A. Schumpeter, *The Theory of Economic Development*, Cambridge, MA: Harvard University Press, 1968.
33 J. A. Schumpeter, *Capitalism, Socialism and Democracy*, New York: Harper Perennial, 1976, p. 106. (First edition published by Harper and Brothers in 1942.) M. Blaug (*The Disease of Formalism in Economics, or Bad Games that Economists Play*, Jena: Lectiones Jenenses, 1998, p. 7) has expressly used the term 'dynamic efficiency' in reference to Schumpeter's point of view.
34 H. Leibenstein, 'Allocative Efficiency vs. X-Efficiency', *American Economic Review*, no. 56 (1966), pp. 392–415.
35 G. J. Stigler, 'The Existence of X-Efficiency', *American Economic Review*, no. 66 (1976), pp. 213–216.
36 I. Kirzner, *Perception, Opportunity and Profit*, Chicago, IL: University of Chicago Press, 1979, pp. 120–136.
37 On x-efficiency, see also R. Frantz, *X-Efficiency: Theory, Evidence and Applications*, Boston, MA and Dordrecht: Kluwer Academic Publishers, 1988.
38 D. C. North, *Institutions, Institutional Change and Economic Performance*, Cambridge and New York: Cambridge University Press, 1990, pp. 80–82, 99, 136; *Understanding the Process of Economic Change*, London: Institute of Economic Affairs (IEA), 1999, pp. 17–18. Stromberg has written the best critical, Austrian evaluation of North's view. See J. R. Stromberg, 'Douglas C. North and Non-Marxist Institutional Determinism', *Journal of Libertarian Studies* 16, no. 4 (autumn) (2002), pp. 101–137.
39 Of the most recent discussions on the subject, see R. O. Zerbe, *Economic Efficiency in Law and Economics*, Cheltenham: Edward Elgar, 2001.
40 I. Kirzner, *Competition and Entrepreneurship*, Chicago, IL: University of Chicago Press, 1973, pp. 225–234.
41 Harold Demsetz has criticized the *nirvana approach* of many neoclassical economists (Arrow and others) who insist on comparing actual institutions with ideal ones that could never exist in the real world, since the transaction costs involved in transporting the existent system to 'nirvana' would be impossible to bear. Though we regard Demsetz's position as a step forward in the realism of the analysis, it is nevertheless not completely suitable, since it still fails to acknowledge that the fundamental problem is not one of transaction costs, but one of a purely entrepreneurial nature. See H. Demsetz, *Efficiency, Competition and Policy*, London: Basil Blackwell, 1989, chapter 1, 3–24.
42 Coase's thesis on the irrelevance of the layout of property rights (with zero transaction costs) has been labelled by Gary North as the 'Don Corleone theory of property rights,' and it radically contradicts the approach we present, one based on the relationship between ethics and dynamic efficiency. See G. North, 'Undermining Property Rights: Coase and Becker', *Journal of Libertarian Studies* 16, no. 4 (autumn) (2002), pp. 75–100.
43 The sample of manuals consulted comprises well-known textbooks by the following authors: Samuelson, Lipsey, Friedman (Milton), Friedman (David), Stiglitz, Kreps, Fisher-Dornbusch-Schmalense, Mankiw, Wonnacott and Wonnacott, Alchian and Allen, Sloman, Boulding, Bresciani-Turroni, Gwartney and Stroup, Dolan and Lindsay, Barre, Kasper and Streit, Hardwick–Khal-Langmead, Gimeno and Guirola, González Paz, Mochón, and O'Driscoll and Rizzo.

44 J. D. Gwartney and R. Stroup, *Economics: Private and Public Choice*, third edition, New York and London: Academic Press, 1983, especially pp. 416–419.
45 E. G. Dolan and D. E. Lindsay, *Economics*, fifth edition, New York: Dryden Press, 1988, pp. 489–492.
46 W. Kasper and M. E. Streit, *Institutional Economics*, Aldershot: Edward Elgar, 1998, p. 58.
47 G. P. O'Driscoll and M. J. Rizzo, *The Economics of Time and Ignorance*, London: Routledge, 1998, especially p. 88 and following.
48 P. Wonnacott and R. Wonnacott, *Economics*, New York: McGraw-Hill, 1986, pp. 492, 771.
49 As we have seen, we can arrive at a similar conclusion via Coase's theorem.
50 Our example of a pathological, antisocial envious person would constitute the exception.
51 See J. Huerta de Soto, *Socialismo, cálculo económico y función empresarial*, op. cit.
52 The drive of entrepreneurial creativity also manifests itself in help to the needy and in the prior search for and systematic detection of situations in which others are in need. In fact, coercive state intervention, through the mechanisms typical of the so-called welfare state, neutralizes and to a great extent blocks the entrepreneurial search for situations of urgent human need and for opportunities to help one's neighbours (both close and distant) who are experiencing difficulties. In this way, intervention drowns the natural desire to support one's fellow man and blocks the actions that would tend to aid those in distress through the voluntary, spontaneous cooperation most people prize. Pope John Paul II stressed these and other issues in his 1991 encyclical, *Centesimus Annus: On the Hundredth Anniversary of Rerum Novarum* (Rome: Vatican Press, chapter 4, section 49).
53 For a more detailed analysis of the above considerations, see J. Huerta de Soto, 'Socialismo, corrupción ética y economía de mercado', chapter 8 in *Nuevos estudios de economía política*, Madrid: Unión Editorial, 2002, pp. 193–219.
54 These institutions (the family, religion) also play an indispensable role in instilling habitual adherence to the more general norms of social ethics (concerning property rights). All of the state's coercive power would be insufficient to enforce the most basic standards of social cooperation without the help of such institutions.
55 Deep-seated religious convictions and behaviour that is consistent with them act as a sort of 'certificate of guarantee' concerning the future fulfilment of family obligations. Such a 'guarantee' lessens (though it does not eliminate) the uncertainty inherent in any marital decision, and although it does not exclude the possible disappointment of expectations, it promotes the adjustment and coordination which make a prosperous and dynamically efficient society possible.
56 J. Huerta de Soto, *Socialismo, cálculo económico y función empresarial*, op. cit., p. 69, note 37.
57 J. Huerta de Soto, 'Historia, ciencia económica y ética social', in *Estudios de economía política*, Madrid: Unión Editorial, 1994, pp. 105–109 (English version chapter 3 of this book).
58 The traditional static analysis presumes that the supply and demand functions are constant and known, and therefore that it is possible to calculate the corresponding elasticities necessary for the operative application of the Ramsay–Pigou rule: the optimal rate of taxation is that inversely proportional to the elasticity of the demand for each good compensated for by its price.
59 In the field of public finance, the proposed approach reveals the non-existence of public goods in a dynamic sense (as the problems of joint supply and exclusion of consumption tend to be detected and solved through entrepreneurial creativity), and hence what has, up to now, been considered the main theoretical justification for the existence of the state disappears.

60 I. Kirzner, 'Los objetivos de la política *antitrust*: una crítica', *Información comercial española*, no. 775 (1999), pp. 67–77. On the dynamically efficient nature of collusion between private companies which is not directly or indirectly encouraged by the state, see P. Salin, 'Cartels as Efficient Productive Structures', *Review of Austrian Economics* 9, no. 2 (1996), pp. 29–42.

61 I devoted my entire book, *Money, Bank Credit, and Economic Cycles*, op. cit., to the analysis of these phenomena. Incidentally, the rejection of the hypothesis of efficiency and equilibrium in capital markets will give rise to a reformulation of the now obsolete theory of financial markets, which was responsible for so much damage as the theoretical basis of the past speculative bubble during the years of the so called 'New Economy'. In contrast, the new theory must conceive the stock market as a dynamic process of entrepreneurial creativity, a process never perfectly efficient in a static sense, but which always tends toward dynamic efficiency in terms of the discovery and creation of profit opportunities and entrepreneurial coordination. See J. Huerta de Soto, *Money, Bank Credit, and Economic Cycles*, op. cit., especially chapters 5 and 6.

2 The ongoing *Methodenstreit* of the Austrian School

1 This paper was written at the request of Gary Becker, who asked me to represent the Austrian viewpoint in a panel discussion where this was contrasted with the neoclassical stance. The discussion took place during the general meeting of the Mont Pèlerin Society held in September 1996 in Vienna. Also on the panel were Sherwin Rosen, Leland Yeager and Eric Streissler. A summary of the main points in the debate appeared in separate articles by Rosen and Yeager in the *Journal of Economic Perspectives*, vol. 2, no. 4 (1997), pp. 153–165. The original English version of my paper was published as 'The Ongoing *Methodenstreit* of the Austrian School' in the *Journal des économistes et des études humaines*, vol. VIII, no. 1 (March 1998): 75–113.

2 Ludwig von Mises, *Notes and Recollections*, South Holland, IL: Libertarian Press, 1978, p. 36.

3 Carl Menger, *Grundsätze der Volkswirtschaftslehre*, Wilhelm Braumüller (ed.), Vienna 1871. Translated by James Dingwall and Bert F. Hoselitz, with an introduction by F. A. Hayek, *Principles of Economics*, New York and London: New York University Press, 1981.

4 Israel M. Kirzner, *Competition and Entrepreneurship*, Chicago, IL: Chicago University Press, 1973, p. 33.

5 Israel M. Kirzner, *The Meaning of Market Process: Essays in the Development of Modern Austrian Economics*, London: Routledge, 1991, pp. 201–208.

6 Lionel Robbins, *An Essay on the Nature and Significance of Economic Science*, London: Macmillan, 1932 and 1972.

7 F.A. Hayek, *The Counter-Revolution of Science: Studies in the Abuse of Reason*, Illinois: Free Press of Glencoe, 1952, p. 209.

8 The Austrian subjectivist concept allows economics to be generalized into a science that deals with all human actions and has full *objective* validity, which is paradoxical only in appearance.

9 Ludwig von Mises, *Human Action: A Treatise on Economics*, 4th revised edition, New York: The Foundation for Economic Education, 1996, p. 92.

10 Ibid., pp. 809–811.

11 Israel M. Kirzner, 'A Tale of Two Worlds', *Advances in Austrian Economics*, Greenwich, CT, and London: Jay Press, 1994, vol. I, pp. 223–226.

12 See Jesús Huerta de Soto, 'The Economic Analysis of Socialism', Chapter 14 of *New Perspectives on Austrian Economics*, Gerrit Meijer (ed.), London and New York: Routledge, 1995.

13 Regarding the Austrian criticism of Grossman–Stiglitz's theory of information, see Esteban Thomsen, *Prices and Knowledge: A Market Process Perspective*, London: Routledge, 1992; and also Israel M. Kirzner, 'Entrepreneurial Discovery and the Competitive Market Process', *Journal of Economic Literature*, March 1997, vol. XXXV, no. 1, pp. 60–85.
14 Rothbard and Kirzner have criticized the extreme subjectivist position held by some theorists who, like Lachmann and Shackle, believe that there is no coordinating tendency in the market. This error originates from ignorance of the coordinating force of all entrepreneurial human action. See Murray N. Rothbard, 'The Present State of Austrian Economics', in *Journal des économistes et des études humaines*, vol. 6, no. 1, March 1995, especially pp. 56–59; and Israel M. Kirzner, 'The Subjectivism of Austrian Economics', Chapter 1 of *New Perspectives on Austrian Economics*, op. cit., pp. 11–22.
15 My Austrian School colleagues usually refer to the fact that entrepreneurial processes tend to lead the system towards equilibrium, although they acknowledge that this is never reached. I prefer to talk about a different model, which I have described as the 'social big bang', that allows unlimited growth of knowledge and civilization in a way that is as adjusted and harmonious (i.e. coordinated) as is humanly possible in each historical situation. This is the case because the entrepreneurial process of social coordination never ceases or becomes exhausted. In other words, the entrepreneurial act consists basically of creating and transmitting new information that will inevitably modify the general perception of goals and means of all the actors involved in society. This in turn leads to the unlimited appearance of new disorders which imply new opportunities of entrepreneurial gain that tend to be discovered and coordinated by the entrepreneurs. This repeats itself successively, in a never-ending dynamic process that constantly makes civilization advance (model of the coordinated 'social big bang'). See Jesús Huerta de Soto, *Socialismo, cálculo económico y función empresarial*, Madrid: Unión Editorial, 1992, pp. 78–79 (English version forthcoming).
16 A.M. Endres even refers to the 'Mengerian principle of non-maximization'. See his article 'Menger, Wieser, Böhm-Bawerk and the Analysis of Economic Behaviour', *History of Political Economy*, vol. 23, no. 2, Summer 1991, pp. 275–295, especially footnote 5 on p. 281.
17 'Modern economics does not ask what "iron" or "bread" is worth, but what a definite piece of iron or bread is worth to an acting individual at a definite date and a definite place. It cannot help proceeding in the same way with regard to money. The equation of exchange is incompatible with the fundamental principles of economic thought. It is a relapse to the thinking of ages in which people failed to comprehend praxeological phenomena because they were committed to holistic notions. It is sterile, as were the speculations of earlier ages concerning the value of "iron" and "bread" in general' (Ludwig von Mises, *Human Action*, op. cit., p. 400).
18 Mises calls equilibrium an 'evenly rotating economy' and considers it an imaginary construction with a strictly instrumental value for improving the analytical comprehension of only *two* problems in our science: the emergence of entrepreneurial profits in a dynamic environment and the relationship that exists between the price of consumer goods and services and the price of the production factors necessary to produce them. In this specific aspect, I would go even further than Mises himself, as I believe that it is perfectly possible to explain the emergence of entrepreneurial profits and the trend toward fixing the prices of the production factors in accordance with the discounted value of their marginal productivity, without any reference to models of equilibrium (either general or partial), but merely to the dynamic process which tends towards what Mises calls a 'final state of rest' (which is never reached). See Ludwig von Mises, *Human Action*, op. cit., p. 248.

19 L. Walras, *Correspondence of Léon Walras and Related Papers*, W. Jaffé (ed.), Amsterdam: North Holland, vol. II, 1965, p. 3.
20 Hans Mayer, 'The Cognitive Value of Functional Theories of Price: Critical and Positive Investigations Concerning the Price Problem', Chapter XVI of *Classics in Austrian Economics: A Sampling in the History of a Tradition*, Israel M. Kirzner (ed.), London: William Pickering, 1994, vol. II, p. 92.
21 Hans Mayer tells us that when 'all wants differing in kind or quality are not reciprocally present to one another, then the postulate of the law of equal marginal utility becomes impossible in the real world of the psyche'. And he very descriptively adds, commenting on the theoretical absurdity of the forced synchronization of utility estimations, that 'It is as if one were to express the experience of aesthetic value of hearing a melody – an experience determined by successive experiences of individual notes –in terms of the aesthetic value of the simultaneous harmonization of all notes of making up the melody' (Hans Mayer, 'The Cognitive Value of Functional Theories of Price', op. cit., pp. 81 and 83). Very similar critical analyses may be made with regard to the indifference–preference curves and the income effect–substitution effect. See, in this respect, Pascal Salin, 'The Myth of the Income Effect', *Review of Austrian Economics*, vol. IX, no. 1, 1996, pp. 95–106.
22 Ludwig von Mises, *Human Action*, op. cit., pp. 102–104. And, likewise, Murray N. Rothbard, 'Toward a Reconstruction of Utility and Welfare Economics', in *Austrian Economics*, Stephen Littlechild (ed.), Aldershot: Edward Elgar, 1990, Vol. III, p. 228 onwards.
23 Thus, an outstanding example is the demonstration of the Law of Diminishing Returns which Mises sets out in exclusively logical terms (point 2 of Chapter VII of *Human Action*). This logical demonstration is based on the fact that, in *sensu contrario*, if the mentioned law were not true in the world of human action, the production factor considered as fixed would have an unlimited production capacity and, therefore, would be a free good. Karl Menger, the son of the great Austrian economist, has tried, in our opinion fruitlessly, to refute Mises' theorem on the strictly praxeological nature of the Law of Diminishing Returns. See Karl Menger, 'Remarks on the Law of Diminishing Returns. A Study in Meta-Economics', Chapter 23 of *Selected Papers in Logic and Foundations, Didactics, Economics*, Dordrecht, Holland: D. Reidel Publishing Co., 1979, pp. 279–302.
24 The former is the position upheld by Rothbard and the latter by Mises. See the summary of the Austrian methodological position by Hans-Hermann Hoppe in his *Economic Essence and the Austrian Method*, Auburn, AL: The Ludwig von Mises Institute, Auburn University, 1995, as well the most recent and clarifying article of Barry Smith, 'In Defense of Extreme (Fallibilistic) Apriorism', *Journal of Libertarian Studies*, vol. 12, no. 1, Spring 1996, pp. 179–192.
25 A favourable and dispassionate explanation of the methodological paradigm of the Austrians may be found in Bruce Caldwell, *Beyond Positivism: Economic Methodology in the Twentieth Century*, 2nd edition, London: Routledge, 1994, pp. 117–138. On the relationship between theory and history, the most important work is Ludwig von Mises, *Theory and History*, Yale, CT: Yale University Press, 1957, together with Hayek's classic work *The Counter-Revolution of Science*, Indianapolis, IN: Liberty Press, 1979.
26 It would be preferable to say 'praxeological'. According to Mises, logic may be distinguished from praxeology because the former is constant and atemporal and the latter includes time and creativity. Ludwig von Mises, *Human Action*, op. cit., pp. 99–100.
27 See Sherwin Rosen, 'Austrian and Neoclassical Economics: Any Gains from Trade?', *Journal of Economic Perspectives*, vol. II, no. 4, Fall 1997, pp. 139–152.

28 F.A. Hayek, 'The Pretence of Knowledge', *American Economic Review*, December 1989, pp. 3–7.
29 Although it does not fully coincide with our description of the different controversies between the Austrians and the neoclassicals, Lawrence A. White's summary, *The Methodology of the Austrian School Economists*, Auburn, AL: The Ludwig von Mises Institute, Auburn University, 1984, should be consulted.
30 See especially headings 2, 3 and 4 of Chapter I of Carl Menger, *Principles of Economics*, New York: New York University Press, 1981, pp. 51–71. The quotation given in the text is on p. 67 (emphasis added).
31 The most brilliant and concise explanation of Menger's theory can be found in his article which was published in English with the title 'On the Origin of Money', *Economic Journal*, June 1892, pp. 239–255. This article has been reedited by Israel M. Kirzner in his *Classics in Austrian Economics: A Sampling in the History of a Tradition*, op. cit., vol. I, pp. 91–106, especially pp. 98–99.
32 The term 'historicism' has at least three different meanings. The first of them, identified with the Historical School of Law (Savigny, Burke) and opposed to Cartesian rationalism, is the meaning defended by the Austrian School in its theoretical analysis of institutions. The second meaning corresponds to the Historical School of Economics of the German professors of the nineteenth century and the twentieth century American institutionalists. They deny the possibility of the existence of universally valid abstract economic theory, as defended by Menger and the Austrian economists. The third kind of historicism is found in the basis of methodological positivism or scientism, which tries to use empirical observation (history) to verify or falsify theories, which, according to Hayek, is merely another manifestation of the Cartesian rationalism so much criticized by the Austrians. See Raimondo Cubeddu, *The Philosophy of the Austrian School*, London and New York: Routledge, 1993, pp. 29–30.
33 Regarding Say as a forerunner of the Austrian method, see, especially, Murray N. Rothbard, *Classical Economics: An Austrian Perspective on the History of Economic Thought*, Adershot: Edward Elgar 1995, vol. II, pp. 12–18.
34 Bruno Leoni, *Freedom and the Law*, Indianapolis, IN: Liberty Fund, 1991, p. 88.
35 Among others, the following have studied the contribution of the Spanish scholastics to economic theory: Murray N. Rothbard, 'New Light on the Prehistory of the Austrian School', in *The Foundations of Modern Austrian Economics*, E. G. Dolan (ed.), Kansas City, MO: Sheed Andrews and McMeel, 1976, pp. 52–74; and *Economic Thought before Adam Smith: An Austrian Perspective on the History of Economic Thought*, Adershot: Edward Elgar, 1995, vol. I, Chapter 4, pp. 97–133; Lucas Beltrán, 'Sobre los orígenes hispanos de la economía de mercado', *Cuadernos del Pensamiento Liberal*, Madrid: Unión Editorial, 1996, pp. 234–254; Marjorie Grice-Hutchinson, *The School of Salamanca: Readings in Spanish Monetary Theory 1544–1605*, Oxford: Clarendon Press, 1952; and *Economic Thought in Spain: Selected Essays of Marjorie Grice-Hutchinson*, Laurence S. Moss and Christopher K. Ryan (eds), Aldershot: Edward Elgar, 1993; Alejandro Chafuen, *Christians for Freedom: Late-Scholastic Economics*, San Francisco, CA: Ignatius Press, 1986; and Jesús Huerta de Soto, 'New Light on the Prehistory of the theory of Banking and the School of Salamanca', *Review of Austrian Economics*, vol. 9, no. 2 (1996), pp. 59–81. The intellectual influence of the Spanish theorists of the School of Salamanca on the Austrian School is not, however, a pure coincidence or a mere whim of history. It originates from and exists because of the intimate historical, political and cultural relations which, as from the reigns of Carlos V and his brother Fernando I, arose between Spain and Austria and which were to continue for several centuries. In addition, Italy also played an important role in these relations, acting as an authentic cultural, economic and financial bridge over which the relations between the two furthest points of the Empire (Spain and

Vienna) flowed. In this respect, Jean Berenguer's book *Histoire de l'empire des Habsbourg 1273–1918*, Paris: Librairie Arthème, Fayard, 1990, should be consulted.
36. The former, wondering what the equilibrium price was, reached the conclusion that it depends on such a large number of specific circumstances that only God is able to know ('Pretium iustum mathematicum licet soli Deu notum', *Disputationes de Iustitia et Iure*, Lyon: Sumptibus Petri Prost, 1643, vol. II, D.26, S.4, N.40, p. 312); and Juan de Salas, referring to the possibilities of knowing specific information on the market, says that it is so complex 'quas exacte comprehendere et ponderare Dei est non hominum' (*Commentarii in Secundam Secundae D. Thomas de Contractibus*, Lyon: Sumptibus Horatij Lardon, 1617, IV, no. 6, p. 9).
37. Murray N. Rothbard, *Economic Thought before Adam Smith: An Austrian Perspective on the History of Economic Thought*, op. cit., vol. I, pp. 268, 369, 387 and 388.
38. Covarrubias' work on money is quoted by Carl Menger on p. 157 of the first German edition of his *Grundsätze* (p. 317 of the English edition published by New York University Press in 1981).
39. Leland B. Yeager, 'Book Review' of *Economic Thought before Adam Smith (Vol. I)* and *Classical Economics (Vol. II), An Austrian Perspective on the History of Economic Thought* (Aldershot: Edward Elgar, 1995), published in *Review of Austrian Economics*, vol. 9, no. 1 (1996), p. 183. I do not understand how anyone who has read Rothbard's two volumes in depth can continue to uphold the thesis that Adam Smith was a forerunner of the Austrian School. Furthermore, if Rothbard is right, there would be important arguments to defend the thesis that, at its roots, the Austrian School was a Spanish school and that the German predecessors of Menger, rather than influenced by Smith, were influenced by the Catholic subjectivist tradition they received from Jean-Baptiste Say through Hufeland and others.
40. John Bates Clark, 'The Genesis of Capital', *Yale Review*, November 1893, p. 312.
41. Eugen von Böhm-Bawerk, 'Professor Clark's Views on the Genesis of Capital', *Quarterly Journal of Economics*, IX, 1895, pp. 113–131, reproduced on pp. 131–143 of *Classics in Austrian Economics*, Israel M. Kirzner (ed.), op. cit. Furthermore, Böhm-Bawerk points out, with great foreknowledge, that, if Clark's static view were to prevail, the doctrines on under-consumption, which were refuted by economists previously, would again emerge, as actually happened with the Keynesianism that emerged from the neoclassical Marshall: 'When one goes with Professor Clark into such an account of the matter, the assertion that capital is not consumed is seen to be another inexact, shining figure of speech, which must not be taken at all literally. Any one taking it literally falls into a total error, into which, for sooth, science has already fallen once. I refer to the familiar and at one time widely disseminated doctrine that saving is a social evil and the class of spendthrifts a useful factor in social economy, because what is saved is not spent and so producers cannot find a market'. *Ibidem*, p. 137.
42. Frank H. Knight, for example, considers Menger's theory on economic goods of first order and higher order (concept of human action made up of stages) to be one of his less important economic contributions. See the 'Prologue' he wrote for the first English edition of *Principles of Economics*, J. Dingwall y B. Hoselitz (eds), Free Press of Glencoe, Illinois, 1950. With regard to the most important articles within the polemic with the School of Chicago, they are Fritz Machlup's article 'Professor Knight and the 'Period of Production', *Journal of Political Economy*, October 1935, vol. 43, no. 5, included in *Classics in Austrian Economics*, Israel M. Kirzner (ed.) op. cit., vol. II, pp. 275–315; and F.A. Hayek's 'The Mythology of Capital', *Quarterly Journal of Economics*, February 1936, pp. 199–228.
43. Eugen von Böhm-Bawerk, *Capital and Interest*, South Holland, IL: Libertarian Press, 1959, vol. I, pp. 241–321, and *Shorter Classics of Eugen von Böhm-Bawerk*, South Holland, IL: Libertarian Press, 1962, pp. 201–302.

44 See Eugen von Böhm-Bawerk 'On the Value of Producer's Goods and the Relationship between Value and Cost', *Capital and Interest*, South Holland, IL: Libertarian Press, 1959, vol. III, Chapter VIII, pp. 97–115; and 'The Ultimate Standard of Value', *Shorter Classics of Eugen von Böhm-Bawerk*, op. cit., pp. 303–370. The subjective concept of cost of opportunity was originally developed by Friedrich von Wieser in 1876. (See his article 'On the Relationship of Costs to Value', Chapter 8 of vol. I of *Classics in Austrian Economics*, op. cit., pp. 207–234.) Mises has shown, however, that Wieser was the member of the Austrian School who was closest to the neoclassical paradigm of the School of Lausanne: 'Wieser was not a creative thinker and in general was more harmful than useful. He never really understood the gist of the idea of subjectivism in the Austrian School of Thought, which limitation caused him to make many unfortunate mistakes. His imputation theory is untenable. His ideas on value calculation justify the conclusion that he could not be called a member of the Austrian School, but rather a member of the Lausanne School (Léon Walras et al and the idea of economic equilibrium)'. See Ludwig von Mises, *Notes and Recollections*, South Holland, IL: Libertarian Press, 1978, p. 36.
45 Ludwig von Mises, *Human Action*, op. cit., p. 206.
46 Frank H. Knight, 'Review of Ludwig von Mises' *Socialism*', *Journal of Political Economy*, no. 46, April 1938, pp. 267–268.
47 These were the only explanations that, for example, were mentioned by Gary Becker in his 'Presidential Address' at the Regional Meeting of the Mont Pèlerin Society which took place in Prague, Czechoslovakia, from November 3–6, 1991, under the general title 'In Search of a Transition to a Free Society'.
48 Wlodzimierz Brus and Kazimierz Laski, *From Marx to the Market: Socialism in Search of an Economic System*, Oxford: Clarendon Press, 1985, p. 60. And Robert L. Heilbroner himself has concluded that 'Mises was right: socialism has been the great tragedy of this century'. See his articles 'Analysis and Vision in the History of Modern Economic Thought', *Journal of Economic Literature*, September 1990, pp. 1,097–1,110; 'The Triumph of Capitalism', *New Yorker*, January 23, 1989, pp. 90–91, and 'Reflections after Communism', *New Yorker*, September 10, 1990, pp. 91–100 (especially p. 98).
49 J.E. Stiglitz, *Whither Socialism?*, Cambridge, MA: MIT Press, 1994, pp. ix–xii.
50 See, for example, F.A. Hayek, *Contra Keynes and Cambridge*, vol. IX of *The Collected Works of F.A. Hayek*, London: Routledge, 1995.
51 This is a slightly corrected and expanded version of the chart included in F.A. Hayek, *The Pure Theory of Capital*, Routledge, London, 1976, pp. 47–49; see also Mark Skousen, *The Structure of Production*, New York: New York University Press, 1990, p. 370.
52 However, this process took some time, which explains the dictum of Fritz Machlup, according to which 'the real triumph of the Austrian School is that its contributions became so much part of the economic mainstream that no one realized any more that they were Austrian'. Surprisingly, Mises himself said something similar in 1932. Israel Kirzner, 'Introduction' to vol. I of *Classics in Austrian Economics*, op. cit., p. xvi onward.
53 Chapter 16 of vol. II of *Classics in Austrian Economics*, op. cit., pp. 55–168. This article is the English translation of the article published by Hans Mayer in 1932 with the title 'Der Erkenntniswert der funktionellen Preistheorien', in the book *Die Wirtschaftheorie der Gegenwart*, Vienna, 1932, vol. II, pp. 147–239b. An expanded version of this article was published in Italian some years later: Hans Mayer, 'Il concetto di equilibrio nella teoria economica: richerche sulla trattazione matematica del problema dei prezzi', *Economia Pura*, Gustavo del Vecchio (ed.), *Nuova collana di economisti stranieri e italiani*, vol. 4, Turin: Unione Tipografico-Editrice Torinese, 1937, pp. 645–799.

54 F.A. Hayek, *The Counter-Revolution of Science: Studies in the Abuse of Reason*, Illinois: Free Press of Glencoe, 1952.
55 Milton Friedman, *Essays in Positive Economics*, Chicago, IL: University of Chicago Press, 1953.
56 F.A. Hayek, *Hayek on Hayek*, London and New York: Routledge, 1994, p. 145. Elsewhere, Hayek clarified even further his methodological differences with Friedman and the neoclassicals as follows:

> Friedman is an arch-positivist who believes nothing must enter scientific argument except what is empirically proven. My argument is that we know so much detail about economics, our task is to put our knowledge in order. We hardly need any new information. Our great difficulty is digesting what we already know. We don't get much wiser by statistical information except by gaining information about the specific situation at the moment. But theoretically I don't think statistical studies get us anywhere. ... Milton's monetarism and Keynesianism have more in common with each other than I have with either. ... The Chicago School thinks essentially in 'macroeconomic' terms. They try to analyze in terms of aggregates and averages, total quantity of money, total price level, total employment, all these statistical magnitudes. ... Take Friedman's 'quantity theory', I wrote forty years ago that I have strong objections against the quantity theory because it is a very crude approach that leaves out a great many things: I regret that a man of the sophistication of Milton Friedman does not use it as a first approach but believes it is the whole thing. So it is really on methodological issues, ultimately, that we differ

See Robert Pool and Virginia Postrel's interview with Hayek published in *Free Minds and Free Markets*, Pacific Research Institute for Public Policy, California, 1993, pp. 129–130.
57 Thus, George Stigler considered that the two parties to the debate on socialism failed when appreciating the 'empirical' consequences of their respective positions, since only 'empirical evidence' can resolve the differences that exist between the advocates of capitalism and those of socialism. See his book *The Citizen and the State*, Chicago: The University of Chicago Press, 1975, pp. 1–13; and the critical comment on Stigler's position put forward by Norman P. Barry, 'The Economics and Theory of Socialism', *Il Politico*, Pavia: University of Pavia, 1984, year XLIX, no. 4, pp. 573–592.
58 See Israel M. Kirzner, 'Book Review' of the book by Bridget Berger (ed.) *The Culture of Entrepreneurship*, published in *Advances in Austrian Economics*, vol. I, Greenwich, CT, and London: Jay Press, 1994, p. 328.
59 Hans-Hermann Hoppe, *Economic Science and the Austrian Method*, op. cit., p. 54. And also Murray N. Rothbard, 'The Hermeneutical Invasion of Philosophy and Economics', *Review of Austrian Economics*, no. 3, 1989, pp. 45–59; and 'Intimidation by Rhetoric', *Review of Austrian Economics*, vol. IX, no. 1, 1996, pp. 173–178.
60 For the same reason, neither can we accept Barry Smith's thesis (*Austrian Philosophy: The Legacy of Franz Brentano*, Illinois: Open Court, 1994, pp. 330–331), whereby the Austrian methodology would be appropriate for establishing the basic foundations of the discipline, while neoclassical empiricism would handle above all problems of applied economics. Again, Barry Smith's approach would be correct if the scientific methodology of the neoclassicals did not tend to conceal the problems of real interest by generating defects in the theoretical analysis that affect, to a great extent, the validity of its conclusions.
61 F.A. Hayek, *The Sensory Order*, Chicago, IL: University of Chicago Press, 1952, pp. 184–194.

62 Stiglitz even entitles one section of his book 'Hayek versus Stiglitz'. Joseph E. Stiglitz, *Whither Socialism?*, op. cit., pp. 24–26. Unfortunately, Stiglitz tries to reconstruct the neoclassical models using a static methodology based on equilibrium and formalized language, failing, from the Austrian point of view, to avoid the methodological errors of the same models as he himself is criticizing. See Stephen Sullivan's 'Signifying Nothing: A Review Essay of Joseph Stiglitz' *Whither Socialism?*', *Advances in Austrian Economics*, vol. III, Greenwich, CT, and London: Jay Press, 1996, pp. 183–189.
63 Vilfredo Pareto, *Manual of Political Economy*, New York: Augustus M. Kelley, 1971, p. 120. Pareto is referring specifically to the instrument of the indifference–preference curves, the use of which is, in our opinion, very negative for economic science as it does not recognize the sequential and non-synchronic nature of all human actions, does not take into account the fact that the human being only considers the combinations thought most appropriate for each specific end (*indifference* does not involve any human action) and does not adequately reflect the most universal and relevant phenomenon of the *complementary* nature of goods.
64 See Joseph Alois Schumpeter, *Das Wesen und der Hauptinhalt der Theoretischen Nationalökonomie*, Leipzig: Dunker & Humblot, 1908, p. 227. The best-known criticism of Schumpeter's scientific book was written by Friedrich von Wieser, 'The Nature and Substance of Theoretical Economics', *Classics in Austrian Economics*, Israel M. Kirzner (ed.), op. cit., vol. I, pp. 285–303.
65 Two examples of what we are saying are the 'prediction' of the fall of real socialism that is implicit in the Austrian analysis of the impossibility of socialism and the Austrians' prediction of the Great Depression of 1929. Neither of these very significant historical events were predicted by the neoclassical economists. In this respect, see Mark Skousen, 'Who Predicted the 1929 Crash?', in *The Meaning of Ludwig von Mises*, Jeffrey M. Herbener (ed.), Amsterdam: Kluwer Academic Publishers, 1993, pp. 247–284. Lionel Robbins, in his 'Introduction' to the first edition of *Prices and Production* by F.A. Hayek (London: Routledge, 1931, p. xii), referred to Mises and Hayek's prediction of the inexorable advent of the Great Depression as a result of the monetary and credit excesses committed in the 1920s, which appeared expressly in an article by Hayek published in 1929 in the annals of the *Monatsberichte des Österreichischen Instituts für Konjunkturforschung*. This Austrian prediction contrasted with the optimism of many neoclassicals (Keynes and monetarists like Fisher), who, even a few months before the Crash, still publicly affirmed that the economic boom of the 1920s and the high stock market index which characterized it would be maintained indefinitely.
66 See, for example, the harsh observations made by Samuelson, who even commits the excess of stating that the existence of the Austrian economists made him 'tremble for the reputation' of my subject' (*The Collected Scientific Papers of Paul A. Samuelson*, R.C. Merton (ed.), Cambridge, MA: The MIT Press, 1972, vol. III, p. 761). And also the accusations against the Austrian School made by Blaug in his book on *The Methodology of Economics*, Cambridge and London: Cambridge University Press, 1980, pp. 91–93. However, as we will see later, more recently Mark Blaug has gradually changed his position and is increasingly inclining towards the propositions of the Austrian School, if not in his deductive methodology, at least in his acceptance of the dynamic entrepreneurial approach and criticism of the model of equilibrium of the neoclassical-Walrasian paradigm.
67 Bruce Caldwell, *Beyond Positivism: Economic Methodology in the Twentieth Century*, London: Routledge, 1994, pp. 118–119.
68 An example of this neoclassical habit of assuming a complete exclusive on the 'correct' conception of the 'economic point of view' could be Gary Becker's speech on receiving the Nobel Prize, 'The Economic Way of Looking at Behaviour', reproduced as Chapter 26 of *The Essence of Becker*, Ramón Febrero and

Pedro S. Schwartz (eds.), Stanford, CA: Hoover Institution, Stanford University, pp. 633–658.
69 J.E. Stiglitz, *Whither Socialism?*, op. cit., p. 273.
70 Israel M. Kirzner, *The Meaning of the Market Process: Essays in the Development of Modern Austrian Economics*, London: Routledge, 1992, p. 207. However, the accusation of imperialism is not justified when it refers exclusively to the scope of application of economic science, and not to the use of the neoclassical approach: from the Austrian point of view as well, since economics is considered a general theory of human behaviour, it is applicable to all fields in which the human being acts. Only when the conception based on the strictly rational *homo oeconomicus* is applied is the accusation of imperialism clearly justified, not with regard to the scope of application of the economic point of view correctly understood, but in respect of the neoclassical attempt to apply the strictly rationalist approach to all human fields.
71 For Menger, this (neoclassical) approach 'contrary to the intention of its representatives inexorably leads to socialism'. Carl Menger, *Problems of Economics and Sociology*, Champaign, IL: University of Illinois Press, 1963, p. 177 (pp. 207–208 of the original German edition of the *Untersuchungen über die Methode der Socialwissenschaften und der polistischen Oekonomie insbesondere*, Leipzig: Verlag von Ducker & Humblot, 1883).
72 Edward H. Crane, 'A Property Rights Approach to Social Security and Immigration Reform', comment on Gary S. Becker's paper 'An Open Door for Immigrants?', presented at the Regional Meeting of the Mont Pèlerin Society that took place in Cancun, Mexico, in January 1996, manuscript pending publication, p. 6. Also, William H. Hutt, in his excellent book *Politically Impossible ... ?*, London: The Institute of Economic Affairs, 1981, lists several specific examples where the neoclassical libertarian economists have directly or indirectly justified interventionist measures.
73 Murray N. Rothbard even referred to how 'the case of Jeremy Bentham should be instructive to that host of economists that tend to weld utilitarian philosophy with free market economics'. Murray N. Rothbard, *Classical Economics*, op. cit., p. 55.
74 Hans-Hermann Hoppe, 'The Intellectual Cover for Socialism', *The Free Market*, February 1988.
75 Sherwin Rosen, 'Austrian and Neoclassical Economics: Any Gains from Trade?', op. cit., p. 145. Another surprised theorist was Ronald H. Coase: 'Nothing I'd read or known suggested that the collapse was going to occur'. 'Looking for Results', *Reason: Free Minds and Free Markets*, January 1997, p. 45.
76 See *Appraising Economic Theories*, Mark Blaug and Neil de Marchi (eds.), London: Edward Elgar, 1991, p. 508. Even more recently, in the *Economic Journal* (November 1993, p. 1,571), Blaug has again referred to the neoclassical paradigm in relation to its application in order to justify the socialist system as something 'so administratively naive as to be positively laughable. Only those drunk on perfectly competitive static equilibrium theory could have swallowed such nonsense. I was one of those who swallowed it as a student in the 1950s and I can only marvel now at my own dim-wittedness'.
77 Ludwig von Mises, *Human Action*, op. cit., p. 869.
78 Illustrations of regression in the evolution of economic thought would be, for example, the revival of the objective theory of value by the neo-Ricardian School, Keynesian economic analysis, the abandonment of the time dimension and the theory of capital in modern macroeconomic thought and the narrow concepts of rationality, maximization and equilibrium upon which neoclassical analysis is constructed.
79 Additional arguments against the so-called market test on Austrian Economics are given in the most brilliant paper of Leland Yeager 'Austrian Economics,

Neoclassicism and the Market Test', *Journal of Economic Perspectives*, vol. II, no. 4, Fall 1997, pp. 153–165.
80 F.A. Hayek, *The Counter-Revolution of Science*, New York: Free Press of Glencoe, 1952, p. 31. Hayek adds in note 24 (on p. 210) that subjectivism 'has probably been carried out most consistently by Ludwig von Mises and I believe that most peculiarities of his views which at first strike many readers as strange and unacceptable are due to the fact that in the consistent development of the subjectivist approach he has for a long time moved ahead of his contemporaries'.

3 Conjectural history and beyond

1 Published in the *Humane Studies Review*, Fairfax, VI: George Mason University, vol. 6, no. 2, Winter 1988–1989, p. 10.
2 F. A. Hayek, *The Fatal Conceit: The Errors of Socialism*, Chicago, IL: University of Chicago Press, 1989, p. 69.

4 Entrepreneurship and the economic analysis of socialism

1 Published as chapter 14 of the Book *New Perspectives on Austrian Economics*, Gerrit Meijer (ed.), London and New York: Routledge, 1995, pp. 228–253.
2 With regard to the concept of human action and its main elements, Ludwig von Mises' *Human Action: A Treatise on Economics*, third revised edition, Chicago, IL: Henry Regnery Company, 1966, pp. 11–29 and 251–256, should be especially consulted. Mises textually states that 'every actor is always an entrepreneur and a speculator' (p. 252) and that 'entrepreneur means *acting man* in regard to the changes occurring in the market' (p. 254).
3 The main writer on the concept of entrepreneurship discussed in this article is Israel M. Kirzner, Professor of Economics at the University of New York. Kirzner is the author of a trilogy (*Competition and Entrepreneurship, Perception, Opportunity and Profit* and *Discovery and the Capitalist Process*, published by Chicago, IL: University of Chicago Press, 1973, 1979 and 1985, respectively), in which Professor Kirzner expands upon and makes an impeccable in-depth study of the different aspects of the concept of entrepreneurship which was initially developed by Ludwig von Mises and Friedrich A. Hayek. Moreover, Kirzner has written a fourth book, *Discovery, Capitalism and Distributive Justice*, Oxford: Basil Blackwell, 1989, which studies the implications of his concept of entrepreneurship in the field of *social ethics*.
4 *The Oxford English Dictionary*, 2nd edition, vol. V, Oxford: Clarendon Press, 1989, p. 293, meanings 3 and 1.
5 Israel M. Kirzner, *Competition and Entrepreneurship*, op. cit., pp. 65–69.
6 Saint Thomas of Aquinas defines particular circumstances as 'accidentia individualia humanorum actuum' (i.e. the individual accidents of human acts) and states that, apart from time and place, the most important of such particular circumstances is that which refers to the end pursued by the actor ('principalissima est omnium circunstantiarum illa quae attingit actum ex parte finis'). See *Suma Teológica de Santo Tomás de Aquino*, parts I–II, Q7, art. 1 & 2, vol. IV, B.A.C., Madrid, 1954, pp. 293–294 and 301. In addition, it must be pointed out that we owe the distinction between 'practical knowledge' and 'scientific knowledge' to Michael Oakeshott (*Rationalism in Politics*, London: Methuen, 1962; this book has been re-edited and expanded under the title *Rationalism in Politics and Other Essays*, Indianapolis, IN: Liberty Press, 1991, pp. 12 and 15 being especially relevant. Equally essential is Oakeshott's book *On Human Conduct*, Oxford: Oxford University Press, 1975, re-edited by Oxford: Clarendon Paperbacks, 1991, pp. 23–25, 36, 78–79 and 119–121).

7 See especially the seminal articles by F.A. Hayek 'Economics and Knowledge' (1937) and 'The Use of Knowledge in Society' (1945), which are included in the book *Individualism and Economic Order*, Chicago, IL: Henry Regnery, 1972, pp. 33–56 and 77–91.
8 This distinction has become generalized since it was given in 1949 by Gilbert Ryle in his well-known article 'Knowing How and Knowing That', included in *The Concept of Mind*, London: Hutchinson's University Library, 1949.
9 Michael Polanyi, *The Study of Man*, Chicago, IL: The University of Chicago Press, 1959, pp. 24–25.
10 Don Lavoie, *Rivalry and Central Planning*, Cambridge: Cambridge University Press, 1985. Lavoie adds that, if costs were something which could be established objectively, scientifically and universally, the taking of decisions in economic life could be reduced to obeying a series of completely articulated and specified rules but, given that costs are something subjective and can only be known within the context of each specific action by the actor, the practice of entrepreneurship cannot be articulated in detail or replaced by any objective criterion of a scientific nature (op. cit., pp. 103–104).
11 The word 'calculation' proceeds etymologically from the Latin expression *calx-calcis*, used, among other things, to name the chalk used on the Greek and Roman abacuses.
12 The *Dictionary* of the Spanish Royal Academy defines coercion (in Spanish: 'coacción') as 'force or violence performed upon a person to make him execute something'. It comes from the Latin *cogere*, to impel, and *coactionis*, which refers to the collection of taxation. Regarding the concept of coercion and its effects on the human actor, the reader should consult pp. 20–21 of *The Constitution of Liberty* by F.A. Hayek (London: Routledge, 1959), which was reprinted in 1990. Murray N. Rothbard defines aggression as follows: 'Aggression is defined as the initiation of the use or threat of physical violence against the person or property of someone else'. See Murray N. Rothbard, *For a New Liberty*, New York: Macmillan Publishing, 1973, p. 8. There are three types of coercion: *autistic*, *binary* and *triangular*. Autistic coercion is the aggression arising from a command addressed strictly towards one actor, modifying the behaviour of the coerced party in such a way that his interaction with other human beings is not affected. Binary coercion, according to our definition, is that in which the controlling organism coerces the actor in order to obtain something from him against his will, i.e. the controlling organism forces, in his own favour, an interchange between itself and the coerced actor. Triangular coercion is where the commands and coercion by the controlling organism are aimed to force an interchange between two different actors. We owe this classification to Murray N. Rothbard, *Power and Market: Government and the Economy*, Menlo Park, CA: Institute for Human Studies Inc., 2nd edition, 1970, pp. 9 and 10.
13 We do not, of course, consider the concept of systematic aggression described in the text to include the minimum level of institutionalized coercion necessary to guard against and correct the negative effects produced by arbitrary non-institutionalized or non-systematic aggression. This minimum level of institutionalized coercion is that which even the non-institutionalized aggressor would wish to be provided to him, outside the scope of his non-systematic aggression, in order to pacifically take advantage thereof.
14 Ludwig von Mises has already stated that 'the idea of socialism is at once grandiose and simple. We may say, in fact, that it is one of the most ambitious creations of the human spirit, so magnificent, so daring, that it has rightly aroused the greatest admiration. If we wish to save the world from barbarism we have to refute socialism, but we cannot thrust it carelessly aside'. *Socialism: An Economic and Sociological Analysis*, Indianapolis, IN: Liberty Classics, 1981, p. 40.

15 Ludwig von Mises, *Human Action*, op. cit., p. 696.
16 Mises even states that the director (or controlling organism) 'has at his disposal all the technical knowledge of his age. Moreover, he has a complete inventory of all the material factors of production available and a roster enumerating all manpower employable. In these respects the crowd of experts and specialists which he assembles in his offices provide him with *perfect information* and answer correctly all questions he may ask them. Their voluminous reports accumulate in huge piles on his desk'. (*Human Action*, op. cit., p. 696.) Furthermore, Mises assumes that 'the director has made up his mind with regard to the valuation of ultimate ends' and that 'everyone agrees with one another and with the director in the valuation of ultimate ends' (*ibidem*). However, when Mises refers to 'perfect information' and to the availability of 'a complete inventory of all the factors of production', this must be understood in its technological sense ('all the technological knowledge of his age') and as a concession referring only to the first reason against socialism that we have given in the text (it is impossible to assimilate the enormous volume of information spread over society, even if it is correctly articulated – i.e. without errors, as Mises concedes). But Mises is not making any concessions regarding the other three reasons for the impossibility of socialism, which could only be solved assuming *perfect knowledge* (in the neoclassical sense), i.e. an *omniscient* capability to know: (1) inarticulate knowledge; (2) knowledge not yet created by the entrepreneurs; and (3) knowledge that can only be created by the entrepreneurs if not coerced. So, Mises explicitly states that 'it would be nothing short of idiocy to assume that (the directors) are omniscient and infallible', adding that the question is 'whether any *mortal* man, equipped with the logical structure of the *human* mind, can be equal to the tasks incumbent upon a director of a socialist society' (*ibidem*); concluding that 'It is vain to comfort oneself with the hope that the organs of the collective economy will be 'omnipresent' and 'omniscient'. We do not deal in praxeology with the acts of the omnipresent and omniscient Deity, but with the actions of man endowed with a human mind only. Such a mind cannot plan without economic calculation' (p. 710). This long note was necessary because very recently some Austrian economists, in their obsession with dehomogenizing Mises and Hayek, have concluded that Mises was assuming that socialism was impossible even under 'perfect knowledge' (i.e. 'omniscient' conditions), as if Mises argument were a mere computational problem inside the static framework of the pure logic of choice. See Joseph T. Salerno, 'Ludwig von Mises as Social Rationalist', *Review of Austrian Economics*, no. 4, 1990, pp. 36–41; idem, 'Postscript: Why a Socialist Economy Is 'Impossible'', in Ludwig von Mises, *Economic Calculation in the Socialist Commonwealth*, Auburn, AL: Praxeology Press, 1990, pp. 51–71; idem, 'Mises and Hayek Dehomogenized', *Review of Austrian Economics*, vol. 6, no. 2, 1993, pp. 113–146; Murray N. Rothbard, 'The End of Socialism and the Calculation Debate Revisited', *Review of Austrian Economics*, vol. 5, no. 2, 1991, pp. 51–76; idem, *The Present State of Austrian Economics*, working paper from the Ludwig von Mises Institute, Auburn, Alabama, November 1992, pp. 4–5.
17 For Mises, 'The essence of socialism is this: all the means of production are in the exclusive control of the organized community. This and this alone is socialism. All other definitions are misleading'. Ludwig von Mises, *Socialism*, New York: New York University Press, 1983, p. 211. And three years earlier (1919), we can read almost exactly the same definition in *Nation, State and Economy*, op. cit., p. 172. For the reasons put forward in the text, we believe that Mises was mistaken to make such an emphatic statement.
18 Hans-Hermann Hoppe, *A Theory of Socialism and Capitalism*, Boston, MA: Kluwer Academic Publishers, 1989, p. 2. Hoppe states that 'Socialism, by no means an invention of XIX century Marxism but much older, must be con-

ceptualized as an institutionalized interference with or aggression against private property and private property claims'.

19 The first one to use the term 'interventionism' in its economic sense was Ludwig von Mises in his book *Kritik des Interventionismus*, published in 1925 by Gustav Fischer Verlag in Jena (translated into English and published by Arlington House under the title *A Critique of Interventionism*, New York, 1976). See also Don Lavoie's article on 'The Development of the Misesian Theory of Interventionism', *Method, Process and Austrian Economics: Essays in Honor of Ludwig von Mises*, I.M. Kirzner (ed.), Lanham, MD: Lexington Books, 1982, pp. 169–193.

20 Thus, for example, Don Lavoie concludes that 'interventionism'

> can be shown to be self-defeating and irrational on much the same grounds on which Mises pronounced complete central planning impossible ... piecemeal government interference into the price system must be seen as similarly obstructive of this same necessary discovery procedure, and therefore as distortive of the knowledge which it generates. Thus the calculation argument may be used to explain many of the less-than-total failures resulting from government *tinkering* with the price system, in fundamentally the same way that it explains the utter economic ruin inevitably resulting from the attempted *abolition* of the price system.

See 'Introduction', *Journal of Libertarian Studies*, vol., no. 1, Winter 1981, p. 5. Israel Kirzner, on his part, has referred on several occasions to the *parallelism* between 'socialism' and 'interventionism'. See his 'Interventionism and Socialism: A Parallel', in 'The Perils of Regulation: A Market-Process Approach', Chapter 6 of *Discovery and the Capitalist Process*, op. cit., p. 121 onwards. We must criticize the idea, even defended by Mises on occasions, that economic calculation is possible in interventionist systems, as such calculation is impossible precisely in the areas where intervention takes place and, if, in general, some calculations may be made, it is because the system does not extend its intervention to the whole society (at least to the degree which characterizes real socialism).

5 The crisis of socialism

1 Professor Pascal Salin has dedicated his long academic career to the analysis and defence of free market and libertarian principles. This note on the Crisis of Socialism was written in his honour.

6 Entrepreneurship and the theory of free market environmentalism

1 Included in *Festschrift in Honour of Jacques Garello*, Kurt R. Leube, Angelo M. Petroni and James Sadowsky (eds), Turin: La Rosa Editrice, 1997, pp. 175–188.

2 This seminar was organized by Liberty Fund within the scope of the Huitième Université d'Été de la Nouveelle Économie, which took place from 5–14 September 1985 in Aix-en-Provence (School of Law of the University of Aix-Marseille). In addition to the author, the following professors took part in this seminar: John Baden (University of Montana); Baudouin Bouckaert (University of Gante); Jean-Pierre Centi (University of Aix-Marseille); Jacques Garello (University of Aix-Marseille); Michel Glais (University of Rennes); Jean-Louis Harouel (University de Poitiers); Jean-Dominique Lafay (University of Poitiers); Henri Lepage (Paris Business Institute); Leonard P. Liggio (Institute for Humane Studies); Jean-Philippe Mangin (RIP) (University of Nice); Christian Mouly (Uncitral International Centre of Vienna); Pascal Salin (University of Paris Dauphine); Alain Siaens (University of Louvaine) and Richard Stroup (University of Montana).

3 Corresponds to the original title of the work on this subject by Anderson and Leal (Terry L. Anderson and Donald R. Leal, *Free Market Environmentalism*, San Francisco, CA: Pacific Research Institute for Public Policy, 1991). These authors consider free market environmentalism as a 'new socio-political movement which advocates the defence of nature' through the market and free enterprise.

4 In fact, as Richard Stroup points out, the intellectual movement in favour of free market environmentalism starts to be conceived in the second half of the 1970s by a group of young nature-loving economists concerned about the environment, grouped around the University of Montana, the University of California in Los Angeles (UCLA) and the Public Choice Center. This group of economists gradually gave rise to a new discipline which, under the name of 'New Natural Resource Economics', is based on three theoretical bodies which are different but complementary: first, the theory of the Austrian School of Economics based on the study of the processes of social interaction which result from the creative force of entrepreneurship; second, the School of Public Choice, which makes theoretical analyses of the incentives, conditioning factors and results of the combined action of politicians, bureaucrats and voters; and, third, the evolution, development and basis of the economic theory of property rights. See Richard Stroup's work 'Natural Resource Scarcity and the Economics of Hope', published in *Economics and the Environment: A Reconciliation*, Walter E. Block (ed.), Canada: The Fraser Institute, 1990, p. 132. These ideas reached Europe at the now historic seminar organized by Liberty Fund in Aix-en-Provence in September 1985, cited in note 2.

5 See Jesús Huerta de Soto, *Socialismo, cálculo económico y función empresarial*, Madrid: Unión Editorial, pp. 45, 54 and, above all, 84–85.

6 First definition of the term '*ecología*' in the *Diccionario* of the Spanish Royal Academy, Madrid: Espasa Calpe, 1992 edition, p. 555.

7 What is more, as Walter Block states, it is not that there is a simple analogy between the market and the ecosystems, but that the laws of evolution and interaction in the two processes are very similar and, therefore, it could be said that environmentalism is simply a part of economic science (giving rise to the term 'free market environmentalism'), or, if one prefers, that economics itself would be a discipline included in another broader discipline, environmentalism. See Walter Block's article 'Environmental Problems, Private Rights Solutions', in *Economics and the Environment: A Reconciliation*, op. cit., p. 289.

8 Elsewhere I have defended the thesis that socialism should be defined as 'any system of institutional aggression against the free practice of entrepreneurship' and have tried to demonstrate that such an aggression has the effect of preventing the creation and discovery of the practical information necessary to adjust and coordinate the behaviour of human beings, thus making the development of civilization impossible. When, in any social area, specifically in those related to the natural environment, freedom of human action is prevented, there is the paradoxical result that human beings are unable to realize that they are acting inefficiently and uncoordinatedly, meaning that numerous social adjustments are not discovered and the most flagrant cases of environmental aggression are neither discovered nor remedied. In this respect, see Jesús Huerta de Soto, *Socialismo, cálculo económico y función empresarial*, op. cit., Chapters II and III, especially pp. 117–118.

9 The theory of the evolutionary development of institutions originates from Carl Menger, *Untersuchungen über die Methode der Socialwissenschaften und der Politischen Ökonomie insbesondere*, Leipzig: Duncker Humblot, 1883, p. 182, and Jesús Huerta de Soto, *Socialism, cálculo económico y función empresarial*, op. cit., pp. 68–73.

10 See, especially, Ludwig von Mises' judicious pioneer considerations in this respect in 'The Limits of Property Rights and the Problem of External Costs and Exter-

nal Economies', heading 6 of Chapter XXIII of *Human Action: A Treatise on Economics*, Chicago: Henry Regnery, third edition, 1966 (the first edition was published in 1949), pp. 614–663.

11 With regard to the basic principles of property law which are necessary for a free enterprise economy to function and their specific application to the case of environmental problems, see Murray N. Rothbard's thought-provoking article entitled 'Law, Property Rights and Air Pollution', included in *Economics and the Environment: A Reconciliation*, Walter Block (ed.), op. cit., pp. 233–279. In this article Rothbard defends and develops the application of the traditional principles of property law, which emerged through evolution and entrepreneurship in the way explained in the main text, to the new circumstances which unpredictably arise, refining their historical impurities and logical errors and proposing their application to the new realities which emerge as a result of the evolution of civilization. In this way, Rothbard explains the great advantages of, for example, the privatization of roads, air corridors, the different uses of the sea, air and subsoil, also indicating, with a great deal of ingenuity and imagination, how this could and should be put into practice technically and legally.

12 Although the literal expression was created by Garrett Hardin, the first analysis of the 'tragedy of the commons' was made by Mises in 1940 in his 'Die Grenzen des Sondereigentums und das Problem der external costs und external economies', heading VI of Chapter 10 of part IV of *Nationalökonomie: Theorie des Handelns und Wirtschaftens*, Geneva: Editions Union, 1940, 2nd edition Munich: Philosophia Verlag, 1980, pp. 599–605. Garrett Hardin's contribution, 'The Tragedy of the Commons', was published almost thirty years later, *Science*, December 1968, republished on pp. 16–30 of the book *Managing the Commons*, Garrett Hardin and John Baden (eds), San Francisco, CA: Freeman & Co., 1970. Hardin's analysis offers little more than Mises' and, moreover, reaches certain neo-Malthusian conclusions which we cannot share and which show that Hardin is a biologist rather than an economist. In particular, Hardin ignores the fact that having more children does imply a cost which is discounted *a priori* by the parents more or less explicitly. Moreover I have defended elsewhere the idea that the increase in the population is a necessary condition for all economic and social development and that the problem of the current underdeveloped societies is derived, rather than from the population, from the coercive imposition of institutions and economic systems which do not permit the creative practice of entrepreneurial capacity or the coordinated development of free and efficient markets (socialism and interventionism). See Jesús Huerta de Soto, *Socialismo, cálculo económico y función empresarial*, op. cit., pp. 80–83.

13 As Mises rightly points out (*Human Action*, op. cit., p. 917), the problem of public goods emerges from the existence of *external positive effects* with regard to the resources where there is a joint offer and no rivalry in their consumption and has, therefore, an intrinsic entity, completely different from the cases of *external costs* which arise whenever the definition and/or defence of property rights over natural resources is prevented, giving rise to the 'tragedy of the commons'. It is, therefore, analytically erroneous to apply the concept of 'public good' to the problem of the deterioration of the environment with which we are dealing. Incidentally, I have argued elsewhere that public goods as a whole tends to become empty of content in a non-intervened economy and that, therefore, the static analysis of its supposed existence cannot be used to justify the existence of the state. See Jesús Huerta de Soto, *Socialismo, cálculo económico y función empresarial*, op. cit., pp. 36–37.

14 'It is true that where a considerable part of the costs incurred are external costs from the point of view of the acting individuals or firms, the economic calculation established by them is manifestly defective and their results deceptive. But this is

not the outcome of alleged deficiencies inherent in the system of private ownership of the means of production. It is on the contrary a consequence of loopholes left in this system. It could be removed by a reform of the laws concerning liability for damages inflicted and by rescinding the institutional barriers preventing the full operation of private ownership'. Ludwig von Mises, *Human Action: A Treatise on Economics*, op. cit., pp. 657–658.

15 Moreover, those who defend the theory of public property commit an irresolvable logical contradiction when they try to resolve the management thereof through the democratic political system. This is the case because they try to solve a problem of 'external effects' by creating another similar problem which is much greater. In fact, given that the effort of obtaining information on political matters and acting and voting thereon on the basis of sound knowledge benefits the whole community, implying a high individual cost for each actor, a typical case of positive external effects is generated, which leads human beings to, in general, ignore the democratic processes, tending not to obtain adequate information or participate. How will the democrats resolve this contradiction inherent in their system? By justifying institutional coercion on the citizens so that they obtain the information necessary and vote in the democratic system? Would this not mean the death of the democratic system and the emergence of an iron dictatorship? It is evident, therefore, that the attempt to define and manage public property through political processes generates a much greater public good problem, which cannot be solved by political means.

16 Effectively, according to Israel M. Kirzner, we cannot have today the knowledge which will only be created tomorrow by entrepreneurs acting in an appropriate institutional environment and trying to solve the problems and face the challenges related to the environment. But precisely what prevents us from knowing the specific solutions to be adopted (entrepreneurship) is what paradoxically allows us to feel secure and confident that the most appropriate solutions to the environmental problems will be adopted at any given moment. See Israel M. Kirzner, *Discovery and the Capitalist Process*, Chicago, IL: The University of Chicago Press, 1985, p. 168.

17 *Second-best* solutions, of a temporary and subsidiary nature, have also been considered for the areas in which the immediate privatization appears less viable and, in general, are based on the creation of 'markets' of *permits* or rights to pollute, capture certain species, etc. This system could, in some cases, be somewhat more efficient than those currently employed, although it leaves a great weight on bureaucratic intervention to fix, for example prices and the total amount of pollution or fishing which can be carried out. It should be reiterated that *second-best* solutions must always be put into practice on a temporary and subsidiary basis, without losing sight of the fact that the fundamental goal must be to make the free practice of entrepreneurship possible and that the latter should creatively discover the technical innovations and solutions which are necessary to define and defend appropriately the corresponding property rights. Second-best solutions are parallel to those 'market socialism' reforms that were so deep a failure in the former communist countries of Eastern Europe. The theoretical reasons for the failure of second-best solutions and market socialism can be found in Jesús Huerta de Soto, *Socialismo, cálculo económico y función empresarial*, op. cit., pp. 365–386.

18 It is disheartening that, up to now, the tendency in Spain has been the exact opposite of the tendency indicated by the conclusions of free market environmentalism. It is enough to remember the Water Act promulgated by the socialist government which eliminated the existing property rights over subsoil water. We hope that this tendency will change in the future, above all in the non-socialist local or regional administrations which study the environmental problems less dogmatically. Thus, it would be very easy to start by privatizing numerous items

of public property (zoos, natural parks, garbage collection services, etc.) and equally easy, in relative terms, to introduce *second-best* solutions in relation, for example, to the pollution rights of heating fuelled by coal and gas-oil in the buildings of the major Spanish cities, specifically Madrid. They are measures with a low political cost which could be taken quickly, the benefits of which would make it easier to take the subsequent steps ahead in the reform process tending towards the privatization of other natural resources and environmental areas which, today, appear more problematic.

19 The essential political principle which must be defended is not, therefore, 'he who pollutes pays', as has been clumsily established in the political programmes of the Spanish centre-right politicians, but rather the principle that 'he who pollutes indemnifies those who are polluted and, possibly, is penalized through a criminal process if there is culpability or negligence in the damage and no voluntary agreement is reached with the prejudiced parties'.

20 Another of the great advantages of the *free market environmentalism* theory is that it demolishes the entire analysis based on *sustained development*, which has been prevalent to date due to the support of many ingenuous environmentalists and natural scientists who are not familiar with economic theory.

7 A theory of liberal nationalism

1 I use the term *liberal* in its traditional Spanish sense.
2 Published in *Il Politico*, Pavia: University of Pavia, Year LX, no. 4 (175), October–December 1995, pp. 583–598.
3 Thus, as an example, it may be seen how the autonomous Treasury of the Basque Country, following the example of the local legislation of Navarra, has eliminated *de facto* inheritance tax between relatives for the Basques, which means a very important improvement in comparison with the citizens of the rest of Spain.
4 On the Austrian theory of social institutions and the concept of society, understood as a spontaneous process, see Carl Menger, *Investigations into the Method of the Social Sciences with Special Reference to Economics*, New York: New York University Press, 1985, p. 158.
5 On the consideration of nations as spontaneous orders or subgroups of civil society which compete in the social process with other national orders, see Ludwig von Mises' book *Nation, State and Economy: Contributions to the Politics and History of our Time*, New York and London: New York University Press, 1983. This book is the English translation of the book originally published by Ludwig von Mises just after the First World War with the title *Nation, Staat und Wirtschaft: Beiträge zur Politik und Geschichte der Zeit*, Vienna and Leipzig: Manzsche Verlags-und Universitäts-Buchhandlung, 1919. It is very significant that this important book has also been very recently published in Italian with the title *Stato, Nazione ed Economia*, Turin: Bollati Boringheri, 1994. Mises' suggestive ideas on nationalism were subsequently developed in his outstanding book *Omnipotent Government: The Rise of the Total State and Total War*, New York: Arlington House, 1969 (the first edition was published in 1944 by Yale University Press). Ludwig von Mises was a unique and specially qualified witness of the serious events which resulted in the two world wars of the last century and which, with his normal discernment, he explains and comments in great depth in the two books mentioned above.
6 See my article 'Entrepreneurship and the Economic Analysis of Socialism', included in Gerrit Meijer (ed.), *New Perspectives on Austrian Economics*, London and New York: Routledge, 1995, pp. 228–253 (Chapter 4 of this book).
7 Perhaps the diagnosis of Fernando Pessoa is more exact, when he considers that there are three different nations in Iberia, Castilian, Catalonian and the Galician-

Portuguese nation, included in two different states: Spain and Portugal. Pessoa does not refer to the Basque nation, perhaps because he considers it a nation in regression which has almost completely disappeared and been included in others. See his articles 'Para o Ensaio "Iberia"' and 'Principios do Nacionalismo Liberal', included in Fernando Pessoa, *Obra Poética e em Prosa*, vol. III, Lello & Oporto: Irmâo editores, 1986, pp. 979–1,009 and 1,125–1,136.

8 See, in this respect, the interesting article by Hans-Hermann Hoppe, 'Against Centralization', published in *Salisbury Review*, June 1993, pp. 26–28. And also Murray N. Rothbard, 'Nations by Consent: Decomposing the Nation State', *Journal of Libertarian Studies*, vol. II, no. 1, Fall 1994, pp. 1–10.

9 On the beneficial consequences of the population increase and immigration, see the works of Julian L. Simon, especially his *Population Matters: People, Resources, Environment and Immigration*, London: Transaction Publishers, 1990, and also *The Economic Consequences of Immigration*, Oxford: Basil Blackwell, 1989.

10 This is the position of most of the population of Catalonia and, above all, of the Basque Country, whose nationality is basically Castilian and whose political rights are indisputable, as they have resided in these geographical regions for many years, or even generations.

11 This phenomenon is precisely what the European socialist leaders aim to avoid when they aspire to create a social and interventionist European state, for example Felipe González when he negatively criticises 'the Europe of the merchants' designed in the Treaty of Rome.

12 This mission, therefore, of the states, included exclusively within the jurisdictional field of defence of personal rights and freedom of trade, is to prohibit, for example, limitations on commercial hours and other measures of coercive intervention which have recently been taken in Catalonia and other Spanish regions and which, in view of their special nature, are more defended against the beneficial effects of inter-regional competition.

13 In the words of Mises:

> The way to eternal peace does not lead through strengthening state and central power, as socialism strives for. The greater the scope the state claims in the life of the individual and the more important politics becomes for him, the more areas of friction are thereby created in territories with mixed population. *Limiting state power to a minimum, as liberalism sought, would considerably soften the antagonisms between different nations that live side by side in the same territory.* The only true national autonomy is the freedom of the individual against state and society. The 'statification' of life and of the economy leads with necessity to the struggle of nations.

See *Nation, State and Economy*, op. cit., p. 96 (emphasis added).

14 This is what happened historically when Catalonian protectionism was imposed on the free trading Castile, or in the case of the promulgation of the bankruptcy law, made to measure to meet the requirements of Catalonia after the bankruptcy of the Bank of Barcelona, or, more recently, in the political support provided to the interventionist and corrupt regime which is currently in power in Madrid to the detriment of the rest of Spain, thanks to the support received from Catalonian nationalism.

15 As Ludwig von Mises has correctly shown, 'within a system of interventionism the absence of inter-state trade barriers shifts the political centre of gravity to the federal government'. See *Omnipotent Government*, op. cit., p. 268 onwards, which sets out the reasons why, from the point of view of economic theory, measures of intervention and socialisation in a free trade environment are always detrimental to the nations which constitute the state and favour the political centre of the latter.

16 'A nation that believes in itself and its future, a nation that means to stress the sure feeling that its members are bound to one another not merely by accident of birth but also by the common possession of a culture that is valuable above all to each of them, would necessarily be able to remain unperturbed when it saw individual persons shift to other nations. A people conscious of its own worth would refrain from forcibly retaining those who wanted to move away and from forcibly incorporating into the national community those who were not joining it of their own free will. To let the attractive force of its own culture prove itself in free competition with other peoples – that alone is worthy of a proud nation, that alone would be true national and cultural policy. The means of power and of political rule were in no way necessary for that'. Ludwig von Mises, *Nation, State and Economy*, op. cit., p. 76. Rarely have words of greater content, courage and exactitude been written than these of Ludwig von Mises in relation to the concept and ideal of liberal nationalism.

8 A libertarian theory of free immigration

1 This article originally appeared in English under the title 'A Libertarian Theory of Free Immigration', in the *Journal of Libertarian Studies*, vol. 13, no. 2, Summer 1998, pp. 187–197. It was my contribution to the immigration symposium which this journal published and in which Ralph Raico, Julian Simon, John Hospers, Tibor Machan, Gary North and Hans-Hermann Hoppe also participated.
2 Murray N. Rothbard himself became aware of the problem posed by forced immigration at international level as follows: 'I began to rethink my views on immigration when, as the Soviet Union collapsed, it became clear that ethnic Russians had been encouraged to flood into Estonia and Latvia in order to destroy the cultures and languages of these people'. See Murray N. Rothbard, 'Nations by Consent: Decomposing the Nation-State', *Journal of Libertarian Studies*, vol. 11, no. 1, Fall 1994, p. 7.
3 Rothbard, 'Nations by Consent', op. cit., p. 6.
4 This process is explained in detail in Jesús Huerta Soto, *Socialismo, cálculo económico y función empresarial*, Madrid: Unión Editorial, 1992, pp. 80–83.
5 F.A. Hayek, *The Fatal Conceit: The Errors of Socialism*, Chicago, IL: University of Chicago Press, 1988, p. 133.
6 It should be recognized, however, that the technological revolution in the computer communications field (Internet etc.) means that geographical movements are becoming increasingly unnecessary in order to achieve the ends pursued by human action. A good summary of other advantages of emigration and immigration, which acknowledges the importance of the entrepreneurial capacity of emigrants but which, in my opinion, is too much rooted in neoclassical economic analysis, may be found in Julian L. Simon, *Population Matters: People, Resources, Environment and Immigration*, New Brunswick, NJ: Transaction Publishers, 1996, pp. 263–303.
7 We can, however, imagine many of the entrepreneurial solutions that would emerge spontaneously by simply observing, as a point of comparison, how the great problems that were initially posed by the huge flows of tourists that are today so common all over the world were solved. The development of means of transport, the hotel, tourist and leisure industries, the proliferation of travel agencies, and all kinds of intermediaries that organize and guarantee the trips from start to finish are all institutions which, in a much broader field, would emerge in an anarcho-capitalist state. We should remember that the volume of movements for tourist or business reasons is enormous. Thus, for example, my own country, Spain, receives more than 40 million tourists each year – more than the number of inhabitants of the country!

8 Hans-Hermann Hoppe, 'Small Is Beautiful and Efficient: The Case for Secession', *Telos* 107, Spring 1996, p. 101. On the same issue, see Rothbard, 'Nations by Consent', op. cit.; also Jesús Huerta de Soto, 'A Theory of Liberal Nationalism', *Il Politico*, vol. 60, no. 4, pp. 583–598 (Chapter 7 of this book).
9 Hoppe, 'Small Is Beautiful and Efficient', op. cit., p. 101.
10 It is paradoxical to note how Julian Simon, in his enthusiasm to justify free emigration and highlight its positive effects, is willing for significant economic damage to be inflicted on emigrants, not only in cases where the value of their contributions to the public social security system is much higher than the benefits they receive, but also when he defends an auction system for immigration rights which, in his own words, 'will transfer a considerable part of the 'profit' from the pocket of the immigrants to the pockets of the natives'. Julian L. Simon, *Population Matters*, op. cit., p. 293.
11 The above principles should be applied today to both intranational and international emigration. Although it is true that, within the borders of the present-day nation-states, the greater cultural and economic uniformity means that, in general, the problems are not so serious, many external cost problems (for example problems of beggars and tramps) would be solved by consistently applying the mentioned principles. It is, however, in relation to international emigration that the need to apply these principles is most urgent. In any event, other measures that have sometimes been proposed – even by supposedly libertarian theorists – such as immigration quotas or auction systems for the right to be an immigrant, should be ruled out, since they conflict with libertarian ideals.

9 The crisis and reform of social security

1 Paper presented at the Mont Pèlerin Society Regional Meeting, Rio de Janeiro, 5–9 September 1993 and published in the *Journal des économistes et des études humaines*, Bilingual Journal of Interdisciplinary Studies, Paris and Aix-en-Provence, vol. 5, no. 1, March 1994, pp. 127–155.
2 This theoretical principle was empirically illustrated with the historical case of the United States social security system in 1971 by Martin Feldstein in 'Social Security, Induced Retirement and Aggregate Capital Accumulation', *Journal of Political Economy*, vol. 82, September–October 1974. Furthermore, some simulation studies suggest that unfunded social security systems of the scale observed in the 1980s in many developed economies could reduce the long-run capital stock of these economies by 20–30 per cent (see, for example, Laurence J. Kotlikoff, 'Social Security and Equilibrium Capital Intensity', *Quarterly Journal of Economics*, vol. 93, no. 2, May 1979, pp. 183–207; and A.J. Auerbach and L. J. Kotlikoff, *Dynamic Fiscal Policy*, Cambridge: Cambridge University Press, 1987). In addition, Gary Becker doubts that social security reduces the rate of private savings (see 'The Family, Altruism and Public Policy', Mont Pèlerin Society Meeting, St Vincent, Italy, September 1986, p. 9). In note 14 we will criticize Becker's neoclassical rationalization of public social security systems.
3 See my article 'Experiencias Internacionales sobre la Crisis de la Seguridad Social', *Boletín de Estudios Económicos*, vol. XL, Bilbao, August 1985, pp. 327–378, in which I also refer to the bibliography corresponding to the cases of Switzerland, France and Japan (p. 328).
4 I have attempted elsewhere to integrate the effects of savings from pension planning with the Austrian theory of economic cycles, as it has been developed by Ludwig von Mises and F.A. Hayek. See my article 'Interés, Ciclos Económicos y Planes de Pensiones', International Congress of Pension Funds, Madrid, 1984, pp. 458–468, together with my 'La Teoría Austriaca del Ciclo Económico', *Moneda y Crédito*, no. 152, Madrid, March 1980.

5 'Denn die Versicherungsbeiträge gehen immer zu Lasten des Lohnes, gleichviel, ob sie von den Unternehmern oder von den Arbeitern eingehoben werden. Auch das, was der Unternehmern für die Versicherung aufwenden muß, belastet die Grenzproduktivität der Arbeit und schmälert damit den Arbeitslohn.' See Ludwig von Mises, *Die Gemeinwirtschaft; Untersuchungen über den Sozialismus*, Gustav Fischer, Jena, 1922 and 1932, Munich: Philosophia Verlag, 1981, p. 442. The English translation can be found, for instance, on p. 430 of the best English edition, *Socialism: An Economic and Sociological Analysis*, translated by J. Kahane, Indianapolis, IN: Liberty Classics, 1981. Almost thirty years later, von Mises developed this same idea in much more detail, not only in a more generalized way, referring it to all 'social gains' (see *Human Action*, third edition, Henry Regnery, 1966, p. 617), but also specifically elaborating on the question of upon whom the incidence of the cost of public social security systems falls. See Ludwig von Mises, 'Economic Aspects of the Pension Problem', Chapter VII of *Planning for Freedom and Twelve Other Essays and Addresses*, South Holland, IL: Libertarian Press, first edition 1952, third memorial edition 1974, pp. 83–86. Finally, we should mention an interesting empirical illustration of this important argument that has been prepared with the historical data of several countries by John A. Prittain, in 'The Incidence of Social Security Payroll Taxes', *American Economic Review*, March 1971.

6 This trend is similar to that in other developed countries, although there are some differences. For example, in France, there were 4 contributors per pensioner in 1974 and, only ten years later, in 1984, this ratio had been reduced to 3.4 contributors per pensioner. An accelerated decrease in this ratio continues at present. In the United States, there were 17 workers for each pensioner in 1950; in 1970, there were only 3 persons working per pensioner and it is estimated that, at the beginning of the next century, the ratio will have been reduced to 2 active persons for each pensioner. By the year 2040, it is expected that two-fifths of the total population of the USA will be over 64. See Laurence J. Kotlikoff, 'Social Security', *The New Palgrave Dictionary of Economics*, John Eatwell, Murray Milgate and Peter Newman (eds), London: Macmillan, 1987, vol. IV, p. 415. This trend is also reproduced in the less developed countries in accordance with their economic and cultural growth, the standard of living and health care improving and the birth rate subsequently decreasing. The increase in the lifespan and the gradual aging of the population appear, historically, to accompany the maturing stages in the economic development process. See my 'Crisis de la Seguridad Social y el Papel de los Planes de Pensiones Privados en su Reforma', in *Prospects for Social Insurance and Private Employee Benefit Plans*, Transactions of the 23rd International Congress of Actuaries, vol. II, Helsinki, 1988, pp. 477–498.

Finally, it should be pointed out that the social security always originated from the wish to favour groups near to retirement who, without having made any contribution, acquired the right to receive a life pension at moments in history when the aging of the population which we describe above had not been felt. This demagogic utilization of social security, at an initial cost which was apparently easy to support, together with the destruction of people's savings habits as a result of inflation and the Keynesian economic policy are the main reasons which explain the emergence of the public social security in almost all countries (see Ludwig von Mises, 'Pensions, the Purchasing Power of the Dollar and the New Economics', in *Planning for Freedom*, op. cit., pp. 86–93).

7 See my book *Socialismo, Cálculo Económico y Función Empresarial*, Madrid: Unión Editorial, 1992, in which, after proposing a new definition of socialism as 'any system of institutionalized aggression against human action or entrepreneurship', I develop a joint integrated theory on the theoretical impossibility of socialism and interventionism, together with its inevitable secondary effects of

lack of creativity and coordination, corruption and moral destruction. An English version of Chapter 3 of this book has been written under the title 'Economic Analysis of Socialism' and was presented in the First European Conference on Austrian Economics, Maastricht, 9–11 April 1992 (Chapter 4 of this book). My theory of socialism is the natural result of putting together the Austrian analysis of entrepreneurship, developed mainly within the framework of Israel M. Kirzner, with the theory of coercion as the main defining characteristic of socialism, which we owe to Murray N. Rothbard and Hans H. Hoppe (see his *A Theory of Socialism and Capitalism*, Amsterdam: Kluwer Academic Publishers, 1989, p. 2). Incidentally, it is very easy to realize that, within the well-known classification of types of intervention owed to Rothbard, social security systems are a typical case of *binary* coercion, in which the state 'enforces a coerced *exchange* between the individual subject and himself' (M.N. Rothbard, *Power and Market; Government and the Economy*, Menlo Park, CA: Institute for Humane Studies, 1970, pp. 9 and 135–136).

8 Social security 'is the target of complaints from all sides. Persons securing payments complain that the sums are inadequate to maintain the standard of life they had been led to expect. Persons paying social security taxes complain that they are a heavy burden. Employers complain that the wedge introduced by the taxes between the cost to the employer of adding a worker to his payroll and the net gain to the worker of taking a job creates unemployment. Taxpayers complain that the unfunded obligations of the social security system total many trillions of dollars, and that not even the present high taxes will keep it solvent for long. And all complaints are justified'. Milton and Rose Friedman, *Free to Choose; A Personal Statement*, New York: Harcourt Brace Jovanovich, 1980, p. 102. On p. 106 of the same book, Friedman, moving away from Becker's analysis which we will criticize in note 14, indicates the fundamental problem when he states that

> The difference between Social Security and earlier arrangements is that Social Security is compulsory and impersonal – earlier arrangements were voluntary and personal. Moral responsibility is an individual matter, not a social matter. Children helped their parents out of love and duty. They now contribute to the support of someone else's parents out of compulsion and fear. The earlier transfers strengthened the bonds of the family; the compulsory transfers weaken them.

9 See the Austrian analysis of the effects of social security on the allocation of capital and labour produced by Roger W. Garrison, 'Misdirection of Labor and Capital under Social Security', *Cato Journal*, vol. 3, no. 2, Fall 1983, pp. 513–529.
10 See Chapter 19, on 'Social Security', of F.A. Hayek's *The Constitution of Liberty*, Chicago, IL: The University of Chicago Press, 1960, pp. 285–323 and 509–515. Hayek concludes that

> there can be little doubt, indeed, that for the tasks of the magnitude of, say, the provision of Social Security services for the whole nation, the single comprehensive organization is not the most efficient method, even for utilizing all the *knowledge* already available, and still less the method most conducive to a rapid development and spreading of *new knowledge*. As in many other fields, the very complexity of the task requires a technique of coordination which does not rely on the conscious mastery and control of the parts by a directing authority but is guided by an impersonal mechanism.

(p. 511). Along the same line of reasoning, see the even more developed and deep analysis of Israel M. Kirzner included in his 'The Perils of Regulation: A Market

Process Approach', *Discovery and the Capitalist Process*, London: Routledge, 1991, pp. 136–145.
11 This idea was first written by Ludwig von Mises in 1949, *Human Action*, first edition, Yale University Press, p. 613. F.A. Hayek endorsed it entirely when he stated eleven years later that the social security system 'produces the paradox that the same majority of the people whose assumed inability to choose wisely for themselves is made the pretext for administering a large part of their income for them is, in its collective capacity, called upon to determine how the individual incomes are to be spent'. See Chapter 19 on 'Social Security', *The Constitution of Liberty*, op. cit., p. 290.
12 Ludwig von Mises concludes that 'Social Security does not enjoin upon the employers the obligation to expend more in buying Labor. It imposes upon the wage earners a restriction concerning the spending of their income. *It curtails the worker's freedom to arrange his household according to his own decisions*' (emphasis added). *Human Action*, third revised edition, Chicago, IL: Henry Regnery, 1966, p. 617.
13 I cannot agree with Gary Becker's neoclassical rationalization of public social security systems. According to Becker, referring to public social security, 'children would be *happy* (!) to enter into a social compact with their parents whereby the children support their parents when old at current levels in return for a commitment to the current level of public support for children' (*A Treatise on the Family*, Cambridge, MA: Harvard University Press, 1991, p. 373). In our opinion, Becker's analysis is methodologically misguided, precisely for the same reasons as explained by the theorists of the Austrian School of Economics in the critical analysis of the Neoclassical-Walrasian School which they developed in the course of the debate on the impossibility of economic calculation under socialism. Specifically, we should criticize the too short-sighted static equilibrium analysis and concept of 'rationality' used by Becker, together with the pure Robbinsian maximizer approach that agents follow in Becker's well-known economic analysis of the family. This typical methodological approach of the Chicago School of Economics has been brilliantly criticized by Israel M. Kirzner in his 'Self-Interest and the New Bashing of Economics' (*Critical Review*, vol. 4, nos. 1–2, Winter–Spring 1990, pp. 38–39, republished in *The Meaning of Market Process*, London: Routledge, 1992, pp. 207–208). Becker's analysis seems to be a mere ad hoc rationalization of aggregative phenomena, simply rooted in the view that 'people get what they want'. A dynamic theory of social process moved by the entrepreneurial creativity and coordinative efforts of real human beings, with an open universe of feelings, beliefs, goals and valuations, is completely lacking in Becker's analysis. This explains that, in the typical scientific Chicagoan tradition, the institutionalized aggression upon which social security is based is not even mentioned by Becker and in no way seems to worry him. Furthermore, he considers himself to have helped to 'understand the widespread government interventions into family arrangements' (*ibidem*, p. 379), as well as the way in which 'public expenditures on the elderly, together with public expenditures on children's education and other human capital, can fill the void left by the breakdown in the social norms' (*ibidem*, p. 370). Becker seems to confuse the crucial Hayekian distinction between family law in its material sense, which has been formed by evolution, well-known since the development of Carl Menger's theory of institutions, with the legislation of state commands enacted to establish public social security systems. The former is an unintended and spontaneous product of social interaction, and the latter a typical manifestation of institutionalized and deliberate aggression (i.e. socialism) on a specific area of the social body, with all the standard effects of the theoretical impossibility of reaching certain goals, lack of coordination and the creative trial of new solutions, and systematic moral corruption. For this reason we should maintain that the reality seems to be exactly the opposite to the

one mentioned before by Becker: social security, far from 'filling the void left by the breakdown of social norms', has been one of the main forces leading to the corruption and destruction of moral values and social norms. The explanation of social security, together with socialism in its different brands and manifestations, seems to be much more closely related to the scientistic error of constructivism and the historical political pressure of well-known privileged groups than with the spontaneous disappearance of traditional family values (see especially the last paragraph of note 8).

14 F.A. Hayek, 'Social Security', Chapter 19 of *The Constitution of Liberty*, op. cit., p. 292.
15 F.A. Hayek, 'The Mirage of Social Justice', vol. II of *Law, Legislation and Liberty*, Chicago, IL and London: The University of Chicago Press, 1976.
16 This is almost the title of the book by Peter J. Ferrara from which we draw extensively in this section. See Peter J. Ferrara, *Social Security; The Inherent Contradiction*, San Francisco, CA: Cato Institute, 1980.
17 This theoretical principle is illustrated by Peter J. Ferrara and John R. Lott, Jr in 'Rates of Return Promised by Social Security to Today's Young Workers', in *Social Security: Prospects for Reform*, ed. Peter J. Ferrara, Washington, DC: Cato Institute, 1985, pp. 13–32.
18 According to Hayek, 'It is easy to see how such a complete abandonment of the insurance character of the arrangement, with the recognition of the right of all over a certain age (and all the dependents or incapacitated) to an 'adequate' income that is currently determined by the majority (of which the beneficiaries form a substantial part), *must turn the whole system into a tool of politics, a play ball for vote-catching demagogues*'. 'Social Security', Chapter 19 of *The Constitution of Liberty*, op. cit., p. 296 (emphasis added).
19 Or, as Milton and Rose Friedman have graphically set out, 'In addition to the transfer from young to old, Social Security also involves a transfer from the less well-off to the better-off. True, the benefit schedule is biased in favour of persons with lower wages, but this effect is much more than offset by another. Children from poor families tend to start work – and start paying employment taxes – at a relatively early age; children from higher income families at a much later age. At the other end of the life cycle, persons with lower incomes on the average have a shorter lifespan than persons with higher incomes. The net result is that the poor tend to pay taxes for more years and receive benefits for fewer years than the rich – all in the name of helping the poor!' *Free to Choose*, op. cit., pp. 106–107.
20 I say 'initially' because the government is also very inefficient in providing help to needy people, and cannot compete technically and economically in this task with an army of competitive entrepreneurs who devote their efforts and ingenuity to discovering the actual needs of the poor, constantly finding and trying out new ways to resolve them in any specific circumstance of time and space. In the specific area of human solidarity, free human interaction and entrepreneurship, i.e. private charity, is much more efficient and ethical than governmental and systematic coercion (i.e. socialism).
21 'It is something of a paradox that the state should today advance its claims for the superiority of the exclusive single-track development by authority in a field that illustrates perhaps more clearly than any other how new institutions emerge not from design but by a gradual evolutionary process. Our modern conception of providing against risk by insurance is not the result of anyone's ever having seen the need and devising a rational solution. It has been well said that we owe our present life insurance techniques to a gradual growth in which the successive steps due to the uncounted contributions of anonymous or historical individuals have in the end created a work of such perfection that, in comparison with the whole, all clever conception due to single creative intelligences must seem very primitive.'

F A. Hayek, 'Social Security', Chapter 19 of *The Constitution of Liberty*, op. cit., p. 291.

22. 'A man who is forced to provide of his own account for his old age must save a part of his income or take out an insurance policy. A nation cannot prosper if its members are not fully aware of the fact that what alone can improve their condition is more and better production. And this can only be brought about by increased saving and capital accumulation.' Ludwig von Mises, 'Economic Aspects of the Pension Problem', *Planning for Freedom*, op. cit., pp. 92–93.

23. Of course, we cannot know today the knowledge that will be created by the entrepreneurs in the future to solve all the problems and challenges related to the proposed privatization of social security. However, in this specific field, we are particularly lucky, as we can grasp very important hints simply by observing the past evolution of the life insurance and private pension plan institutions. As Kirzner has clearly stated, 'The circumstance that precludes our viewing the future of capitalism as a determinate one is the very circumstance in which, with entrepreneurship at work, we are no longer confined by any scarcity framework. It is therefore the very absence of this element of determinacy and predictability that, paradoxically, permits us to feel confidence in the long run vitality and progress of the economy under capitalism'. Israel M. Kirzner, *Discovery and the Capitalist Process*, Chicago, IL: The University of Chicago Press, 1985, p. 168.

24. Incidentally, the traditional institution of life insurance can also be corrupted, especially when its principles are more or less abandoned under the pretext of 'financial deregulation' or the mixture with the alien banking institution. A historical example of this corruption effect on the life insurance industry is the one protagonized by John Maynard Keynes during the years that he was chairman of the National Mutual Life Assurance Society of London. Under his chairmanship, he promoted not only *ad hoc* equity investments against the traditional fixed rate bond investments, but also non-orthodox accounting principles at market value and even the distribution of dividends to policy-holders against unrealized gains. All these typical Keynesian aggressions against the traditional principles almost cost him the insolvency of his company when the Great Depression arrived. The negative influence of Keynes on the British life insurance sector can still be felt and, to some extent, has also affected the US market. The return to the basic traditional principles of the life insurance industry is a prerequisite for any serious reform based on the privatization of the public social security system. See Nicholas Davenport, 'Keynes in the City', in *Essays on John Maynard Keynes*, Milo Keynes (ed.), Cambridge: Cambridge University Press, 1975, pp. 224–225.

25. The standard work on this line of reasoning is the outstanding book by the late William H. Hutt, *Politically Impossible ... ?*, London: Institute of Economic Affairs, 1971.

26. A fifth stage could be envisaged, in which even the help to the poor with demonstrated need would be privatized and would be in the hands of private charity. For the reasons given in note 20, this entirely private system would be much more ethical and efficient than the intervention of the government, even if it acted in a very limited and purely subsidiary role.

27. This is the most urgent reform for many countries of continental Europe and South America. For those countries like Switzerland, the US, Chile, etc. which are much more advanced in the necessary reforms, the final jump to the fourth and fifth stages should also be planned.

28. I entirely agree with Roger Garrison when he states that 'Politically viable reforms may involve distortions of their own, such as the distortions associated with the tax-exempt status of retirement savings. These distortions, though lamentable, may be an unavoidable feature of any successful strategy designed to hasten the end of the coercive and inefficient Social Security program'. See his 'Misdirection

of Labor and Capital under Social Security', *Cato Journal*, vol. 3, no. 2, Fall 1983, p. 529.

29 We will now summarize the characteristics of these two models for the reform of social security which show the right direction and which may be a guide for the reform of many European and Latin-American countries in the near or more distant future. The most important feature of the reform of British social security is that it allowed a large part of the benefits to be contracted privately, outside the social security system. The history of the political struggle in favour of private contracting of social benefits began in 1960. Initially, the Conservative Party was in favour of the privatization system and the Labour Party opposed it. Whenever one of the parties came into power, it established its own programme for the reform of social security, modifying the system which had been established by the other party in the previous legislature. This continued until, in 1978, the most extensive system which exists to date of private contracting out of social security benefits was established in Great Britain as a result of a consensus between the Conservative and Labour Parties.

Essentially, Great Britain has two types of social security benefits. The first level, which is compulsory, pays a minimum pension which is received by all workers upon retirement, regardless of their income and the contributions they have paid. The second level, however, is calculated according to the income. The most important feature of the British system is that it allowed companies to contract the second level of pensions outside the state social security system, through a private instrument for financing pension schemes. This possibility was allowed on the condition that the company's private pension scheme provided benefits which were at least equally as good as those which the workers would have received if they had remained within the state social security system.

In the British system, each worker who, through his company, contracted out the second level of the social security through a private system received an annual reduction of £227 in his contributions, in exchange for repudiating the right to obtain an annual pension from the state social security system of £40.63 (all these data are calculated in accordance with the average salary earned in April 1978). In April 1983, *after five years, more than 45 per cent of British workers had contracted the second level of the social security through private pension schemes*. And, even more important, the British state had reduced the *future liabilities represented by the pensions corresponding to the second level of the social security, to which it was already committed, to half their current value*. Overall, the decrease in the current value of the future liabilities of all the benefits of the British social security may be estimated at 30 per cent over a period of only five years, thanks to the adoption of the system of private contracting. The results are highly encouraging, as they show to be untrue what many voices say when they consider themselves sufficiently authorized to affirm the impossibility of establishing a system based on capitalization due to its high cost, unless it is over a period of several generations (see, for instance, Michael T. Boskin, 'Alternative Social Security Reform Proposals', statement prepared for the National Commission of Social Security Reform, 20 August 1982).

It must be emphasized that, originally, the choice to contract social security benefits outside the social security was not an individual choice, but was an option granted only to the employers. That is to say, it was the employers who could contract the second level of social security benefits through a private pension scheme. However, in many cases, the contracting was the result of collective negotiation between employers and workers. The employers could not contract through private pensions schemes for part of their workers and leave the other part in the state social security system. If they took the decision to establish a private pension scheme system, they had to do so for all their workers, including those who would benefit most from the change, as they were closer to retirement, the cost for whom is very high through private pension schemes. Finally, it should be mentioned that the reduction in contributions arising from contracting the second level of benefits outside the social security is identical for all the workers, regardless of their age and income level.

The main differences between the Chilean and the British systems were the following: in the first place, to the contrary of Great Britain, the choice as to whether or not to contract social benefits privately was made at an individual level by each worker, not at company level as the result of the employer's decision. *In this respect, the Chilean system was socially much more advanced than the British one*; in the second place, the reduction in social security contributions for the workers who decide to contract the benefits outside it is 10 per cent. That is to say, the workers who remain within the system will pay a total contribution of 27 per cent of their salary; those who decide to contract the benefits outside the state system will pay a contribution of 17 per cent. This means that the 10 per cent difference is, theoretically, used to constitute the funds of the private pension schemes. Another distinctive feature of the Chilean system is that the administration has issued vouchers to cover the value of the contributions made up to the date of the reform of social security. These vouchers will lead to retirement pensions which will increase those obtained from the private system. The reform of the Chilean social security has met with enormous success, as in only one year more than 50 per cent of Chilean workers decided to contract their social security through private systems.

It must be pointed out that, in the Chilean and British models, there is a significant reduction in the contribution of the workers who, through their companies or for themselves, decide to contract the second level of social security benefits through private systems. However, in spite of the reduction, the contributions to the state social security systems continue to be very high. These contributions are necessary for the system to be able to continue to pay out the pensions currently payable to workers who are near retirement age and have not opted to transfer to the private social security system. The fact that the reduction in the contributions is considerably less than would correspond from an actuarial viewpoint shows that *the majority of the public, both in Chile and Great Britain, have been willing to pay a greater amount in contributions in exchange for contracting out a significant part of the social benefits through private systems*. That is to say, people are prepared and willing to pay to 'get out of' the state social security system and this is very favourable, as it allows the incentivation of the greater financing of the transitional reform process of the social security and, above all, the continuance of the financing of the pensions currently being paid to all those for whom the necessary reform has arrived too late.

30 See James Buchanan, 'Dismantling the Welfare State', Chapter 16 of *Liberty, Market and State; Political Economy in the 1980's*, Brighton: Harvester Press, 1986, pp. 178–185. I agree with Buchanan that any successful programme to reform the social security must be based on making it clear to the public that changing the current structure will benefit everyone (or at least that no one will lose), although I think that the *contracting out* mechanism which I propose is simpler than his proposal to 'pay off' individually in capital sums all the outstanding liabilities, financing those payments through the issue of additional public debt (*ibidem*, p. 182). Furthermore, the contracting out system seems to be the best mechanism to reveal social preferences on the reform of social security, and especially if the public at large is willing to pay voluntarily a greater overall amount in contributions in exchange for contracting out a significant part of the social benefits through private systems, as happened in the cases of England and

Chile, where a majority of the population showed that they were willing to pay to 'get out of' the public social security system.

31 'Political economists fulfil their proper role when they can show politicians that there do exist ways to close down the excesses of the welfare sate *without* involving default on the contracts that this state has obliged itself to. This approach to reform not only meets ordinary precepts of fairness; it also facilitates the political leader's task of organizing the consensus necessary to allow any institutional changes to be made at all.' James M. Buchanan, 'Dismantling the Welfare State', Chapter 16 of *Liberty, Market and State*, op. cit., p. 184.

32 See, for instance, the following example prepared with real data in Spain (US $1:100 Spanish pesetas (Ptas)).

Let us take the employer and employee's social security contribution figures of a bank clerk, single, with the grade of second administrative official and three years in the post. This person costs the company 1,080,060 Ptas, which he receives in 16 payments of 41,231 Ptas and the regularizations of the extra payments which amount to 673,522 Ptas. The worker also pays 45,500 Ptas to the social security and there is a withholding tax on his earnings of 88,880. This gives him a gross annual salary of 807,952 Ptas, the difference up to 1,080,060 Ptas (272,108 Ptas) being the employer's social security contribution.

From this starting point, making the simple assumption that the worker continues to work until he is 65 (45 more years), with the investment of his contributions (made by himself and the company) at an accumulative rate of 10 per cent, assuming that such contributions show an annual increase of 10 per cent, so that his contributions over the remaining years of his working life can be totalled, and placing them at the same compound interest rate of 10 per cent until the moment of his retirement, *the result would be that the capital so formed would amount to 574.9 million pesetas*, a figure which is reached thanks to the compound interest rate which should be applied. It is clear that if the workers knew these kinds of figures, they would exert very strong pressure in favour of the privatization of social security (this example has been taken literally from the book by Joaquín Trigo Portela and Carmen Vázquez Arango, *La Economía Irregular*, published in Barcelona in 1983 by the Servicio Central de Publicaciones de la Generalitat de Cataluña, pp. 181–190).

33 See the interesting article by Stuart Butler and Peter Germanis, 'Achieving Social Security Reform: A "Leninist" Strategy', *Cato Journal*, vol. 3, no. 2, Fall 1983, pp. 547–556.

34 The book edited by Peter J. Ferrara, *Social Security; Prospects for Reform*, Washington, DC: Cato Institute, 1985, must be strongly recommended with regard to all this section.

35 Again, the first economist to assert this fact was Ludwig von Mises, when he stated that 'there is no clearly defined frontier between health and illness. Being ill is not a phenomenon independent of conscious will and of psychic forces working in the subconscious'. And he concludes that 'by weakening or completely destroying the will to work, social insurance creates illness and inability to work. In short, it is an institution which tends to encourage disease and to intensify considerably the physical and psychic results of accidents and illnesses'. Ludwig von Mises, *Socialism; An Economic and Sociological Analysis*, op. cit., pp. 431–432.

36 'In a field that is undergoing as rapid change as medicine is today, it can, at most, be the bad average standard of service that can be provided equally for all. Where systems of state medicine operate, we generally find that those who could be promptly restored to full activity have to wait for long periods because all the hospital facilities are taken up by people who will never again contribute to the needs of the rest.' F.A. Hayek, *The Constitution of Liberty*, op. cit., pp. 299–300.

37 A voucher system or, even better, a mixed voucher/contracting out system could very easily be developed to privatize the public health insurance system, without harming anybody and significantly reducing the current excessive costs and inefficiencies. Among the ample literature that has been appearing in this field, we could mention the following: J.C. Goodman and G.L. Musgrave, *Patient Power; Solving America's Health Care Crisis*, Washington, DC: Cato Institute, 1992; *Health Care in America; The Political Economy of Hospitals and Health Insurance*, H.E. Frech III (ed.), San Francisco, CA: Pacific Research Institute for Public Policy, 1988; J.L. Bast, R.C. Rue and S.A. Wesburg, *Why We Spend too Much on Health Care*, Chicago, IL: The Heartland Institute, 1992; and regarding the situation in the United Kingdom all the publications of the Health and Welfare Unit of the Institute of Economic Affairs are very valuable.

10 A critical analysis of central banks and fractional-reserve free banking from the Austrian School perspective

1 Originally published in the *Review of Austrian Economics*, vol. 8, no. 2 (1995), pp. 25–38. The author dedicates this article to James M. Buchanan, in gratitude for his having publicly defended and supported the author when he put forward the most important ideas contained herein at the regional meeting of the Mont Pèlerin Society, which took place in Rio de Janeiro, September 1993. The author would also especially like to give his thanks to the late Professor Murray N. Rothbard, who took great trouble to make the exposition more readable.
2 F.A. Hayek, *The Fatal Conceit: The Errors of Socialism*, Chicago, IL: University of Chicago Press, 1989, pp. 102–104.
3 Vera C. Smith, *The Rationale of Central Banking and the Free Banking Alternative*, Indianapolis, IN: Liberty Press, 1990, Chapter 12, p. 169.
4 Israel M. Kirzner, *Discovery and the Capitalist Process*, Chicago, IL: University of Chicago, 1985, p. 168.
5 F.A. Hayek, *Denationalization of Money: The Argument Refined*, second edition, London: Institute of Economic Affairs, 1978, pp. 119–120. Hayek concludes: 'I expect that it will soon be discovered that the business of creating money does not go along well with the control of large investment portfolios or even control of large parts of industry'. I am afraid, however, that Hayek gives insufficient recognition of the fact – central to Mises's theory of money – that free market money must be *a commodity* money, and that competing kinds of money are dysfunctional of the very purpose of a medium of exchange, as the free market always generates a tendency of the convergence *toward one, universally* employed commodity money.
6 Before Mises, the most distinguished author who defended the 100 per cent reserve requirement was David Hume in his essay 'Of Money' (1752), where he states that 'no bank could be more advantageous, than such a one as locked up all the money it received, and never augmented the circulating coin, as is usual, by returning part of its treasure into commerce'. David Hume, *Essays: Moral, Political and Literary*, Indianapolis, IN: Liberty Classics, 1985, pp. 284–285.
7 On juridical considerations of the traditional legal principle in question, see not only all Title 3, Book 16 of the Digest, especially sections 7 and 8 on the bankruptcy of bankers (*El Digesto de Justiniano*, vol. 1, pp. 606–617, especially p. 112, published by Aranzadi, Pamplona, 1968), but also the fine argument by the Spanish Jesuit Luis de Molina, for whom the banker with a fractional reserve '*sins* by endangering his own capacity to meet his debts, even if in the long run he suffers no legal difficulties because his speculations with the clients' funds turned out well (quoted from *De Iustitia et Iure,* Maguntiae [1614], in Alejandro Chafuen, *Christians for Freedom: Late Scholastic Economics*, San Francisco, CA:

Ignatius Press, 1986, p. 146, notes 1–7). See also the refined conclusions of Pasquale Coppa-Zuccarí included in his definitive work *Il Deposito Irregolare* (Modena, 1901), quoted by, among others, Joaquín Garrigues in his *Contratos Bancarios*, second edition, Madrid, 1975, p. 365. All these considerations are also applicable to so-called financial operations with repurchase agreements at any moment and at face value (and not at a fluctuating secondary market price), since they disguise, by fraudulently using the law for a purpose for which it was not intended, what are really deposit contracts.

8 Ibid., pp. 367–368.
9 With regard to the class probability (objective), which is insurable, and the single event probability, influenced and determined by human action (not insurable), see Ludwig von Mises, *Human Action: A Treatise on Economics*, third revised edition, Chicago, IL: Henry Regnery, 1966, pp. 106–115; and also Jesús Huerta de Soto, *Socialismo, Cálculo Económico y Función Empresarial*, Madrid: Unión Editorial, 1992, pp. 46–48.
10 The temptation was enormous and almost irresistible, given how lucrative it was. We must remember that, in the final analysis, the system of fractional-reserve banking consists of creating loans from nothing and requiring that the borrowers return them in real money and with interest, too!
11 Sir James Steuart, *An Inquiry into the Principles of Political Economy: Being an Essay on the Science of Domestic Policy in Free Nations*, London: A. Miller and T. Caddell in the Strand, 1767, vol. 2, p. 301.
12 David Hume, 'Of Money', p. 284.
13 'The Bank of Amsterdam professes to lend out no part of what is deposited with it, but for every gilder which it gives credit in its books, to keep in its repositories the value of a gilder, either in money or bullion'. Adam Smith, *The Wealth of Nations*, London: W. Strahan and T. Caddell in the Strand, 1776, vol. 2, book 4, chapter 3, p. 72).
14 It is curious to observe how the bankers used all their influence and social power (enormous, in view of the large numbers of the public who received loans from them or were their shareholders) to impede and discourage the depositors from withdrawing their deposits, in the vain hope of avoiding the crisis. Thus, State Senator Condy Raguet of Pennsylvania concluded that the pressure was almost irresistible and that 'an independent man, who was neither a stockholder nor a debtor, who would have ventured to compel the banks to do justice, would have been persecuted as an enemy of society'. Letter from Raguet to Ricardo dated 18 April 1821, published in David Ricardo, *Minor Papers on the Currency Question 1805–1823*, Jacob Hollander (ed.), Baltimore, MD: The Johns Hopkins University Press, 1932, pp. 199–201; quoted in Murray N. Rothbard, *The Panic of 1819: Reactions and Policies*, New York: Columbia University Press, 1962, pp. 10–11.
15 A brief explanation of the Austrian theory of economic cycles, together with the most significant bibliography on the topic, may be found in my article 'The Austrian Theory of Economic Cycles', originally published in *Moneda y Crédito*, no. 152, Madrid, March 1980, and republished in vol. 1 of my *Lecturas de Economía Política*, Madrid: Unión Editorial, 1986, pp. 241–256. And also my book *Money, Bank Credit, and Economic Cycles*, Auburn, AL: Ludwig von Mises Institute, 2006.
16 See her article 'The Theory of Free Banking,' presented at the regional meeting of the Mont Pèlerin Society in Rio de Janeiro from September 1993, especially p. 5.
17 Mises, *Human Action*, pp. 648–88.
18 Ludwig von Mises, *The Theory of Money and Credit*, Indianapolis, IN: Liberty Press, 1980, p. 447.
19 Ludwig von Mises, 'Monetary Stabilization and Cyclical Policy', in *On the Manipulation of Money and Credit*, Irvington-on-Hudson, NY: Free Market Books, 1978, pp. 167–168.

20 Mises, *The Theory of Money and Credit*, p. 481.
21 F.A. Hayek, *Monetary Nationalism and International Stability*, New York: Augustus M. Kelley, 1971, pp. 81–84.
22 F.A. Hayek, *Denationalization of Money*, pp. 119–120.
23 See particularly Murray N. Rothbard's books *The Case for a One Hundred Percent Gold Dollar*, second edition, Auburn, AL: Ludwig von Mises Institute, 1991; and *The Mystery of Banking*, New York: Richardson & Synder, 1983; and his articles 'The Myth of Free Banking in Scotland,' *Review of Austrian Economics*, vol. 2, 1988, pp. 229–245, and 'Aurophobia: or, Free Banking on What Standard?', *Review of Austrian Economics*, vol. 6, no. 1, 1992, pp. 99–108.
24 Maurice Allais, 'Le Retour à l'État du privilège exclusif de la creation monétaire', in *L'Impôt sur le capital et la réforme monétaire*, Paris: Hermann Editeurs, 1985, pp. 200–210; and also his article 'Les Conditions monétaires d'une économie de marchés: des enseignements du passé aux réformes de demain,' *Revue d'économie politique*, vol. 3, May/June 1993, pp. 319–367.
25 This tradition was initiated by an anonymous 26-page pamphlet on 'Banking and Currency Reform', circulated in 1933 by Henry C. Simons, Aaron Director, Frank H. Knight, Henry Schultz, Paul H. Douglas, A. G. Hart and others and subsequently articulated by Henry C. Simons, 'Rules *Versus* Authorities in Monetary Policy', *Journal of Political Economy*, vol. XLIV, no. 1, February 1936, pp. 1–30; Albert G. Hart, 'The "Chicago Plan" of Banking Reform', *Review of Economic Studies*, vol. 2, 1935, pp. 104–116; and Irving Fisher, *100 Percent Money*, Aldelphi, New York, 1936, culminating in 1959 with the publication of Milton Friedman's book *A Program for Monetary Stability*, New York: Fordham University Press, 1960.
26 Mises, *Human Action*, p. 443. In short, according to Mises, it is a question of replacing the current tangle of administrative banking legislation by clear and simple articles in the commercial and criminal codes.
27 Thus, for example, see the works of Lawrence H. White, *Free Banking in Britain: Theory, Experience and Debate, 1800–1845*, Cambridge: Cambridge University Press, 1984; and *Competition and Currency: Essays on Free Banking and Money*, New York: New York University Press, 1989; those of George A. Selgin, *The Theory of Free Banking: Money Supply under Competitive Note Issue*, Totowa, NJ: Rowman and Littlefield, 1988; and *The Experience of Free Banking*, George A. Selgin and Kevin Dowd (eds), London: Routledge, 1992; and those of Kevin Dowd, *The State and the Monetary System*, New York: St Martin's Press, 1989, and *Laissez Faire Banking*, London: Routledge, 1993.
28 Quoted by Mises in *Human Action*, p. 446.
29 Only in the sense of indirectly getting closer to the ideal should we understand Cernuschi's position, mentioned by Mises (in *Human Action*, p. 446), when, in 1865, he said: 'I believe that what is called freedom of banking would result in a total suppression of banknotes in France. I want to give everybody the right to issue banknotes so that nobody should take banknotes any longer'.
30 The practical problems posed by the *transition* from the current monetary and banking system to a system in which, at last, the creation of money and the banking business were completely separated from the State have been theoretically analysed and solved by, among others, Murray N. Rothbard in his *Mystery of Banking*, pp. 249–269.

11 A critical note on fractional-reserve free banking

1 Originally published in the *Quarterly Journal of Austrian Economics*, vol. 1, no. 4, Winter 1998, pp. 25–49. I wrote it in response to the doctrinal controversy aroused in the US by my paper 'A Critical Analysis of Central Banks and Frac-

tional-Reserve Free Banking from the Austrian Perspective', which appeared in the *Review of Austrian Economics*, vol. 8, no. 2, 1995, pp. 25–38. This article, in which I criticized the modern economists who favour fractional-reserve free banking, was challenged by George A. Selgin and Lawrence H. White in their paper 'In Defence of Fiduciary Media – or, We Are *Not* Devo(lutionists), We Are Misesians!' which also appeared in the *Review of Austrian Economics*, vol. 9, no. 2, 1996, pp. 83–107. Before I had had a chance to reply to Selgin and White's criticism of my analysis, Professors Hans-Hermann Hoppe, Jörg Guido Hülsmann and Walter Block defended my position in their article 'Against Fiduciary Media', also printed in the *Review of Austrian Economics*, vol. 10, no. 2, 1997, pp. 125–163. Finally, I published this 'critical note' to sum up the key points in the debate and especially to show that even under the conditions Selgin and White regard as most favourable, fractional-reserve free banking can generate economic cycles.

2 We consider that the classification into four schools included by Vera C. Smith in the double-entry table in her well-known book (Banking School – Free or Central – and Currency School – Free or Central) is more accurate and provides greater clarification than the classification into only three schools proposed by Anna J. Schwartz. See Vera C. Smith *The Rationale of Central Banking and the Free Banking Alternative*, Indianapolis, IN: Liberty Press, 1990, pp. 144–145; and Anna J. Schwartz, 'Banking School, Currency School, Free Banking School', *The New Palgrave: A Dictionary of Money and Finance*, vol. I, London and New York: Macmillan Press, 1992, pp. 148–152. Given that, according to Vera C. Smith, the great majority of Banking School theorists (with the sole exceptions of Tooke, Bonamy Price, Cairnes and Collet) also defended a system of complete banking freedom, it could be considered not completely inaccurate to call the modern Free Banking School the Neobanking School.

3 As David Laidler points out, the recent interest in free banking and the development of the Fractional-Reserve Free Banking School stems from the book published by Friedrich A. Hayek in 1976 entitled, in its second edition, *Denationalization of Money: The Argument Refined, An Analysis of the Theory and Practice of Concurrent Currencies*, London: Institute of Economic Affairs, 1978. Before Hayek, Benjamin Klein had made a similar proposal in his article 'The Competitive Supply of Money', *Journal of Money, Credit and Banking*, no. 6, November 1974, pp. 423–453. See David Laidler, 'Free Banking Theory', *The New Palgrave: A Dictionary of Money and Finance*, London and New York: Macmillan Press, 1992, vol. II, pp. 196–197.

4 Lawrence H. White, *Free Banking in Britain: Theory, Experience and Debate, 1800–1845*, New York and London: Cambridge University Press, 1984, second edition, London: Institute of Economic Affairs, 1995; *Competition and Currency: Essays on Free Banking and Money*, New York: New York University Press, 1989; and also the articles written jointly with George A. Selgin, 'How Would the Invisible Hand Handle Money?', *Journal of Economic Literature*, vol. XXXII, no. 4, December 1994, pp. 1,718–1,749; and, more recently, 'In Defense of Fiduciary Media – or, We are *Not* Devo(lutionists), We are Misesians!', *Review of Austrian Economics*, vol. 9, no. 2, 1996, pp. 83–107. In addition, Lawrence H. White has compiled the most important works of the School in three volumes on *Free Banking: Volume I, 19th Century Thought*; *Volume II, History*; and *Volume III, Modern Theory and Policy*, Aldershot: Edward Elgar, 1993.

5 George A. Selgin, 'The Stability and Efficiency of Money Supply under Free Banking', *Journal of Institutional and Theoretical Economics*, no. 143, 1987, pp. 435–456, republished in *Free Banking: Volume III, Modern Theory and Policy*, Lawrence H. White (ed.), op. cit., pp. 45–66; *The Theory of Free Banking: Money Supply under Competitive Note Issue*, Totowa, NJ: Rowman & Littlefield, 1988; and also the article written jointly with Lawrence H. White, 'How Would the

Invisible Hand Handle Money?', op. cit.; 'Free Banking and Monetary Control', *Economic Journal*, vol. 104, no. 427, November 1994, pp. 1,449–1,459; and 'In Defense of Fiduciary Media – or, We are *Not* Devo(lutionists), We are Misesians!', op. cit.

6 Steven Horwitz, 'Keynes' Special Theory', *Critical Review: A Journal of Books and Ideas*, Summer–Autumn 1989, vol. III, nos. 3–4, pp. 411–434; 'Misreading the Myth: Rothbard on the Theory and History of Free Banking', published as Chapter XVI of *The Market Process: Essays in Contemporary Austrian Economics*, Peter J. Boettke and David L. Prychitko (eds), Aldershot: Edward Elgar, 1994, pp. 166–176; and also his book *Monetary Evolution, Free Banking and Economic Order*, Oxford: Westview Press, 1992.

7 Kevin Dowd, *The State and Monetary System*, New York: St Martin's Press, 1989; *The Experience of Free Banking*, London: Routledge, 1992; and *Laissez-Faire Banking*, London and New York: Routledge, 1993.

8 David Glasner, *Free Banking and Monetary Reform*, Cambridge University Press, Cambridge, 1989; 'The Real-Bills Doctrine in the Light of the Law of Reflux', *History of Political Economy*, vol. 24, no. 4, Winter 1992, pp. 867–894.

9 Leland B. Yeager and Robert Greenfield, 'A Laissez-Faire Approach to Monetary Stability', *Journal of Money, Credit and Banking*, no. XV (3), August 1983, pp. 302–315, republished as Chapter XI of *Free Banking*, Lawrence H. White (ed.), op. cit., vol. III, pp. 180–195; and Leland B. Yeager and Robert Greenfield, 'Competitive Payment Systems: Comment', *American Economic Review*, no. 76 (4), September 1986, pp. 848–849.

10 Richard Timberlake, 'The Central Banking Role of Clearinghouse Associations', *Journal of Money, Credit and Banking*, no. 16, February 1984, pp. 1–15; 'Private Production of Scrip-Money in the Isolated Community', *Journal of Money, Credit and Banking*, no. 4, October 1987 (19), pp. 437–447; 'The Government's License to Create Money', *Cato Journal: An Interdisciplinary Journal of Public Policy Analysis*, vol. IX, no. 2, Autumn 1989, pp. 302–321.

11 Milton Friedman and Anna J. Schwartz, 'Has Government Any Role in Money?', *Journal of Monetary Economics*, no. 17, 1986, pp. 37–72, republished as Chapter XXVII of the book *The Essence of Friedman*, Kurt R. Leube (ed.), Stanford, CA: Hoover Institution Press, Stanford University, 1986, pp. 499–525.

12 George Selgin also includes Gottfried Haberler (1931), Fritz Machlup (1940) and (with qualifications) F.A. Hayek (1935) among the continental European theorists who also upheld the analytical framework of monetary equilibrium. Regarding Keynes, Selgin concludes that 'Despite ... important differences between Keynesian analysis and the view of other monetary-equilibrium theorists, many Keynesians might accept the prescription for monetary equilibrium offered' in his book. See Selgin, *The Theory of Free Banking: Money Supply under Competitive Note Issue*, op. cit., pp. 56 and 59.

13 George A. Selgin, *The Theory of Free Banking: Money Supply under Competitive Note Issue*, op. cit., p. 34. The detailed analysis of this theory can be found in Chapters IV, V and VI of this book, and especially on pp. 64–69.

14 In fact, these and other banking doctrines had already been set forth at an embryonic stage by the anti-bullionist theorists of eighteenth-century Great Britain. See 'The Early Bullionist Controversy', 'The Bullion Report and the Return to Gold' and 'The Struggle over the Currency School', Chapters 5, 6 and 7 of Murray N. Rothbard, *Classical Economics: An Austrian Perspective on the History of Economic Thought*, vol. II, Edward Elgar, Aldershot, England, 1995, pp. 159–274; and also F.A. Hayek, 'English Monetary Policy and the Bullion Debate', Part III, Chapters 9–14 of *The Trend of Economic Thinking: Essays on Political Economists and Economic History*, W.W. Bartley III and Stephen Kresge (eds), *The Collected Works of F.A. Hayek*, vol. III, London: Routledge, 1991, pp. 127–344.

15 According to Stephen Horwitz, Lawrence White 'expressly rejects the real-bills doctrine and endorses a different version of the 'needs of trade' idea. For him the 'needs of trade' means *the demand to hold bank notes*. On this interpretation, the doctrine states that the supply of bank notes should vary in accordance with the demand to hold notes. As I shall argue, this is just as acceptable as the view that the supply of shoes should vary to meet the demand for them'. Stephen Horwitz, 'Misreading the Myth: Rothbard on the Theory and History of Free Banking', op. cit., p. 169.
16 'Free banking thus works against short-run monetary disequilibrium and its business cycle consequences.' George A. Selgin and Lawrence H. White, 'In Defense of Fiduciary Media – or, We are *Not* Devo(lutionists), We are Misesians!', op. cit., pp. 101–102.
17 It is curious to observe how the modern theorists of the Free Banking School, like the Keynesians and the monetarists, seem obsessed by short-term unilateral mutations in the demand for money. However, such mutations historically have been produced over an economic cycle (during the last stages of booms and in crises) which almost always begins as the result of *previous* mutations in the supply of new money created by the banking system. Apart from this, only exceptional disasters like wars and other catastrophes (natural or otherwise) could explain a sudden increase in the demand for money. Seasonal variations in the demand for money are of comparatively minor importance and a 100 per cent free banking system could easily adjust to them through some seasonal movements of gold and variation of prices. Moreover, for Mises, increases in the demand for money do not pose any problem of coordination, even if the banks do not try to adapt themselves to them by creating new credits. Thus, even in the event of an increase in savings (in other words, a decrease in consumption) which materializes entirely in an increase in cash balances (hoarding) and not in direct loans in the form of capital goods expenditure, there will be effective saving of the community's goods and services and a process whereby the productive structure will lengthen and become more capital intensive. If this occurs, the increase in cash balances will simply give rise to an increase in the purchasing power of money and, therefore, to a decrease in the nominal prices of consumer goods and the services of the different production factors which, however, will generate among themselves, in relative terms, the price disparities which are typical of a period in which savings grow and the structure of production becomes more capital intensive. See Ludwig von Mises, *Human Action: A Treatise on Economics*, Chicago, IL: Henry Regnery, 1966, pp. 520–523; and also the corresponding comment of Joseph T. Salerno included in 'Mises and Hayek De-Homogenized', *Review of Austrian Economics*, vol. VI, no. 2, 1993, especially pp. 144 onwards.
18 Hayek wrote that, in order to be neutral, 'the supply of money should be invariable'. F.A. Hayek, *Prices and Production*, London: Routledge, 1935, and New York: Augustus M. Kelley, 1967, p. 108. Remember also that Hayek's goal in *Prices and Production* was 'to demonstrate that the cry for an "elastic" currency which expands or contracts with every fluctuation of "demand" is based on a serious error of reasoning'. See p. xiii of Hayek's preface to the first edition, *Prices and Production*, London: Routledge, 1931.
19 Mark Skousen notes how a 100 per cent free banking system and pure gold standard is more elastic than Hayek's proposal and does respond to the 'needs of business': price deflation would stimulate new gold discoveries and would eventually cause an expansion in the gold-money supply without creating a boom–bust cycle. Skousen concludes that, 'Based on historical evidence, the money supply (the stock of gold) under a pure gold standard would expand between 1 to 5 per cent. And, most importantly, there would be virtually no chance of a monetary deflation under 100 per cent gold backing of the currency'. Mark Skousen, *The*

Structure of Production, New York and London: New York University Press, 1990, p. 359.

20 'Mises' support for free banking is based in part on his agreement with Cernuschi, who (along with Modeste) believed that freedom of note issue would automatically lead to 100 per cent reserve banking'. See George A. Selgin, *The Theory of Free Banking: Money Supply under Competitive Note Issue*, op. cit, p. 62; and also p. 164, where Selgin says that Mises 'believed that free banking will somehow lead to the suppression of fractionally-based inside monies'. A different interpretation of Mises' position has been given by Lawrence H. White, 'Mises on Free Banking and Fractional Reserves', *A Man of Principle: Essays in Honor of Hans F. Sennholz*, John W. Robbins and Mark Spangler (eds), Grove City, PA: Grove City College Press, 1992, pp. 517–533. Salerno criticizes White for defending the thesis that Mises was the prototype of the modern Fractional-Reserve Free Banking School theorists without realizing that Mises always criticized the essential positions of the Banking School and that, if he defended free banking, it was as an indirect procedure for attaining the final goal of a banking system with a 100 per cent reserve requirement. Salerno concludes that 'To the extent that Mises advocated the freedom of banks to issue fiduciary media, he did so only because his analysis led him to the conclusion that this policy would result in a money supply strictly regulated according to the Currency Principle. Mises' desideratum was to completely eliminate the destructive influences of fiduciary media on monetary calculation and the dynamic market process'. Joseph T. Salerno, 'Mises and Hayek De-Homogenized', *Review of Austrian Economics*, op. cit., p. 137 onwards and p. 146.

21 Ludwig von Mises, *Human Action*, p. 442 (emphasis added). A little later Mises adds that 'Free banking ... would not hinder a slow credit expansion' (ibid., p. 443). I think that Mises was, in *Human Action*, probably too optimistic when evaluating the role of free banking in limiting credit expansion. However, Ludwig von Mises from the second German edition of his book *The Theory of Money and Credit* (1924) had already stated that 'It is clear that banking freedom *per se* cannot be said to make a return to gross inflationary policy impossible'. Ludwig von Mises, *Theory of Money and Credit*, Indianapolis, IN: Liberty Fund, 1981, p. 436. (Ludwig von Mises, *Theorie des Geldes und der Umlaufsmittel*, Munich and Leipzig: Verlag von Duncker & Humblot, 1924, p. 408).

22 'The Banking School failed entirely in dealing with these problems. It was confused by a spurious idea according to which the requirements of business rigidly limit the maximum amount of convertible banknotes that the bank can issue. They did not see that the demand of the public for credit is a magnitude dependent on the banks' readiness to lend, and that the banks which do not bother about their own solvency are in a position to expand circulation credit by lowering the rate of interest below the market rate. ... Lowering the rate of interest is tantamount to increasing the quantity of what is mistakenly considered as the fair and normal requirements of business.' Ludwig von Mises, *Human Action*, op. cit., pp. 439–440.

23 Ludwig von Mises, *Human Action*, op. cit., pp. 427–428.

24 See Jörge Guido Hülsmann, 'Free Banking and Free Bankers', *Review of Austrian Economics*, vol. 9, no. 1, 1996, especially pp. 40–41.

25 See David Laidler, 'Free Banking Theory', *The New Palgrave Dictionary of Money and Finance*, op. cit., vol. II, pp. 197.

26 George A. Selgin, *The Theory of Free Banking: Money Supply under Competitive Note Issue*, op. cit., p. 82.

27 See, for example, Anna J. Schwartz, 'The Theory of Free Banking', manuscript presented at the 1993 Regional Meeting of the Mont Pèlerin Society, p. 3.

28 See Mark Skousen, *The Structure of Production*, op. cit., Chapter 8, pp. 269 and 359.

29 The possibility of greater credit expansions induced by commodity-money supply shocks should not either be discarded, although Selgin tends to minimize its importance. See George A. Selgin, *The Theory of Free Banking: Money Supply under Competitive Note Issue*, op. cit., pp. 129–133.
30 We should remember (note 21) that, for Mises, 'It is clear that banking freedom *per se* cannot be said to make a return to gross inflationary policy impossible', especially if an inflationary ideology prevails in the economic world:

> Many authors believe that the instigation of the banks' behaviour comes from outside, that certain events induce them to pump more fiduciary media into circulation and that they would behave differently if these circumstances fail to appear. I was also inclined to this view in the first edition of my book on monetary theory. I could not understand why the banks didn't learn from experience. I thought they would certainly persist in a policy of caution and restraint, if they were not led by outside circumstances to abandon it. Only later did I become convinced that it was useless to look for an outside stimulus for the change in the conduct of the banks. ... We can readily understand that the banks issuing fiduciary media, in order to improve their chances for profit, may be ready to expand the volume of credit granted and the number of notes issued. What calls for special explanation is why attempts are made again and again to improve general economic conditions by the expansion of circulation credit in spite of the spectacular failure of such efforts in the past. The answer must run as follows: according to the prevailing ideology of businessman and economist-politician, the reduction of the interest rate is considered an essential goal of economic policy. Moreover, the expansion of circulation credit is assumed to be the appropriate means to achieve this goal.

Ludwig von Mises, *On the Manipulation of Money and Credit*, Percy L. Greaves, Jr (ed.), New York: Free Market Books, 1978, pp. 135–136.
31 'Crises have reappeared every few years since banks began to play an important role in the economic life of people.' Ludwig von Mises, *On the Manipulation of Money and Credit*, Percy L. Greaves, Jr (ed.), op. cit., p. 134.
32 F.A. Hayek, *The Pure Theory of Capital*, London: Routledge & Kegan Paul, 1941 and 1976, p. 378.
33 F.A. Hayek, *The Pure Theory of Capital*, op. cit., p. 394. This seems to be the extreme case of the increase in saving all of which materializes in new holdings of bank money used by Selgin and White to illustrate their theory. See George A. Selgin and Lawrence H. White, 'In Defense of Fiduciary Media – or, We are *Not* Devo(lutionists), We are Misesians!', op. cit., pp. 104–105.
34 This hypothesis is perfectly possible, as Selgin and White themselves recognize when they say that 'An increase in *savings* is neither necessary nor sufficient to warrant an increase in fiduciary media'. George A. Selgin and Lawrence H. White, 'In Defense of Fiduciary Media – or, We are *Not* Devo(lutionists), We are Misesians!', op. cit., p. 104.
35 See F.A. Hayek, *Prices and Production*, op. cit., Lecture II, pp. 32–62; and Mark Skousen, *The Structure of Production*, op. cit., Chapters 5–6, pp. 133–214.
36 Selgin and White implicitly acknowledge this when they say that 'Benefits accrue to bank borrowers who enjoy a more ample supply of intermediated credit, and to everyone who works with the economy's consequently larger stock of capital equipment'. George A. Selgin and Lawrence H. White, 'In Defense of Fiduciary Media – or, We are *Not* Devo(lutionists), We are Misesians!', op. cit., p. 94.
37 'We deny that an increase in fiduciary media *matched by an increased demand to hold fiduciary media* is disequilibrating or sets in motion the Austrian business

cycle.' George A. Selgin and Lawrence H. White, 'In Defense of Fiduciary Media – or, We are *Not* Devo(lutionists), We are Misesians!', op. cit., p. 102–103.
38 John Maynard Keynes, *The General Theory of Employment, Interest and Money*. London: Macmillan, 1936, p. 83.
39 George A. Selgin, *The Theory of Free Banking: Money Supply under Competitive Note Issue*, op. cit., p. 54.
40 George A. Selgin, *The Theory of Free Banking: Money Supply under Free Note Issue*, op. cit., pp. 54–55. Selgin's thesis reminds us of the tautological identification of investment and savings which underlies Keynes' works and, according to Benjamin Anderson, is the equivalent of considering inflation identical to savings:

> One must here protest against the dangerous identification of bank expansion with savings, which is part of Keynesian doctrine. This doctrine is particularly dangerous today, when we find our vast increase in money and bank deposits growing out of war finance described as 'savings', just because somebody happens to hold them at a given moment of time. From this doctrine, the greater the inflation, the greater the savings!

Benjamin M. Anderson, *Economics and the Public Welfare: A Financial and Economic History of the United States, 1914–1946*, Indianapolis, IN: Liberty Press, 1979, pp. 391–392 (first edition, Van Nostrand, 1949). Selgin himself acknowledges that Keynesians 'who do not regard the liquidity trap as an important factual possibility would probably accept it [Selgin's framework of monetary equilibrium] as entirely adequate'. *Ibidem*, p. 59.
41 George A. Selgin, 'The Stability and Efficiency of Money Supply under Free Banking', op. cit., p. 440.
42 How can it be conceived that a banknote or bank deposit, which are money, constitute a financial asset and, therefore, represent, in turn, for the holder, the delivery of present money to a third party in exchange for future money? The conception of bank money as a financial asset clearly shows that duplicate payment means are created from nowhere: the money which is lent to, enjoyed and held by a third party, and the financial asset that the loan represents and which, in turn, is *also* said to be money.
43 Gerald P. O'Driscoll, 'Money: Menger's Evolutionary Theory', *History of Political Economy*, no. 18, 4, 1986, pp. 601–616.
44 George A. Selgin, *The Theory of Free Banking: Money Supply under Competitive Note Issue*, op. cit., p. 184, no. 20. In the example of our diagrams, for Selgin, the entire surface A of our triangles would be 'transfer credit' because it is 'credit granted by banks in recognition of people's desire to abstain from spending by holding balances of inside money' (*ibidem*, p. 60), whereas, for me (and Machlup) at least surface B would represent 'created credit' as the economic agents have not restrained their consumption by the volume represented by surface C.
45 See Kevin Dowd (ed.), *The Experience of Free Banking*, op. cit., pp. 39–46.
46 Kurt Schuler and Lawrence H. White, 'Free Banking History', *The New Palgrave Dictionary of Money and Finance*, op. cit., vol. II, p. 198.
47 See Jesús Huerta de Soto, 'New Light on the Prehistory of the Theory of Banking and the School of Salamanca', *Review of Austrian Economics*, vol. 9, no. 2, 1996, pp. 62–63; and Carlo M. Cipolla, *Il Governo della Moneta: La Moneta a Firenze nel Cinquecento*, Bologna: Societá editrice Il Mulino, 1990.
48 Sidney J. Checkland, *Scottish Banking: A History, 1695–1973*, Glasgow: Collins, 1973.
49 Thus, for example, George A. Selgin, discussing the period of fractional-reserve free banking in Chile from 1866 to 1874, states how it gave rise to an 'era of remarkable growth and progress, free of monetary crisis'. And he adds that,

during this period, 'Chile's railroad and telegraph systems were developed, the port of Valparaiso was enlarged and improved, and fiscal revenues increased by one-quarter'. All these phenomena suggest, according to the Austrian theory of economic cycles, that, during these eight years, there was a period of acute credit expansion, as Murray N. Rothbard points out in 'The Other Side of the Coin: Free Banking in Chile', *Austrian Economics Newsletter*, Winter 1989, pp. 1–4. Selgin, however, considers that the subsequent serious bank crisis was not due to the fractional-reserve free banking system but to the fact that the government maintained an artificial parity between gold and silver which, as gold was undervalued, meant a massive exit of the gold reserves from the country. See George A. Selgin, 'Short-Changed in Chile: The Truth about the Free Banking Episode', *Austrian Economics Newsletter*, Spring–Summer 1990, pp. 5 and 6 and note 3 of p. 7.
50 George A. Selgin, 'Are Banking Crises a Free-Market Phenomenon?', paper presented at the 1993 Mont Pèlerin Society Regional Meeting, Rio de Janeiro, Table 1(b), p. 27.
51 Murray N. Rothbard, *Classical Economics: An Austrian Perspective on the History of Economic Thought*, op. cit., vol. II, p. 491. Elsewhere, Murray N. Rothbard also argued that the fact that, in relative terms, there were fewer bankruptcies of banks in the supposedly free Scottish fractional-reserve banking system than in the English system does not in any way mean that the Scottish system was *superior*. In fact, bankruptcies of banks have been almost completely eliminated under the present systems based on a central bank and this does not mean that they are superior to a free banking system subject to the law, but rather the contrary. The existence of bank bankruptcies, far from indicating that the system works badly, may be a sign of the healthy social process of economic reaction that takes place in the market against the aggression implied by the privileged practice of banking with a fractional reserve. Thus, where there is a fractional-reserve free banking system and bank bankruptcies and suspensions of payments do not occur regularly, *it is inevitable to suspect that there are institutional reasons which defend the banks from the normal consequences of practising their activity with a fractional reserve and which are able to play a role similar to the one currently played by a modern central bank.* In short, the alleged historical case would not be a truly free banking system and, therefore, its supposed greater stability could not be considered as a historical illustration to support the conclusions of the theory of monetary equilibrium under free banking. Murray N. Rothbard, 'The Myth of Free Banking in Scotland', *Review of Austrian Economics*, vol. II, Lanham, MD: Lexington Books, 1988, pp. 229–245. Rothbard's thesis appears to be confirmed by Raymond Bogaert when he points out how, of the 163 banks known to have emerged in Venice since the end of the Middle Ages, there is documentary proof that at least 93 of them went bankrupt. Raymond Bogaert, *Banques et banquiers dans les cités grecques*, Leyden, Holland: A.W. Sijthoff, 1968, footnote 513 on p. 392.
52 George A. Selgin, 'Are Banking Crises a Free-Market Phenomenon?', op. cit., p. 2.
53 Kevin Dowd (ed.), *The Experience of Free Banking*, op. cit., pp. 40–45 and 46. It must be acknowledged that, in most cases, all these causes have coincided. This was the case, for example, in Chile, where the 'bad apples' or unscrupulous bankers went into alliance with the politicians and the latter, in turn, exploited the system for fiscal purposes. See George A. Selgin, 'Short-Changed in Chile: The Truth about the Free-Banking Episode', op. cit., pp. 5–7.
54 The multidisciplinary nature of the critical analysis of the fractional-reserve free banking system and, therefore, the importance of the juridical considerations, together with the economic ones, have also been brought into relief by Walter Block in his article 'Fractional Reserve Banking: An Interdisciplinary Perspective', published as Chapter III of the book *Man, Economy and Liberty: Essays in*

Honour of Murray N. Rothbard, Walter Block and Llewellyn H. Rockwell (eds), Auburn, AL: The Ludwig von Mises Institute, Auburn University, 1988, pp. 24–32. Walter Block also points out that it is very curious to note that none of the theorists of the modern Free Banking School have made any systematic critical analysis against the proposal to establish a banking system with a 100 per cent reserve. In fact, apart from some isolated comments by Horwitz, the Fractional-Reserve Free Banking School theorists still have not tried to show why a banking system with a 100 per cent reserve would not guarantee 'monetary equilibrium' free from economic cycles. See Stephen Horwitz, 'Keynes' Special Theory', *Critical Review*, vol. III, nos. 3–4, Summer–Autumn 1989, footnote 18 on pp. 431–432. The possible criticisms of a 100 per cent reserve free banking system have been handled systematically and refuted by Jörg Guido Hülsmann, 'Free Banking and Free Bankers', *Review of Austrian Economics*, op. cit., pp. 10–17.

55 Juan Iglesias, *Derecho Romano: Instituciones de Derecho Privado*, Barcelona: Ediciones Ariel, 1972.

56 Furthermore, the mere fact that the whole of this controversy on fractional-reserve free banking is taking place is also an indication that something strange is happening to the juridical foundation of this institution.

57 These problems have even been handled by European case law on several occasions during the last century. See the rulings cited in Jesús Huerta de Soto, 'A Critical Analysis of Central Banks and Fractional-Reserve Free Banking from the Austrian Perspective', *Review of Austrian Economics*, vol. 8, no. 2, 1995, pp. 29–32.

58 The legally-invalid (i.e. criminal) historical origin of fractional-reserve banking seems to me to be unquestionable. With regard to the dual economic availability of the same amount of money generated from nowhere by fractional-reserve free banking, see Hans-Hermann Hoppe, 'How Is Fiat Money Possible? – or, The Devolution of Money and Credit', *Review of Austrian Economics*, vol. VII, no. 2, 1994, p. 67.

59 The subjectivist conception on which Austrian economic theory is based is completely parallel to the legal point of view set forth, which considers, above all, the different causes or purposes of the parties in order to make one kind of contract or the other. This subjectivist approach (typically Austrian) is neglected by Selgin when he criticizes Mises' distinction between *time* liabilities and demand deposits because, according to Selgin, 'Mises confuses a difference of degree [the duration of 'call loans' is unspecified] with one of substance'. However, Mises' distinction is entirely correct because from the *subjective* point of view of bank clients, there is an extremely important difference of *substance*: whereas demand deposits are considered as perfect money substitutes, time liabilities are true loans that imply the loss of money available to the clients during its maturation period. See George A. Selgin, *The Theory of Free Banking: Money Supply under Competitive Note Issue*, op. cit., p. 62.

60 The great Spanish jurist Felipe Clemente de Diego described this type of contract as *monstrous* or a *juridical abortion*, since it includes causes or purposes of the parties which essentially contradict each other. See *La cuenta corriente de efectos de un sector de la banca catalana*, Madrid, 1936, pp. 370–371.

61 As a general rule, the bankers, in the contracts, general conditions and forms of the transactions they enter into, never explain the exact nature of the contract, the obligation of holding and custody that they acquire, or whether or not the depositor has authorized them to invest the funds deposited. Everything is usually expressed vaguely and confusedly and, therefore, it is no rash allegation to suggest that the real contractual consent of the depositors is lacking.

62 The fact that the depositors sometimes receive interest does not in any way change the essential purpose of the deposit (holding or custody of the money). 'Nobody says no to a bit of luck' and, therefore, the *ingenuous* depositor to whom interest is offered will accept it immediately if his trust in the banker is main-

tained. The receipt of interest *contra naturam* does not detract from the basic cause of the contract (continous availability of the cash balance) or convert it into a loan. It merely shows that the banker is making undue use of the money deposited with him. The interest on deposit contracts is an advantage *contra naturam* which greatly reminds us of the advantages *contra naturam* which confidence tricksters use to tempt the victims of their confidence tricks, who always fall into the trap as a result of their illegitimate desire to obtain something extraordinary that does not correspond to them.

63 Few criminal acts of negligent driving cause accidents or damages to third parties but, however, all of them are offences since they imply a breach of public order.

64 Thus, similarly, a contract between a member of the Mafia and a professional killer can be: (1) completely voluntary; and (2) based on a perfect agreement in relation to the legal nature of the covenant. However, even in an entirely free libertarian society, it is a contract totally null and void because it is damaging to a third party (the potential victim).

65 Hans-Hermann Hoppe, 'How Is Fiat Money Possible? – or, The Devolution of Money and Credit', *Review of Austrian Economics*, op. cit., pp. 70–71.

66 We do not agree, therefore, with White and Selgin's comments in this respect. See 'In Defense of Fiduciary Media – or, We are *Not* Devo(lutionists), We are Misesians!', op. cit., pp. 92–93.

67 'The following will be sentenced to imprisonment for a period between twelve years and a day and twenty years, with loss of civil rights for the duration of the sentence: 1) Those who manufacture false money', art. 283 of the Spanish Criminal Code. It should be noted that, in a credit expansion, as in the case of the forgery of money, the social damage is very much diluted and, therefore, it will be very difficult for this offence to be prosecuted as a result of evidence brought at the request of the damaged party. For this reason, the offence is described in terms of the conduct (forgery of banknotes) and not in terms of the identification of the specific personal damages to which it leads. The same procedure will have to be followed if, at any time, it is decided to apply the same treatment as a criminal offence to the creation of money by the banks.

68 These 'option clauses' were already in force in the Scottish banks from 1730 to 1765 and reserved the right to temporarily suspend cash payment of the notes they had issued. Thus, referring to bank panics, Selgin says that 'Banks in a free banking system might however avoid such a fate by issuing liabilities contractually subject to a "restriction" of base money payments. By restricting payments banks can insulate the money stock and other nominal magnitudes from panic-related effects'. George A. Selgin, 'Free Banking and Monetary Control', *Economic Journal*, November 1994, p. 1455.

69 A similar conclusion is reached by Murray N. Rothbard, 'The Present State of Austrian Economics', *Journal des économistes et des études humaines*, vol. VI, no. 1, March 1995, pp. 80–81.

12 The ethics of capitalism

1 Originally published in *Journal of Markets & Morality*, vol. 2, no. 2, Fall 1999, pp. 150–163.

2 John Paul II, Encyclical Letter *Veritatis Splendor*, 6 August 1993, pp. 97–98. In his criticism of consequentialism, John Paul II states that 'each person knows the difficulties, or rather, the impossibility of evaluating all the good or evil effects of his own actions: an exhaustive rational calculation is not possible. Therefore, what should be done in order to establish proportions that depend on an evaluation the criteria of which remain in the dark? How could an absolute obligation resulting from such debatable calculations be justified?'

3 This theorem was discovered by theorists of the Austrian School of Economics (i. e. Ludwig von Mises and Friedrich A. Hayek) and has been articulated and refined in the course of the long polemic on the impossibility of socialism, which took place in the last century. The Austrians also made the crisis of the neoclassical-Walrasian paradigm evident, together with the static concept of economics, which presupposes that the ends and means are known and given and that the economic problem is merely a technical question of maximization. See D. Lavoie, *Rivalry and Central Planning: The Socialist Calculation Debate Reconsidered*, Cambridge and New York: Cambridge University Press, 1985; Jesús Huerta de Soto, 'The Ongoing *Methodenstreit* of the Austrian School', *Journal des économistes et des études humaines*, vol. VIII, no. 1, March 1998, pp. 75–113.
4 These are basically the arguments employed by Murray N. Rothbard, *The Ethics of Liberty*, Atlantic Highlands, NJ: Humanities Press, 1982, pp. 201–213, in his critical analysis of the position of Ludwig von Mises.
5 'Economics does currently inform us, not that *moral principles* are subjective, but that utilities and costs are indeed subjective.' Ibid., 202.
6 However, economic theory alone is not considered to be capable of *determining* moral issues and, therefore, there are no grounds for Roland Kley's criticism of Israel Kirzner. *Hayek's Social and Political Thought*, Oxford: Clarendon Press, 1994, p. 228, note 9.
7 Therefore, the trade-off would exist, at most, between one binomial constituted by what is just and efficient and another arising from an inefficient and unjust action (in which the free practice of entrepreneurship is systematically coerced and the total appropriation of the results of human creativity is prevented). In addition, the inefficiency arising from the immoral systematic coercion that the state exercises over the economy is very different from that which the neoclassical economists think they identify within the static paradigm of the so-called 'welfare economics'. Ultimately for these economists, measures of institutional coercion (e.g. the forced redistribution of income) give rise to the effects of distortion that distance the economic system from the points of the maximum production possibilities frontier of the economy without realizing that the damage caused by these measures is much deeper. This occurs because these measures *dynamically* prevent entrepreneurs from coordinating and discovering new opportunities that continually move the society's production possibilities curve toward the right.
8 See Friedrich von Hayek, 'The Mirage of Social Justice', in *Law, Legislation and Liberty*, vol. 2, *The Mirage of Social Justice*, Chicago, IL and London: University of Chicago Press, 1976.
9 The ideas of Israel Kirzner on social ethics began to be forged in section 4 (Chapters 11–13) of his book *Perception, Opportunity and Profit*, University of Chicago Press, Chicago and London, 1979, concerning 'Entrepreneurship, Justice and Freedom', were even more clearly profiled in his article 'Some Ethical Implications for Capitalism of the Socialist Calculation Debate', in *Capitalism*, Ellen Frankel Paul, Fred D. Miller, Jr, Jeffrey Paul and John Ahrens (eds), Basil Blackwell, Oxford, 1989, which culminated in his book *Discovery, Capitalism and Distributive Justice*, Oxford and New York: Basil Blackwell, 1989.
10 See John Rawls, *A Theory of Justice*, Cambridge, MA: Harvard University Press, 1972.
11 This impetus and entrepreneurial creativity also appears in the field of aid to the needy and the prior search for and systematic detection of situations of need. Thus, state coercion or intervention through the mechanisms of the welfare state neutralizes and, to a great extent, makes impossible the entrepreneurial search for urgent human need and the possibility of aid to others, thus stifling the natural aspirations of solidarity and collaboration that are so important to most persons. This idea has been well understood by John Paul II, who has stated that 'by

intervening directly and depriving Society of its responsibility, the Social Assistance State leads to a loss of human energies and an inordinate increase of public agencies, which are dominated more by bureaucratic ways of thinking than by concern for serving their clients, and which are accompanied by an enormous increase in spending. In fact, it would appear that those needs are best understood and satisfied by people who are closest to them and who act as neighbours to those in need'. John Paul II, Encyclical Letter *Centesimus Annus* (1 May 1991), no. 48.

12 'During the last months of his life, Hayek had the opportunity for a long conversation with Pope John Paul II. There are signs of Hayek's influence in certain portions of the Pope's encyclical *Centesimus Annus*. In paragraphs 31 and 32, in particular, *Centesimus Annus* employs unmistakably Hayekian insights.' Michael Novak, 'Two Moral Ideas for Business', *Economic Affairs*, September–October 1993, p. 7.

13 Michael Novak, *The Catholic Ethic and the Spirit of Capitalism*, The Free Press, New York, 1993, p. 117; Karol Wojtyla, *The Acting Person*, Boston, MA: D. Reidel, 1979.

14 See *Centesimus Annus*, 1991, 25, ch. IV, nos. 32–33.

15 See Kirzner, *Discovery, Capitalism and Distributive Justice*, pp. 126–127, 176–177.

16 Ibid., p. 176.

17 See Israel Kirzner, 'Knowledge Problems and Their Solutions: Some Relevant Distinctions', in *The Meaning of Market Process: Essays in the Development of Modern Austrian Economics*, London and New York: Routledge, 1992, pp. 163–179; *The Limits of the Market: The Real and the Imagined*, Proceedings of the Regional Meeting of the Mont Pèlerin Society, Rio de Janeiro, 5–8 September 1993.

18 'There appears to be no obvious way in which any private entrepreneur could be attracted to notice the superiority of the metric system – let alone any chance of it being within his power to affect its adoption. The externality of the relevant benefit to society arising from a change in the metric system appears to block the translation of this unexploited opportunity, jointly available to members of society, into concrete, privately attractive opportunities capable of alerting entrepreneurial discovery.' Kirzner, 'Knowledge Problems and Their Solutions', op. cit., p. 174.

19 'The happy idea of proceeding in this way could strike the shrewdest individuals, and the less resourceful could imitate the former's method.' Mises, *Human Action*, third revised edition, Regnery, Chicago, 1966, p. 406. Perhaps there is no more concise or precise way of referring to the dominant role played by entrepreneurial alertness and creativity in the emergence of institutions than these words written by Mises in his comment praising Menger's contribution.

20 This consideration does not legitimate the neoclassical analysis of law and juridical institutions – which it has been used for – by assuming a context of constancy, equilibrium and the strict rationality of the economic agents based on the principle of profit maximization. The contradiction contained in the economic analysis of law is obvious since, in the static framework described, laws and institutions would not be necessary: simple commands that included the full information assumed to be available would be sufficient to coordinate society. Over against this paradigm, we urge that juridical rules and institutions should not be judged in the narrow terms of static efficiency that originate from Pareto, comparing costs with supposedly known profits, but rather should be judged by a criterion of dynamic efficiency. In other words, depending on whether they promote and encourage the entrepreneurial creativity and coordination of the market. Therefore, rather than 'optimal' case-law rules and decisions from the Paretian point of view, what should be sought after are *just* case-law rules and

322 *Notes*

decisions which, from the point of view of the dynamic efficiency of the entrepreneurial market processes, drive the coordination therein.

13 A Hayekian strategy to implement free market reforms

1 Originally published in J. Backhaus, W. Heijmann, A. Nantjes and J. Van Ophem (eds), *Economic Policy in an Orderly Framework: Liber Amicorum for Gerrit Meijer*, Münster: LIT Verlag, 2003, pp. 231–254.
2 Jesús Huerta de Soto, *Socialismo, cálculo económico y función empresarial*, Madrid: Unión Editorial, 1992.
3 In other words, the democratic system generates, in neoclassical terminology, a giant insoluble problem of 'public good' or 'free rider', as each voter fully internalizes the high cost of voting responsibly with the necessary information, while almost all the benefits of his or her action are diluted among the rest of his fellow citizens, thus making it practically impossible that each individual voter can take advantage of the benefits of his or her action in acting as an informed and responsible voter.
4 We could enumerate many other previous liberalizing reforms and even go back to the failed reform attempted by Turgot in the eighteenth century. However, for our purposes, we feel the examples we put forward in the main text to be sufficient.
5 On Erhard's reform, see the book by Ludwig Erhard himself, *Wohlstand für alle*, Econ-Verlag, Düssledorf, 1957, together with the compilation of his works included in Ludwig Erhard, *Deutsche Wirtschaftspolitik: Der Weg der sozialen Marktwirtschaft*, published by Econ-Verlag, Düsseldorf and Vienna, 1992; and, likewise, the work by Samuel Brittan and Peter Lilley, *The Delusion of Income Policy*, London: Temple Smith, 1977, Chapter IV.
6 On Reagan's reforms and their philosophical foundations, see Martin Anderson, *Revolution*, New York and London: Harcourt Brace Jovanovich, 1988; and Bruce Bartlett, *Reaganomics*, Westpool, CT: Arlington House, 1981.
7 On the meaning and impact of the Thatcherist revolution, see, above all, Margaret Thatcher's own books *The Downing Street Years*, London: HarperCollins, 1993, and *The Path to Power*, London: HarperCollins, 1995.
8 This is the case, for example, of Carlos Menem in Argentina. The liberalizing measures in Chile have been very successful and served as a model for the rest of the Latin-American countries, even though they were initiated under the dictatorship of General Pinochet. The Chileans, however, have been wise enough to maintain and even reinforce the liberalizing reforms initially promoted by Pinochet, now that democracy has been re-established in their country.
9 Jesús Huerta de Soto, 'Conjectural History and Beyond', *Humane Studies Review*, vol. 6, no. 2, Winter 1988–1989, p. 10 (Chapter 3 of this book).
10 This is the case, for example, of the Marxist theory of exploitation, invented by Karl Marx to justify his previously existing revolutionary position, and, more recently, of Keynes' *General Theory*, which owed its great popularity precisely to the fact that it seemed to provide theoretical support and scientific respectability to the interventionism which had always been applied by governments in the fiscal, monetary and credit fields, against the principles of correct economic theory.
11 It is exciting to read how the most conspicuous former socialist theorists, such as Robert L. Heilbroner, acknowledge the failure of socialism and the triumph of the theories of the Austrian School, concluding that 'Mises was right ... socialism has been the great tragedy of this century'. Robert L. Heilbroner, 'Analysis and Vision in the History of Modern Economic Thought', *Journal of Economic Literature*, vol. 28, September 1990, pp. 1097 and 1010–1011. See also his articles published in the *New Yorker*, 'The Triumph of Capitalism', 23 January 1989, and 'Reflections after Communism', 10 September 1990, pp. 91–100. A detailed analysis of the controversy on the theoretical impossibility of socialism may be found in Jesús

Huerta de Soto, *Socialismo, cálculo económico y función empresarial*, Madrid: Unión Editorial, 1992. In this book, I also explain the theory that the fall of the Berlin Wall and of real socialism will have a strong impact on the way in which economics is carried out, which, to date, has been dominated by the scientistic neoclassical paradigm, the models and theoretical developments of which have often been used to justify interventionist economic policies and to argue that socialism, as a system, could work. Also see in this respect J.E. Stiglitz, *Whither Socialism?*, Cambridge, MA: The MIT Press, 1994, pp. xi–xii.

12 F.A. Hayek, 'On Being an Economist', Chapter 2 of *The Trend of Economic Thinking: Essays on Political Economists and Economic History*, vol. III of *The Collected Works of F.A. Hayek*, W.W. Bartley III and Stephen Kresge (eds), London: Routledge, 1991, pp. 45–46.

13 Very recently, one of the distinguished members of the Mont Pèlerin Society regretted that 'it is frustrating when our Chicago allies employ their manifest talents in helping the state to do more efficiently that which it either shouldn't be doing or of which it should be doing much less'. Edward H. Crane, 'A Property Rights Approach to Social Security and Immigration Reform', comment on Gary S. Becker's paper 'An Open Door for Immigrants', presented at the Mont Pèlerin Society Regional Meeting, Cancun, Mexico, January 1996, p. 6.

14 William H. Hutt, *Politically Impossible ... ?*, The Institute of Economic Affairs, London, 1971. I have tried to apply the principles of this *dual strategy* in the specific field of the analysis of the crisis and reform of the social security in my article 'The Crisis and Reform of Social Security: An Economic Analysis from the Austrian Perspective', *Journal des économistes et des études humaines*, vol. V., no. 1, Paris and Aix-en-Provence, March 1994, pp. 127–155 (Chapter 9 of this book).

15 In a similar way many libertarian theorists of the School of Chicago often fell victims of what we could call the 'paradox of libertarian "social engineer"'. In fact, they fully share the scientific arrogance of the neoclassical social engineers, pretending, in turn, to justify, with the analytical outlook and tools described, supposedly 'libertarian' policies which often contradict the essential principles of freedom. Thus, in the long run, they end up by encouraging the institutional coercion typical of interventionism without realizing it.

16 See Jesús Huerta de Soto, 'The Ongoing *Methodenstreit* of the Austrian School', *Journal des économistes et des études humaines*, vol. 8, no. 1, March 1998, pp. 75–113 (Chapter 2 of this book).

17 The static concept of Paretian efficiency should be abandoned and replaced by a 'dynamic' concept based on the creative capacity of entrepreneurship. According to the dynamic criterion we propose, the most important thing is to promote entrepreneurial creativity and constantly move the 'maximum production possibilities curve' towards the right (alternative criterion of 'dynamic efficiency'), rather than merely to avoid waste and place the system at any point of said curve (Paretian criterion). As is logical, when we refer to the 'maximum production possibilities curve', we are merely using a metaphor to enable our readers from the neoclassical tradition to understand us, without forgetting that this curve *does not exist*, as its points are not given (they constantly vary) and can never be known.

18 This seems to be the opinion of Pope John Paul II, who, on wondering whether capitalism is the path to economic and social progress, unambiguously concludes the following:

> If by 'capitalism' is meant an economic system which reorganizes the fundamental and positive role of business, the market, private property and the resulting responsibility for the means of production, as well as free human creativity in the economic sector, then the answer is certainly in the affirma-

tive, even though it would perhaps be more appropriate to speak of a 'business economy', 'market economy' or simply 'free economy'.

See John Paul II, *Centessimus Annus*, London: Catholic Truth Society, 1991, Chapter IV, no. 42, p. 31.

19 See Jesús Huerta de Soto, 'Entrepreneurship and the Economic Analysis of Socialism', in *New Perspectives on Austrian Economics*, Gerrit Meijer (ed.), London and New York: Routledge, 1995, Chapter 14, pp. 228–253 (Chapter 4 of this book).

20 See Murray N. Rothbard, *The Ethics of Liberty*, Atlantic Highlands, NJ: Humanities Press, 1982, pp. 207–208.

21 'The supremacy of public opinion determines not only the singular role that economics occupies in the complex of thought and knowledge. It determines the whole process of human history. The flowering of human society depends on two factors: the intellectual power of outstanding men to conceive sound social and economic theories, and the ability of these or other men to make these ideologies palatable to the majority.' Ludwig von Mises, *Human Action: A Treatise on Economics*, fourth revised edition, New York: The Foundation for Economic Education, 1996, pp. 863–864.

22 For example, we cannot minimize the harmful effect of the novels of Dickens in spreading the erroneous idea that the Industrial Revolution was seriously damaging to ordinary people when, in fact, it has been demonstrated that the exact opposite occurred. Unfortunately, for every novelist who, like Ayn Rand, interprets reality in accordance with an adequate theory and morality based on libertarian principles, there are many others who, like Dickens, reflect only a partial reality or even declare themselves to be against the essential principles of the capitalist economic system, doing incalculable social damage to civilization in the long run and becoming directly (although 'diffusely') responsible for the most serious social conflicts and violence. See F.A. Hayek (ed.), *Capitalism and the Historians*, Chicago, IL: The University of Chicago Press, 1954. With regard to Ayn Rand, author of, among others, the novels *The Fountainhead* and *Atlas Shrugged*, and her influence on the American libertarian movement, see D.M. Sciabarra, *Ayn Rand: The Russian Radical*, University Park, PA: The Pennsylvania State University Press, 1995.

23 A detailed analysis of the history and importance of this type of institute and foundation in the libertarian revolution of recent decades can be found in Richard Cockett's book *Thinking the Unthinkable: Think-Tanks in the Economic Counter-Revolution, 1931–1983*, London: HarperCollins Publishers, 1994, especially pp. 123–124, in which Anthony Fisher explains how F.A. Hayek was determinant in his decision to found the Institute of Economic Affairs (IEA):

> Hayek first warned against wasting time – as I was then tempted – by taking up a political career. He explained his view that the decisive influence in the battle of ideas and policy was wielded by intellectuals whom he characterised as the 'second hand dealers of ideas'. ... If I shared the view that better ideas were not getting a fair hearing, his counsel was that I should join with others in forming a scholarly research organization to supply intellectuals in universities, schools, journalism and broadcasting with authoritative studies of the economic theory of markets and its application to practical affairs.

24 With regard to the Mont Pèlerin Society, see R.M. Hartwell, *A History of the Mont Pèlerin Society*, Indianapolis, IN: Liberty Press, 1995.

25 'The best theories are useless if not supported by public opinion. They cannot work if not accepted by a majority of the people. Whatever the system of gov-

ernment may be, there cannot be any question of ruling a nation lastingly on the ground of doctrines at variance with public opinion. In the end the philosophy of majority prevails. In the long run there cannot be any such thing as an unpopular system of government. The difference between democracy and despotism does not affect the final outcome.' Ludwig von Mises, *Human Action*, op. cit., p. 863.
26 Quoted by Lucas Beltrán in his article 'Seis nombres para una visión de Cataluña', *La Vanguardia Española*, Barcelona, 2 September 1976, p. 15.
27 On the origin and role of the professional politician as a diffuser of second-hand ideas, see Max Weber's classic work *Politik als Beruf, Wissenschaft als Beruf*, Berlin and Munich: Dunker & Humblot, 1926.
28 This group should also include the politicians who, rightly or wrongly, believe that the political circumstances do not allow them to go any further and await a change in circumstances in order to become politicians belonging to the *fourth* group, able to drive forward more radical reforms. Whether this is true or whether it is merely an illusion in order to justify their own shortcomings is something which will have to be evaluated in each specific case.
29 Following the English example, it would be helpful for a committee of libertarian observers, who published their results regularly, to classify the politicians existing at any given moment into one of these four groups, in order to make it clear which of them followed the most contradictory and/or harmful courses of action, while, at the same time, encouraging healthy competition between libertarian politicians to move up the scale of classification, increase their knowledge and try to improve their professional behaviour.
30 A paradigmatic example of irreversible reform was the privatization of the English council houses that Thatcher's government sold to their tenants (mostly millions of modest workers), who thus became owners from whom no party, not even one belonging to the left, will dare expropriate their property in the future.
31 In any case, the interventionist parties should not be allowed to have a monopoly on demagoguery and, although we must acknowledge that it is more difficult for a free market politician to have recourse to it, this does not mean that there do not exist important libertarian recommendations the demagogic content of which may, on occasions, be exploited advantageously.
32 This is, for example, the name given by S. Butler and P. Germanis to the strategy they propose for libertarian reforms in their article 'Achieving Social Security Reform: A Leninist Strategy', *Cato Journal*, vol. 3, no. 2, Autumn 1983, pp. 547–556. On the most fitting strategy in order to achieve the triumph of freedom, see Murray N. Rothbard's suggestive remarks on 'A Theory of the Struggle for Liberty' in *The Ethics of Liberty*, op. cit., pp. 253–268.
33 'When the politician has reflected on the reform he is preparing; when it is agreed that it is opportune and beneficial, then he should throw it out into the world and make it prosper with all his force. Tenacity should be one of the first qualities of the politician. He should never abandon the work he began certain that it was pertinent and useful. He should work earnestly for it; devote all his time and energy to it. If his efforts do not attain the gratification of success, the time will come when his good will be recognized, when all eyes will look towards him to seek his initiatives'. José Martínez Ruiz (Azorín), *El político (con un epílogo futurista), Obras completas*, vol. VIII, Madrid: Rafael Caro Raggio, Editor, 1919, pp. 194–195.
34 This is one of the aspects that had the greatest influence on the people's acceptance of the Liberalization Plan carried out by Erhard in Federal Germany in 1948, which, to the contrary of all the predictions of the occupying powers, gave rise to the *Wirtschaftswunder*, or 'German economic miracle'.
35 Furthermore, in these periods when the more 'tepid' politicians (groups 1, 2 and 3) are in control, it is nevertheless advisable not to break all links with the party,

in order to continue to play a necessary role as the critical libertarian conscience that constantly draws attention to the contradictions and errors of those in power.
36 We should remember, among other cases, the unsuccessful libertarian reform attempted by Jacques Turgot in eighteenth century France and, in the twentieth century, the presidential candidatures of Barry Goldwater in the United States and Mario Vargas Llosa in Peru, together with the failure of the libertarian programme of Forza Italia designed for Italy by Antonio Martino.

14 The future of liberalism

1 This is the article I presented at the general meeting of the Mont Pèlerin Society held in Santiago, Chile, 24–27 November 2000. I made a joint presentation with James M. Buchanan and Bruno S. Frey on the future of democracy, and my part was to comment on Frey's paper, 'The Future of Democracy: In Search of Greater Citizen Participation through Direct Democracy', in which Frey calls for the spread of the Swiss referendum system to all countries.
2 Hans-Hermann Hoppe, 'Small is beautiful and efficient: the case for secession', *Telos*, no 107, 1996, p. 107.
3 J. Huerta de Soto, 'A theory of liberal nationalism' and 'A libertarian theory of free immigration', chapter 7 and 8 of this book.
4 Hoppe, op.cit., p. 101.
5 Bruno Frey, 'A Utopia? Government without territorial monopoly', *The Independent Review*, VI, no 1, Summer 2001, pp. 92–112.
6 Frank A. Fetter, *The Principles of Economics*, New York, 1913, pp. 394 and 410.
7 William Hutt, 'The concept of consumer's sovereignty', *Economic Journal*, March 1940, pp. 66–77; Murray N. Rothbard, *Man, Economy, and State*, Los Angeles, CA: Nash Publishing, 1970, pp. 561–566.
8 Mises, *Human Action*, op. cit., p. 471.
9 Murray, N. Rothbard, *For a New Liberty*, New York: Macmillan, 1973; David Friedman, *The Machinery of Freedom*, Illinois: Open Court, 1989.

15 Juan de Mariana and the Spanish scholastics

1 Published as chapter 1 of the Book *15 Great Austrian Economists*, Randall G. Holcombe (ed.), Auburn, AL: Ludwig von Mises Institute, 1999, pp. 1–11.
2 In the paper entitled 'New Light on the Prehistory of the Austrian School' which Rothbard presented at the conference held in South Royalton and which marked the beginning of the notable re-emergence of the Austrian School over recent decades. This paper was published two years later in *The Foundations of Modern Austrian Economics*, Edwin Dolan (ed.), Kansas City, MO: Sheed & Ward, 1976, pp. 52–74.
3 Murray N. Rothbard, *Economic Thought before Adam Smith: An Austrian Perspective on the History of Economic Thought*, vol. I, Aldershot: Edward Elgar, 1995, pp. 97–133.
4 Bruno Leoni, *Freedom and the Law*, Indianapolis, IN: Liberty Fund, 1991.
5 One of the Hayek's best pupils, Marjorie Grice-Hutchinson, specialized in Spanish literature and translated the main texts of the Spanish scholastics into English in what is now considered a short classic, *The School of Salamanca: Readings in Spanish Monetary Theory, 1544–1605*, Oxford: Clarendon Press, 1952, together with *Economic Thought in Spain*, Laurence Moss and Christopher Ryan (eds), Aldershot: Edward Elgar, 1993. I even have a letter from Hayek, dated 7 January 1979, in which he asked me to read Murray Rothbard's article on 'The Prehistory of the Austrian School' because he and Grice-Hutchinson 'demonstrate that the basic principles of the theory of the competitive market were worked out by the

Spanish Scholastics of the 16th century and that economic liberalism was not designed by the Calvinists but by the Spanish Jesuits'. Hayek concludes his letter saying that 'I can assure you from my personal knowledge of the sources that Rothbard's case is extremely strong'.

6 The most up to date work on the Spanish scholastics is the book by Alejandro Chafuen, *Christians for Freedom: Late Scholastics Economics*, San Francisco, CA: Ignatius Press, 1986.

7 Mariana describes the tyrant as follows:

> He seizes the property of individuals and squanders it, impelled as he is by the unkingly vices of lust, avarice, cruelty, and fraud. ... Tyrants, indeed, try to injure and ruin everybody, but they direct their attack especially against rich and upright men throughout the realm. They consider the good more suspect than the evil; and the virtue which they themselves lack is most formidable to them. ... They expel the better men from the commonwealth on the principle that whatever is exalted in the kingdom should be laid low. ... They exhaust all the rest so that they can not unite by demanding new tributes from them daily, by stirring up quarrels among the citizens, and by joining war to war. They build huge works at the expense and the suffering of the citizens. Whence the pyramids of Egypt were born. ... The tyrant necessarily fears that those whom he terrorizes and holds as slaves will attempt to overthrow him. ... Thus he forbids the citizens to congregate together, to meet in assemblies, and to discuss the commonwealth altogether, taking from them by secret-police methods the opportunity of free speaking and freely listening so that they are not even allowed to complain freely.

Murray N. Rothbard, *Economic Thought before Adam Smith*, op. cit., pp. 118–119.

8 See Juan de Mariana, *Discurso de las enfermedades de la Compañía*, printed by Don Gabriel Ramírez, calle de Barrionuevo, Madrid, 1768, 'Dissertation on the author, and the legitimacy of this discourse', p. 53.

9 I will be quoting *in extenso* from the latest Spanish edition of this book, which was published with the title of *Tratado y discurso sobre la moneda de vellón*, with an introduction by Lucas Beltrán, Instituto de Estudios Fiscales, Madrid, 1987.

10 Murray N. Rothbard, *Economic Thought before Adam Smith*, op. cit., p. 120.

11 I quote from Covarrubias, *Omnia Opera*, published in Venice in 1604, vol. II, Book 2, Chapter 4, p. 131.

12 Luis Saravia de la Calle, *Instrucción de mercaderes*, Pedro de Castro, Medina del Campo, 1544; republished in *Colección de Joyas Bibliográficas*, Madrid, 1949, p. 53. All the content of Saravia's book is addressed to business entrepreneurs (in Spanish 'mercaderes'), following a continental Catholic tradition that can be traced back to San Bernardino of Siena (1380–1444). See Murray N. Rothbard, *Economic Thought Before Adam Smith*, op. cit., pp. 81–85.

13 Juan de Lugo (1583–1660), *Disputationes de iustitia et iure*, Lyon: Sumptibus Petri Prost, 1642, vol. II, D. 26, S. 4, N. 40, p. 312.

14 Juan de Salas, *Commentarii in secundam secundae D. Thomae de contractibus*, Lyon: Sumptibus Horatij Lardon, 1617, IV, no. 6, p. 9.

15 Jerónimo Castillo de Bovadilla, *Política para corregidores*, Salamanca, 1585, II, Chapter IV, no. 49. See also the important comments on the scholastics and their dynamic concept of competition written by Oreste Popescu, *Estudios en la historia del pensamiento económico latinoamericano*, Buenos Aires: Plaza & Janés, 1987, pp. 141–159.

16 Luis de Molina, *De iustitia et iure*, Cuenca, 1597, II, disp. 348, no. 4, and *La teoría del justo precio*, Francisco Gómez Camacho (ed.), Madrid: Editora Nacional, 1981, p. 169. Raymond de Roover, ignoring the work of Castillo de Bovadilla,

refers how 'Molina even introduces the concept of competition by stating that concurrence or rivalry among buyers will enhance prices'. See his article 'Scholastic Economics: Survival and Lasting Influence from the Sixteenth Century to Adam Smith', *Quarterly Journal of Economics*, vol. LXIX, no. 2, May 1955, p. 169.
17 Included in Covarrubias, *Omnia Opera*, op. cit., vol. I, pp. 669–710.
18 Carl Menger, *Principles of Economics*, New York and London: New York University Press, 1981, p. 317.
19 Martín Azpilcueta Navarro, *Comentario resolutorio de cambios*, Madrid: Consejo Superior de Investigaciones Científicas, 1965, pp. 74–75.
20 See Jesús Huerta de Soto, 'New Light on the Prehistory of the Theory of Banking and the School of Salamanca', *Review of Austrian Economics*, vol. 9, no. 2, 1996, pp. 59–81 (Chapter 16 of this book).
21 Luis de Molina, *Tratado sobre los cambios*, with an introduction by Francisco Gómez Camacho, Instituto de Estudios Fiscales, Madrid, 1990, p. 146. Also James Pennington's memo dated 13 February 1826 'On the Private Banking Establishments of the Metropolis', included as an Appendix in Thomas Tooke, *A Letter to Lord Grenville; On the Effects Ascribed to the Resumption of Cash Payments on the Value of the Currency*, London: John Murray, 1826.
22 However, according to Father Bernard W. Dempsey, if the members of this second group of the School of Salamanca had had a detailed theoretical knowledge of the functioning and implications of the economic process to which fractional-reserve banking gives rise, it would have been described as a perverse, vast and illegitimate process of *institutional usury*, even by Molina, Lessius and Lugo themselves. See Father Bernard W. Dempsey, *Interest and Usury*, Washington, DC: American Council of Public Affairs, 1943, p. 210.
23 Quoted by Bernard W. Dempsey, *Interest and Usury*, op. cit., footnote 31 on p. 214.
24 Juan de Mariana, *Discurso de las enfermedades de la Compañía*, op. cit., pp. 151–155 and 216.
25 'Adam Smith dropped earlier contributions about subjective value, entrepreneurship and emphasis on real-world markets and pricing and replaced it all with a labour theory of value and a dominant focus on the long run "natural price" equilibrium, a world where entrepreneurship was assumed out of existence. He mixed up Calvinism with economics, as in supporting usury prohibition and distinguishing between productive and unproductive occupations. He lapsed from the laissez-faire of several eighteenth-century French and Italian economists, introducing many waffles and qualifications. His work was unsystematic and plagued by contradictions'. See Leland B. Yeager, 'Book Review', *Review of Austrian Economics*, vol. 9, no. 1, 1996, p. 183.
26 Jaime Balmes, 'Verdadera idea del valor o reflexiones sobre el origen, naturaleza y variedad de los precios', in *Obras Completas*, vol. 5, BAC, Madrid, 1949, pp. 615–624. Balmes also described the personality of Juan de Mariana with the following graphic words:

> The overall impression that Mariana offers is unique: an accomplished theologian, a perfect Latin scholar, a deep knowledge of Greek and the eastern languages, a brilliant man of letters, an estimable economist, a politician with great foresight; that is his head; add an irreproachable life, strict morality, a heart which does not know untruth, incapable of flattery, which beats strongly at the mere name of freedom, like that of the fierce republicans of Greece and Rome; a firm, intrepid voice, that is raised against all types of abuse, with no consideration for the great, without trembling when it addressed kings, and consider that all this has come together in a man who lives in a small cell of the Jesuits of Toledo, and you will certainly find a set of virtues and circumstances that seldom coincide in a single person.

See the article 'Mariana', in *Obras Completas*, op. cit., vol. 12, pp. 78–79.

16 New light on the prehistory of the theory of banking and the School of Salamanca

1 The idea for this article arose from a conversation with Murray N. Rothbard at the regional meeting of the Mont Pèlerin Society held in Rio de Janeiro in September 1993. The original English version of the article appeared in *Review of Austrian Economics*, vol. 9, no. 2, 1996, pp. 59–81. This issue was actually a tribute to the memory of Murray N. Rothbard, who had passed away on 7 January 1995.

2 See Murray N. Rothbard, 'New Light on the Prehistory of the Austrian School', *The Foundations of Modern Austrian Economics*, E.G. Dolan (ed.), Kansas City, MO: Sheed and Ward, 1976, pp. 52–74. I have a letter from F.A. Hayek dated 7 January 1979, in which he states that, apart from Raymond de Roover, the researchers to whom we owe the establishment of the link between the School of Salamanca and the Austrian School are, chronologically, H.M. Robertson (*Aspects of the Rise of Economic Individualism*, Cambridge: Cambridge University Press, 1933), Marjorie Grice-Hutchinson (*The School of Salamanca*, Oxford: Clarendon Press, 1952) and, especially, Murray N. Rothbard in his above-mentioned article.

3 Ramón Carande, *Carlos V y sus Banqueros*, three volumes, Barcelona and Madrid: Editorial Crítica, 1987.

4 Finally, with a great deal of effort, he managed to obtain 200,000 ducats, but, as he wrote, 'I am afraid of causing the bankruptcy of all the banks of Seville'. See Ramón Carande, *Carlos V y sus Banqueros*, Barcelona and Madrid: Editorial Crítica, 1987, vol. I, pp. 299–323, especially pp. 315–316, which deal with Gresham's visit to Seville.

5 See Carlo M. Cipolla's important article 'La moneda en Florencia en el Siglo XVI', published in *El Gobierno y la Moneda: Ensayos de Historia Monetaria*, Barcelona: Editorial Crítica, 1994, pp. 11–142, especially p. 96 onwards. This book is the Spanish edition of the work originally published in Italian with the title *Il Governo della Moneta: La Moneta a Firenze nel Cinquecento*, Bologna: Societá editrice Il Mulino, 1990.

6 Cipolla tells us how the Ricci Bank, from the 1970s onwards, was not able to meet the demand for payments in cash and, *de facto*, suspended payments, as it paid simply 'with ink' or 'with bank policies'. The authorities of Florence, looking only at the symptoms and trying, with typical good intentions, to resolve this worrying situation merely by decrees, imposed on the bankers the obligation to pay their creditors in cash without any delay, but did not attack the fundamental causes of the phenomenon (the undue appropriation of the deposits as loans and failure to hold a 100 per cent cash ratio). This meant that the successive decrees issued met with inevitable failure and the crisis became gradually more serious until it broke out with its full virulence in the mid-1570s. See Carlo M. Cipolla, 'La Moneda en Florencia en el Siglo XVI', op. cit., pp. 102–103.

7 Among others, the following have recently studied the contribution of the Spanish scholastics to economic theory: Lucas Beltrán in his 'Sobre los orígenes hispanos de la economía de mercado', published in *Cuadernos del Pensamiento Liberal*, no. 10 (1), 1989, pp. 5–38; Marjorie Grice-Hutchinson, *Economic Thought in Spain: Selected Essays of Marjorie Grice-Hutchinson*, Laurence S. Moss and Christopher K. Ryan (eds), Edward Elgar, Aldershot, England, 1993; Jesús Huerta de Soto, 'Génesis, esencia y evolución de la Escuela Austriaca de Economía', *Estudios de Economía Política*, Unión Editorial, Madrid, 1994, pp. 17–55; and especially, and most recently, Murray N. Rothbard, *Economic Thought before Adam Smith: An Austrian Perspective on the History of Economic Thought*, vol. I, Edward Elgar,

Aldershot, England 1995, pp. 101–127. The intellectual influence of the Spanish theorists of the School of Salamanca on the Austrian School is not, however, a pure coincidence or a mere whim of history. It originates from and exists because of the intimate historical, political and cultural relations which, as from the reigns of Carlos V and his brother Fernando I, arose between Spain and Austria and which were to continue for several centuries. In addition, Italy also played an important role in these relations, acting as an authentic cultural, economic and financial bridge over which the relations between the two furthest points of the Empire (Spain and Vienna) flowed. In this respect, Jean Berenguer's book *El Imperio de los Habsburgos*, Editorial Crítica, Barcelona, 1993, should be consulted, particularly pp. 133–335. This book is the Spanish edition of the French original, which was entitled *Histoire de l'empire des Habsbourg 1273–1918*, Paris: Librairie Arthème, Fayard, 1990.

8 Luis Saravia de la Calle, *Instrucción de Mercaderes*, Pedro de Castro, Medina del Campo, 1544; republished in *Colección de Joyas Bibliográficas*, Madrid, 1949.
9 Saravia de la Calle, *Instrucción de Mercaderes*, op. cit., p. 180.
10 Saravia de la Calle, *Instrucción de Mercaderes*, op. cit., p. 181.
11 Saravia de la Calle, *Instrucción de Mercaderes*, op. cit., p. 195.
12 Saravia de la Calle, *Instrucción de Mercaderes*, op. cit., p. 196.
13 Saravia de la Calle, *Instrucción de Mercaderes*, op. cit., p. 197.
14 Saravia de la Calle, *Instrucción de Mercaderes*, op. cit., p. 197.
15 See Jesús Huerta de Soto, 'A Critical Analysis of Central Banks and Fractional-Reserve Free Banking from the Austrian School Perspective', *Review of Austrian Economics*, vol. 8, no. 2, pp. 25–38, especially pp. 29–30 (footnote 6) (Chapter 10 of this book).
16 Saravia de la Calle, *Instrucción de Mercaderes*, op. cit., p. 186.
17 Saravia de la Calle, *Instrucción de Mercaderes*, op. cit., p. 190 (emphasis added).
18 Saravia de la Calle, *Instrucción de Mercaderes*, op. cit., p. 198.
19 Martín de Azpilcueta, *Comentario Resolutorio de Cambios*, Consejo Superior de Investigaciones Científicas, Madrid, 1965, pp. 57–58. When studying the position of Doctor Navarro, I have worked with the first Spanish edition published by Andrés de Portonarijs in Salamanca in 1556, and also with the first Portuguese edition published by Ioam de Barreyra in Coimbra in 1560 with the title *Comentario Resolutorio de Onzenas*. The quotations contained in the main text appear in Portuguese on pp. 77–80 of this edition.
20 Martín de Azpilcueta, *Comentario Resolutorio de Cambios*, op. cit., pp. 60–61.
21 Ibid., p. 61.
22 I quote the edition of the Instituto de Estudios Fiscales published in Madrid in 1977, edited and introduced by Nicolás Sánchez Albornoz, vol. II, p. 479. There is another edition, by Restituto Sierra Bravo, published by the Editora Nacional in 1975, which includes the quotation given in the main text on p. 401. The original edition was published in Seville in 1571 'en casa de Hernando Díez Impresor de Libros, en la calle de la Sierpe'.
23 Tomás de Mercado, *Suma de Tratos y Contratos*, op. cit., vol. II, p. 480 of the edition of Instituto de Estudios Fiscales and p. 401 of the edition of Restituto Sierra Bravo.
24 Ibid., p. 480.
25 This is the quotation from Mercado that Ramón Carande includes in vol. I of *Carlos V y sus Banqueros* in the introduction to his analysis of the bankers of Seville and the crisis which led them all into bankruptcy. See Tomás de Mercado, *Suma de Tratos y Contratos*, op. cit., vol. II, pp. 381–382 of the 1977 edition of Instituto de Estudios Fiscales and p. 321 of the edition of Restituto Sierra Bravo.
26 According to Restituto Sierra Bravo, *El Pensamiento Social y Económico de la Escolástica*, Consejo Superior de Investigaciones Científicas, vol. I, Madrid, 1975,

p. 215, this phrase of Domingo de Soto implies his acceptance of the banking business with a fractional-reserve ratio.
27 It is very significant that various authors, among them Marjorie Grice-Hutchinson, are in doubt as to whether Luis de Molina should be included among the theorists of the School of Salamanca: 'The inclusion of Molina in the School seems to me now to be more dubious'. Marjorie Grice-Hutchinson, 'The Concept of the School of Salamanca: Its Origins and Development', Chapter 2 of *Economic Thought in Spain: Selected Essays of Marjorie Grice-Hutchinson*, op. cit., p. 25.
28 Luis de Molina, *Tratado sobre los Cambios*, edition and introduction of Francisco Gómez Camacho, Madrid: Instituto de Estudios Fiscales, 1990, pp. 137–140.
29 Luis de Molina, *Tratado sobre los Préstamos y la Usura*, edition and introduction of Francisco Gómez Camacho, Madrid: Instituto de Estudios Fiscales, 1989, p. 13.
30 Luis de Molina, *Tratado sobre los Cambios*, op. cit., p. 137.
31 Luis de Molina, *Tratado sobre los Cambios*, op. cit., p. 138–139 (the emphasis is not in the original).
32 R.P. Joannis de Lugo Hispalensis, S.I., *Disputationum de Iustitia et Iure, Tomus Secundus*, Lugduni, 1642, Disp. XXVIII, Sec. V, pp. 406–407. I would like to thank the Jesuit father Professor Enrique M. Ureña and the Dominican father Rodrigo T. Hidalgo who provided me with different copies of de Lugo's original book.
33 See, above all, the research which Marjorie Grice-Hutchinson published under the direction of F.A. Hayek with the title of *The School of Salamanca: Readings in Spanish Monetary Theory, 1544–1605*, Oxford: Clarendon Press, 1952; Murray N. Rothbard, 'New Light on the Prehistory of the Austrian School', published in *The Foundations of Modern Austrian Economics*, op. cit., pp. 52–74; Alejandro A. Chafuen, *Christians for Freedom: Late-Scholastics Economics*, San Francisco, CA: Ignatius Press, 1986, pp. 74–86; and Murray N. Rothbard, *Economic Thought before Adam Smith: An Austrian Perspective on the History of Economic Thought*, vol. I, op. cit., pp. 101–127.
34 The edition which I have used is the *Omnia Opera*, published in Venice in 1604, which includes the treaty on money by Diego de Covarrubias in volume I, under the full title of *Veterum Collatio Numismatum, cum his, quae modo expenduntur, publica, et Regia authoritate perpensa*, pp. 669–710. This work by Diego de Covarrubias is often quoted by Davanzati and, at least once, in Chapter 2 of Galiani's famous *Della Moneta*, written in 1750.
35 Martín de Azpilcueta, *Comentario Resolutorio de Cambios*, edition of Consejo Superior de Investigaciones Científicas, Madrid, 1965, pp. 74–75 (the emphasis is not in the original).
36 Not even in the most brilliant and recent work by Murray N. Rothbard, *Economic Thought before Adam Smith: An Austrian Perspective on the History of Economic Thought*, vol. I, op. cit., to which the present article should be considered a humble addendum.
37 Luis de Molina, *Tratado sobre los Cambios*, op. cit., p. 145.
38 Ibid., p. 146.
39 See James Pennington's memo dated 13 February 1826, 'On the Private Banking Establishments of the Metropolis', included as an Appendix in Thomas Tooke, *A Letter to Lord Grenville; On the Effects Ascribed to the Resumption of Cash Payments on the Value of the Currency*, London: John Murray, 1826; Murray N. Rothbard, *Classical Economics: An Austrian Perspective on the History of Economic Thought*, vol. II, Aldershot: Edward Elgar, 1995, pp. 230–233; and F.A. Hayek, 'The Dispute between the Currency School and the Banking School, 1821–1848', Chapter 12 of *The Trend of Economic Thinking: Essays on Political Economists and Economic History*, W.W. Bartley III and Stephen Kresge (eds), vol. III of *The Collected Works of F.A. Hayek*, London: Routledge, 1991, p. 224.

40 Luis de Molina, *Tratado sobre los Cambios*, op. cit., p. 147.
41 Luis de Molina, *Tratado sobre los Cambios*, op. cit., p. 149.
42 'Quare magis videntur pecuniam precario mutuo accipere, reddituri quotiscumque exigetur a deponente. Communiter tamen, pecunia illa interim negotiantur, et lucrantur, sine ad cambium dando, sine aliud negotiationis genus exercendo.' I quote literally from p. 406, Section 5, no. 60, 'De Cambiis', Joannis de Lugo Hispalensis, Societatis Iesu, *Disputationum de Iustitia et Iure, Tomus Secundus*, Lugduni 1642.
43 Perhaps Juan de Lugo is the person who best summarizes and expresses this principle: 'Qui bene advertit, eiusmodi bancarios depositarios peccare graviter, & damno subsequuto, cum obligatione restituendi pro damno, quoties ex pecuniis apud sed depositis tantam summan ad suas negotationes exponunt, ut inhabiles maneant ad solvendum deposentibus, quando suo tempore exigent. Et idem est, si negotiationes tales aggrediantur, ex quibus periculum sit, ne postea ad paupertatem redacti pecunias acceptas reddere non possint, v.g. si euenrus ex navigatione periculosa dependeat, in qua navis hostium, vel naufragij periculo exposita sit, qua iactura sequnta, ne ex propio quidem patrimonio solvere possint, sed in creditorum, vel fideiussorum damnum cedere debet'. R.P. Joannis de Lugo Hispalensis, S.I., *Disputationum de Iustitia et Iure, Tomus Secundus*, Lugduni, 1642, Disp. XXVIII, Sec. V, pp. 406–407.
44 That is to say, in the terminology of Israel M. Kirzner ('Economics and Error', *Perception, Opportunity and Profit*, Chicago, IL: The University of Chicago Press, 1979, pp. 120–136), committing sheer or pure entrepreneurial error (which cannot be insured by the law of large numbers) which causes serious entrepreneurial losses, regardless of the degree of prudence with which one has acted.
45 Published by the journal *Pensamiento: revista trimestral de investigación e información filosófica publicada por las Facultades de Filosofía de las Compañías de Jesús en España*, no. 73, vol. 19, January–March 1963, Madrid, pp. 64–89.
46 Father Francisco Belda, op. cit., pp. 63 and 69.
47 Ibid., p. 87. The reference to Juan de Lugo corresponds to vol. 2, Disp. XXVIII, Section V, nos. 60–62 of the aforementioned work by Juan de Lugo.
48 Bernard W. Dempsey, *Interest and Usury*, published with an introduction by Joseph A. Schumpeter by the American Council of Public Affairs, Washington, DC, 1943. Attention should be drawn to the fact that Father Belda's article arose as a criticism, from the Keynesian point of view, of the theses upheld by Dempsey in this book. I would like to thank Professor James Sadowsky of Fordham University, who provided me with a copy of Dempsey's book, which was not available in Spain.
49 Father Dempsey's broad theoretical knowledge and familiarity with the economic doctrines of Ludwig von Mises, Friedrich A. Hayek, Wicksell, Keynes and others is very much emphasized in Schumpeter's 'Introduction' to his book. Moreover, Schumpeter quotes and praises Dempsey in his *History of Economic Analysis*, New York: Oxford University Press, 1980, pp. 95–96 and 104.
50 'The credit expansion results in the depreciation of whatever circulating medium the bank deals in. Prices rise; the asset appreciates. *The bank absolves its debt by paying out on the deposit a currency of lesser value.* ... No single person perhaps would be convinced by a Scholastic author of the sin of usury. But the *process* has operated usuriously; again we meet systematic or institutional usury. ... The modern situation to which theorists have applied the concepts of divergence of natural and money interest, divergences of saving an investment, divergences of income disposition from tenable patterns by involuntary displacements, all these have a sufficient common ground with late medieval analysis to warrant the expression 'institutional usury' for the movement heretofore described in the above expressions'. Father Bernard W. Dempsey, *Interest and Usury*, op. cit., pp. 225 and 227–228.

51 Bernard W. Dempsey, *Interest and Usury*, op. cit., p. 210. Incidentally, Father Dempsey points out that the theory of time preference may even date from Saint Thomas Aquinas, as it was expressly stated by one of the latter's most brilliant pupils, Giles Lessines, for whom 'res futurae per tempora non sunt tantae existimationis, sicut eaedem collectae in instanti nec tantam utilitatem inferunt possidentibus, propter quod oportet quod sint minoris existimationis secundum iustitiam', i.e. 'future goods are not valued so highly as the same goods available at an immediate moment of time, nor do they allow their owners to achieve the same utility. For this reason, it must be considered that they have a more reduced value in accordance with justice'. See p. 426 of Opusculum LXVI, *De usuris in communi et de usurarum contractibus*, written by Aegidius Lessines in 1285 (quoted by Bernard Dempsey in note 31 of p. 214). Dempsey's discovery of Lessines exposition of time preference was not included in Murray N. Rothbard's cited book on *Economic Thought before Adam Smith*, in which Rothbard considers San Bernardino of Siena and Conrad Summenhart to have been in 1431 and 1499 the first expositors of time preference theory (pp. 85 and 92).
52 This is the same argument given by the great libertarian Jesuit Juan de Mariana in his book *De monetae mutatione* ('On the Alteration of Money') published in 1609. Mariana condemns as robbery any government debasement of coins, whereas Dempsey follows the same reasoning in relation to the even more disturbing credit inflation created by banks. On Juan de Mariana, see the most brilliant analysis of Murray N. Rothbard, *Economic Thought before Adam Smith: An Austrian Perspective on the History of Economic Thought*, vol. I, op. cit., p. 119.

17 Ludwig von Mises' *Human Action* as a textbook of economics

1 Originally published in *Journal for the New Europe*, vol. 1, no. 1, 2004, pp. 5–62.
2 See Jesús Huerta de Soto, 'La crisis del paradigma walrasiano' and 'Método y crisis en la Ciencia Económica', in *Estudios de Economía Política*, Madrid: Unión Editorial, 1994, pp. 56–82.
3 All those who ingenuously believe that 'scientific meliorism' applies to economics fall into the trap of what Murray N. Rothbard appropriately called the 'Whig theory of the history of science'. According to this viewpoint, 'the latest is always the best' in any scientific discipline and, consequently, also in economics. This belief assumes that everything constructed scientifically at any given time is correct or, at least, 'better' than what had been constructed previously. This inevitably leads to the self-complacence and unjustified optimism which are so dangerous in the search for and preservation of the scientific truth. In fact, the 'scientific meliorism' position is merely an artificial 'safety belt' which the different paradigms implicitly and surreptitiously create in order to invalidate from the outset any possibility that a whole school of economic thought may be based on error, or that the evolution of Economic Science itself may stagnate or, as has often been the case, undergo phases of evident regression over determined time periods. Against this doctrine, Rothbard maintains that

> There can be therefore no presumption whatever in economics that later thought is better than earlier, or even that all well-known economists have contributed their sturdy mite to the developing discipline. For it becomes very likely that, rather than everyone contributing to an ever-progressing edifice, economics can and has proceeded in contentious, even zig-zag fashion, with later systemic fallacy sometimes elbowing aside earlier but sounder paradigms, thereby redirecting economic thought down a total erroneous or even tragic path. The overall path of economics may be up, or it may be down, over any give time period.

Murray N. Rothbard, *Economic Thought before Adam Smith: An Austrian Perspective of the History of Economic Thought*, Aldershot: Edward Elgar, 1995, vol. I, p. x. Illustrations of regression in the evolution of economic thought would be, for example, the revival of the objective theory of value by the Neo-Ricardian School, Keynesian economic analysis, the abandonment of the time dimension and the theory of capital in modern macroeconomic thought and the narrow concepts of rationality, maximization and equilibrium upon which neoclassical analysis is constructed.

4 Joseph E. Stiglitz, *Economics*, W.W. Norton & Company, 1993, Chapter 4, p. 84. As Mises rightly explains, 'acting man does not measure utility. He arranges it in scales of gradation. Market prices are not expressive of equivalence, but of a divergence in the valuation of the two exchanging parties'. *Human Action*, Chicago, IL: Henry Regnery, 1966, p. 703. (From now onwards, unless otherwise stated, all the quotations from *Human Action* will refer to the aforementioned third English edition of 1966.)

5 With regard to the possibility of using the rule 'price equals marginal cost' to organize a socialist economy 'optimally', it is, for example, set out categorically, among other places, in the well-known textbook by J.C. Gould and C.E. Ferguson, *Microeconomic Theory*, Richard D. Irwin, Illinois, 1980, p. 445. The serious fallacies contained in this idea are demonstrated in detail in Jesús Huerta de Soto, *Socialismo, cálculo económico y función empresarial*, Unión Editorial, Madrid, 1992, pp. 319 onwards.

6 It is not, therefore, surprising that concepts are constantly used which, like 'elasticity', are merely unfortunate transpositions (in this case, by Alfred Marshall) to the economics field of concepts which belong to the world of physics. This has been recently shown by authors who, like Philip Mirowski, have demonstrated that the neoclassical paradigm is simply a bad copy of the (now obsolete) conception of energy in nineteenth century physics. See Philip Mirowski, *More Heat than Light: Economics as Social Physics, Physics as Nature's Economics*, Cambridge: Cambridge University Press, 1991.

7 Mises refers to the damage that this scientistic conception of economics does to the students as follows:

> The students are bewildered. In the courses of the mathematical economists they are fed formulas describing hypothetical states of equilibrium in which there is no longer any action. They easily conclude that these equations are of no use whatever for the comprehension of economic activities. In the lectures of the specialists they hear a mass of detail concerning interventionist measures. They must infer that conditions are paradoxical indeed, because there is never equilibrium, and wage rates and the prices of farm products are not so high as the unions or the farmers want them to be. It is obvious, they conclude, that a radical reform is indispensable. But what kind of reform? The majority of the students espouse without any inhibitions the interventionist panaceas recommended by their professors. Social conditions will be perfectly satisfactory when the government enforces minimum wage rates and provides everybody with adequate food and housing, or when the sale of margarine and the importation of foreign sugar are prohibited. They do not see the contradictions in the words of their teachers, who one day lament the madness of competition and the next day the evils of monopoly, who one day complain about falling prices and the next day about rising living costs. They take their degrees and try as soon as possible to get a job with the government or a powerful pressure group.
>
> *Human Action*, op. cit., p. 875.

8 Compare, for example, Paul A. Samuelson and William N. Nordhaus, *Economics*, twelfth edition, New York: McGraw Hill, 1986, with Paul A. Samuelson and William N. Nordhaus, *Economics*, fourteenth edition, New York: McGraw-Hill, 1992. Also in the fourteenth edition of Samuelson's manual the disgraceful treatment (at least from the standpoint of the events that have taken place in Eastern European countries, which have fully confirmed Mises' theoretical analysis of socialism) which Samuelson had traditionally given to this subject, according to which 'the Soviet economy is proof that, contrary to what many sceptics had earlier believed, a socialist command economy can function and even thrive' (Paul A. Samuelson, *Economics*, thirteenth edition, New York: McGraw-Hill, 1989, p. 837), has disappeared without any explanation.

9 The only examples I know of intellectual honesty in this field are the manuals of Bresciani-Turroni and Röpke, both of whom at least mention the important critical works of Hans Mayer on the neoclassical functional theory of price determination. See C. Bresciani-Turroni, *Corso di Economia Politica*, Milan: A. Guiffrè Editore, 1960, Chapter 2, and Wilhelm Röpke, *Die Lehre von der Wirtschaft*, Zurich: Eugen Rentsch, 1968, note 2 of Chapter I. With regard to Hans Mayer's work, originally published under the title 'Der Erkenntniswert der funktionellen Preistheorien: kritische und positive Untersuchungen zum Preisproblem', in *Die Wirtschaftstheorie der Gegenwart*, Hans Mayer (ed.), Verlag von Julius Springer, vol. II, Vienna, 1932, pp. 147–239b, it has fortunately recently been translated and published in English under the title 'The Cognitive Value of Functional Theories of Price: Critical and Positive Investigations Concerning the Price Problem', in *Classics in Austrian Economics: A Sampling in the History of a Tradition*, Israel M. Kirzner (ed.), London: William Pickering, 1994, vol. II, pp. 55–168.

10 As Mises rightly states in his criticism of Samuelson's 'revealed preference' theory which appears on page 103 of *Human Action*,

> The attempt has been made to attain the notion of a nonrational action by this reasoning: If a is preferred to b and b to c, logically a should be preferred to c. But if actually c is preferred to a, we are faced with a mode of acting to which we cannot ascribe consistency and rationality. This reasoning disregards the fact that two acts of an individual can never be synchronous. If in one action a is preferred to b and in another action b to c, it is, however short the interval between the two actions may be, not permissible to construct a uniform scale of value in which a precedes b and b precedes c. Nor is it permissible to consider a later third action as coincident with the two previous actions.

See also Murray N. Rothbard, 'Toward a Reconstruction of Utility and Welfare Economics', in *Austrian Economics*, Stephen Littlechild, Aldershot: Edward Elgar, 1990, vol. III, pp. 228 onwards. Also see note 40.

11 The only exception I am aware of where reference is made to methodological positions other than positivist ones is Richard G. Lipsey, who, at least up to the eighth edition of his well-known manual *An Introduction to Positive Economics*, said the following with regard to Mises' *Human Action* and Robbins' *An Essay on the Nature and Significance of Economic Science*: 'All specialists in economics should read this interesting book. It sets out a conception of the nature of economic theory and its relationship with empirical observations which directly contradicts the one presented in our book'. Richard G. Lipsey, *An Introduction to Positive Economics*, London: Weidenfeld and Nicolson, 1967, footnote 19 of Chapter 16.

12 Thus, for example, in Chapters XXIX–XXXI of *Human Action*, Mises presents a theoretical analysis of the logic of the concatenation of events in relation to

protectionism, interventionist measures and exchange controls which is especially brilliant and shows a great capacity for reflection, wisdom and practical experience.
13 Friedrich A. Hayek, winner of the Nobel Prize for Economics in 1974, specifically referred to these characteristics of Mises' book in one of the first reviews he made of the first edition published in German, reaching the conclusion that 'there appears to be a width of view and an intellectual spaciousness about the whole book which are much more like that of an eighteenth-century philosopher than of a modern specialist'. F.A. Hayek, *The Economic Journal*, April 1941, pp. 124–127. In fact, Mises, with his general treatise on economics *Human Action* aims, among other things, to respond to the intellectual challenge originally launched by Max Weber relating to the need to prepare an integrated theoretical *corpus* which would permit history to be interpreted and made; in other words, a whole *unified social theory* which would make the interpretation of historical reality possible. In the neoclassical field, there have been some attempts to draw up this unified scientific *corpus*, such as, for example, James Coleman's book *The Foundations of Social Theory* (Cambridge, MA: Harvard University Press, 1990). However, as Coleman works on the basis of the neoclassical paradigm in its School of Chicago version, his book has not only the virtues, but also all the defects and insufficiencies which are typical of this paradigm and which, in our opinion, have been adequately eliminated and overcome by Mises in his Treatise.
14 Thus, for example, Toshio Murata, professor of economics at the University of Yokohama in Japan, recently referred to how 'Mises' *Human Action* is filled with his precious wisdom, written in a very concise style, extending into many spheres. It is a treasury of thoughts and ideas, any one of which may be explored further and developed into a new thesis or a new book'. Toshio Murata, 'Fascinated by Mises for Thirty-Five Years', *Shunjo (Shunjo-sha)*, no. 330, July 1991, p. 4.
15 'Around Christmas, 1903, I read Menger's *Grundsätze der Volkswirtschaftslehre* for the first time. It was the reading of this book that made an "economist" of me.' Ludwig von Mises, *Notes and Recollections*, South Holland, IL: Libertarian Press, 1978, p. 33. See Carl Menger, *Grundsätze der Volkswirtschaftslehre*, Vienna: Wilhelm Braumüller, 1871; translated by James Dingwall and Bert F. Hoselitz, with an introduction by F.A. Hayek, New York and London: New York University Press, 1981.
16 The connections between theories of the Austrian School and those of the Spanish scholastics have been studied in detail by two of Mises' students, F.A. Hayek and, particularly, Murray N. Rothbard. See, above all, the latter's article 'New Light on the Prehistory of the Austrian School', published in *The Foundations of Modern Austrian Economics*, Kansas City, MO: Sheed & Ward, 1976, pp. 52–74 and, more recently, volume I of his posthumous work *Economic Thought before Adam Smith: An Austrian Perspective on the History of Economic Thought*, op. cit., pp. 97–177. Curiously, this intimate relationship between the members of the School of Salamanca and the Austrian School theorists is not expressly mentioned by Mises in the reference which he makes, in passing, to the predecessors of the subjective theory of value at the end of point 3 of Chapter XII of *Human Action* (p. 219).
17 F.A. Hayek stated that 'it is probably no exaggeration to say that every important advance in economic theory during the last hundred years was a further step in the consistent application of subjectivism'. *The Counter-Revolution of Science*, New York: Free Press of Glencoe, 1955, p. 31. Hayek adds, referring to Mises (note 24, pp. 209–210), that subjectivism

> has probably been carried out most consistently by Ludwig von Mises and I believe that most peculiarities of his views which at first strike many readers as strange and unacceptable are due to the fact that *in the consistent devel-*

opment of the subjectivist approach he has for a long time moved ahead of his contemporaries. Probably all the characteristic features of his theories, from his theory of money to what he calls his *apriorism*, his views about mathematical economics in general, and the measurement of economic phenomena in particular, and his criticism of planning all follow directly from his central position.

(The italics are mine.) This subjectivist conception is the most typical stamp of Mises and is the main element which differentiates the Austrian School from the other marginalist schools of Walras and Jevons. See William J. Jaffé, 'Menger, Jevons and Walras De-Homogenized', *Economic Enquiry*, no. 14 (4), December 1976, pp. 511–524. Also see note 36.

18 Böhm-Bawerk's *magnum opus* which is, in spite of its title, an economic treatise in the true sense of the term, is *Kapital und Kapitalzins*, Wagner, Insbruck, 1884–1903. There is an English translation by Hans Sennholz, published under the title *Capital and Interest*, South Holland, IL: Libertarian Press, 1959.

19 Ludwig von Mises, *Theorie des Geldes und der Umlaufsmittel*, Munich and Leipzig: Duncker & Humblot, 1912 (second edition in 1924). The best English edition (translated from German by H.E. Batson) was published, with a foreword by Murray N. Rothbard, Indianapolis, IN: Liberty Classics, 1981.

20 Unfortunately, an author of the prestige of John Maynard Keynes could not extract sufficient meaning out of Mises' work because, as he himself confesses, 'In German I can only clearly understand what I already know – so that new ideas are apt to be veiled from me by the difficulties of the language'. John Maynard Keynes, *A Treatise on Money*, London, 1930, vol. I, p. 199, note 2. Neither could Paul A. Samuelson take advantage of Mises' contribution, as shown by the comments he makes on Mises' monetary theory in his *Foundations of Economic Analysis*, Cambridge, MA: Harvard University Press, 1947, pp. 117–118.

21 The radical separation between the 'micro' and 'macro' aspects of Economic Science is another of the insufficiencies characteristic of modern introductory manuals and textbooks on political economy. Instead of providing a unified treatment of economic problems, as Mises does, they always present Economic Science as divided into two different disciplines ('microeconomics' and 'macroeconomics') with no connection between them and which, therefore, can be studied separately. As Mises rightly says, this separation originates from the use of concepts which, like the *general price level*, ignore the application of the subjective theory of the value of money and continue to be anchored in the pre-scientific stage of economics, when it was still attempted to make analyses in terms of global classes or aggregates of goods, rather than in terms of incremental or marginal units of them. This explains the fact that, to date, a whole 'discipline' based on the study of the mechanical relationships which supposedly exist between macroeconomic aggregates has been developed, the connection of which with individual human action is difficult, if not impossible, to understand.

22 See Mark Skousen, 'Who Predicted the 1929 Crash?', included in *The Meaning of Ludwig von Mises*, Jeffrey M. Herbener (ed.), Amsterdam: Kluwer Academic Publishers, 1993, pp. 247–284. Lionel Robbins, in his 'Introduction' to the first edition of F.A. Hayek's *Prices and Production* (London: Routledge, 1931, p. xii), also referred to this prediction made by Mises and Hayek of the inexorable advent of the Great Depression, which had appeared expressly in an article by Hayek which was published in 1929 in *Monatsberichte des Österreichischen Instituts für Konjunkturforschung*.

23 'The illusion that a rational order of economic management is possible in a society based on public ownership of the means of production owed its origin to

the value theory of the classical economists and its tenacity to the failure of many modern economists to think through consistently to its ultimate conclusions the fundamental theorem of the subjectivist theory. ... In truth it was the errors of these schools that made socialist ideas thrive.' Ludwig von Mises, *Human Action*, p. 206. More recently, Joseph E. Stiglitz has also expressed his opinion that the neoclassical paradigm which has prevailed to date has been, to a great extent, the cause for maintaining the erroneous belief that the socialist economic system could work. He concludes that 'the standard (neoclassical) models were partly to blame for the disastrous situation in which so many Eastern European countries found themselves. A strong case could be made for the proposition that ideas about economics have led close to half the world's population to untold suffering'. J.E. Stiglitz, *Whither Socialism?*, Cambridge, MA: The MIT Press, 1994, pp. ix–xii. Along the same lines, see the declarations made two years earlier by Jesús Huerta de Soto, *Socialismo, cálculo económico y función empresarial*, op. cit., pp. 33 onwards.

24 The concept and analysis of economic calculation and its importance for human action and interaction constitute one of the most essential aspects of Misesian thought and Mises devotes the whole of the Third Part (Chapters XI–XIII) of *Human Action* to studying it. Perhaps the merit of Mises stems from the fact that he knew how to establish in theoretical terms the connection which exists between the subjective world of individual valuations (ordinal) and the external world of market price estimations fixed in monetary units (cardinal world typical of economic calculation). The *bridge* between the two worlds is made possible whenever an act of interpersonal exchange takes place and, driven by the different subjective valuations of the parties, is set forth in a monetary market price or historical exchange relationship in monetary units with a real determined quantitative existence, which can be subsequently used by the entrepreneur as valuable information to estimate the future evolution of events and take decisions (economic calculation). It becomes, therefore, evident that, if free human action is impeded by force, voluntary interpersonal exchanges will not take place, thus destroying the bridge or connection which they represent between the subjective world of the creation of information and direct valuations (ordinal) and the external world of prices (cardinal). This makes economic calculation totally impossible. See especially Murray N. Rothbard, 'The End of Socialism and the Calculation Debate Revisited', *Review of Austrian Economics*, vol. 5, no. 3, 1991, pp. 64–65.

25 Ludwig von Mises, *Die Gemeinwirtschaft: Untersuchungen über den Sozialismus*, Gustav Fischer, Jena, 1922. Translated into English by J. Kahane and published with a foreword by F.A. Hayek under the title *Socialism: An Economic and Sociological Analysis*, Indianapolis, IN: Liberty Classics, 1981. This treatise includes almost literally Mises' first seminal contribution on socialism, which appeared in his article 'Die Wirtschaftsrechnung im Sozialistischen Gemeinwesen', published in *Archiv für Sozialwissenschaft und Sozialpolitik*, no. 47, 1920, pp. 106–121. It was translated into English by S. Adler under the title 'Economic Calculation in the Socialist Commonwealth' and included in *Collectivist Economic Planning*, F.A. Hayek (ed.), Clifton: Augustus M. Kelley, 1975.

26 See the 'Foreword' written by F.A. Hayek for the fourth English edition of Mises' *Socialism*, published in 1981 (*Socialism: An Economic and Sociological Analysis*, op. cit., p. xix). Mises, in turn, acknowledges that, when he started university, he was ideologically a great statist and only slowly did his studies in political economy make him change his mind:

> When I entered the university, I, too, was a thorough statist (interventionist). But in contrast to my fellow students I was consciously anti-Marxian. My first doubts about the excellence of interventionism came to me when, in my

fifth semester, Professor Philippovich induced me to research housing conditions and when, in the following semester in the Seminar on Criminal Law, Professor Löffler asked me to research the changes in law regarding domestic servants, who at that time were still subject to corporal punishment by their employers. It then dawned on me that all real improvements in the conditions of the working classes were the result of capitalism; and that social laws frequently brought about the very opposite of what the legislation was intended to achieve.

Ludwig von Mises, *Notes and Recollections*, op. cit., pp. 16 and 19–20.

27 The other three controversies are, chronologically, the *Methodenstreit*, in which Menger confronted the German Historicist School in the nineteenth century; second, the controversy on the concept of capital and the theory of interest, which was originally maintained between Böhm-Bawerk and J.B. Clark and subsequently between Mises, Hayek and Machlup, on one side, and Frank H. Knight and the School of Chicago, on the other; the third is the well-known controversy of Hayek against Keynes during the 1930s (see F.A. Hayek, *Contra Keynes and Cambridge: Essays, Correspondence*, vol. 9 of *The Collected Works of F.A. Hayek*, Bruce Caldwell (ed.), London: Routledge, 1995). The evolution of historical events (the fall of real socialism) and economic thought (crisis of Keynesian economics) are demonstrating how the Austrian theorists were right in these four doctrinal controversies.

28 Jesús Huerta de Soto, *Socialismo, cálculo económico y función empresarial*, op. cit. Likewise, see Donald A. Lavoie, *Rivalry and Central Planning*, Cambridge: Cambridge University Press, 1985.

29 'Mises was right. ... Socialism has been the great tragedy of this century.' Robert L. Heilbroner, 'The Triumph of Capitalism', *New Yorker*, January 23, 1989, and 'Analysis and Vision in the History of Modern Economic Thought', *Journal of Economic Literature*, vol. 28, September 1990, pp. 1097 and 1110–1111. The economists Wlodzmierz Brus and Kazimierz Laski also conclude that Oskar Lange and the socialist theorists 'never succeeded in confronting the Austrian challenge'. *From Marx to the Market: Socialism in Search of an Economic System*, Oxford: Clarendon Press, 1985, p. 60. Mises summarizes, re-evaluates and gives his final opinion on the impossibility of socialist calculation in the Fifth Part of *Human Action*, Chapters XXV and XXVI.

30 Mises' great merit is that he was the first person to tackle the problem of the theoretical impossibility of socialism, which nobody before him (from 1848 to 1920) had dared to touch and that he showed that, if it was possible to maintain the socialist idea for so long a period of time, it was the result of the errors of the neoclassical paradigm (see heading 2 of Chapter XXVI) and constructivist rationalism (which Mises calls 'rationalistic romanticism'). See *Human Action*, pp. 507 and 702.

31 As Tullio Bagiotti, who was professor of economics at the Bocconi University of Milan, rightly said, 'Il titolo non mancherà di sorprendere un poco. Nessun economista prima di lui l'aveva usato, anche se l'economia spesso forzava i suoi cànoni presentandosi com norma all'azione'. Tullio Bagiotti, 'Presentazione' to the Italian edition of *L'Azione Umana: Trattato di Economia*, Turin: Unione Tipografico-Editrice Torinese, 1959, p. vi.

32 Mises expressly states that the essential element of entrepreneurship is its creative capacity ('Only the human mind that directs action and production is creative', p. 141). Likewise, he strongly criticizes the popular fallacies that consider that profit is derived from simply assuming risks (when risk only gives rise to an additional cost of the production process, which has nothing to do with entrepreneurial profit, pp. 809–810) and the essentially erroneous idea that entrepre-

neurship is a management production factor which can be bought and sold on the market. On the contrary, says Mises, 'In order to succeed in business a man does not need a degree from a school of business administration. These schools train the subalterns for routine jobs. They certainly do not train entrepreneurs. An entrepreneur cannot be trained. A man becomes an entrepreneur in seizing an opportunity and filling the gap. No special education is required for such a display of keen judgement, foresight and judgement' (p. 314).

33 Kirzner has told me that his whole academic career was due to the historical accident of having chosen, in order to complete some credits which he needed, to attend the seminar on economics which Mises held at the University of New York from 1949 to 1969, applying the decisive criterion of the number of works published by each lecturer. The basic works of Israel M. Kirzner are the following: *Competition and Entrepreneurship*, Chicago, IL: Chicago University Press, 1973; *Perception, Opportunity and Profit*, Chicago, IL: Chicago University Press, 1979; *Discovery and the Capitalist Process*, Chicago, IL: Chicago University Press, 1985; *Discovery, Capitalism and Distributive Justice*, Oxford: Basil Blackwell, 1989; and *The Meaning of the Market Process*, London: Routledge, 1992.

34 Mises' emphatic affirmations that economics is a science which deals with means and not ends (p. 15) should be understood to mean that economics never analyses the specific content or makes value judgements on the ends desired by human beings when they act. However, in economic analysis, the ends, like the means, are taken into account, always in strictly formal terms, as a result of the continuous flow of creation of information which arises from the entrepreneurial process of human interactions. Moreover, economics also studies which established rules or precepts of behaviour are in accordance with the spontaneous process of human coordination driven by the force of entrepreneurship and which, on the contrary, make it difficult or impossible. We are, therefore, in complete agreement with the position of Murray N. Rothbard (*The Ethics of Liberty*, Atlantic Highlands, NJ: Humanities Press, 1982, p. 202) when he criticizes Mises because the latter considers that the ethical principles of behaviour are also purely subjective (see note 73). In addition, it was a reductionist and narrow interpretation of Mises' clear position on the role of ends and means in economic analysis which induced Lionel Robbins to commit the error of considering that the ends are 'given' (not in the sense that they should not be judged, but in the sense that they are known and constant) and, therefore, economic behaviour should be reduced to a simple optimization or maximization aimed at getting the maximum of previously fixed ends using means which are also known (p. 21).

35 Jesús Huerta de Soto, *Socialismo, cálculo económico y función empresarial*, op. cit., pp. 150 and 406–407. As Mises states, theory comes before empirical facts and is indispensable in interpreting the social reality that constitutes history. The latter, in order to be formed as a discipline, also requires a non-scientific judgement of relevance (*Verstehen*, or understanding) which, as it is not objective, varies from one historian to another (Chapter II of *Human Action*).

36 'Economics is not about things and tangible material objects; it is about men, their meanings and actions. Goods, commodities and wealth and all other notions of conduct are not elements of nature; they are elements of human meaning and conduct. He who wants to deal with them must not look at the external world; he must search for them in the meaning of acting men. ... Production is not something physical, material and external; it is a spiritual and intellectual phenomenon' (pp. 92 and 141). Therefore, in economics, the 'restrictions' are not imposed by the material factors of the external world (for example, in the energy field, by the oil reserves), but by entrepreneurial human knowledge (the discovery, for example, of a carburettor which doubles the efficiency of the internal combustion engine has the same economic effect as the duplication of the total physical oil reserves).

37 Thus, an outstanding example is the demonstration of the Law of Diminishing Returns which Mises sets out in exclusively logical terms (heading 2 of Chapter VII of *Human Action*). This logical demonstration is based on the fact that, in *sensu contrario*, if the mentioned law were not true in the world of human action, the production factor considered as fixed would have an unlimited production capacity and, therefore, would be a free good. Karl Menger, the son of the great Austrian economist, has tried, in our opinion fruitlessly, to refute Mises' theorem on the strictly praxeological nature of the Law of Diminishing Returns. See Karl Menger, 'Remarks on the law of Diminishing Returns. A Study in Meta-Economics', Chapter 23 of *Selected Papers in Logic and Foundations, Didactics, Economics*, Dordrecht, Holland: D. Reidel Publishing Co., 1979, pp. 279–302.

38 Ludwig von Mises, *Human Action*, p. 58. A recent, favourable and objective explanation of the methodological paradigm of Mises is given by Bruce Caldwell, *Beyond Positivism: Economic Methodology in the Twentieth Century*, second edition, London: Routledge, 1994, pp. 117–138. On Mises' methodology in general and, particularly, on the relationships between theory and history, see the thirty-six bibliographical references contained in my article on 'Crisis y método en la Ciencia Económica', *Hacienda Pública Española*, no. 74, 1982 (republished in Jesús Huerta de Soto, *Estudios de Economía Política*, Madrid: Unión Editorial, 1994, pp. 59–84), together with Mises' *Theory and History*, New Haven, CT: Yale University Press, 1957, and Hayek's 'The Facts of the Social Sciences', in *Individualism and Economic Order*, Chicago, IL: Henry Regnery, 1972, and *The Counter-Revolution of Science*, Indianapolis, IN: Liberty Press, 1979.

39 Mises calls equilibrium an 'evenly rotating economy' and considers it an imaginary construction with a strictly instrumental value for improving the analytical comprehension of only two problems in our science: the emergence of entrepreneurial profits in a dynamic environment and the relationship that exists between the price of consumer goods and services and the price of the production factors necessary to produce them (p. 248). In this specific aspect, I would go even further than Mises himself, as I believe that it is possible to explain the emergence of entrepreneurial profits and the trend toward fixing the prices of the production factors in accordance with the discounted value of their marginal productivity, without any reference to models of equilibrium (either general or partial), but merely to the dynamic process which tends towards what Mises calls a 'final state of rest' (which is never reached). In any case, it must be stressed that, according to Mises, 'What distinguishes the Austrian School and will lend it immortal fame is precisely the fact that it created a theory of economic action and not of economic equilibrium or non action'. Ludwig von Mises, *Notes and Recollections*, op. cit., p. 36. Moreover, according to Mises, 'The imaginary construction of the final state of rest is marked by paying full regard to change in the temporal succession of events (p. 246). This is what differentiates it from the model of equilibrium or 'evenly rotating economy' in which the time factor is radically eliminated (p. 247).

40 'There are, in the field of economics, no constant relations, and consequently no measurement is possible'. Ludwig von Mises, *Human Action*, op. cit., p. 55. Furthermore, as we have already seen in note 10, the axiomatic criteria of rationality proposed by Samuelson and other mathematical economists do not make sense either, as, if an actor prefers a to b and b to c, he may perfectly well prefer c to a, without ceasing to be 'rational' or consistent, if he has simply changed his mind (although it has only occurred during the hundredth of a second for which he has considered this problem in his own reasoning).

41 The critical analysis of the use of mathematics in economics is included under heading 5 of chapter XVI of *Human Action* and is one of the most important parts of the book. Mises' contributions on this subject were, in turn, parallel to

those which were also developed by the Austrian economist Hans Mayer, who succeeded Menger and Wieser as professor of economics at Vienna. For Mayer, the neoclassical theory of functional or mathematical price determination does not make sense, as it presupposes that a system of equations should integrate, *simultaneously*, information on the prices and quantities of goods and services produced in the market. In reality, these are heterogeneous magnitudes which are never given at the same time in society, but rather emerge s*equentially* throughout a process, as a result of specific human actions driven by the force of entrepreneurship. Hans Mayer's essential work is the previously mentioned 'Der Erkenntniswert der funktionellen Preistheorien', in *Die Wirtschaftstheorie der Gegenwart*, vol. 2, Springer, Vienna, 1932, pp. 147–239b (translated into English under the title 'The Cognitive Value of Functional Theories of Price' and published in volume II of *Classics in Austrian Economics: A Sampling in the History of a Tradition*, Israel M. Kirzner (ed.), London: William Pickering, 1994, pp. 55–71). The mathematicians are left with the challenge of conceiving and developing a new 'mathematics' capable of including and permitting the analysis of the human being's creative capacity and its implications, without resorting, therefore, to the hypotheses of constancy which come from the world of physics and upon which all the mathematical languages known to date are based. In our opinion, however, the ideal scientific language for including this creative capacity is precisely the language that human beings have spontaneously created in their day-to-day entrepreneurship, which materializes in the different languages and forms of speech which prevail in the world today.

42 Economic problems would be eliminated and substituted by strictly technological problems if, as Mises rightly states (pp. 206–207), a relationship of perfect substitution existed between all the production factors in given proportions, or if all the production resources were completely specific. Apart from these cases, all problems are economic according to our definition in the main text unless, as is the case of the neoclassical economists, the functions of supply and demand and the corresponding prices of equilibrium are presupposed. In this case, although there are no relationships of perfect substitution in fixed proportions between the production factors, and the latter are not completely specific, the economic problems which occur in the real world are also reduced to strictly technical problems of maximization.

43 The conversion of Mark Blaug, who has deserted the model of general equilibrium and the static neoclassical-Walrasian paradigm, has caused a great sensation. He concludes that 'I have come slowly and extremely reluctantly to view that they (the Austrian School) are right and that we have all been wrong'. See *Appraising Economic Theories*, Mark Blaug and Neil de Marchi (eds), London: Edward Elgar, 1991, p. 508. In the same respect, see also his *Economics through the Looking-Glass*, Institute of Economic Affairs, Occasional Paper 78, London, 1988, p. 37. Even more recently, in the *Economic Journal* (November 1993, p. 157), Blaug again referred to the neoclassical paradigm in relation to its application in order to justify the socialist system as something 'so administratively naive as to be positively laughable. Only those drunk on perfectly competitive static equilibrium theory could have swallowed such nonsense. I was one of those who swallowed it as a student in the 1950s and I can only marvel now at my own dim-wittedness'. It is not even necessary to mention the fact that the neoclassical analysis of 'imperfect' information which emerges from G.J. Stigler's article on 'The Economics of Information' (*Journal of Political Economy*, no. 69, June 1961, pp. 213–225) is not capable of including the true creative capacity of the human being, or the ineradicable ignorance which characterizes him in the analysis, as it considers that both the possible alternatives of future events and their distribution of probabilities are known. In fact, in real processes of human

interaction, not even the possible alternatives are known, and much less their distribution of probabilities (entrepreneurial creativity continuously generates new options). Therefore, the neoclassical theory is a caricature of the concept of entrepreneurial information in the market and, although it claims that its models include the 'imperfect' nature of the information, it continues, in fact, to be anchored in the presupposition of constancy and complete information (even though in probabilistic terms) in respect of the possible alternatives. See, for example, Israel M. Kirzner, 'Economics and Error', Chapter 8 of *Perception, Opportunity and Profit*, op. cit., pp. 120–136.

44 The definitive bibliographical work on Mises is by Bettina Bien Greaves and Robert McGee, published under the title *Mises: An Annotated Bibliography*, New York: The Foundation for Economic Education, 1993, 391 pp. On Mises' life and intellectual evolution, apart from his valuable autobiography (*Notes and Recollections*, op. cit.), we can read the works of Murray N. Rothbard, among which his article 'Ludwig Edler von Mises', *The New Palgrave: A Dictionary of Economics*, London: Macmillan, 1987, vol. III, pp. 479–480, second edition 2008, vol. 5, pp. 624–26; his monographic work *Ludwig von Mises: Scholar, Creator, Hero*, Auburn, AL: The Ludwig von Mises Institute, Auburn University, 1988; and *The Essential von Mises*, Michigan: Oakler R. Bramble, 1973, stand out. Other very interesting works include the biography written by his wife, Margit von Mises, *My Years with Ludwig von Mises*, New York: Arlington House, 1976, and the glossary on *Human Action* prepared by Percy L. Greaves, entitled *Mises Made Easier: A Glossary for Ludwig von Mises' Human Action*, New York: Free Market Books, 1974.

45 *The Annals of the American Academy of Political and Social Science*, no. 239, November 1944, pp. 192–193.

46 *The University of Chicago Magazine*, no. 67, Autumn 1974, p. 16.

47 'A man of an exceptional intelligence whose contributions to economic science have all been of the first order.' See Maurice Allais, *L'Impôt sur le capital et la réforme monétaire*, Paris: Hermann Editeurs, 1989, p. 307. This praise from Allais is of special value as it comes from a mathematical economist who is very distant from Misesian methodology, although it should be pointed out that Allais, from the beginning, recognized the importance of the Misesian theory on the impossibility of socialist economic calculation and the need to develop a dynamic theory of social processes in disequilibrium. See, for example, Maurice Allais, *Traité d'économie pure*, third edition, Paris: Clément Juglar, 1994, pp. 549–551 and 653–657 (which includes more than five literal quotations from Mises).

48 Lord Robbins, *Autobiography of an Economist*, London: Macmillan, 1971, p. 108.

49 This is a conservative estimate, considering an average of 3,000 copies for each reprint in English and an average of 2,000 copies for each reprint in other languages.

50 Ludwig von Mises, *Nationalökonomie: Theorie des Handelns und Wirtschaftens*, Geneva: Editions Union, 1940, 756 pp.

51 'My objective in writing the treatise was to provide a comprehensive theory of economic behaviour which would include not only the economics of a market economy (free-enterprise system) but no less the economics of any other thinkable system of social cooperation, viz., socialism, interventionism, corporativism and so on. Furthermore I deemed it necessary to deal with all those objections which, from various points of view have been raised against the validity of economic reasoning and the soundness of the methods hitherto applied by economists of all schools and lines of thought. Only such an exhaustive treatment of all critical objections can satisfy the exacting reader and convince him that economics is a science both conveying knowledge and able to guide conduct. The treatise is purely scientific and certainly not a popular book. However, as it does not use any technical terms but those precisely defined and explained, it can be understood by every

educated man.' Ludwig von Mises wrote these words in December 1944 to his American publisher Norman V. Davidson of Yale University Press. They are quoted by Margit von Mises, *My Years with Ludwig von Mises*, op. cit., pp. 105–106.
52 This appears, specifically, on pp. 439–444 of the German edition of *Nationalökonomie*, which have been translated into English by Percy L. Greaves and published in his book *Mises Made Easier: A Glossary for Ludwig von Mises' Human Action*, op. cit., pp. 150–157.
53 Ludwig von Mises, *Nationalökonomie: Theorie des Handelns und Wirtschaftens*, second edition, The International Carl Menger Library, Munich: Philosophia Verlag, 1980.
54 See, among others, the reviews published by E. Tuchtfeldt in the *Neue Zürcher Zeitung* (no. 207) on September 8, 1981; in *Unsere Wirtschaft* (Düsseldorf, August 1981); the review by Wilhelm Seuss in the *Frankfurter Allgemeine Zeitung* (9 December 1980); and the one by Karl Graber, *Die Presse*, Vienna (23 November 1981).
55 Ludwig von Mises, *Human Action: A Treatise on Economics*, New Haven, CT: Yale University Press, 1949, 889 pp. plus the index. The British edition also appeared in 1949 with the same title and format, published by William Hodge in London.
56 Margit von Mises gives full details of the headaches which the errors in the second edition of *Human Action* caused to Ludwig von Mises. See *My Years with Ludwig von Mises*, op. cit., Chapter 8.
57 Ludwig von Mises, *Human Action: A Treatise on Economics*, third revised edition, Chicago, IL: Henry Regnery, 1966, 907 pp. plus the index.
58 Ludwig von Mises, *Human Action: An Abridged Audiotape Version*, Ashland, OR: Classics on Tape, 1990, read by Bernard Mayes.
59 Ludwig von Mises, *Human Action: A Treatise on Economics*, fourth revised edition, with a foreword by Bettina Bien Greaves, Irvington-on-Hudson, NY: The Foundation for Economic Education, 1996 (this is available on the Internet via the Ludwig von Mises Institute website).
60 Ludwig von Mises, *Human Action: A Treatise on Economics, The Scholar's Edition*, with an introduction by Jeffrey H. Herbener, Hans-Hermann Hoppe and Joseph T. Salerno, Auburn, AL: Ludwig von Mises Institute, 1998.
61 Ludwig von Mises, *L'Azione Umana: Trattato di Economia*, translation and foreword by Tullio Bagiotti, Turin: Unione Tipografico-Editrice Torinese, in the collection Sociologi ed Economisti, 1959, 861 pp. In 1988 a book in homage to the memory of Tullio Bagiotti was published, *Studi in memoria di Tullio Bagiotti*, Padova, 1988.
62 Chinese translation of *Human Action* by Tao-Ping Hsia, revised by Hui-Lin Wu, Taipei, Taiwan: Yuan Liu Publishing, 1991, nos. 1 and 2 of the series 'Famous Books on Libertarianism', two volumes, the first of which includes pp. 1 to 506 and the second pp. 507–1,074.
63 Ludwig von Mises, *L'Action humaine: Traité d'économie*, translation by Raoul Audouin, Paris: Presses Universitaires de France, January 1985, 942 pp. Raoul Audouin has also translated the main works of Hayek into French, including *La Présomption fatale: Les Erreurs du socialism*, Presses Universitaires de France, Paris, 1988, and *La Constitution de la liberté*, Paris: Litec, 1994 (the latter was translated into French in collaboration with professor Jacques Garello).
64 *Human Action*, translated into Korean and published in Seoul by Kyung Mun Sa Publishing Co., vol. I, 1987 (Chapters 1–19, 519 pp.) and vol. II, 1988, (Chapters 20–39, 459 pp.), both with forewords by Toshio Murata.
65 Ludwig von Mises, *Açào humana: um tratado de economia*, translated into Portuguese by Donald Stewart, Jr, Rio de Janeiro: Instituto Liberal, 1990, 972 pp. plus indices.

66 Ludwig von Mises, *Ningen-Kôi-Gaku*, Tokyo: Shunjü Sha, 1991, 995 pp. plus the index.
67 This thesis earned a 'cum laude' award. Mariano Puigdoller Oliver presided over the tribunal judging, which also included Professors Nicolás Pérez Serrano, Juan del Rosal Fernández, José María Naharro Mora and Gaspar Bayón Chacón. As an anecdote, we should mention that the censorship which then prevailed in the Spain of General Franco issued an official communication dated 25 April 1958 of the Directorate General of Information of the Ministry of Information and Tourism, Inspection of Books (file 842–58) stating that, before publishing the thesis, 'the indicated parts of pages 13, 34–36 and 42–44, the whole of page 56, and the indicated parts of pages 62–65, 72–78, 96–125 and 142–197 should be deleted, ordering the submission of printed galley proofs which included the deletions ordered by the authority'.
68 Ludwig von Mises, *La acción humana (tratado de economía)*, Fundación Ignacio Villalonga, Valencia, 1960, vols I and II. I have a copy which was revised by the censorship authorities, in which instructions are also given to delete several paragraphs of Mises' work which were considered politically dangerous for the regime of General Franco, then in power in Spain. The Foundation created by the entrepreneur Ignacio Villalonga, who in his youth had been a deputy for Francesc Cambó's *Lliga Regionalista*, was a pioneer in the difficult task of publishing, in Franco's Spain, a magnificent collection of books on libertarianism, democracy and market economy, which was directed by Joaquín Reig Albiol in the 1960s. See also 'Ignacio Villalonga: Semblanza de un político, banquero y liberal', in Jesús Huerta de Soto, *Nuevos Estudios de Economía Política*, Madrid: Unión Editorial, 2002, ch. XV, pp 379–394.
69 Ludwig von Mises, *La acción humana (tratado de economía)*, second edition in Spanish, Madrid: Editorial Sopec, 1968, translated by Joaquín Reig Albiol, 1,066 pp. This is the edition that I first read more than thirty five years ago, when I began my studies in economics at the Complutense University of Madrid.
70 Other important books by Mises translated into Spanish and published by Unión Editorial are: *Burocracia*, translated by Dalmacio Negro Pavón, Madrid: Unión Editorial, 1974; *Teoría e Historia*, translated by Rigoberto Juárez Paz, Madrid: Unión Editorial, 1975 and 2003; *Sobre liberalismo y capitalismo* – a collection of essays which includes *Liberalism* (third edition), *The Anticapitalist Mentality* (second edition) and *Six lessons of capitalism* (second edition), Madrid: Unión Editorial, 1995; *La teoría del dinero y del crédito*, Madrid: Unión Editorial, 1997; *Socialismo, Análisis económico y sociológico*, Madrid: Unión Editorial, 2003; *Crítica del intervencionismo*, translated by Jesús Gómez Ruiz, Madrid: Unión Editorial, 2001; *Autobiografía de un liberal*, Madrid: Unión Editorial, 2001; and *Gobierno omnipotente*, translated by Pedro Elgoibar, Madrid: Unión Editorial, 2002.
71 Ludwig von Mises, *La acción humana: tratado de economía*, Madrid: Unión Editorial, 1980, third edition, 1,302 pp.; fourth edition of 1985, 1,302 pp. These are the editions which have basically been used as a textbook by my students over the last fifteen academic years in which I have been teaching political economy at the School of Law of the Complutense University of Madrid. The subsequent editions were used at my chair at King Juan Carlos University (from 2000 onwards).
72 As Margit von Mises points out in her biography of her husband, 'Ludwig's most ardent readers and admirers always have been in the Spanish-speaking countries. Apparently, the more subjugated the country is, the deeper the longing for freedom'. Margit von Mises, *My Years with Ludwig von Mises*, op. cit., p. 109. The main academic trips made by Mises to Latin America were the following: from 30 July to 28 August 1949, to the School of Economics of the University of

Mexico; from 31 March to 16 April 1950, to the University of Peru, under the auspices of the Peruvian Banco Central; from 19–28 September 1958, again to Mexico, under the auspices of the Instituto de Investigaciones Sociales y Económicas; and, lastly, the important visit made from 2 to 15 July 1959 to the University of Buenos Aires, under the auspices of the Centro de Estudios para la Libertad. The speeches he made on this trip were transcribed and published in English under the title *Economic Policy: Thoughts for Today and Tomorrow*, Chicago, IL: Henry Regnery, 1979. Subsequently translated into Spanish by Joaquín Reig Albiol, they were published under the title *Seis lecciones sobre el capitalismo*, Madrid: Instituto de Economía de Mercado and Unión Editorial, 1981, 107 pp. (republished in 1991 in the book *Sobre liberalismo y capitalismo*, op. cit.).

73 See pp. 405–408 and, particularly, pp. 264–267, where Mises expressly states that 'The market economy is the product of a long evolutionary process'. What is more, on p. 33, Mises explains how the aprioristic nature of thought categories is perfectly compatible with the theory of evolution, coinciding with the thesis that Hayek develops *in extenso* in his book *The Sensory Order*, Chicago, IL: The University of Chicago Press, 1976. In the light of these passages from *Human Action*, perhaps Hayek's criticism of the utilitarian rationalism of Mises in the foreword he wrote for the latest English edition of *Socialism* is somewhat exaggerated. See F. A. Hayek, 'Foreword', *Socialism: An Economic and Sociological Analysis*, Indianapolis, IN: Liberty Classics, 1981, pp. xxiii–xxiv, and Jesús Huerta de Soto, *Estudios de Economía Política*, Madrid: Unión Editorial, 1994, pp. 114–115.

74 F.A. Hayek, *Law, Legislation and Liberty*, Chicago, IL: The University of Chicago Press, three vols, 1973, 1976 and 1979, and *The Fatal Conceit: The Errors of Socialism*, London: Routledge, 1988.

75 'The moral precepts and the laws of the country are means by which men seek to attain certain ends.' *Human Action*, op. cit., p. 761.

76 'Economics does currently inform us, not that *moral principles* are subjective, but that utilities and costs are indeed subjective.' Murray N. Rothbard, *The Ethics of Liberty*, Atlantic Highlands, NJ: Humanities Press, 1982, p. 202.

77 See Hans-Hermann Hoppe, *A Theory of Capitalism and Socialism*, Holland: Kluwer Academic Publishers, 1989, especially Chapter 7, pp. 127–144; and *The Economics and Ethics of Private Property*, Holland: Kluwer Academic Publishers, 1993, Chapters 8–10, pp. 173–208.

78 See Israel M. Kirzner, *Discovery, Capitalism and Distributive Justice*, London: Basil Blackwell, 1989.

79 I set out my theory of the three levels (theoretical, historical-evolutionary and moral) of approach to the study of the social reality in 'Historia, ciencia económica y ética social', Jesús Huerta de Soto, *Estudios de Economía Política*, Madrid: Unión Editorial, 1994, Chapter VII, pp. 105–110. See also my note on 'Conjectural History and Beyond', '"The Fatal Conceit" by F.A. Hayek. A Special Symposium', *Humane Studies Review*, vol. 6, no. 2, Winter 1988–1989, p. 10 (Chapter 3 of this book).

80 For Mises, practical knowledge as a 'specific anticipative understanding of the conditions of the uncertain future defies any rules and systematization. It can be neither taught nor learned'. *Human Action*, op. cit., p. 585. Also see Jesús Huerta de Soto, *Socialismo, cálculo económico y función empresarial*, op. cit. pp. 52–85.

81 See Jesús Huerta de Soto, *Socialismo, cálculo económico y función empresarial*, op. cit. pp. 80–82.

82 Murray N. Rothbard, 'Monopoly and Competition', Chapter 10 of *Man, Economy, and State*, Nash Publishing, Los Angeles, 1970, pp. 560–666; and Israel M. Kirzner, 'Competition and Monopoly', Chapter 3 of *Competition and Entrepreneurship*, Chicago, IL and London: The University of Chicago Press, 1973, pp. 88–134.

83 Effectively, Margit von Mises, in her biography of her husband, tells us that

> in Stresa, during the 1965 Mont Pèlerin meeting, Joaquín Reig once spoke to Ludwig von Mises about monopoly and Rothbard's *Man, Economy, and State*, which had been published in 1962. Reig directed Ludwig's attention to the fact that Rothbard, one of Ludwig's most able and admiring pupils, did not completely agree with Ludwig's analysis of monopoly. Ludwig replied: 'I would subscribe to every word Rothbard has written in his study'. About this Reig told me: 'That was such a generous statement of Ludwig von Mises to say that one of his own students had exposed one of his own ideas better than he himself had been able to do it, that my admiration for this man jumped sky-high.'

Margit von Mises, *My Years with Ludwig von Mises*, op. cit., p. 158. Another explicit acknowledgement of having committed an error which shows Mises' great humility and intellectual generosity, in strong contrast to the arrogance of modern authors, appears on p. 786, where, referring to the gold standard (with a fractional reserve and controlled by the State), Mises regrets having been unable to see from the beginning that this system made it excessively easy for governments to manipulate the monetary supply as they wished: 'In dealing with the problems of the gold exchange standard all economists – including the author of this book – failed to realize the fact that it places in the hands of governments the power to manipulate their nation's currency easily'.

84 See Jesús Huerta de Soto, 'Entrepreneurship and the Economic Analysis of Socialism', in *New Perspectives on Austrian Economics*, Gerrit Meijer (ed.), London and New York: Routledge, 1995, especially pp. 247–250 (Chapter 4 of this book).

85 Thus, for example, in Part Four, 'Monetary Reconstruction', which he included in the English republication of *The Theory of Money and Credit* in 1953, four years after the publication of the first edition of *Human Action*, he concludes that: 'The main thing is that the government should no longer be in a position to increase the quantity of money in circulation and the amount of chequebook money not fully – that is, 100 percent – covered by deposits paid in by the public'. Ludwig von Mises, *The Theory of Money and Credit*, Indianapolis, IN: Liberty Classics, 1981, pp. 481 and 491.

86 The most important bibliography of the mentioned authors may be consulted in Jesús Huerta de Soto, 'A Critical Analysis of Central Banks and Fractional-Reserve Free Banking from the Austrian School Perspective', *Review of Austrian Economics*, vol. 8, no. 2, 1995, pp. 25–38 (Chapter 10 of this book). It is important to clarify that Mises and the Austrian School economists who favour a free banking system based on a 100 per cent cash ratio are really upholding a position which is radically different to that of the School of Chicago theorists, who also defended a 100 per cent cash ratio for demand bank deposits. In fact, the theorists of the School of Chicago defend the need for the existence of a monopolistic central bank which is responsible for monetary supply and, if they propose a 100 per cent cash ratio, it is precisely to make the monetary policy of the governments easier and its effects more 'predictable'. On the contrary, the Austrian economists defend the complete disappearance of State intervention in the monetary and credit fields, together with the reprivatization of the banking system with a cash ratio of 100 per cent for demand deposits of the commodity used as money which, depending on the evolutionary process, prevails in the market (gold and, to a lesser extent, silver). The Austrian position is, therefore, contrary to the monetarist (general equation of exchange) and Keynesian hypotheses, as both the latter share the macroeconomic approach and ignore the

application of the theory of marginal utility to money and the effects of microeconomic discoordination of inflation on capital goods. See Jesús Huerta de Soto, 'A Critique of Monetarist and Keynesian Theories', Chapter VII of *Money, Bank Credit, and Ecomonic Cycles*, Auburn, AL: Ludwig von Mises Institute, 2006.

87 'As far as there is unhampered capitalism, there is no longer any question of poverty in the sense in which this term is applied to the conditions of a non-capitalist society. The increase in population figures does not create supernumerary mouths, but additional hands whose employment produces additional wealth.' Ludwig von Mises, *Human Action*, op. cit., p. 836.

88 See F.A. Hayek, *The Fatal Conceit: The Errors of Socialism*, London: Routledge, 1988, pp. 120–134; and Jesús Huerta de Soto, *Socialismo, cálculo económico y función empresarial*, op. cit., pp. 80–82.

89 See Julian L. Simon, *The Economic Consequences of Immigration*, Basil Blackwell, London, 1989; and *The Ultimate Resource*, Princeton, NJ: Princeton University Press, 1994 (second edition).

90 Also see Mises' detailed study of *Bureaucracy* (the first English edition was published by Yale University Press in 1944), where he concludes that: 'It was a purposeful confusion on the part of the German metaphysicians of statolatry that they clothed all men in the government service with the gloriole of such altruistic self-sacrifice' (p. 78). The Misesian analysis had such a great influence on William A. Niskanen that, in his now classic book on economic analysis of bureaucracy, he profusely quotes Mises' pioneering study. See William A. Niskanen, *Bureaucracy and Representative Government* (second edition included in *Bureaucracy and Public Goods*, Aldershot: Edward Elgar, 1994), pp. 3, 7–9, 19, 36, 68–69, 201 and 208.

91 'Democracy guarantees a system of government in accordance with the wishes and plans of the majority. But it cannot prevent majorities from falling victims to erroneous ideas and from adopting inappropriate policies which not only fail to realize the ends aimed at but result in disaster.' Ludwig von Mises, *Human Action*, op. cit., p. 193.

92 'The gold standard makes the determination of money's purchasing power independent of the changing ambitions and doctrines of political parties and pressure groups. This is not a defect of the gold standard; it is its main excellence.' Ludwig von Mises, *Human Action*, op. cit., p. 474.

93 Quoted by Thomas J. DiLorenzo, 'The Subjective Roots of James Buchanan's Economics', *Review of Austrian Economics*, vol. 4, 1990, p.108. DiLorenzo acknowledges, notwithstanding, that the School of Public Choice is not fully influenced by subjectivism and that a large amount of its analysis is still very much influenced by the positivist and scientist methodology of the Neoclassical School. Also see Thomas J. DiLorenzo, 'Competition and Political Entrepreneurship: Austrian Insights into Public Choice Theory', *Review of Austrian Economics*, vol. 2, pp. 59–71.

94 In short, to use a not very appropriate expression which is today in common use among economists, the detailed study of *Human Action* will mean a very profitable 'investment in human capital' for them. Incidentally, the pioneering nature of Mises' contributions to what is inappropriately called the theory of 'human capital' and the processes of investment in education and training and its eminently speculative and entrepreneurial nature may also be seen on pp. 624 and 625 of *Human Action*. The same may be said in respect of the small amount of truth contained in the so-called 'theory of rational expectations' (*Human Action*, p. 797, and also Mises' article 'Elastic Expectations in the Austrian Theory of the Trade Cycle', *Economica*, August 1943, pp. 251–252), the errors of which are pointed out by Mises on p. 871 and have been subsequently clarified even further

by, among others, Gerald P. O'Driscoll and Mario J. Rizzo in *The Economics of Time and Ignorance*, Oxford: Basil Blackwell, 1985, pp. 222 onwards, and Jesús Huerta de Soto, *Money, Bank Credit, and Ecomonic Cycles*, op. cit., Chapter VII.

95 With regard to the study of *Human Action* at a strictly individual level, I can say from my own experience that it can be done intensively over a one-month period, with some three hours a day of detailed reading.

96 Eugen von Böhm-Bawerk, *Capital and Interest*, vol. II, *Positive Theory of Capital*, Book III, 'Value and Price', South Holland, IL: Libertarian Press, 1959, pp. 207–256.

97 This gap may easily be filled by referring to Murray N. Rothbard, 'General Pricing of the Factors', Chapter 7 of *Man, Economy, and State*, Los Angeles, CA: Nash Publishing, 1970, pp. 387–433 (fourth edition by the Ludwig von Mises Institute, Auburn University, 1994).

98 See Jesús Huerta de Soto (ed.), *Lecturas de Economía Política*, three vols, Madrid: Unión Editorial, 1986–1987. This includes, among other things, Spanish versions of the works quoted in the two preceding notes, Eugen von Böhm-Bawerk, 'La ley básica de determinación del precio' (vol. I, pp. 99–142) and Murray N. Rothbard, 'La fijación general del precio de los factores de producción' (vol. II, pp. 21–48).

99 Murray N. Rothbard's posthumous work on the history of economic thought from the standpoint of the Austrian School is made up of the two volumes of *An Austrian Perspective on the History of Economic Thought*, *Economic Thought before Adam Smith* (vol. 1) and *Classical Economics* (vol. 2), Aldershot: Edward Elgar, 1995.

100 We cannot leave aside, in this respect, the notable economic treatise written by Murray N. Rothbard, *Man, Economy, and State*, of which five editions have been published to date (Van Nostrand, New Jersey, 1962; Nash Publishing, Los Angeles, 1970; New York University Press, 1979; and Ludwig von Mises Institute, Auburn University, 1994, and Scholar's Edition 2004) and which is completed by the book *Power and Market* (Institute for Humane Studies, 1970, New York University Press, 1977, and Scholar's Edition 2004). Although Rothbard's treatise provides extraordinary clarification of many issues and, in many aspects, even exceeds *Human Action*, we feel, notwithstanding, that there still exists the challenge of writing *A Treatise on Modern Political Economy* which incorporates and integrates the latest contributions of the Austrian School, providing an even greater impetus for its development in the next century.

18 In memoriam of Murray N. Rothbard

1 Published in the *Journal des économistes et des études humaines, Bilingual Journal of Interdisciplinary Studies*, Paris and Aix-en-Provence, vol. 6, no. 1. March 1995, pp 15–20.

2 M. N. Rothbard, *Man, Economy, and State*, New Jersey: Van Nostrand Press, 1962. Subsequently, three new editions appeared, one published by Nash Publishing, Los Angeles, 1970; another by New York University Press in New York in 1979; and the third by the Ludwig von Mises Institute, Auburn University, 1994 and 2004. Various sections of this book have been translated into Spanish and published in Volumes I and II of my *Lecturas de Economía Política*, Madrid: Unión Editorial, 1986–1987, and also by ESEADE, Buenos Aires, 2004.

3 M. N. Rothbard, *Power and Market*, Menlo Park, CA: Institute for Humane Studies, 1970 (Ludwig von Mises Institute Scholar's Edition, 2004)

4 Rothbard's defence of the Thomist *ius naturalism* was so vigorous that it was rumoured that he had been converted to Catholicism. Although Rothbard denied

this rumour, he nevertheless continued to be an 'agnostic Thomist', as he has recently been described by Father Robert Sirico (in 'Murray N. Rothbard, 1926-1995', in the magazine *Liberty*, vol. VIII, no. 4, March 1995, p. 13).

5 One of these marathon sessions was the root of Robert Nozick's interest in liberal theory, as Nozick himself acknowledges: 'It was a long conversation about six years ago with Murray Rothbard that stimulated my interest in individualist anarchist theory' (R. Nozick, *Anarchy, State and Utopia*, New York: Basic Books, 1974, p. xv).

6 Joseph Soberan, in his recollections of Rothbard, tells us how 'Murray's earliest memory of a political conversation was of a family gathering in the 30s at which his relatives, most of them communists, were denouncing Franco. The prepubescent Murray Rothbard shocked them by asking 'what's so bad about Franco anyway?' In that setting the question was heretical. Murray started young' (*Liberty*, vol. 8, no. 4, March 1995, p. 26). Although the young Rothbard's question may have seemed heretical to his communist relatives, he had right on his side, above all if one considers the great similarity between the dictatorial and coercive nature of Franco's regime and the regime which its communist opponents were also trying to impose by force.

7 M. N. Rothbard, 'New Light on the Prehistory of the Austrian School', chapter 3 of *The Foundations of Modern Austrian Economics*, Dolan, E. (ed.), Kansas City, MO: Sheed & Ward, 1976, pp. 52–74.

8 See M. N. Rothbard, *Economic Thought before Adam Smith: An Austrian Perspective on the History of Economic Thought*, vol. I, Aldershot: Elgar, 1995; and *Classical Economics: An Austrian Perspective on the History of Economic Thought*, vol. II, Aldershot: Elgar, 1995. In these volumes, he expands upon and profoundly analyses in extensor the importance of the continental Catholic tradition as opposed to the Anglo-Saxon tradition of Protestant origin. On this subject, see my article J. Huerta de Soto, 'Génesis, esencia y evolución de la Escuela Austriaca de Economía', in Estudios de Economía Política, Madrid: Unión Editorial, 1994.

9 Rothbard, *The Ethics of Liberty*, New Jersey: Humanities Press, 1982. There is a French translation published under the title *L'Ethique de la Liberté*, Paris: Les Belles Lettres, 1991. The Spanish edition, entitled *La Ética de la Libertad* was published under the auspices of the author of this article in the collection of libertarian books he is editing for Unión Editorial (Madrid 1995).

10 M. N. Rothbard, 'Nations by Consent: Decomposing the Nation-State?', *Journal of Libertarian Studies*, vol. XI, no. 9 (Autumn), 1994, pp.1–10.

11 J. Huerta de Soto, 'A Critical Analysis of Central Banks and Fractional Reserve Free Banking from the Austrian School Perspective', *Review of Austrian Economics*, vol. VIII, no. 2, 1995, pp. 25–38 (Chapter 10 of this book).

19 Hayek's best test of a good economist

1 Originally published in *Procesos de Mercado: Revista Europea de Economía Política*, vol. I, no. 2, autumn 2004, pp. 121–124.
2 F.A. Hayek, *The Pure Theory of Capital*, London: Routledge, 1976, p. 439.
3 Huerta de Soto, J. (2006). *Money, Bank Credit, and Economic Cycles*, Auburn, AL: Ludwig von Mises Institute, 2006, pp. 265–395.
4 Mises, L. von, *Notes and Recollections*, South Holland, IL: Libertarian Press, 1978, p. 36.

20 The Ricardo effect

1 Originally published in *An Eponymous Dictionary of Economics*, edited by Julio Segura and Carlos Rodríguez Braun, Cheltenham: Edward Edgar, 2004, pp. 217–218.

Appendix

1 This is an interview which appeared in the 1997 summer issue (vol. 17, no. 2, pp. 1–7) of the *Austrian Economics Newsletter* (*AEN*). The occasion for the interview was provided by my visit to the Ludwig von Mises Institute at Auburn University in Alabama in April 1997 to present an address on the 'Spanish Roots of the Austrian School'. Jeff Tucker conducted the interview.

Index

action 63; three levels 186
adaptive efficiency 1, 15
adjustment 70–1
aggression 72–4, 82
Alchian, A. 7
alertness, and entrepreneurship 64
Allais, Maurice 145
Allen, W.R. 7
anarcho-capitalist model 113
antitrust legislation 26–7
aprioristic-deductive methodology 238–9
Arrow, K. 6
assumptions, simplifying 52–3
Atlas Research Foundation 193
Austria, cultural relations with Spain 268–9
Austrian Institute of Economic Research 236
Austrian School: criticism of neo-classical school 43; criticisms of 51–6; differences from neoclassical 31–43, 32–3; dogmatism 55–6; entrepreneurial coordination 37–9; entrepreneurial error 36; entrepreneurship 35–6; lack of empirical criteria 54–5; lack of empirical work 53–4; macroeconomics 49; methodological position 43–51; re-emergence 51; relation with empirical world 40–3; renunciation of prediction 54; Spanish origins 204, 209–10; subjective information 36; subjectivism 35; theory of action 34; verbal formalism 39–40
Austrian theory of the economic cycles 236
Aznar, José María 271
Azpilcueta Navarro, Martin de 45, 207, 208, 217–18, 223, 267

Balmes, Jaime 210, 269
Bank Charter Act 1844 (Peel's Act) 141
Bank of Amsterdam 143
banking contracts 162–8
banking issues, multidisciplinary analysis 162
Banking School 223, 224, 268
banking system, evolution 141–3
banking theory 267–8; need for new approach 139
bankruptcies: banks 317n51; Seville bankers 212–13
Basque Country 200–1
Becker, Gary 272, 302n13
Belda, Francisco SJ 226–7
Bentham, Jeremy 5, 57
Bergson, A. 6
Blaug, Mark 58, 341n43
Böhm-Bawerk, Eugen von 46–7, 235
Buchanan, James M. 183–4

calculation, economic 96–8
Caldwell, Bruce 55
Cantillon, Richard 45, 210, 269
Capitalism, Socialism and Democracy (Schumpeter) 13
Carande, Ramón 212, 213
Carlos V y sus Banqueros (Carande) 212
Casa de Contratación (Trade House) 212
Castillo, Cánovas del 194
Castillo de Bovadilla, Jerónimo 206
Catalonia 108–9, 110
Catholic Church 176–7, 274
Cato Institute 193
Centesimus Annus (John Paul II) 177
central banking 141–3, 167–8
Central European Bank 146–7
Charles V 211–12, 268
Chicago School 1, 145, 187–8, 259

Chile 271, 316n49
Cipolla, Carlo M. 161, 213–14
cities, development of 114
Clark, John Bates 46–7
Coase, Ronald H. 15–16
coercion 72–4, 85, 290n12; property rights and the environment 95–6
Comentario Resolutorio de Cambios (Azpilcueta) 217–18
competition 9–10, 206
complementarity, Austrian and neo-classical schools 51–2
Complutense University 264
conjectural history 61
consequentialism, failure of 169–70
consumer goods, supply and demand 154
coordination 10–11, 70–1
Cordato, Roy E. 12–13
corruption 90–2
cost 39
cost-benefit analysis 40
Covarrubias y Leyva, Diego de 206, 222
Crane, Edward H. 57
creative destruction 13
creativity: and coordination 10–11; innate 19–20, 87, 190, 240; and need 279n52, 320n11
credit expansion 151–3, 166, 208, 226, 228, 236
currencies, freedom of choice 147
Currency School 223
currency school theorists 140–1

De monetae mutatione (Mariana) 205
De rege et regis institutione (Mariana) 205
decisions, ex post rationalization 36
democracy, direct 200–3
Dempsey, Bernard W. SJ 227–8
Demsetz, H. 17, 278n41
Denationalization of Money (Hayek) 145
deposit of money: appropriation by bankers 216; demand 215–16, 217–18, 218–20, 220–2; as different to loan of money 164; term 215
development, economic theory of 27
Die Gemeinwirtschaft: Untersuchungen über den Sozialismus (Mises) 237
direct democracy 200–3
Discovery, Capitalism and Distributive Justice (Kirzner) 177–8
Discurso de las enfermedades de la Compañía (Mariana) 209
dispersed knowledge 65–7
distributive justice 174

documents, in lieu of cash 224–5 *see also* fiduciary media
dogmatism, of Austrian School 55–6
Dolan, E.G. 17
Dowd, Kevin 146, 148, 162
dual strategy 188, 196, 272
dynamic concept of action 46–7
dynamic efficiency 1

Eastern Europe, fall of socialism 185
economic analysis, law, legal regulations and social institutions 28–9
economic calculation 96–8; and human action 338n34
economic theory of development 27
economics: definition 338n36; emergence of 61; influence of mechanical physics 3–5; micro- and macro-337n21; Xenophon 2–3
Economics (Xenophon) 2–3
'Economics and Mechanics' (Walras) 4
Economics: Private and Public Choice (Gwartney and Stroup) 17
economics textbooks: concept of dynamic efficiency 16–18; shortcomings 229–33
ecosystems 94
education 192
efficiency: definitions 4; etymology 2; and morality 172–4
efficient allocation, definition 4
emigration *see also* immigration: freedom of 104–5; solution to problems posed by flows 115–16
empirical criteria, for validation of theories 54–5
empirical success criteria 58–9
empiricism 40–3
empirical work, lack of in Austrian school 53–4
energy 3; efficiency 4
English Banking School 224
entrepreneurial coordination 37–9
entrepreneurial error 36
entrepreneurship 2–3, 8–10, 29, 35–6; and alertness 64; and concept of socialism 72–4; creative nature 68–9; essence of 63–72; ethical implications 175; etymology 63–4; information and knowledge 64–5; understanding concept 84–5
environmental damage 89
environmental problems, entrepreneurial solution 98–9

environmentalism: free market 94–9; and impossibility of socialist economic calculation 96–8
equilibrium 10, 206, 281n18, 341n39; general and/or partial 37–9
equity 173
Erhard, Ludwig 185
Essays in Positive Economics (Friedman) 50
essential principle 71–2
estate, increasing 2–3
ETA 200–1
ethical principles 1–2; entrepreneurship 175; evolution 24–5; relativism 177–8; Rothbard 12
ethics: compatibility with dynamic efficiency 29–30; contribution of Kirzner 174–6; critique of Kirzner 177–80; foundation for freedom 170–1; as necessary and sufficient condition 19–22; relationship with dynamic efficiency 18–25; and social security 122–5
'Ética de la creación de créditos según la doctrina de Molina, Lesio y Lugo' (Belda) 226–7
European Economic Community (EEC) *see* European Union
European Union 105–6, 107, 118–19
evolutionist theory of social processes 170
ex post rationalization of past decisions 36

facts 41
family relationships 23–4
Fetter, Frank Albert 203
fiduciary media *see also* documents, in lieu of cash; money: changes in demand as exogenous variable 149–51; demand for 148–9, 313n17; issuing 152–3, 154
first theorem of welfare economics 6
formalism, verbal versus mathematical 39–40
fractional-reserve banking 142, 143–5, 163–8, 208, 223, 226, 267–8
fractional-reserve free banking: historical illustrations 160–2; juridical arguments 162–8; monetary equilibrium theory 153–8
Fractional-Reserve Free Banking School 148
fraud 163
free banking 140–1, 146, 211, 313n19, 314n20

Free Banking in Britain (White) 149
free market environmentalism 94–9, 293n4
free market, private property anarchism 203
free market reforms *see also* libertarian reform: analysis of strategy 186; dual strategy 188, 196; ethical level of action 186, 189–92; historical level of action 186, 192–4; levels of action required 186–94; reasons for political impossibility 183–4; refuting pessimism 184–5; specialization and division of labour 194; theoretical level of action 186, 187–9
free society, monetary and banking system 145–7
freedom: of emigration/immigration 104–5; importance of ethical foundation 170–1; of trade 103–4
Frey, Bruno 200–3
Friedman, Milton 50, 148
Functional Overlapping Competing Jurisdictions (FOCJs), deconstruction of state 202–4

Garello, Jacques 94
'German Economic Miracle' 185
German Historical School 44, 48, 51
Glasner, David 148
González, Felipe 106
Gresham, Thomas 213
Grice-Hutchinson, Marjorie (Baroness Marjorie von Schlippenbach) 266
Grotius, Hugo 269
Gwartney, J.D. 17

Hardin, Garrett 96
Hayek, F.A. 1, 17, 34, 41, 42–3, 47, 48, 50, 52, 60, 61–2, 65, 88, 89, 113–14, 124, 139, 141–2, 143, 145, 154–8, 176, 187, 190, 191, 204, 236, 237, 247, 258–60, 262, 266
hermeneutics 51
Hicks, J. 6
historicism 283n32
homo oeconomicus 35–6, 238
Hoppe, Hans Hermann 51, 57, 82, 116–17, 165–6, 248
Horwitz, Stephen 148
human action 63
Human Action (Mises) 50, 229, 238 *see also* Mises, Ludwig von; development of economic science 247–51; English

editions 243–4; as forerunner of Public Choice School 250–1; importance of 234, 254; *Nationalökonomie: Theorie des Handelns und Wirtschaftens* 243; potential readership 251–2; Spanish translations 245–6, 263–4; studying and teaching 251–4; successive editions 242–6; teaching 253–4; translations, not Spanish 244–5
human capital theory 272
human nature 25
human reality, levels of study 61–2
humans: innate creativity 87, 190, 240; interactions 101
Hume, David 143
Hutt, William H. 188, 203
ideological intermediaries 192
immigration *see also* emigration: freedom of 104–5; libertarianism 112; principles 116–19; problems of coercive state intervention 114–15; pure theory of movements of persons in a libertarian environment 113–14; and right to vote 118–19; solution to problems posed by flows 115–16; and welfare benefits 117
inarticulate knowledge 67–8
indifference-preference curves 287n63
inflation 205–6, 207
information *see also* knowledge: creation of 69–70; knowledge and entrepreneurship 64–5; objective 36; subjective 36, 87; tacit 76–7; transmission of 70; volume 86–8
innate creativity 19–20, 87, 190, 240
Institute for Humane Studies 193
institutions: entrepreneurship and moral behaviour 178–80; essential 24–5
Instrucción de Mercaderes (Saravia de la Calle) 206, 214–17, 223
intellectuals 192
interest 215, 318n62
Interest and Usury (Dempsey) 227–8
international coordination 193
interventionism 83, 108, 292n20
introspection 44
Italy 213–14

John Paul II, Pope 92, 177, 323n18
Juan Carlos, King 274
justice 22, 91; distributive 174; and efficiency 173

Kaldor-Hicks approach 6
Kaldor, N. 6
Kasper, Wolfgang 17
Keynes, John Maynard 5, 48, 158, 273–4
Keynesians, macroeconomics 49
Kirzner, Israel M. 1, 11–12, 14, 15–16, 34, 48, 50, 51, 56, 63, 64, 172, 174–81, 238, 248, 249
Knight, Frank H. 47, 48
knowledge *see also* information: information and entrepreneurship 64–5; as not 'given' 86; private and dispersed 65–7; subjective and practical non-scientific 65; tacit 67–8, 76–7, 87

la Calle, Luis Saravia de 45
La Justicia y el Derecho (Soto) 220
Lange, Oskar 48
language, and national identity 101
Latin America 185
Lavoie, Don 51
law: economic analysis 28–9, 321n20; prostitution of 91
law of conservation of energy 3
Law of Diminishing Returns 282n23, 341n37
law of equal marginal utility 282n21
law of equality of weighted marginal utilities 40
learning effect 70–1
legal institutions, economic analysis 28–9
legal principles 25
Leibenstein, Harvey 1, 14
Leoni, Bruno 45, 204, 266
Lessines, Giles 208–9
Lessius, Leonard SJ 224
liberal nationalism: conversion of national socialists 109–11; economic and social advantages 105–7; essential principles 102–5; role of the state 107–8; and socialist nationalism 108–9
libertarian environment, immigration within 113–14
libertarian principles, application 182
libertarian reform *see also* free market reforms: role of politicians 194–6
Liberty Fund 193
liberty, theory of 182
Lindsay, D.E. 17
Lipsey, R.G. 7
liquidity crises 226
loans 221–2

Locke's proviso 20, 175
logical-deductivism 41
Ludwig von Mises Institute 193
Lugo, Juan de SJ 206, 208, 220, 222, 224, 225, 226–7, 268
lying, by politicians 196–8

Machlup, Fritz 47
macro-, separation from micro- 38
macroeconomics 27–8, 48; two ways of conceiving 49
Madrid 110
mainstream 50–1
Mariana, Juan de SJ 209, 268, 328n26; biography 204; debasement of coinage 205–6, 207; defence of tyrannicide 205; on taxation 205
market defects 179
market economies, ethical basis 20
marriage 23–4
Marshall, Alfred 47
Marx, Karl 47
mathematical formalism 39–40, 53
mathematics 341n41
Mayer, Hans 4, 39–40, 50, 273, 282n21
McCloskey, Deirdre 51
mechanical physics, influence on economic thought 3–5
media 193
medical assistance, problem of 136–8
medical socialism 271
megalomania 91
Menem, Carlos 194
Menger, Carl 27–8, 39, 43–6, 57, 61, 180, 204, 210, 238, 247
Mercado, Tomás de 208, 218–20, 223, 226
Methodenstreit 43–51
methodological pluralism 52
methodology, neoclassical economics 56, 286n56
micro-, separation from macro- 38
Mirowski, Philip 4
Mises, Ludwig von 1, 34, 35, 37, 38, 47–8, 50, 59, 61, 81, 86, 121, 140–1, 143, 144–5, 150–1, 190, 191, 229, 259, 270, 281n18, 282n23, 291n16 see also *Human Action*; aprioristic-deductive methodology and criticism of scientistic positivism 238–9; biography 241–2; editions of *Human Action* 242–6; impossibility of socialism 237; influence of Carl Menger 234–5; practical knowledge as distinct from scientific knowledge 248; publication of collected works 263; socialism and theory of interventionism 249; theory of credit and the banking system 250; theory of dynamic processes 240; theory of entrepreneurship 237–8; theory of evolution 247; theory of money, credit and economic cycles 235–6; theory of monopoly 248–9; theory of Natural Law 247–8; theory of population 250
model of perfect competition 10
Molina, Luis de SJ 45, 206, 208, 220–1, 224–5, 226–7, 267–8
monetarism, macroeconomics 49
monetary and banking system, in free society 145–7
monetary equilibrium-disequilibrium 148
monetary equilibrium theory, fractional-reserve free banking 153–8
monetary theory 27–8; need for new approach 139
money 27–8 see also fiduciary media; demand for, and savings 158–60
Mont Pèlerin Society 193
Montesquieu, Charles-Louis de Secondat, Baron de 61–2
moral principles 173
morality 90, 92; and efficiency 172–4; institutions and entrepreneurship 178–80; traditional 191

nation, concept and characteristics 100–2
nationalism, as problem 100
Nationalökonomie: Theorie des Handelns und Wirtschaftens (Mises) 243
needs of trade theory 149
neo-Austrians 50–1
neoclassical economics 4; equilibrium, general and/or partial 37–9; ex post rationalization of past decisions 36; homo oeconomicus 35–6; macroeconomics 49; mathematical formalism 39–40; need to re-work 56; objective information 36; objectivism 35; polemics against 47–8, 50, 51; relation with empirical world 40–3; theory of decision 34
nihilism 52; methodological 50–1
nirvana 25, 278n41
North, Douglas C. 1, 14–15

Novak, Michael 176–7
novelty, in economics textbooks 230

objective information 36
objectivism 35
occupatio rei nullius 20, 175
O'Driscoll, G.P. 17–18
On the Principles of Political Economy and Taxation (Ricardo) 261–2
'option clauses' 166–7
Opus Dei 274
original sin 88

paradigms, measuring success 58–9
Pareto efficiency 1, 6
Pareto, Vilfredo 53, 287n63
paternalism 123
pattern predictions 41, 239
pay as you go 120–1, 126
Peel's Act 1844 (Bank Charter Act) 141
pensions 120, 270, 300n6 *see also* private pension schemes; social security
personal morality 22–4
Philip IV 269
Pigou, A.C. 5, 7
Pigouvian analysis 5
pluralism, methodological 51, 52
Polanyi, Michael 67
polemics 47–8, 50, 51
politicians: dislike of referenda 200; lying 196–8; pragmatism 195; recommendations for 198–9; role in libertarian reform 194–6
Popper, Karl 51
population aging 121–2
positivism 41, 50, 231, 238–9
potential compensation 6
practical applications 26–9
practical knowledge 65
pragmatism 272; political 130–1, 188–9; of politicians 195
praxeology 55, 61, 238
prediction 40–3, 239, 287n65; renunciation by Austrian school 54
pride 88
principles: importance of study in Economic science 233–4; legal 162–3; libertarian 182; moral 173
Principles of Economics (Menger) 43
private knowledge 65–7
private ownership, of results of entrepreneurship 21
private pension schemes 128–9 *see also* pensions; social security

private property 21
private property anarchism 203
propanganda 90–1
property rights 99, 294n11; coercion and the environment 95–6; distribution 16; and immigration 117, 119
Protestant Reformation 45
prudence 226
Public Choice School 183–4, 250–1
Public Choice theory 184
public good 179, 279n59, 294n13
public opinion 192, 194
public ownership 97–8
publication 192, 265
Pufendorf, Samuel 269
pure entrepreneurial profits 68–9
Pure Theory of Capital (Hayek) 258

qualitative success criterion 59

Ramsay-Pigou rule 279n58
rationality 168, 190
Rawls, John 175–6
Reagan, Ronald 185
referenda 200
regression theorem of purchasing power 236
regrettable errors 36
Reig, Joaquín 263–4, 273
Reiter, Stanley 4
religion 24, 274–5, 279n55
reserve banking 142
reserve ratios 268
Resolutary Commentary on Exchanges (Navarro) 207
resources, as given/not given 19–20
Ricardo, David 261–2
Ricci Bank 214, 329n6
rigour, lack of in economics textbooks 231
risk 35–6
rivalry, entrepreneurship 10
Rizzo, M.J. 17–18
Robbins, Lionel 7, 34, 237
Röpke, Wilhelm 237
Rosen, Sherwin 57
Rothbard, Murray N. 1, 12–13, 113, 116, 145, 161, 204, 208, 211, 248, 249, 255–7, 265–6

saints 275
Salamanca, banking and currency points of view 222–6
Salas, Juan de SJ 206

Samuelson, P.A. 6
Saravia de la Calle, Luis 206, 208, 214–17, 223, 267–8
Savigny, Friedrich Carl von 162
savings 121, 128; and concept of demand for money 158–60
Say, Jean-Baptiste 45, 210, 269
Schumpeter, Joseph Alois 1, 13–14, 15, 266
Schwartz, Anna J. 144
scientific meliorism 230
scientism 42, 189, 190, 231, 238–9, 334n7
secession 201–3
second-best solutions 295n17
second fundamental theorem of welfare economics 6, 18–19
'second-hand dealers of ideas' 192
self-determination 102–3
self-interest 80
Selgin, George 146, 148, 149, 153, 158, 161, 268
Sen, Amartya K. 6
separation, micro- and macro- 38
Seville, development of banks 212–14
simplification, in economics textbooks 230
sin 215, 216, 226
Smith, Adam 143, 269, 328n25
Smith, Vera C. 311n2
social assistance 128
social big bang 281n15
social coordination 37
social ethics: formal theory 62; possibility of theory 171–2
social institutions 44; economic analysis 28–9; emergence and evolution 101; study of 25; transmission of personal morality 22–3
social justice 173–4
social processes, evolutionist theory 170
social security 301n8, 302n13, 303n19 see also pensions; private pension schemes; basic strategic principles 130–1; company contributions 121; diagnosis of problem 120–7; ethical problems 122–5; ideal model from libertarian perspective 127–30; inherent contradiction 125–7; lines of reform 132–4; political influences 127; problems posed 120; reform 305n29, 306n30; reform in Spain 270–2; relative position of different countries *131*; stages in reform *131*, 131–2; strategy for reform 130–6;

technical problems 120–2; voucher system 308n37
social-welfare function 6, 7, 19
socialism 48, 50; arguments against 86–8; criticism of alternative concepts 81–4; definition 85, 190–1; dynamic argument 77–9; and entrepreneurship 72–4; environmental damage 89; fall of 182, 185, 187; impossibility from perspective of controlling organism 79–81; impossibility from perspective of society 76–9; as intellectual error 74–6; and interventionism 83; lack of rigour 88–9; Mises' analysis of impossibility 237, 291n16; paradox of 86; possibility of conversion to liberal nationalism 109–11; static argument 76–7; and theory of interventionism 249; traditional definition 81; as unethical 21
Socialism (Mises) 237, 270
socialist economic calculation, controversy 237
socialist nationalism, and liberal nationalism 108–9
Soto, Domingo de SJ 220, 224
Spain 106–7, 121; cultural relations with Austria 268–9
Spanish scholastics 266, 267, 283n35; influence on Austrian School 204, 209–10
St Antonino of Florence 45, 275
St Bernardine of Siena 3, 45, 275
state: deconstruction 200–3; role in liberal nationalism 107–8
static efficiency: critical analysis of evolution 2–8; historical background 2–3; influence of mechanical physics 3–5; as myth 12
steam engine 4
Stigler, G.J. 14
Stiglitz, J.E. 36, 48, 53, 55–6
Streit, Manfred E. 17
Stroup, Richard 17, 293n4
subjective information 36, 87
subjective knowledge 65
subjective theory of value 45, 209
subjectivism 35, 44, 60, 206, 210, 234–5, 318n59
Suma de Tratos y Contratos (Mercado) 218–20

tacit knowledge 67–8, 76–7, 87
taxation theory 26

Taylor, Frederick W. 5
technical efficiency 7–8
textbooks 86
Thatcher, Margaret 106, 185
The Acting Person (John Paul II) 177
The Catholic Ethic and the Spirit of Capitalism (Novak) 176–7
The Counter-Revolution of Science (Hayek) 50
The Fatal Conceit (Hayek) 61, 88
The Principles of Scientific Management (Taylor) 5
The Theory of Economic Development (Schumpeter) 13
The Theory of Money and Credit (Mises) 144–5, 235
theoretical propositions, formalizing 53
theories, empirical criteria for validation 54–5
theory of action 34
theory of credit and the banking system 250
theory of decision 34
theory of dynamic processes 240
theory of economic cycles 143
theory of entrepreneurship 63, 237–8; emergence of institutions and moral behaviour 178–80
theory of evolution 247
theory of interventionism 249
theory of liberty 182; ethical foundations 191
theory of marginal utility 235–6
theory of monetary equilibrium 268
theory of monopoly 248–9
theory of Natural Law 247–8
theory of population 250
theory of public property 295n15
theory of regulation and interventionism 26
theory of social ethics 171–2
theory of spontaneous orders 52
theory of trade cycles 236
theory of value, subjectivist 206
thermodynamics, second law 3
think tanks 193
thoroughness, lack of in economics textbooks 232

Timberlake, Richard 148
trade, freedom of 103–4
tragedy of the commons 97, 144, 294n12, 294n13
transaction costs theory 15–16
Tratado sobre los Cambios (Molina) 221, 224
Tratado sobre los Préstamos y la Usura (Molina) 221
trend predictions 41, 239
triangular diagrams (Hayek) 155, 156, 157
Turgot, Jacques 45, 210, 269
tyrants 327n7

under-consumption 284n41
understanding (verstehen) 41
utilitarianism, impossibility of 40–1
utility, comparisons of 7

verbal formalism 39–40
verstehen (understanding) 41
Veterum Collatio Numismatum (Covarrubias y Leyva) 222
Vitoria, Francisco de OP 205, 268
voting, by immigrants 118

Walras, Leon 4
Walrasian paradigm 58, 171, 191, 229, 252
waste, inherent in market economy 11
Webb, Beatrice and Sydney 5
welfare benefits, and immigration 117
welfare economics: criticism of static efficiency 6–8; first theorem 6; second fundamental theorem 6, 18–19; and static concept of efficiency 5–6; static efficiency 173
welfare state, crisis 187
Whig theory of the history of science 333n3
White, Lawrence 146, 148, 149, 158
Wonnacott, P. 18
Wonnacott, R. 18
x-efficiency 1, 14
Xenophon 2–3

Yeager, Leland B. 45–6, 148